Computing Strategies
in Liberal Arts Colleges

EDUCOM
Strategy Series
on Information Technology

Computing Strategies
in Liberal Arts Colleges

Martin D. Ringle, Editor

Addison-Wesley Publishing Company, Inc.

Reading, Massachusetts • Redwood City, California • New York
Don Mills, Ontario • Wokingham, England • Amsterdam • Bonn
Sydney • Singapore • Tokyo • Madrid • San Juan • Milan • Paris

EDUCOM was assisted in the development of this book by grants from the following corporate associates: Apple Computer, Inc., the Digital Equipment Corporation, International Business Machines Corporation, and NeXT Computer, Inc.

International Business Machines Corporation and Apple Computer, Inc. are EDUCOM Leadership Sponsors.

The opinions expressed in this book are those of the individual authors and are not intended to represent policy statements of EDUCOM, the contributing institutions, or Addison-Wesley Publishing Company.

Executive Editor: Alan Jacobs
Project Manager: Kathy O'Neil
Production Supervisor: Brian Miller
Jacket Design: Karen Stroman
Copyeditor: Jane Kilgore
Composition: Editorial Services of New England, Inc.
Manufacturing Supervisor: Patricia Gordon

*LB
2395.7
C68
1992*

Many of the designations used by manufacturers and sellers to distinguish their products are claimed as trademarks. Where these designations appear in this book, and Addison-Wesley was aware of the trademark claim, the designations have been printed in initial caps or all caps.

Library of Congress Cataloging-in-Publication Data

Computing strategies in liberal arts colleges / Martin D. Ringle, editor
      p. cm. — (EDUCOM strategies series on information technology)
    Includes bibliographical references and index.
    ISBN 0-201-60526-0 : $35.00
      1. Universities and colleges — United States — Data Processing.
  2. Information resources management. 3. Computer networks — United States.
  4. Computer-assisted instruction — United States. I. Ringle, Martin D. II. Series
  LB2395.7.C68 1992
  378.73'0285—dc20
                        91-44855
                            CIP

0-201-60526-0

1 2 3 4 5 6 7 8 9 10-MA-95949392

For Mom and Dad, who taught me everything I really
needed to know.

— M. D. R.

CONTENTS

Foreword

That astute observer of the contemporary scene, Mr. Woody Allen, has developed an all-purpose commencement speech that goes: "Today, as never before in history, humanity faces a crossroad. One path leads to hopelessness and despair, the other to oblivion. Let us pray that we have the wisdom to choose the right path."

In many respects, higher education, like humanity, is at that kind of crossroad. The academic reward structure has, at many institutions, pushed faculty into concentrating on ever more specialized research at the same time social policy is pushing higher education toward access, diversity, and an emphasis on teaching and general education. It is important that these contradictions between the reward structure and social expectations be resolved, for in many research-centered institutions there are complaints that, at least during the freshman and sophomore years, students and faculty are wandering around in two separate worlds. Yet liberal arts colleges have always maintained a balanced relationship between scholarship and teaching, with faculty and students intimately involved in a common learning community.

Another major unsolved problem for higher education is that the cost of a quality education has been rising faster than the consumer price index. There are a number of factors contributing to this problem, including the fact that teaching is a labor-intensive activity, which has largely not benefited from productivity improvements resulting from capital investments in technology. It has been possible to improve the quality of education through the application of information technology, but it has been hard to make it cheaper. Liberal arts colleges that pride themselves on individualized instruction, small class sizes, and excellence in teaching are particularly labor-intensive and consequently are experiencing unusual financial pressures. These pressures have led to very creative and efficient uses of information technology. This confluence of pressures is forcing higher education to seek new paradigms for education in the twenty-first century. In this search, as always, it can learn much from liberal arts colleges.

A primary mechanism EDUCOM uses to communicate important issues to the higher education community is to create a volume dealing with those issues in its Strategy Series. EDUCOM is a higher education association with 600 college and university members and 125 corporate associates. A major mission of EDUCOM is to promote the rational and effective use of information technology in higher education. It attempts to accomplish this through publications, conferences, seminars, workshops, consulting services, and task forces directed toward achieving specific goals. The primary purpose of the Strategies Series is to help colleges and universities in their planning activities.

We at EDUCOM are deeply grateful to the editor of the volume, Marty Ringle, and to the contributors, who devoted their time and energy to share with us the valuable lessons they have learned. These are all people who have done outstanding work in their field. We are also grateful to their home institutions for giving them the opportunity and support they needed to prepare this volume.

We would also like to express our gratitude to Apple Computer, Inc., the Digital Equipment Corporation, the IBM Corporation, and NeXT Computer, Inc., whose financial support made this volume possible. These organizations are EDUCOM Corporate Associates and are continuing supporters of the goals of higher education.

Information technology is starting to change higher education in major ways, and institutions working on the frontier of instruction and research need to make major investments in this technology in order to prepare students adequately for the world in which they will live and work. In times when resources are tight, it is particularly important that these investments be informed. Information technology has the power to transform learning from a passive process to one that is interactive, participatory, and exploratory. Liberal arts colleges are in many respects on the cutting edge of this transformational process. I believe that their story will be valuable to all segments of education.

Ken King
President, EDUCOM

The Importance of Computing at Liberal Arts Colleges— A Presidential Perspective

Robert M. Gavin, Jr.
President, Macalester College

Twenty-five years ago the president of a liberal arts college would not be writing about the importance of computing. In the late 1960s computing was still the bailiwick of engineers and physical scientists, not a key resource for both the curricular and administrative activities of a college. In fact, most liberal arts colleges had just begun to think about using computers for routine tasks in the business, development, and registrar's offices, and the prospect of integrating computing into the curriculum was rarely taken seriously. When I was a newly appointed assistant professor of chemistry at Haverford College, it was difficult for me to imagine the revolutionary changes in computing that would take place during the next two-and-a-half decades.

Today the computer is ubiquitous on the liberal arts college campus. Students and faculty in practically every discipline make extensive use of computers, from the most basic operations of word processing to the most sophisticated and elaborate exercises in computer simulation. Today many faculty members in the humanities and social sciences are as dependent on computers for their scholarship and teaching as are their colleagues in the natural sciences. Our faculty and students expect to be able to browse through automated library catalogues and to probe databases, not only on campus but all around the country. The college library itself has become a centerpiece for technological innovation. And administrative offices from the registrar to the physical plant depend on computers for their operation. All of this, however, is a fairly recent phenomenon.

In June 1985, the presidents of 49 of the nation's leading colleges met at Oberlin College to discuss ways of improving science education at liberal arts colleges. When the presidents reconvened the following year, it was discovered that there was another topic of shared interest: information technology. Many, if not all, of our institutions were struggling with the same set of problems: What kind of computing resources did we need on our campuses? What role should computing play in teaching and research at the small liberal arts college? And how much of an investment in computing was it reasonable for us to make?

The high level of interest led to the formation of a Committee on Computing and Telecommunications, comprised of both presidents and technology administrators. Two years later, the committee split into a governing board and a steering committee and the group of schools—now numbering 55—came to refer to itself as the Consortium of Liberal Arts Colleges, or *CLAC*. Having served as the chair of the Committee on Computing and Telecommunications, I agreed to continue my participation in the group's activities as chair of the governing board.

The principal mission of the consortium—to gather and distribute information about technology on member campuses—has given me a rare opportunity to witness the evolution of liberal arts college computing in this critical period of its development. I have been struck by the rapid and yet carefully controlled growth of computing resources. Though funding did rise appreciably at the end of the eighties, liberal arts colleges did not translate their recognition of the importance of computing into massive budget drains.

I have been continually impressed by the manner in which colleges have introduced computing into the liberal arts environment. Debates about computing have ranged far and wide on the topics of curricular impact, quality of student life, and the relationship to other institutional priorities. The participants have included representatives from every constituency within the college. The number of committees, policy statements, and organizational changes that have resulted from the introduction of computing on our campuses during the past decade has been extraordinary.

Yet for all the changes that have come about, I believe that in the long run we shall see that computing has not changed the liberal arts environment so much as the liberal arts environment has changed computing. While many universities and technical institutions have hastened to modify their curricula and instructional methods to accommodate changes in technology, liberal arts colleges have insisted instead that the technology adapt to an educational approach that has proven effective for the past thousand years. The widespread use of computing in the liberal arts college environment has contributed to a number of initiatives designed to make the technology less obtrusive, more flexible, and more suitable for classroom instruction.

The attention focused on computing has grown rapidly at liberal arts colleges during the past few years and we now have some of the answers to the questions that were raised in 1985 by the presidents at the Oberlin meeting. The chapters of this book provide a broad set of perspectives on the kind of technology we need, the relationship of computing to the curricular mission, the required organizational structure, and the appropriate level of planning and financial support necessary to maintain adequate computing resources.

The question of financial support is especially important in these times of fiscal uncertainty. Computing and information technology are major elements in the financial planning of any institution. Each of our budgets reflects the need to provide computing technology across the academic departments as well as throughout the administration. We face growing demands for information resources from all constituents of the college community. Our faculty need and want to communicate with their colleagues at other universities through national and international networks; our libraries are becoming increasingly computerized and are being linked electronically to other libraries and to databases throughout the world; our students are coming to rely on computing to register for their courses, communicate with their instructors, and prepare their research reports. The resources are expanding rapidly and all of this costs money.

In this climate of rapid technological change, it is easy to fall prey to extremes. A common mistake is that of inaction. Liberal arts colleges are often tempted to wait until the rate of change in a technology area has stabilized before deciding which computers, networks, or software packages to purchase. The flaw in this approach is that rapid change seems to be an inherent part of the high technology industry and there may never be an "ideal" time to jump in. Waiting for the "right time" may result in waiting too long. Prospective students may elect to go elsewhere, faculty may become handicapped in their ability to keep up with their colleagues at other institutions, opportunities for streamlining and improving administrative operations may fall by the wayside.

On the other hand, however, moving too rapidly can also prove to be a serious mistake. Being at the cutting edge of academic disciplines does not mean being the first with each new technological advance. There are few, if any, liberal arts colleges that have the resources to be always at the forefront of technology when technology is changing by the day. The amount of money necessary to replace equipment and train staff to keep up with every new advance is far too high. While technical institutes and research universities may be forced to maintain leadership roles in technology development, liberal arts colleges can afford to hold back and let others test the viability of new products and strategies before investing significant portions of their limited budgets in these areas.

A general rule of thumb I have used is to delay making significant investments in certain technologies until standards have been mutually agreed upon in the field. Those of us who have been involved in computing for the last thirty years recognize the tremendous advances that come about once standards are established. Fortunately, national educational computing organizations, such as EDUCOM, CLAC, CAUSE, and others, have helped to promote standardization of technology on our campuses, and individual institutions are now in a better position to make technology decisions based on trends and standards than ever before. This is increasingly true of the technology for hardware and networks, though standards for software are still somewhere in the future.

As you review the essays in this book you will come across a number of very creative ideas for planning and implementing programs on liberal arts campuses. I believe the crucial element in planning is to recognize that as undergraduate liberal arts colleges we have a different perspective from that of an engineering school, a research university, or a company engaged in a high-technology business. Our primary concern is to improve the quality of education offered to our students. Computing and information technology can do that in a number of different ways. Our task is to provide a mechanism through which needs in the area of computing and information technology can be incorporated into each of our planning processes.

Contributors

Joanne M. Badagliacco
Director of Academic Computer Services
Pomona College

Gai Carpenter
Director, Library Center
Hampshire College

Marianne M. Colgrove
Associate Director, Computing and Information Systems
Reed College

David V. Cossey
Director, Computer Services
Union College

Paul A. Dobosh
Director of Computing and Information Systems
Mount Holyoke College

Ann C. Edmonds
College Librarian
Mount Holyoke College

William Francis
Director of Computing
Grinnell College

Robert M. Gavin, Jr.
President
Macalester College

Carol Lennox
Director of Academic Computing and Campus Networks
Mills College

Thomas C. Makofske
Director of Computing and Information Services
Connecticut College

Thomas F. Moberg
Vice-President, Information and Computing Services
Kenyon College

Martin D. Ringle
Director of Computing and Information Systems
Reed College

David L. Smallen
Director, Information Technology Services and Institutional
Research
Hamilton College

H. David Todd
Director of University Computing
Wesleyan University

Thomas A. Warger
Director of Computing Services
Bryn Mawr College

Liberal Arts Colleges and Computing

Martin D. Ringle
Reed College

The Game of Leapfrog

Many faculty and staff who have worked within the liberal arts college environment are familiar with the fact that innovation often defers to tradition. This is nowhere more evident than in the case of computer technology. During the late seventies and early eighties, when research universities, community colleges, and other segments of higher education were scrambling to acquire as much technology as possible, many liberal arts colleges were quietly deliberating on the value of computing to their institutional mission of high-quality humanistic instruction. They were paying careful attention to the long-term impact computing might have on the fabric of campus life as well as on the college's budget. Strategic planning for computing was undertaken within the context of larger institutional goals, and committees were formed to oversee the integration of technology into all aspects of academic endeavor.

Critics of computing appeared on almost every campus and their criticisms were often well founded. Small colleges have very few resources to devote to fads, and poor decisions in an area such as technology can have catastrophic effects on other, more vital, areas, including the curriculum. As a result of such concerns, technology arrived at liberal arts colleges in a slower, more restrained, and more coordinated fashion than it did at most large universities. In some respects, small colleges are still years behind the rest of higher education when it comes to computing and information services. At some colleges, skepticism regarding computerization still lingers, though most of the key concerns regarding the perils of technology have been effectively addressed.

Ironically, however, the rapidly changing nature of technology that caused many small colleges to fall behind in the early eighties has enabled them to leapfrog ahead in the nineties. Unlike many large universities, small colleges are not burdened by investments in massive mainframes or supercomputers that were rendered obsolete long before they could be amortized. Most do not have to face the grim and expensive tasks of replacing hundreds of first-generation personal computers or exchanging thousands of feet of copper wire for fiberoptic cable. For the most part, small liberal arts colleges have avoided both the thrill of pioneering and the agony of rectifying the results of technological innovation.

The wait-and-see approach to computing technology has served colleges well. Though they are unable to take advantage of many of the economies of scale available to larger universities, they have the luxury of being able to let others take technical and financial risks while they sit back and learn from the mistakes of their predecessors. The debt liberal arts colleges owe to the leaders in educational computing—Stanford, Brown, Carnegie-Mellon, MIT, Dartmouth, Michigan, and others—cannot be overestimated. Were it not for the examples provided by these schools, both good and bad, on how to implement technology, the task for small colleges would be nearly impossible.

For all their conservatism, however, many liberal arts colleges are now making tremendous strides in computing. For example, though colleges began their network installation five or ten years later than most universities, the smaller size of the colleges has enabled them to complete their networks years ahead of the universities. Lack of investment in "big ticket" items such as supercomputing, has made it possible for small colleges to update their equipment faster and with more regularity than many universities. And the specialized computing facilities for music and graphics at liberal arts colleges are on par with some of the best university facilities in the country.

The majority of liberal arts colleges, however, are still feeling their way toward the right level of computing resources. While computing environments and organizations at small colleges continue to grow, it is becoming increasingly clear that growth will level off during the next few years and that the shape of computing in the latter part of the nineties is likely to set the standard at liberal arts colleges for decades to come. We are beginning to see a natural change in small college computing from one of initial implementation and expansion to one of consolidation and maintenance. Senior administrators and faculty alike are beginning to acquire a sense of the boundaries of information technology, from the viewpoint of both applicability and institutional commitment.

With some of the excitement and much of the fanfare behind us, faculty, staff, and administrators at small colleges are now abandoning the policy question, Should we acquire information technology? Instead they are asking the pragmatic question, How much is enough? The quest for the nineties is to integrate computing and information technology into the regular business of the college and to remove its aura of glamour, mystery, and urgency.

As a fundamental aspect of institutional support—both academic and administrative—computing requires a sound organization that fits well with other college structures. It requires budgetary and planning processes that are stable, yet are able to accommodate the ever-changing nature of technology. And above all it demands an understanding on the part of faculty and administrators of its potential benefits as well as its inherent limitations within the liberal arts environment. I hope this volume will provide a good road map for technology development, both for schools that are just beginning the process of strategic planning for computing and for those that are pausing to take stock of their progress thus far.

About the Book

When the idea of putting together a volume on computing at liberal arts colleges was first conceived, it was thought that a set of case studies from a dozen or so campuses would suffice. It quickly became apparent, however, that faculty members, computing staff, and administrators at small colleges need more than just a survey of *what* has been done in computing; they need a discussion of *why* certain strategies are followed. The present volume seeks to provide that discussion by focusing on four key questions:

1. What is the nature of planning and budgeting for technology?

2. How are information services affected by organizational and staffing structures?

3. What technical trends have emerged at small colleges?

4. How does technology relate to other aspects of the college, such as teaching, faculty development, and library resources?

In Part One, *Planning and Finance*, we address the first question. Dave Smallen in chapter 1 focuses on the overall question of technology planning, priorities for the nineties, and the relationship of computing to the mission of the college. In many ways, his discussion provides an excellent overview of issues that make up the entire book. Joanne Badagliacco's chapter (chapter 2) then provides a detailed discussion of the planning process, alternative planning strategies, and insights about why planning for technology sometimes fails. Her discussion is equally useful for schools that wish to assess the impact of their planning activities and schools that are just beginning to develop their first long-range computing plan. Part One closes with chapter 3, by David Todd and myself, addressing the financial questions: How do we pay for computing? How do we manage computing budgets? And how do we set priorities for computer spending?

Part Two, *Organizational Issues*, addresses the effects that different staffing and organizational structures have on a college's ability to deliver computing services to the community. In chapter 4 Tom Warger focuses his attention on the different types of computing organizations, reporting options, and policy-making practices found at small colleges. He discusses the ways in which organizations have evolved to accommodate changes in technology as well as the impact that different organizational structures have had on budgeting and decision making. In chapter 5 Paul Dobosh moves the discussion from organizational issues to staffing issues by considering the number and type of computing positions appropriate for the liberal arts college environment. He looks at the problems of staff development and turnover and concludes with a discussion of goals for computer center directors. In chapter 6 Dave Cossey looks at the role of administrative computing in small college computing environments. He discusses organizational issues, such as the relationship between academic and administrative computing, as well as technical issues, such as the criteria for purchasing a new administrative software package.

Part Three is devoted to a discussion of the technical trends and standards that are emerging at small colleges. Bill Francis outlines in chapter 7 the historical background of networking at small colleges and identifies some of the key policy issues that are used to determine the optimum strategy for each institution. In chaper 8 Tom Moberg picks up where Bill leaves off by examining the technical and pragmatic aspects of campus networking in detail. Moberg's discussion is especially useful for colleges that are just beginning to implement a campus-wide network. It includes an appendix of specifications for standardizing a college's network technology. Tom Makofske rounds out the discussion of campus networking by describing in chapter 9 how telecommunications services can be linked to data services in student residences. He considers a wide variety of issues including technology, legal requirements, institutional policies, and finances.

Part 4, the final section of the volume, examines the influence that computing has on faculty development, curriculum design, and library resources. In chapter 10 Carol Lennox explores both the benefits and the hazards encountered by faculty members who have pursued courseware development activities. She compares the promise of computer-aided instruction of the 1970s to the reality of classroom use of computers in the 1990s. Marianne Colgrove extends the discussion of the curricular impact of computing in chapter 11 by considering specific examples of courseware initiatives that have succeeded or failed. Her analysis provides a firm basis for speculating on the future of instructional computing during the remainder of the decade. Chapter 12, coauthored by Ann Edmonds and Gai Carpenter, gives us a view of the relationship between library resources and computing resources as seen from the librarian's perspective. The discussion, which is both informative and provocative, touches on the complex question of how libraries and computing centers must cooperate in order to best serve the information needs of small colleges in the coming years.

What Does It All Mean?

Though each author draws extensively on personal experiences and the state of information services at his or her own institution, an effort has been made to keep the discussion in each chapter focused on problems and solutions that are relevant to all liberal arts colleges. In some places authors repeat or contradict points that have been made elsewhere in the volume. Rather than editing out such redundancies and inconsistencies, I have preserved them as a way of emphasizing the fact that although there is wide agreement on some points there is equally wide disagreement on others.

Many of the authors' observations are based on data that have been reported in the annual computing surveys of the Consortium of Liberal Arts Colleges (CLAC). CLAC, an organization of 55 colleges distributed throughout the United States, comprises roughly ten percent of all liberal arts colleges in America. In 1990-91, undergraduate enrollments at CLAC institutions ranged from 563 to 3,695; institutional operating budgets ranged from $14,100,000 to $87,500,000; operating budgets for computing ranged from $218,000 to $1,675,000; and staff size in computing ranged from 4 to 35 full-time equivalents (FTE's). The diversity of approaches to computing at CLAC institutions provides us with a fairly broad cross-section of the liberal arts community.

When the contributors to this volume were recruited they were asked to step outside their day-to-day activities of crisis management and to reflect on the future of information technology during the next ten years. Given that all of us are required to prepare long-range plans and annual progress reports, the task seemed fairly straightforward. Unfortunately, it was not. The lesson that each author learned in the course of preparing this volume is that the history of computing provides remarkably little insight into its future.

The accounts of computing strategies included in the book illustrate the priorities that many colleges have established for information technology, the problems they have encountered along the way, and the solutions that have proven to be most effective. That these strategies can be applied successfully in all small colleges, under all circumstances, and at all times, is doubtful. You may find it useful to consider the nature of the institutions, as well as the background of the authors, when assessing the comments made here.

Some Words of Thanks

Producing an anthology of this sort is a happy chore. The chance to collaborate with so many excellent colleagues across the nation is both a privilege and a pleasure. I'm deeply grateful to those who have contributed to the volume as well as to those who were forced by circumstances to drop out along the way. To my friend and comrade, David Todd, I am especially indebted; if I ever suggest doing another anthology, however, please shoot me immediately.

I want to thank Ken King for his encouragement as well as his patience. The volume took a long time to prepare and went through many twists and turns during its development. Despite the delays and uncertainties, Ken maintained a high level of enthusiasm. I'm extremely grateful to Ken for his unwaivering support as well as his periodic pep talks.

Working on an anthology is also a tiring and time-consuming chore. It's easy to become so absorbed in reading and rereading chapter drafts that you lose sight of your daily obligations. Fortunately, the staff in Computing and Information Systems at Reed work well under stress. Marianne Colgrove provided the required amounts of supervision, expertise, patience, and moral support necessary to keep CIS running smoothly while I dithered over each of the chapters. Rebecca Kilgore, *administrative assistant extraordinaire*, dotted all the i's, crossed all the t's, and kept the project on track despite numerous catastrophes, mysterious file erasures, and general chaos.

More than anyone else, Rebecca deserves the credit for seeing the volume through to completion. I'm also grateful to Ed McFarlane for his feedback on chapter 3 and to all the faculty, staff, and students of Reed College who have made my work in computing here such a wonderful experience.

I would like to thank Steve Gilbert, Suzanne Douglas and the other folks at EDUCOM for their help in nurturing the project along. I would also like to thank the staff at Addison-Wesley, especially Mary Coffey, Brian Miller, and Jenny Kilgore, for doing such an excellent job of turning rough copy into high-quality text.

Most of all, I am grateful to Noel for her patience and understanding, especially during those many evenings and weekends when editing took precedence over excursions to Mount Hood or the Oregon Coast.

Consortium of Liberal Arts Colleges

Member Roster 1991–92

Albion College
Allegheny College
Alma College
Amherst College
Bates College
Beloit College
Bowdoin College
Bryn Mawr College
Bucknell University
Carleton College
Colgate University
College of The Holy Cross
College of Wooster
Colorado College
Connecticut College
Davidson College
Denison University
DePauw University
Earlham College
Franklin & Marshall College
Grinnell College
Hamilton College
Harvey Mudd College
Haverford College
Hope College
Kalamazoo College
Kenyon College
Lafayette College

Lawrence University
Macalester College
Manhattan College
Middlebury College
Mills College
Mount Holyoke College
Oberlin College
Occidental College
Ohio Wesleyan University
Pomona College
Reed College
Skidmore College
Smith College
St. Olaf College
Swarthmore College
Trinity College
Trinity University
Union College
University of the South
Vassar College
Wabash College
Washington College
Wellesley College
Wesleyan University
Wheaton College
Whittier College
Williams College

Part One

Planning and Finance

Chapter 1

Planning for Information Technology Resources: The Issues

David L. Smallen
Hamilton College

David L. Smallen is director, information technology services and institutional research at Hamilton College. In this capacity he is responsible for the planning and management of academic and administrative computing resources, campus voice and data communications, and institutional research.

Dr. Smallen has been a seminar leader at EDUCOM national seminars dealing with strategic planning for computing and computer literacy, as well as a presenter at national conferences dealing with issues of the application of computer technology in higher education. He has written extensively on information technology issues, including chapters in Campus Computing Strategies *(Digital Press, 1983) and* Organizing and Managing Information Resources on Campus *(Academic Computing Publications, 1989). He was one of the authors of* The Evaluation Guidelines for Information Technology Resources *(EDUCOM/CAUSE, 1988).*

He holds B.S. and M.S. degrees from the State University of New York at Albany, and a Ph.D. in Mathematics from the University of Rochester. He served as a member of the board of directors of CAUSE from 1986 to 1990, and as its chair in 1989. He was also a member of the board of trustees of EDUCOM from 1985 to 1990.

The major challenge for the use of technology in higher education is one of planning. In the face of certain change in the technology, it is important to develop a vision and goals for its use that are congruent with the institutional mission and a planning process that will help to realize that vision.

Most liberal arts colleges have been followers rather than pioneers in their use of information technology. This is appropriate given the size and expertise of their support staffs and the size of their technology-related budgets. Further, information technology has not been considered to be of strategic importance to the institution. Planning at such institutions places a heavy emphasis on technology transfer rather than technology development—on applying what has been proven at other institutions, rather than undertaking major experimentation with emerging technologies. "Strategic planning aims to exploit the new and different opportunities of tomorrow while minimizing any negative aspects of the unexpected challenges that will surely occur. This is in contrast with long-range planning, which tries to optimize for tomorrow the trends of today." (Penrod & West, 1989) A key to planning in this environment is to develop strategies that keep the information technology environment flexible and open to adaptation of proven approaches. In addition, information technology planning must be synchronized with institutional planning.

A Changing Climate for Institutional Planning

Most liberal arts colleges have traditionally planned in an informal manner. That is, planning responsibility was limited to a small number of individuals, usually the officers of the college. Often there was no broadly participative long-range planning process that dealt with issues of strategic importance to the institution. The absence of a formal institutional planning process, with its resultant goals, objectives, and close ties to the budget process, made it difficult for information technology planners to develop an appropriate vision. Further, *selective* liberal arts colleges, such as those heavily represented in this book, have been among the most financially healthy— thus they lack a fundamental driving force for more formal long-range planning. There are indications that the environment for these institutions is changing.

Forces are mounting to moderate some of the basic revenue sources available to such institutions, particularly tuition and fees. The antitrust investigation of the Justice Department begun in 1989 is significant, not for any likelihood of discovering wrongdoing, but rather because it is an indication that political pressure may be used to moderate the spiraling costs of higher education. The likely result will be more constrained financial environments at precisely the time that many colleges will need to consider making major investments in information technology resources. In this atmosphere, a planning process that closely ties the use of information technology resources to institutional mission and goals will be necessary if information technology initiatives are to receive their appropriate share of institutional resources.

In addition to tying into the institutional mission, applications of information technology must be consistent with the fundamental characteristics of the institution. Such characteristics provide the foundation for the information technology vision. For liberal arts colleges these include:

1. An institutional focus on teaching. Liberal arts colleges are primarily teaching institutions. Within this environment, the lecture/seminar approach, with small class size, has a long and hallowed tradition. Applications of technology that would radically alter this instructional setting—for example, by creating large classes using computer-assisted methods in place of faculty— are unthinkable.

2. Close faculty/student interaction. The Hamilton College catalogue describes, for example, students *working with* faculty, rather than *taking courses from* faculty. This is part of what makes the small liberal arts college an attractive option for prospective students when it is compared to the large research university.

3. Isolation. Many small liberal arts colleges are physically isolated from other institutions. While this creates a sense of community among those at the institution, it creates problems for faculty trying to remain productive as scholars. This is a particular problem in the more selective colleges where there is a heavier emphasis on continued professional activity as a condition of promotion and tenure.

4. Lack of economies of scale. A characteristic of small-
   ness is the inability to take advantage of economies
   that accrue from having a large number of people sharing
   a resource. This is often manifested in the small size of the
   staff of the information technology services organization.

The institutional mission and goal statements must be the foundation of all information technology planning. However, at many liberal
arts colleges such statements provide only a vague direction for the
planning process. They are often only general reaffirmations of the
value of liberal learning and critical thinking as compared with training
programs. There are exceptions, however. At Hamilton, for example,
the mission statement is unusually clear. Thus it was possible for a
formal planning process for information technology to follow naturally on the heels of the creation of a similar institutional process.

Unique Aspects of Planning at Liberal Arts Colleges

Generalizations about the planning processes at different institutions are prone to oversimplification because planning depends heavily upon the personalities of the leadership and the specific traditions
of those institutions. However, some characteristics of information
technology planning at three major institutional types—the liberal
arts college, the research university, and the community college—can
be distinguished in broad terms. These relate to the degree of centralization, the participants in planning, and the central focus of the
planning process.

The nature of decentralization and power among the three institutional types differs substantially and is reflected in their planning
processes. At research universities, decision making is generally
decentralized, with considerable power vested in the schools, research centers, and sometimes the individual departments that make
up the institution. At a prestigious research university, for example,
expenditures for computing in the school of business alone exceed the
budget for all centrally provided computing. In such an environment,
planning for information technology is generally a decentralized,
though highly coordinated, activity. At public universities the

situation may be further complicated by statewide or systemwide technology planning groups or by quantity purchasing agreements for both hardware and software. Often, the crucial factor that determines if planning is done at the level of the department, the school, the university, or the system is simply the source of funding.

Unlike research universities, which frequently obtain funds for computing from individual research grants, community colleges are principally funded by state allocations and thus have highly centralized decision making processes that focus on the teaching mission of the institution. Decisions for the college, such as requiring the integration of computing into all disciplines, is usually the result of top-down planning at the college (or system) level.

Private liberal arts colleges, especially the selective institutions represented in this book, fall somewhere between these two extremes. While particular departments—for example, computer science, or economics—may represent concentrations of power and knowledge that must be incorporated in the planning process, most planning and decision making tends to be centralized, though not to as great a degree as one finds in community colleges.

Different constituencies play dominant roles in information technology planning across the three institutional types. At community colleges, planning for information technology is usually an administrative responsibility with minor involvement by the faculty. This is partly a reflection of the large number of adjunct faculty at such institutions, individuals who do not have a major stake in the long-term future of the college. At universities, involvement of the faculty is critical, especially with respect to supporting research needs. University–wide planning must recognize the relative power of the various schools and involve faculty from them. At liberal arts colleges, faculty generally serve as representatives of the four major divisions of the liberal arts curriculum—the arts, humanities, social sciences, and natural sciences—and planning is frequently the combined responsibility of a faculty committee and senior administrators.

Finally, the focus for information technology at the three institutional types reflects their missions. Teaching, serving large numbers of students, and efficiency, are important themes in the community college setting. Computing is often viewed pragmatically, as a necessary training component for students who are already in— or who are about to enter—a highly competitive job market. Increasingly, a thorough acquaintance with computing is a prerequisite for a wide range of positions in business, finance, and the health professions, to name a few.

Research needs tend to drive the planning process at universities. At the level of the department or the school, planning may be largely a reactive process that takes advantage of the grant funding available to individual faculty members. University–wide planning is often motivated by the need to find ways of interfacing—rather than homogenizing—the wide array of hardware, software, and local network components across the institution. Interoperability, network standardization, software, and data translation are among the technical concerns that guide university-level information technology planning.

The selective liberal arts institution combines the teaching emphasis of the community college with some of the research motivations of the university. It generally eschews the practical training aspects of computing, although some faculty members, especially in the sciences, acknowledge that hands-on experience with computers is essential for both professional and post-graduate work in their fields. Information technology planning at liberal arts colleges is largely driven by the same forces that motivate library resource planning: the desire to provide students and faculty with the best possible resources for scholarship, including both teaching and research.

Starting a Planning Process for Information Technology Resources

Prior to the 1988–89 academic year, planning at Hamilton followed the traditional informal approach. Planning for information technology was similarly informal, with goals and strategies being the responsibility of the director of information technology services. The small college environment facilitated regular contact between the information technology services organization and the college community. However, as the decade of the eighties came to a close, computing expertise on the campus had significantly increased, departmental and individual requests for information technology resources exceeded available institutional financial resources, and there did not appear to be a clear understanding of institutional priorities.

In the fall of 1988, when Harry C. Payne became Hamilton's seventeenth president, he created a campus long-range planning committee as part of a process to set directions for the future of the institution. The campus committee was designed to parallel a similar committee of the board of trustees. With a capital campaign imminent, the need for a clear sense of priorities for the next decade was apparent. In the spring of 1989, a committee was constituted to plan for the use of information technology resources.

In an academic environment, process is paramount. The planning process for information technology must involve a representative group of campus constituencies and high-level decision makers.[1] Since academic and administrative computing and telecommunications have always been jointly managed at Hamilton, it was reasonable to set up a single committee with responsibility to set appropriate goals. The Information Technology Planning Committee (ITPC) was composed of six faculty, three administrators, two members of the staff, two students, and the director of information technology services and institutional research (ITS/IR). The dean and vice president for administration and finance are ex-officio members of the committee. The committee was charged to:

1. Assess the strengths and weaknesses of the current information technology environment relative to Hamilton's institutional goals and needs for instruction, research, and institutional management

2. Explore alternative approaches to meeting those needs

3. Make recommendations for strategies to guide the growth of information technology resources in the near future

In considering alternative approaches and recommending strategies, the committee realized it would be important to consider both

---

1. This point is discussed thoroughly in chapter 2.

external trends and the college's competitive position with respect to peer institutions. Since Hamilton was due for its decennial Middle States Accreditation visit in the fall of 1990, and since one focus of the self-study was to be the use of information technology in support of the academic program, it was decided to make this the first area of attention for the ITPC.

The starting point for information technology planning was Hamilton's mission statement. "Teaching in all its forms is the central mission of Hamilton College. At Hamilton it is understood that the pivotal commitment of the Faculty to the education of our students is the College's most important and enduring tradition" *(Hamilton College Catalogue* 1989/90).

Because of its representative nature, the ITPC was a large committee, and, therefore, it was difficult to schedule meeting times. In order to move the planning process along, it was decided that after the committee agreed on the major areas that needed to be addressed, the director of ITS/IR would prepare first drafts of goal statements and background materials for discussion purposes. Draft documents would be distributed to committee members a week in advance of the meetings at which they would be discussed. In this manner all members of the committee would have an opportunity to provide input to the revision process, even if they were not able to attend a particular meeting. This turned out to be a very effective way to keep the discussions moving along. The committee met approximately three times a month during the 1989–90 school year. In planning for information technology the committee followed the approach outlined in the remainder of this chapter.

Major Planning Areas

Regardless of the particular committee structure, there are four major areas that must be addressed by any long-range planning process for information technology resources:

1. Building and maintaining the *infrastructure* that
   will facilitate the use of information technology
   resources in support of the institutional mission.

2. Facilitating and supporting the *applications of the technology* for instruction, research, and institutional management.

3. Providing a *stable source of financing* for the first two areas.

4. Setting up an *evaluation process* to monitor progress toward achieving goals in areas 1 through 3.

Fundamental to consideration of alternatives in each area must be the effect the alternatives have on achieving the mission and goals of the institution and the degree to which an alternative is consistent with the fundamental characteristics of the institution. In addition, the institution does not exist in a vacuum, and each of its information technology goals must be constructed in light of reasoned assumptions about technological directions and the institution's competitive position with respect to peers. Being in the position of follower rather than leader, the liberal arts college has the advantage of being able to study those things that have proved effective at the leading research universities. The most technical planning area is the one dealing with the underlying information technology infrastructure.

Infrastructure

Infrastructure issues include networks, access to information technology resources (for faculty, students, and staff), facilities (classrooms, public clusters, and offices), staff providing support services, and availability of information resources (internal and external databases including the library). Planning for the creation and maintenance of the infrastructure is critical to providing an appropriate environment in which applications of information technology can flourish.

Networks

The infrastructure issue receiving the greatest attention in recent years has been the issue of networks. The decentralization of computing over the last decade has fundamentally changed the notion of access to information resources. Computers on the desktop have brought computing to the masses, but decentralization has created new problems as well. These problems include incompatibility of hardware and software, increased support costs to serve a broader spectrum of computer users, and the need for wider access to information databases. With the move to decentralization has come an increased focus on creation of networks of all varieties to tie together valuable institutional resources.

Senior administrators are discovering that the costs of such networks, both the initial capital investment and the ongoing costs, exceed initial projections. They must weigh whether investment in advanced networking technology is a wise use of institutional funds, relative to other possible expenditures. Also, in assessing the various options available for networking the campus, they must decide on the capacity of the network to carry varying degrees of information in the form of voice, data, and video. A legitimate concern is the way such networks contribute to the achievement of the fundamental mission of the institution.

Campus networks can ameliorate some of the fundamental problems related to decentralization, including incompatibility of information technology resources and the need for access to a broad collection of information resources.

For the most part, it does not appear that vendors are interested in making their hardware and software compatible with those of other vendors. Most, however, are willing to work toward assuring network compatibility, that is, making sure their systems observe emerging network standards, such as OSI (Open Systems Interconnection), so that information can be shared among systems. Choosing and promoting such standards must be a central part of any network planning. Thus, networks seem the best hope of getting incompatible equipment to work together. Once compatibility issues are addressed, information of all kinds can be made widely available.

The availability of a wide range of databases, both on and off campus, provide opportunities for improvement of the campus environment. Providing easy access to such databases is clearly a network challenge. The most common example involves automation of the campus library catalogue. On many small campuses, this provides the initial motivation for setting up a campus network. There is, however, much more that will soon be possible. Access to the library resources of other institutions, computer resources at supercomputer facilities, and inter–institutional communication among colleagues are all emerging as natural outgrowths of the development of a national data network. The campus network must be able to provide appropriate access to such resources for members of the college community. Beyond solving some of the problems related to decentralization of resources, campus networks can provide new opportunities for the institution to enhance the central role played by the classroom in the liberal arts environment.

Networks provide opportunities to extend classroom discussions beyond the physical boundaries of the classroom, thereby increasing faculty–student interaction. The availability of campuswide networks (and linkages to national and international networks) will make possible the "virtual classroom"—a resource that contains many of the features of the classroom without requiring students to be physically in the same room, yet providing faculty–student interaction, student–student interaction, and access to the instructor's notes.

The virtual classroom approach can supplement and even improve—but not replace—the regular classroom environment. At Hamilton, for example, we have been experimenting with a networked approach to improving students' critical reading skills. The system, called DISCUSS, facilitates the understanding of assigned reading material through an extension of, and preparation for, classroom discussion. The objective is to improve the quality of classroom discussion, not replace classroom interaction, thus making more effective use of existing classroom time.

In a similar fashion, networks can help reduce professional isolation of the liberal arts college faculty by providing them access to colleagues and databases at other institutions. Access to national networks can make faculty more productive in their scholarship as well as help them maintain close contact with their colleagues on other campuses. For a small institution with limited resources, this may be a cost-effective way to encourage continued scholarship. Further, it encourages the sharing of resources rather than the acquisition of resources, which provides some of the benefits usually associated with economies of scale.

In addition to providing connectivity, planning for the appropriate carrying capacity of the network must be a high priority. Currently most applications of computing on the liberal arts campus can be adequately met by transmission speeds of 19.2 KB or less, supplemented by departmental networks of higher speed. What will be necessary in the future?[2]

Access to Information Technology Resources

The best network will not help to further the institutional mission unless attention is paid to providing appropriate access to information technology resources for members of the college community. From a strategic perspective, providing faculty with personal computers on their desks can enhance the attractiveness of the institution. A number of institutions already provide computer systems to faculty, and more will surely do so as personal computers are recognized as essential tools for meeting the teaching, research, and service needs of the faculty. The coming decade will see an increase in competition for faculty caused by the retirement of those hired in the sixties when many colleges increased faculty size to match increased enrollments. Those liberal arts colleges that can enhance their teaching and learning environments will be in a better position to attract quality faculty.

At Hamilton, the Information Technology Planning Committee felt that it was no longer necessary to debate the value of personal computers in improving faculty productivity. Substantial numbers of faculty members, at almost any institution, will attest to how personal computers enable them to be more productive scholars, to produce higher quality course-related materials, to perform more effectively their committee and administrative responsibilities, and to improve the learning process for their students. Personal computing is not just a substitute for the typing that would otherwise be done by a secretary, but rather the basis of a whole different work style.

Significant national efforts are underway to address the issue of improving teaching and learning through the use of computing. Such efforts are being spearheaded by national disciplinary organizations

---

2. See Part Three for a detailed discussion of this issue.

such as the American Mathematical Society, the American Psychological Association, the American Chemical Society, and the American Sociological Association and by national computing organizations such as EDUCOM (through such efforts as the Educational Uses of Information Technology program).[3] One outcome of these efforts has been the realization that a precondition for faculty success in effective use of computing to improve their teaching is *using a computer for personal productivity,* and this is enhanced by having access to computing in their offices. Making the transition from being a non-user, or an occasional user, to a user in the classroom is nearly impossible unless intermediary steps are taken.

Providing computers in offices should be viewed as the *first step* to providing the tools for teaching, scholarship, and service for faculty. Questions related to campus networking, electronic mail, access to the library, and other internal and external databases are all derivative issues that first require faculty to have convenient access to computer resources. Already those faculty members who have computers in their offices are making use of such services to connect with national data sources and communicate with colleagues at other institutions.

The planning process must deal with providing appropriate access to information technology resources not only to faculty but also to students and staff. For example, is the approach of requiring, or strongly recommending, the purchase of a computer system by students appropriate for the institution?

Contrary to what the public often believes, almost no colleges (except those with a heavy focus on engineering or business) require students to purchase computers. Even strongly recommending a computer purchase is not a decision to be taken lightly. In this age of high tuitions, the additional cost of a computer will require a strong argument that ownership rather than access improves students' educational experience, in order to overcome strong criticism from parents and students.

Institutions often have considered strongly recommending a computer purchase as a way of transferring the burden of technology purchases from the institution to the student. The benefits of such a

---

3. See chapter 10 for further discussion of EUIT.

strategy are obvious: The institution can reduce its costs for equipment acquisition and maintenance; space for public computing facilities can be stabilized and possibly reduced; and the problem of equipment obsolescence and replacement can be held to a minimum.

However, unless some sort of standard is promoted, it is likely that incompatibility on a large scale will take place, compromising the value of computing in connection with work in the classroom. Even with a standard system, annual improvements in technology create internal incompatibilities. For example, freshmen may purchase machines capable of running software that is too sophisticated to operate on older machines purchased when juniors or seniors entered college.

At institutions that provide substantial need-based financial aid to their students, a strong recommendation to purchase a computer can create inequities among students or add an additional burden to an already strained financial-aid budget. It is not surprising that liberal arts colleges generally have been cautious about promoting computer purchases. Ultimately, the decision to require or strongly recommend student purchase of computers must be one that is based on the pedagogical mission of the institution. Other bases for the decision are fraught with peril. And it must be recognized that whatever approach the institution takes to deal with student access will have significant financial implications.

Facilities

Providing appropriate technology-equipped classrooms for faculty is essential if we are to expect infusion of computing into the curriculum. It has been demonstrated that in certain disciplines, concepts that are difficult to communicate in the traditional manner, using blackboard and chalk, can be made understandable by using a computer system and projection equipment. Improvements in technology have made the projection of computer images in the classroom setting affordable and transportable for most liberal arts colleges. Standards need to be developed for the technology-equipped classroom so that planning can be incorporated into the creation and renovation of educational buildings containing such classrooms. Space is a resource often in short supply on our campuses; thus we must be creative in utilizing our existing classrooms for teaching that is supported by technology. This is particularly true at Hamilton, where it has been impossible to find non-classroom space for the creation of new public computer clusters.

Public clusters have sprung up on campuses in response to the infusion of microcomputers into academic work. Long-range planning must deal with the future of such facilities. If most students and faculty own their own systems, what useful role will public clusters serve? On a small campus, should the strategy be to have many small clusters or a few large ones? What support services should be available in such facilities?

Especially on the liberal arts campus, the role of public clusters needs to be considered in the context of the residential nature of the campus. The vast majority of students at small liberal arts colleges live in college residence halls or in housing located very close to the campus. In the last decade many of these institutions have made significant efforts to integrate more closely the academic and residential lives of students. Achieving this end may require that students have access to academic resources in the residence setting. Computing is one of these resources. If this philosophy is adopted, either the location of public clusters must shift from academic buildings to residence halls or the purpose of public clusters must change substantially. On a heavily networked campus, the distributed model of computing in the residence halls largely supported by residence hall staff may be an appropriate approach that supports the integration of the academic and residential goals of the institution.

Support Services

The need for support services is very often underestimated in creating the infrastructure. One example already mentioned is staff necessary to support an advanced network. This is a particularly important planning area, since personnel are often the major ongoing cost of information technology and finding qualified individuals is difficult, especially for the small college. While finding and paying such personnel is difficult, the greater challenge is effectively managing them. Planning should not only involve deciding how many staff positions are necessary. Provision must be made for the continued professional development of those hired. As information technology organizations at liberal arts colleges increase in size, managers of those organizations must devote significantly more time to assuring the growth and professional development of their staffs. However, at a small college the expertise of a support services staff must be supplemented by an informed user community.

The responsibility of each member of the user community to develop his or her own expertise in using information technology resources has been largely ignored as the complexity of the campus environment has increased. Support staffs will always be small in number relative to the user community. Thus, it is critical that an extended support staff be created, consisting of knowledgeable users.

What are appropriate responsibilities of the user of information technology? Is it possible to create structures in which the user community functions as an extended support organization? Controlling the diversity of hardware and software supported on our campus is a necessity if we are to achieve high levels of support for our college communities. What are appropriate methods to assure consensus on standards to achieve controlled diversity?

In the 1990s institutions of higher education will be re-examining the way they operate, in order to survive, and even prosper, in a more constrained financial atmosphere. An area of focus in this examination is the variety of services that exist in support of the institutional mission and the way they are provided. Information technology support services are among the most important and expensive.

As our campuses move to a decentralized model of computing we must examine new paradigms for providing support services. There are numerous tradeoff factors that serve to increase or decrease the cost of support services, as shown in the following list. The more complex the information technology environment, the greater the need for support services and the higher the associated cost. Unless users assume a greater responsibility for their own computing needs there will be a greater need for specialized support personnel. Lack of standards, especially in the area of networking, will lead to incompatibilities and hidden redundancies that ultimately increase the cost of information technology support for the institution. These factors are interrelated; changes in approach to one often require a change in another if the provision of support services is to remain economical. Whatever choices are made, planning for support services is an essential part of constructing the necessary infrastructure.

Cost Accelerators	*Cost Decelerators*
Complexity of the computing environment	Controlled diversity of the computing environment
Centralized responsibility	User responsibility
Lack of standards	Observation of standards
Decentralization of computing	Centralization of computing

Availability of Information Resources

Having all the other pieces of the infrastructure but not having access to abundant information resources is like having a wonderful highway system but no place to go. The library is the central information resource on the liberal arts campus. Facilitating access to the library as well as to external databases should be one of the fundamental planning areas for building the infrastructure. This is an area of particular opportunity for the liberal arts college. The access requirements for information resources for faculty at such institutions often go well beyond the capabilities of the on-campus library. Providing convenient access to resources at other institutions can greatly enhance the research and teaching environment for faculty. Planners should consider the possibility of consortial arrangements with other institutions. With the availability of local, regional, and national networks, the next decade will be a time of emphasis on *access to,* rather than *ownership of,* information resources.

Library collections, especially periodicals and scholarly journals, are becoming increasingly expensive to produce, acquire, and store in printed form. Colleges and universities are collectively paying (the faculty member) to produce the research that goes into journals, then paying to have it printed (through page charges), and finally paying to acquire and house the journals. The shortage of space to house rapidly growing collections is a continuing problem for libraries.

Compact and shared storage can delay the time when new space will have to be constructed, but either approach is expensive.

Only by a fundamental change can the need for increasing space be brought under control. Instead of purchasing and storing information in many individual collections, information can be made available in electronic form and shared among those who need it—with printed copies generated on demand. This long-term strategy recognizes advances that will be made in electronic storage and networking technologies.

National efforts, such as those of the Coalition for Networked Information (CNI), are underway to change the emphasis of libraries from acquisition to access. Federal and private agencies are funding projects that encourage such sharing. Since most of the information that goes into journals is already composed in electronic form there is every reason to believe that the production cost to publishers can be significantly reduced if information is distributed electronically. The resulting savings can be passed on to consumers. Issues of copyright complicate national efforts, but it is likely that initiatives now underway will eventually resolve these problems, impelled by the more constrained financial environment of the coming decade.

Further advances in technology are making information resources available in new formats. Laser disk and CD Rom technologies allow institutions to obtain large information resources for direct use on their campuses. Can these be economically shared across a campus network? Or, on a small campus, does it make sense to provide access to these resources only to persons who go to the library or other information center? Thus far, very few colleges have addressed these issues directly and a viable model has yet to emerge.

Applications of the Technology

Even after the appropriate infrastructure is in place, there is no assurance that information technology will *in fact* be applied to major college activities. While curriculum content has undergone dramatic change in the last 150 years, instructional methodology in higher education has not changed significantly. Faculty and students gather several times a week in classrooms equipped with blackboards and chalk to discuss subject matter related to particular courses. The operational hypothesis is that if you bring talented faculty together with motivated students in a setting conducive to interaction and *let things happen*, quality learning will result. There is no strong evidence to refute the validity of this hypothesis.

Since computers are useful devices for accessing and manipulating information and since information is the basis of most of what goes on in higher education, much effort is being devoted to applying technology to the business of the academy. Natural applications arise in connection with research—creating whole new fields of research. Similarly, applications to administrative functions are equally straightforward, although generally more complex than first imagined. What is not clear is the role that computing can play in improving the main academic mission of the institution, namely teaching and learning. Much interesting work is being done—there have been many false starts, some notable successes, much discussion about the difficulty of creating useful software, and some discussion about assessing improvement attributable to the use of technology.[4] The following can be fairly said.

1. Very good examples exist showing how computing can improve students' understanding of subject matter *in certain disciplines.*

2. Creating instructional software is difficult, consumes a great deal of faculty and staff time, and is expensive.

3. Locating and adapting instructional software developed elsewhere for use in courses is easier than developing it, but is still not trivial.

4. General-purpose software tools such as word processors, spreadsheets, database managers, drawing programs, and statistical packages are being used successfully in connection with the teaching and learning process.

5. All four of these areas are improving to varying degrees as technology advances.

---

4. See chapter 11 for a discussion of the status and use of courseware at liberal arts institutions.

The institution must decide how to approach the important subject of applying technology. Making *major* investments in information technology in hopes of widespread improvements in the teaching and learning process is particularly risky since there is little to suggest that improvements will be recognized if they indeed take place. In that context, the institution must decide whether to be proactive, supportive, or resistive with respect to applications of information technology to the instructional process. There are substantial differences in the amount of resources that will have to be devoted to each approach.

Decisions are also necessary with respect to applications of information technology to the institutional management of the college. Applications of information technology to the administrative functions of the liberal arts college have proven to be more expensive and difficult than most senior administrators first assumed. The glossy brochures promising totally integrated management information systems with decision-support systems, have given way to the reality of expensive hardware, large programming staffs, and application backlogs. Since liberal arts colleges do not yet view institutional information as a strategic resource, it is more appropriate for such institutions, with their less complex and less formal management styles, to view administrative information technology applications as synonymous with automation. Attempting to develop administrative systems for decision support when the senior officers of the institution are not interested in directly accessing this information is wasteful of institutional resources.

Whether the approach taken is oriented towards decision support or merely automation, a clear focus of planning must be data integrity and consistency. Systems must be developed in a manner that assures consistency of data across the offices of the institution. Small institutions will be able to deal with this problem more easily than their highly decentralized university counterparts. The use of advanced software tools has been touted as a way for institutions more effectively to utilize their programming personnel.

What are appropriate investments in tools such as fourth-generation languages, CASE (Computer Assisted Software Engineering), relational databases, and object-oriented programming environments for the liberal arts colleges? Should the liberal arts institution, with its focus on teaching, be more proactive about applications of information technology to improving teaching and learning? Can it afford to be a pioneer in this area rather than a close follower? These questions will challenge planners in the coming years.

Assuring Adequate Financing

Information technology investments have generally been viewed as capital rather than operating expenses. Further, the secondary implications of acquisitions are often not planned. To reverse this trend it is necessary to consider carefully all the associated costs of the use of information technology resources and create a predictable stream of revenues to support those expenditures. Consideration must take place in the context of an environment in which the "library model" of centralized funding for computing has been dominant.

One of the most obvious and pressing financial issues is the problem of equipment amortization. Information technology equipment has been viewed for too long as a *one-time* purchase, rather than something that has a life-cycle. The result is similar to the *deferred maintenance problem* of the institution's physical plant. This thinking needs to be revised. For example, an institutional plan to provide each faculty member with access to computing at the desktop must be coupled with a replacement plan that treats each microcomputer as having a useful lifetime (for example, 3 to 5 years). It is not that the equipment will be *functionally* obsolete in a few years' time, but that on the one hand advances in hardware will make the older equipment less cost-effective to repair and on the other that advances in software will require systems with capabilities beyond those of the existing equipment. Usually, faculty members have different levels of computing expertise and needs. So one way to deal with aging equipment is to recycle it within the institution until it is no longer economical to repair it. Failure to account for life-cycles of information technology resources will create continual periods of dissatisfaction with the information technology environment.

At the same time, the institution must resist vendor pressure continually to invest in the "latest and fastest." An often overlooked strength of the liberal arts environment is the deliberate way in which change is handled. The support structures are not in place for an environment of rapid technological change—rapid change that would be accompanied by serious disorientation of staff and a decrease in the level of support services.

An even larger information technology investment that must receive a steady source of funding is the creation, maintenance, and replacement of institutional administrative information systems. Just as equipment has a useful life cycle, so too do management information systems. The length of the life cycle will depend on the degree to which the mission and strategic goals of the institution change over time. The systems that support the information needs of the institution involve both software and hardware, as well as the personnel who design and operate them.

Are models of funding other than the library model appropriate in this environment? Can liberal arts institutions develop partnerships with vendors that will result in revenue streams to fund continued applications of information technology in a manner similar to research universities? The answers a college develops to these questions play a critical role in the planning process.[5]

The Ongoing Evaluation Process

Higher education is better at setting plans in motion than it is at monitoring how well those plans are going. This is especially true at small colleges, where each person is already covering many functional areas. Further, evaluation requires that objectives be stated in such a manner that progress can be discerned. Finally, evaluation of progress is never quite as much fun as making the progress. Evaluation looks to the past—what has, or has not, been achieved—while planning looks to the future, to the exciting and the possible. Despite all these difficulties, effort should be devoted to building into any planning

---

5. Some answers to these questions are discussed in chapter 3.

process a means of gathering feedback on progress towards achieving the objectives of the planning process. Momentum for long-range planning depends on the credibility of the process, and that credibility can be greatly enhanced by the feedback that comes from a well designed process of evaluation. Some general evaluation guidelines for the use of Information Technology Resources have been jointly developed by CAUSE and EDUCOM (1988).

It is important that a means of evaluation be built into the planning process. In some areas this can be easily done in a quantitative manner. For example, providing a campus network of sufficient bandwidth and density on the campus can be broken down into measurable objectives. On the other hand, enhancing the teaching process through the use of information technology is far more difficult to assess given the general lack of criteria on what constitutes improvement. If progress towards meeting an objective cannot be discerned then the value of the objective itself is subject to debate.

Given these difficulties, the evaluation process should be as simple as possible. For each long-range objective, set a specific time line for achieving that objective, and either designate those observables that will be measured, how they will be measured, and when they will be measured, or create survey instruments that can be used on a periodic basis to collect subjective information that relates to progress on meeting the objective. Information gathered in this process should be regularly summarized and reported back to planning committees.

Let us assume, for example, that the objective is to provide each faculty member who desires one with access to an appropriate work-station at the desktop on a five-year renewal cycle. The time line should start with an accounting of which faculty members have computers and when they were acquired, as well as the number who do not have computers. Each year a "snapshot" of progress towards meeting this objective should be taken. The snapshot should include a report on the cost of the partial implementation during that year. This cost should be compared with the planning estimates for achieving this objective. Such comparisons serve as a check on the accuracy of the projections that were made and can also serve to build credibility into the planning process.

If the objective is to facilitate the improvement of the teaching and learning process by providing appropriate technology-equipped classrooms, the information collected on an annual basis might more appropriately be a combination of objective and subjective assessments. In addition to tabulating the number of courses and students affected by technology-related initiatives, the evaluators might ask each faculty member and student to complete a short survey that gathers their perceptions about the value of such activities. Such information can be useful to other faculty members considering using computing in connection with their courses, as well as to the planning committee in considering expansion of investments in this area.

Conclusion: Opportunities, Risks, and Cautions

The nineties are a decade of technological opportunity for the liberal arts college. Institutions that have been close followers will be presented with opportunities to choose from among a collection of proven information technology alternatives to further teaching and learning. Coupled with these opportunities are significant risks, including the potential to squander significant financial resources, failure to understand the personnel implications of technological change, and overpromising and under-delivering. Many of these risks can be addressed by a well constructed planning process, while others must be recognized as possible consequences of planning.

The application of information technology to the liberal arts setting has a price tag that scares financial vice-presidents at even the most financially healthy liberal arts colleges. If institutional decisions are driven by changes in technology rather than institutional need, financial resources will be wasted. For example, vendor claims of obsolescence of equipment barely out of packing crates have prevented many institutions from developing strategies that recycle aging equipment to less experienced users. A major component of the financial impact of information technology applications that has been poorly planned in the past is the associated cost of knowledgeable support personnel.

Without proper planning colleges will fail to consider the human implications of technological change. In the long run this is the most expensive part of creating an effective information technology environment. Such colleges will be caught in the cycle of high expectations, followed by lack of trained staff to achieve those expectations, followed by failure, and finally discouragement. The result is debilitating to those responsible for meeting these expectations. Without a clear sense of purpose and without adequate resources, substantial staff turnover and burnout will result. The institution will move from crisis to crisis, unable to meet rising user expectations.

Finally, it must be realized that planning itself is time consuming, demanding of both the creative and physical energies of the participants. This is particularly important at the small college where faculty and staff have significant commitments to their teaching, research, and professional service activities. It is not an activity to be entered into casually. Those involved must be committed to do more than compile wish lists. They must be ready to deal with the inevitable tradeoffs among need, feasibility, and financial impact. The process will take more time than expected, but will provide a direction for the use of information technology that will make future decisions less difficult.

As Daphne Layton has pointed out, "institutions oriented primarily toward teaching undergraduates will not—and cannot—make the same choices as large research universities. But they do have to find the right level of technology for their campuses" (1989). An effective long-range planning process for information technology resources is the key to making connections among the institutional mission, user expectations, human resources to support the technology, and the needed financial investments. Central to this process is answering the question: Which investments will have the greatest impact in achieving the institutional mission and goals and in being consistent with institutional characteristics? This is no longer a question that can be answered just by the director of computer services and the financial vice-president, but rather must involve a representative long-range planning process.

References

CAUSE/EDUCOM. 1988. *Evaluation guidelines for institutional information technology resources.*

Decker, Richard, Stuart Hirshfield, David Paris, and Nathanial Strout. 1989. Computer assisted instruction in the liberal arts using a simple authoring system. *Journal of Computing in Higher Education* 1:21–38.

Hamilton College Catalogue, 1989/90, page 11.

Layton, Daphne N., ed. 1989. *Integrated planning for campus information systems.* Dublin, Ohio: OCLC Online Computer Library Center.

Penrod, James, and Thomas W. West. 1989. Strategic planning for computing and communications. In *Organizing and managing information resources on campus*, ed. Brian L. Hawkins. Reading, Mass.: Addison-Wesley.

Planning for Information Technology Resources: The Methods

Joanne M. Badagliacco
Pomona College

Joanne M. Badagliacco is the director of academic computing at Pomona College, where she is responsible for all aspects of instructional and research computing. Prior to coming to Pomona College in 1988, Dr. Badagliacco was the director of academic computing at Hunter College of the City University of New York for eight years.

Dr. Badagliacco is a frequent presenter at national conferences, most recently speaking at EDUCOM, IBM/ACIS, and the Snowmass Seminar on Academic Computing. She has been the program director for several grants to Pomona College to integrate information technology into the curriculum. She has also received personal grants for the development of social science courseware.

In addition to her position as director of academic computing, she is an associate professor of sociology, having received her Ph.D. degree in sociology from Columbia University. She teaches regularly and has conducted research, lectured, published, and participated in panel discussions on gender and race issues in computing and in the sociology of reproduction. She is on the editorial board of Social Science Computer Review, *the Council of the Microcomputer Section of the American Sociological Association, and a former member of the Steering Committee of the Consortium of Liberal Arts Colleges. Dr. Badagliacco frequently consults for colleges and universities on academic and administrative computing planning.*

"Would you tell me, please, which way I ought to go from here?"
"That depends a good deal on where you want to get to," said
   the Cat.
"I don't much care where—" said Alice.
"Then it doesn't matter which way you go," said the Cat.
"—so long as I get *somewhere*," Alice added as an explanation.
"O, you're sure to do that," said the Cat, "if you only walk
   long enough."

Lewis Carroll *Alice's Adventures in Wonderland* (1865)

Planning for information technology can best be defined and justified
as planning in response to the instructional, research, and administrative needs of an institution. The purpose of such planning is to link
the goals of the institution in each of these areas to the actions that
are necessary to achieve those objectives, as we have seen in the
previous chapter.

In this chapter, I address *types* of plans and the *process* of planning
for the future of information technology resources and services in
liberal arts colleges.[1] Planning is necessary because of the following
factors.

- The technological changes of the present and recent
  past take place rapidly.

- The complexity of technological advances needs to
  be approached in an organized fashion in order to
  maximize the potential of these advances.

- Information technology resources are not only
  costly, but are becoming increasingly important in
  all areas of higher education.

- The provision and delivery of information technology
  resources and services need to be professionalized.

- Problems relating to computing services, office automation, data processing, and networking need to be
  dealt with effectively.

---

1. The reader is encouraged to consult the references for more complete and
   detailed information on the topics presented here.

Liberal arts colleges are often involved in planning. At the college-wide level, what we may refer to as *institutional prioritizational plans* are developed. They include an assessment of the mission of the college, its resources, and the projects and other activities that must be undertaken in order to accomplish that mission with the available resources. The adjective "prioritizational" indicates the necessity of choosing among numerous desirable activities and rank ordering them based upon the limitations imposed by the resources and the philosophy of the institution.

The overall structure of the planning process can, and perhaps should be, a fluid process. Many of the ideas for planning discussed in this chapter become important and necessary under very different circumstances, and each college and each planning group must determine the most important issues for the particular setting of that institution. For example, involving faculty in planning decisions may be the normal, accepted mode of operation at one school, while at another this might be seen as quite innovative or even invasive.

In this chapter I describe various types of plans and identify several processes that offer flexibility for planning and their relationship to the philosophy and structure of an institution. I also examine the steps involved in the planning cycle itself. For institutions that have not yet—or not recently—embarked on the adventure of overhauling their computer services, the ideas presented in this chapter may serve as a field guide to the planning process.

Types of Plans

Several types of plans are appropriate to the academic setting and to information technology in particular. *Prospective, operational, initiative-response,* and *budget* plans are discussed in the following sections.

The Prospective Plan

Planning, like many other human activities, is subject to fads, trends, and evolutions in concept and terminology. In the 1960s, colleges were deeply committed to a practice termed *long-range planning.* A long-range plan is an internal blueprint for a fixed period of time that defines explicit activities and outcomes for an institution, usually with little or no provision for modification. For example, during the 1960s many liberal arts colleges devised ten-year building plans that did not include built-in flexibility to respond to changes in demographics or other external forces. As a result, those colleges now have some buildings that for various reasons are inappropriate, are unable to accommodate expansion, and are now prompting the development of costly new building projects.

By the 1980s, the recognition that external factors play an ever increasing role in determining the life of the college led to a trend known as *strategic planning.* While similar in scope and time frame to long-range planning, this approach pays greater attention to external influences upon the institution and incorporates greater flexibility to allow for ongoing plan modifications. As Cope (p. 1) explains, "Long-range plans [focus] upon institutional goals and objectives five years from now; strategic planning asks what decision is appropriate today based upon an understanding of where the critical external variables will be five years from now."

For the sake of simplicity, the term *prospective plan* will encompass both long-range and strategic plans. In the context of information technology planning, prospective plan will refer to any plan with a scope that includes the following:

- A broad variety of such elements as technology, personnel, and organization

- A time line of three years or more

- A direct relationship to the mission and prioritizational planning of the institution as a whole

- A sensitivity to external influences

- A built-in mechanism for ongoing modification

The purpose of a prospective plan for the information technology group is to develop and establish an effective and efficient framework to meet the future responsibilities of the group. It has as its fundamental aims the establishment of both the organizational and the technical infrastructures for information technology on the campus and the definition of broadly related goals such as levels and types of support for instruction, research, and administration.

A prospective plan for *academic* computing involves defining how information technology is going to support instructional and research endeavors at the college. Such a plan takes into account anticipated curricular modifications and developments at the institution and a prediction of research activities. A prospective plan for *administrative* computing involves the application of information technology to various support activities on the campus such as admissions recruitment, fund raising, registration, student services, and so forth. This plan is based on current levels of computerization of administrative functions and projected developments in these and as yet unautomated services.

Smith College, for example, recently completed an extensive three-year plan for academic computing. The plan includes a concise statement of mission, extensive documentation of assumptions regarding the college and other relevant matters, a statement of the present status of academic computing at the college, a detailed list of goals and objectives, a series of proposed steps for implementation of the plan, and a discussion of the budget implications of the plan. The format, scope, and detail of Smith's plan are similar to those of prospective plans developed in the last decade by Grinnell, Kenyon, Bryn Mawr, Reed, Vassar, and many other liberal arts colleges in the forefront of computing.

The Operational Plan

An *operational plan* implements the prospective plan by establishing the objectives and goals for a specific time frame, such as the upcoming academic year. This type of plan contains details of particular projects, activities, and resources that need to be acquired, updated, or installed over the lifetime of the plan.

For example, an administrative operational plan, intended to implement the broad goal of strengthening the development office, might contain details of specific software to be acquired and installed and personnel to be hired or trained. It might also include specifications for additional hardware, such as terminals to be purchased and placed in the appropriate staff offices. An academic computing operational plan, intended to implement the broad goal of strengthening foreign language instruction, might include the choice of which foreign languages are to be addressed in a particular year, the necessary courseware and hardware to be installed, and the plans for training faculty members and support staff.

The Initiative-Response Plan

> Chance favors only the mind that is prepared.
>
> Louis Pasteur (1822–95)   Quoted by René Vallery-Radot
> in *The Life of Pasteur* (1927)

An *initiative-response plan* is a direct and timely proposal defining how the information technology group should react to a particular, usually unanticipated, opportunity. An opportunity such as a major bequest to the college may present itself at any time throughout the planning cycle, and an immediate response is required. The response must be addressed specifically to this particular issue, taking advantage of the unforeseen resources to achieve an objective from the prospective plan that has not as yet been implemented.

For example, Pomona College recently received a major gift to be used for erecting a new social sciences building. This gift provided the opportunity to develop computing resources for the social science disciplines that were part of the prospective plan, but for which funding had not yet been identified. The response from the information technology group was to work directly with the social sciences building committee to create detailed plans for incorporating electronic classrooms, student laboratories, and faculty research facilities. Because the prospective plan contained general outlines of such facilities, it was possible for the response to this initiative to be timely and relevant.

The Budget Plan

A *budget plan* identifies the financial and personnel requirements needed to achieve the short-range operational objectives and to establish the priorities and fiscal boundaries for projects in the following budget period. A budget plan is not a budget. Budgets contain specific line items and dollar amounts in considerable detail. Budget plans, on the other hand, are much more general, theoretical, and goal oriented. In addition, budget plans contain justifications for their contents.

A typical budget plan is developed as a result of prospective, operational, or initiative-response planning. It includes discussions of the costs of implementing various goals, the potential sources of funding and other support, and a schedule for implementation based upon the availability of resources. Realistic budget plans are cast in the light of institutional prioritizational planning—that is, they are not wishful thinking, but rather reasonable interpretations of the institution's resources and intentions for employing those resources.

Budget plans are not designed to stand alone. They are directly related to another plan; they should refer to that other plan and be appended thereto. For example, a prospective plan for information technology might include the goal of installing a fiber optic network backbone throughout the campus. The related budget plan would encompass the major financial implications of such an installation—trenching the campus, laying conduit, pulling cable, wiring buildings, installing terminal servers, and so on. The budget plan also includes a justification for the estimated overall expenditures associated with each aspect of the project.

Budget plans often include personnel expenditures. An operational plan, for example, may include a goal that requires the appointment or retraining of various personnel. The budget plan should include an estimate of the various expenses associated with implementing these personnel activities. It is not necessary in the plan to include specific accounting for all costs (retirement, medical and other fringe benefits, and so on). A rough estimate is sufficient, together with its justification.

The Process of Planning

Regardless of the type of planning that is being undertaken, recognizing and understanding the *process* of planning is important if the plan is to be successful. Several aspects of the planning process can be identified. These phases include assessing the planning environment, defining the objectives for planning, designing the plan, implementing the plan, and the role of evaluation in planning.

The Planning Environment

Planning Approaches. Planning can be initiated from at least two quite different perspectives. Sometimes the highest levels of administration in a college decide that planning is needed. The reasons are many and may include a lapse of time since previous such efforts or a change in institutional goals or top administration. In this case, planning is imposed from the top down, and the information technology group must do its planning following the guidelines imposed from above.

At other times, there may be no institutional imperative, and the impetus for planning comes from within the group itself. For whatever reasons, the information technology group decides that it needs to initiate or review or update its plans. In this case, planning comes from the bottom up. The group determines what its goals and needs are and, using its plan, tries to convince the college to agree.

Organizational Structure. The initial stage of the planning process has been aptly named the "planning audit" by Naylor (p.46). Before the question of how to address the plan can be answered, the organizational structure and the structure of planning of the institution must be examined. It may be necessary to gather some data at this stage of the planning process, but a good understanding of the planning environment does not take very long. The challenge facing a planner is to develop a plan with sensitivity to the existing environment.

A solid understanding of the organizational structure of the institution is fundamental to the preparation for planning. Is the administration of the college centralized or decentralized? How autonomous are departments, faculty members, and special programs, for example? Moreover, who are the important players, and how do they interact with the administration and the trustees of the college? One cannot adequately plan to address the needs of the college if, for example, one assumes that a particular vice-president or provost can make a specific decision—say, to install an electronic classroom in a new building—when in fact the departments to be housed in the new building have been given the autonomy to use the space as they see fit for *departmental* needs, which may or may not include the electronic classroom the *college* needs.

In sum, a beginning step in planning is reflecting on the organization and hierarchy of the institution. This will, undoubtedly, require knowledge of the politics of the campus and familiarity with those whose input matters more than others. One approach is simply to ask faculty, support staff, and students to name those whom they think are important members of the community. Another method is to examine carefully the rationale, effectiveness, and composition of college-wide committees. Regardless of the planning strategy, it is vital to include these important players in the planning process, at least at some level.

The Mission of the College.   Planners must understand the organizational structure of the college, but more importantly, must understand the mission of the college and the philosophy behind that mission. Is there a consensus among the administration and faculty members about the mission? Where is the mission explicitly stated, who authored it, and when was it written? The overarching objective of any planning for information technology and resources will be to answer the question: *How should the computing services group meet the goals of the mission?* If an institution prides itself in placing teaching first, for example, planning for information services must reflect teaching — not to the exclusion of research or administrative services — but certainly first and foremost. For example, Pomona College believes that its purpose

> . . . is the pursuit of knowledge and understanding through study in the sciences and the humanities. A diverse, socially supportive community, the College makes every effort to provide faculty and students with an atmosphere stimulating to intellectual and creative endeavor, yet tranquil enough for the reflection and deliberation on which reason and imagination depend. [*Pomona College Catalog,* 1990–91 front cover]

In planning for the future of computing services, therefore, this mandate must be reflected in all objectives, planning, development, and growth. The ability to define objectives and to provide growth opportunities for administrative and research computing depends crucially on the obligation to fulfill the college's primary goals.

The Larger College Plan. Planning for information technology should always be viewed as only one part of the overall plan for the institution. It is not possible to plan adequately for the future without first having a firm understanding of the larger college plan and the role that the information technology group plays in that plan. Departmental planning within a vacuum is likely to be unsuccessful. Consequently, the planning process begins by finding out if a prospective college plan exists. If so, when was it written and by whom? What were the objectives? In addition, an inventory can be taken of developments that are planned for major areas of the college, such as new construction, new programs, curricular expansion, and administrative changes. Furthermore, it is helpful to ascertain whether the college plan has been updated, evaluated, or revised, and whether there have been any plans written to meet special initiatives. If ad hoc plans have been developed, what were the objectives and were these objectives met?

Another important aspect of the preliminary assessment of the campus planning atmosphere is determining if there is consensus in the community regarding the existing overall college plan and plans in the offing. Questions that are commonly asked include: What attention is paid to the college plan? Is it taken seriously, referred to, and consulted? Or, is it just another piece of administrative paper? Knowing how the college plan is perceived is important, because if everyone feels that the plan is on a steady course, any new departmental plan should ensure that information technology is a solid component of that overall plan for the college. If, on the other hand, little support is expressed for existing plans or future planning, it will be necessary to devise a plan that stands on its own and that can withstand any revising that the college-wide plan may face.

Who Are the Planners?

> In the construction of a country it is not the practical workers but the idealists and planners that are difficult to find.
>
> Sun Yat-sen, *Chung-shan Ch'üan-shu,* vol. 2 (1936)

Another useful determination at the beginning of the planning process is to identify who is responsible for planning at an institution and to find out how this person or persons perceive the future development of information technology. At some colleges it has been necessary to educate this planning group about information services, what is being done presently, and what it is hoped will be accomplished in the future. This education normally does not take the shape of a formal report or presentation; an informal "enlightenment" is generally found to be appropriate.

Most often, grants office or development office staff should be the information technology planner's greatest allies. They have, of course, been given specific initiatives to fund. Once information technology is seen as important among those initiatives, these offices will seek innovative and creative ways to fund information resources. Potentially, every invitation for a college to participate in a funded program can benefit information technology needs—if they have been planned well. One role of the planner is to be ready to seize such an opportunity by writing an initiative-response plan that adapts to specific programmatic needs and creatively spends the donors' money.

To illustrate, one college recently received an invitation from a major foundation to enhance library resources, especially the use of remote databases among the faculty for research and instruction. One of the existing needs of this institution was funding to expand their nascent campus network backbone. The foundation had explicitly excluded initiatives such as networking from their call for proposals. However, the college was able to convince the foundation that in order to achieve their primary goal (database dissemination) it was necessary to support network development.

Because the college had already planned for networking and was seeking funding to continue its growth, the campus development officers were aware of this need and worked cooperatively with the information technology group to write a successful proposal. Nowhere was this proposal specifically aimed at networking. It was pitched as support for library services and database dissemination, but in response to this initiative the college was able to progress toward its networking goals.

Defining the Objectives for Planning

The process of defining the objectives for successful planning should be begun in light of the mandate of the college and its priorities. Among the questions to consider during this definition process are: Who are the users of information technology resources? What are their needs? What are the relevant major developments in computing? What role does an advisory committee play? What is the involvement of the computing staff?

Who Are the Users? It is important first to identify the users of the services of the information technology group. The clientele and the objectives for computing differ from campus to campus. Each campus is idiosyncratic; for example, on some campuses the physical science departments may have their own computing resources paid for and staffed by departmental or grant funds. On other campuses, however, the major consumer of centralized computing resources may be the physical sciences. Some colleges may aim to integrate computing into all instruction, while at other institutions only a few courses use computers. On some campuses academic and administrative computing are strictly separated, while at other schools there is only one computing center. The configuration on a given campus will have clear implications for the political realities of goals and support for computing on that campus. Before any effective planning can be undertaken, the planner must have a clear understanding of the intended users of the information technology services.

The next consideration in the early stages of plan development is to clarify the driving forces behind computing and to understand campus politics. For example, if the goal of the president is to promote equity in the distribution of resources among all academic departments, but the social sciences are demanding mainframe support for large databases while the humanities show no interest whatsoever in computing, the planner must take this apparent inconsistency into consideration. Who should be served? The "squeaky wheels" or the "silent majority?" Or, is it possible to serve some combination of both? The wrong choice can lead to alienating some major users or to the acquisition of equipment and software that remain unused except, perhaps, as doorstops and paperweights.

Often, on small liberal arts campuses, departments consist of five or fewer professors, one of whom may be the college "star." In this case, it is sometimes necessary to cater to the needs of the star at the expense of equity, because of the realities of small campus politics. At small colleges, one does not have the luxury of dealing impersonally. We know everybody and everybody knows us, and we must take individual personalities into account when planning.

What Are the Users' Needs? After the users are identified, their needs must be ascertained. Many techniques have been used in liberal arts colleges to determine user needs. A combination of techniques, chosen to meet the unique environment of a particular college, has proven to be most appropriate. Several strategies have been used successfully at various colleges.

At some colleges a short survey is administered to all students at registration in the fall. From this survey, such information as how many students have their own computers and what software they use for various purposes can be determined. The results of this survey are particularly important in planning for public access facilities and services.

Another technique is to survey the faculty and administration. For example, at Pomona College the faculty are surveyed in several ways. All new faculty members are interviewed by the dean of the college and the director of academic computing to determine their computing needs, both research and instructional. The results of these interviews are used to provide appropriate resources to incoming faculty members. In addition, each semester all current faculty members are asked to complete a form indicating their current computing requirements. These forms provide a basis for planning instructional services. Similar surveys can be developed for administrative users.

At small liberal arts colleges, one of the best ways to keep abreast of the needs of faculty and administrators is to maintain informal contact with those who make significant use of computing. The planner should be prepared to gather information about users' needs whenever the opportunity arises; in a small college community this could be in the gym, the grocery store, the library, and elsewhere.

There are also numerous avenues for making formal contact with divisions, departments, department chairs, program directors, and so forth. At Pomona College, the director of academic computing has taken the opportunity to speak with and listen to the faculty at college-wide faculty meetings, divisional meetings, meetings of individual departments, and meetings of the faculty of specialized programs. To make possible these contacts, she has to locate the groups, invite herself to meetings, and obtain a place on the agenda. Attending these meetings is particularly helpful in prospective planning, because in addition to specific computer-related information, she gets a sense of the direction of the department, division, or program. This same approach can be taken with various groups in administration as well, for example, the registrar's office or the admissions office.

In addition, it can be useful to monitor the use of system resources. Many colleges have found it is helpful to maintain detailed records of the utilization of all resources (hardware, software, and personnel) of the computing center. In this way, it is easy to identify which services are underutilized and which need to be expanded, upgraded, or replaced. Williams College, for example, has used commercially available software designed to monitor utilization of its administrative computing hardware. The results of this monitoring are then used to determine the availability of resources for future projects and whether new hardware or upgrades to the current system are required.

What Are the Relevant Major Developments? Often, events on and beyond the campus will provide a serendipitous opportunity for strengthening computing resources and services. For example, Scripps College took advantage of a major project to trench its campus for a new irrigation system, and added conduit to the trenches to contain communications cabling. Harvey Mudd College has arranged with a local cable television company to lay conduit for computer networking as an adjunct to their primary project of providing cable television to the dormitories.

Another example of a relevant development is the invitation from a foundation to submit a proposal for a grant program or the receipt of a significant gift to the college. As Pasteur said, however, "Chance favors only the mind that is prepared." In other words, serendipitous events should not take planners by surprise. One can and should keep abreast of events on campus and trends in philanthropy.

These situations are good examples of when initiative-response planning comes to the fore. In their prospective planning, Harvey Mudd College could not have known, for example, that a cable television company would want to wire the campus when it did. But they were aware of the nationwide trend toward cabling for television—even dormitories—and were prepared to seize the opportunity when it presented itself.

In order to take advantage of these opportunities, the planner has to be in contact on a regular basis with those persons on the campus who are responsible for the physical plant management and new construction. To achieve this, the planner needs to build a rapport with those persons, to be seen by them as an important consumer of their expertise, one who can save the college considerable expense by avoiding duplication of existing or pending efforts.

Planners must be aware of major developments in the computing industry. Elsewhere in this book important issues for the 1990s are discussed. Such subjects as newer and faster hardware, networking protocols, and production software are important to the planning process. An awareness of these developments is the only way to avoid being saddled with "white elephants." While it is impossible to avoid all errors, without such an awareness these errors are much more likely.

In order to gather this information and develop this awareness computer center staff members must keep up to date on the trade literature, subscribe to various electronic network conferences, maintain close working relations with vendors, undertake beta testing of new products, communicate with their counterparts on other campuses, and attend professional conferences. Much of the knowledge that will be gathered may not be relevant for a particular campus. However, a judicious culling can provide crucial guidance for planning.

One other excellent source of current information for planning is found in professional organizations and consortia. Such national groups as EDUCOM, Educational Uses of Information Technology (EUIT), CAUSE, Association for Computing Machinery Special Interest Group for University and College Computing Services (ACM/SIGUCCS), Consortium of Liberal Arts Colleges (CLAC), among many others, hold professional meetings and produce numerous publications that are indispensable for successful planning. In addition, there are many regional and local groups that make valuable information available. For example, at the Claremont Colleges, designated representatives of the six institutions meet regularly to discuss issues of mutual concern and to exchange information.

Regional and local groups also allow for the coordination of efforts, and sometimes a consequent reduction in cost by economies of scale. Examples of such local coordination involving liberal arts colleges include: the Five College Consortium (Mount Holyoke, Smith, Amherst, Hampshire, and the University of Massachusetts); Haverford, Bryn Mawr, and Swarthmore Colleges; the Claremont Colleges; and Trinity College and Yale University. Informal contact among similar colleges can also prove quite beneficial. By keeping in touch and exchanging ideas, plans, and planning documents, colleges learn from each other and do not have to "reinvent the wheel."

The ability to plan successfully for the future can also be greatly informed by a broad and general understanding of the major developments on the horizon in the educational uses of information technology. Several major national conferences and publications are devoted to new developments in academic computing. These conferences include: EDUCOM, DECUS (Digital Equipment Corporation Users' Society), Macademia and MacWorld, IBM/ACIS (Academic Computing Information Systems); as well as discipline-specific conferences such as ACH/ALLC (Association for Computers and the Humanities/Association for Libraries and Linguistic Computing), ICDBHSS (International Conference on Databases in the Humanities and Social Sciences), and the annual meetings of professional societies. Another source of information regarding the latest developments resides in professional periodicals such as *EDUCOM Review, Edutech Report,* the *EDUCOM Strategies Series on Information Technology, Social Science Computing Review, Computers and the Humanities,* and various others.

It is not possible for one person to be totally knowledgeable regarding all details of the latest applications in all disciplines. The specific details can be left to individual specialists or users. What is important for planning is a general knowledge of trends and developments that transcend individual applications and are indicative of likely new directions for higher education computing. For example, three to five years ago many speakers at national conferences were discussing the likelihood of using hypermedia and interactive video. Today, a large number of such applications are now commonplace. The institutions that incorporated the early information into their planning are now in a position to take advantage of the latest packages.

What Role Does an Advisory Committee Play? Many colleges have found that an advisory committee on information technology provides several benefits directly related to planning.[2] Such a committee can consist of representatives of all user constituencies, including students. It can serve as a liaison between users and planners and as an advocate for special interest groups. The committee can serve to gather information, providing a convenient method for assessing the needs and interests of different users, be they academic or administrative.

It is well to keep in mind that "a camel is a horse that was designed by a committee." An advisory committee as a whole usually cannot be expected to write a prospective plan. The appropriate role of a large committee is to provide information to, feedback from, and liaison with those who will be most directly affected by the plan, the users. In addition, the committee can be one of the most effective vehicles for "selling" a plan to the college community, because its members had a hand in its development and have a stake in its success. On some campuses, a subgroup of the larger committee might be charged with actually writing the plan.

At Pomona College, where academic and administrative computing are separate departments, there are several advisory committees. For example, for academic computing, there is a committee consisting of faculty members representing each division of the college, two students, and the director of academic computing, *ex officio.* This committee advises the director of academic computing; it does not involve itself in day-to-day operations. The committee deals with such larger issues as: Should the dormitories be networked? or, Do we need

---

2. See chapter 4 for a discussion of advisory committees from an organizational rather than a planning perspective.

another computerized classroom? The full committee also has a major role in gathering information and presenting to the community prospective plans for academic computing; a subcommittee (the chair of the advisory committee and the director of academic computing) work together on writing such plans.

Pomona also has a joint academic and administrative committee that is charged with planning for campus networking, consisting of the directors of academic and administrative computing, the vice president and dean of students, the director of campus planning, and the chairpersons of the Academic Computing Advisory Committee and of the executive committee of the faculty. This committee recently delivered its overall recommendations for networking at the college for the next decade. This is an example of how prospective planning for information technology is integrated with and is vital to the planning process of the entire institution. Here, a subject—networking—has to be dealt with specifically in the academic computing plan and the administrative computing plan, but also must be included in the institutional prioritizational planning for the entire college.

What Is the Involvement of the Information Technology Staff? Liberal arts colleges normally have relatively small computer center staffs, frequently fewer than ten persons. Nevertheless, they can be a significant planning resource. Small staff size requires everyone to work closely together, to take on a broad range of responsibilities, and to contribute whenever possible. When people are doing this, they gain a sense of confidence and importance in their own work, and their contributions improve thereby. Many staff members have experience at other institutions and outside of academia that can be invaluable in the planning process. Furthermore, involving the center's personnel provides the added benefit of having them treat the plan as their own.

One way to involve the center's staff is to have each staff member produce a draft plan for his or her areas of responsibility. This draws upon the individual's experience and expertise, provides a formal mechanism for input, and relieves the person responsible for the final draft of the plan of the time-consuming task of developing detailed projections and justifications.

Pomona College also employs the technique of a *planning retreat*. Once every semester, the entire staff of the academic computing center assembles at a location away from campus. There are a number of advantages to this approach. Being distant from the computer center means that staff are distant from the incessant interruptions and daily concerns, and can concentrate on the planning process. Moreover, bringing staff together in an informal setting develops a strong sense of community and camaraderie. The retreat begins on Friday and ends Saturday afternoon, providing attenders with the opportunity to stay on until Sunday evening if they wish. Several members of the student staff are nominated by their supervisors to participate in the retreat. This not only ensures valuable student input, but contributes mightily to morale.

In preparation for the retreat, the director of academic computing, with suggestions from the group, prepares an agenda, so that the planning sessions have structure and direction. She does not lead the discussion, inviting volunteers to do so instead. This strategy achieves two goals. First, the director is free to participate in the discussions as a member of the group, and, second, staff members do not feel constrained by having the director as chair of the meeting. On occasion, particularly when controversial issues need to be discussed, the director will invite an outside facilitator to lead the discussions. After the retreat, it is important to prepare a structured document of the proceedings so that what was said is not lost and so that participants recognize the seriousness of the endeavor.

Designing the Plan

At the beginning of the chapter four basic types of plans were described—prospective, operational, initiative-response, and budget — each of which is appropriate under different circumstances. When the appropriate type of plan has been selected, a model needs to be chosen, goals for the plan should be specified, a schedule for creation and delivery of the plan needs to be established, and various tools can be employed in designing the plan.

Choosing Which Type of Plan to Use. It should be fairly obvious in most situations which type of plan should be developed. However, a common mistake is combining different types of planning in one document. This can lead to confusion in thinking about the plan during its development and disaster in its implementation. For example, a prospective plan should deal only with broad, general goals to be achieved over a substantial period; a short-range operational plan should deal only with specific techniques needed to achieve the goals of the prospective plan within a relatively brief time period, normally an academic year or less.

The type of plan to be chosen depends totally on the planning environment, as I mentioned earlier. At a college where the infrastructure for information technology (hardware, software, staffing, external funding, curricular development, and so forth) was not planned or implemented during the 1980s, the emphasis needs to be placed on developing such a prospective plan and finding ways to have the institution fund it. At colleges fortunate enough to have had the foresight to complete such infrastructure planning during the 1980s, the current emphasis will be on maintenance and avoidance of obsolescence, which can be achieved by short-range operational planning. In both cases, budget planning will follow the completion of the prospective or operational plans.

Choosing a Planning Model. As colleges and universities begin to face the financial realities of the present day, when the institution has to become much more like a business than a traditional nonprofit educational enterprise, increased attention is being paid to corporate planning techniques. A national organization, the Society for College and University Planning (SCUP), is concerned with these issues. However, its concerns tend to be primarily at the level of institutional prioritizational planning. The methodologies employed therein are not necessarily appropriate for information technology planning within a given college.

Traditionally, in business a number of corporate planning models are available. These include *financial planning, market forecasting, econometric market modeling, production planning modeling,* and *management information systems modeling.* Each of these techniques has its strengths and its appropriate place in the arsenal of business planning. There is an extensive literature describing these techniques and considerable effort has gone into their refinement. It is unfortunate that colleges cannot take full advantage of these developments. However, these models do not generally fit the realities of academe, especially in small liberal arts colleges with their unique goals and structure.

For information technology planning in a liberal arts college there is no need for the sophistication and complexity of corporate planning strategies. Certainly there are aspects of corporate planning strategies that can be helpful in information technology planning, and an eclectic combination of techniques borrowed from industry might be of assistance. However, experience at a number of liberal arts colleges has shown that a fairly simple goal-oriented approach has normally proven quite efficacious. Indeed, the application of sophisticated measurement and planning tools, and an unduly large emphasis on planning itself, may overtax the limited resources of a liberal arts college and result in elaborate plans that are never acted upon.

A Goal-Oriented Approach to Planning.

Make no little plans; they have no magic to stir men's blood.

Attributed to Daniel Hudson Burnham (1846–1912)

Burnham's assertion implies that plans should deal with major objectives. But, to achieve such objectives, they must first be broken down into smaller and smaller, attainable sub-objectives. In the goal-oriented approach, the planner first must identify the principal areas of concern for the college, such as networking, mainframe computing, automated registration, and computer-based instruction. Based on the information gathered from the numerous sources discussed in the previous section, individual, limited objectives can be identified and specified. The plan is then developed in direct response to these particular limited objectives. In this way, not only is a considerable saving in development time realized, but the plan, when completed, is far more practical.

For a goal-oriented plan to be successful, it must be realistic. While it can be great fun, and sometimes very helpful, to "blue-sky," a plan is not an appropriate place to do so. The goals should be such that there is a reasonable expectation that they can be attained, not just a wish that this is how it "should be." Goals must be in line with the mandate of the college as expressed explicitly in institutional planning documents and implicitly in the actions and philosophies of faculty and chief administrators.

Furthermore, goals should have somewhat widespread acceptance; it is not a good idea to follow the direction advocated by a particular zealot, no matter how important this one individual happens to be on campus. For example, if there is one faculty member who strongly favors a specific version of text-processing software to the exclusion of all others, no matter how strong his or her arguments and how good the software, it would be inappropriate to adopt such a goal unless it appears acceptable to a wider constituency.

Writing the Plan. Writing a plan is hard and time-consuming work, even after gathering all the requisite information. When several people—such as a subcommittee—are involved in the writing effort, it is very helpful to set a reasonable schedule and keep to it. In order to be successful psychologically, a schedule needs to be realistic. That is, it needs to take into account other obligations such as conferences to be attended, examinations to be written and administered, candidates to be interviewed, and so on. The schedule should establish realistic target dates within the planning cycle and deadlines that can be met.

Because they will be read by many people who have not done the background research that the authors have undertaken, successful plans often contain a history and survey of the state of the art of the subject under consideration. Furthermore, they usually contain a synopsis placing the college in relation to that history and state of the art. This foundational material, when presented in a politically sensitive manner, introduces the goals of the plan and indicates why they are important for the college, setting the stage for support of the plan.

Several tools may prove valuable in constructing a plan. Specialized surveys that have been conducted in the planning process and additional data generally available at all colleges, such as surveys of incoming students, lists of faculty publications, and institutional research files are all useful. The data may have been used during the development of the goals, but they can also be used during the actual writing of the document. Graphs, charts, tables, and statistical analyses all can contribute to strengthening the arguments put forth in support of a plan. For example, the argument for public terminal facilities might be bolstered by the ratio of terminals to students who do not own their own computers, especially when compared with similar data from peer institutions.

There are also many electronic tools that can be of assistance in writing the planning document. Raw data can be manipulated efficiently using a spreadsheet, database software, or a textbase system. In addition, electronic mail can be used very effectively to share ideas, drafts, and schedules among members of the planning team, thereby hastening progress.

One other important technique that has proven quite useful is to incorporate feedback mechanisms in the writing process. Such feedback serves as a reality check. Ideas and drafts can be passed around to various colleagues both within and outside the institution with a request for confidentiality and constructive criticism. An important side benefit of this approach is that those parties who are consulted become involved, whether they intended to or not, and may become strong advocates of the final plan. Care must be exercised, however, that a preliminary document is not seized upon as final and does not become the source of undesired rumor or controversy.

Implementing the Plan

Having a written plan without implementing it is analogous to Mark Twain's definition of a "classic"—a book that people praise and don't read. Implementing the prospective plan requires short-term operational and budget planning, sophisticated public relations, an awareness of campus politics, and utilization of numerous campus groups such as the information technology advisory committee, and members of the staff, the faculty, the students, and the administration.

Operationalizing the Plan.

> I was a-trembling because I'd got to decide forever betwixt two
> things, and I knowed it. I studied for a minute, sort of holding
> my breath, and then says to myself, "All right, then, I'll *go* to
> hell."

> Mark Twain, *Adventures of Huckleberry Finn* (1884)

In order to implement a prospective plan, it must be broken down
into smaller units that can be treated individually. Several of these
units will be combined to form an operational plan and will also be
incorporated into a budget plan. Without such dissection of the
prospective plan, the specifics of what actions must be taken can be
lost in the general nature of the larger plan. This transition from a
general, prospective plan to specific activities frequently is not a
trivial exercise. Numerous options may present themselves, and a
judicious selection among attractive alternatives requires careful
thought and the input of various constituencies.

Some factors that should be considered when planners make these
selections include the overall goals of the institution, the needs of
specific groups of users, the current resources of the information
technology group, trends in the computer industry and in computing
in higher education, and projections of future funding sources.
Furthermore, these decisions must be made with a recognition that
they may be truly *short-term*. That is, they may be subject to recon-
sideration in the near future during other stages of the planning cycle,
and should be structured such that they can be changed without
undue hardship.

Suppose, for example, that an institution's objective is to integrate
computers as deeply as possible into the instructional process. This
has been translated into a prospective goal of acquiring and supporting
electronic classrooms. Now, a short-term goal would be to develop one
such classroom, and choices must be made among a wide variety of
hardware, software, courseware, furniture, personnel for support,
and so on. Some of these choices will have to be semi-permanent; for
example, hiring a specialist cannot be reversed easily, whereas
exchanging one piece of furniture for another is not as traumatic.

Campus Politics and Public Relations. A necessary condition for the success of the implementation of a plan is the support of the key political figures among the constituencies toward whom the plan is aimed. For example, if the prospective goal is to upgrade or automate the registration system, success is doubtful at best without the full support and endorsement of the registrar and his or her staff, no matter what software is chosen.

Some of the techniques discussed in earlier sections are equally appropriate at this point. For example, take a physicist to lunch; take a vice-president to lunch. Good public relations are essential. Involving key people early in the implementation process helps to gain their support, assuages any misgivings they may have, allows them to proceed with their own planning with an accurate knowledge of impending developments, provides the benefit of their input, and gains respected spokespersons for the information technology plan.

Additional tools for public relations include newsletters, general mailings, and posters; open houses; presentations to faculty, student, staff, and administration groups; and demonstrations, seminars, and short courses. For example, at Pomona College a prospective goal was to upgrade and modernize large computing capabilities. This objective was translated into an operational and budgetary goal to replace the existing mainframe computer with a new system. As with any such decision, there was attendant controversy and apprehension among the users, and, therefore, among the administration.

To calm the fears, to prepare the users, and to convince them that they would be better served, the computer center undertook a large public relations campaign. The campaign consisted of personal contacts with every faculty member and many other users of the outgoing system to help them understand the implications and mechanics of making the transition. In addition, the campus was blitzed with newsletters, posters, general mailings, and reminders of the change and what to do about it. The center offered short courses (some taught by staff, some by the vendor) on how to use the new system and how to transfer files from the old to the new computer. The director of academic computing managed to mention the impending change at every faculty meeting during the semester.

Involvement of Others in Implementation. Successful implementation of a plan often depends on the efforts of many individuals and groups — student groups, faculty members, administrators, and so on. One such group, the advisory committee to the information technology group, has an important role to play. It serves as a liaison between the user community and the computer center and, as such, provides an invaluable two-way communication channel. It can broadcast messages explaining the plan and report back any static from the users. Moreover, the combined counsel of its members can be valuable in determining procedures for implementing various aspects of the plan.

Students, particularly those who work in the computer center, can often be of great value in spreading knowledge to their peers. Students work together, help each other, and usually are eager to embrace new developments. Administrators, too, can play an important role in realizing the objectives of a plan. A few well placed words by a respected administrator at a faculty meeting can be invaluable in enlisting the support of others and encouraging them to embrace new ideas.

The information technology staff, too, is central to putting a plan into action. They need to be fully informed and committed to the success of the plan. One of the best ways to achieve this is to involve them from the earliest possible time and to delegate, wherever possible, specifics of implementation that fall within their particular spheres of responsibility and expertise. This approach is particularly beneficial to staff morale, and it significantly decreases the distance between the abstract plan and the practical implementation. Many staff members, especially at the junior level, feel they have not had any meaningful input into or influence upon a plan. By involving them in its implementation they may feel more supportive; they learn from the experience and become more valuable employees.

There is a subtle difference between true involvement in implementing a plan and having the plan and its implications imposed upon a staff member. Consider the case of a mid-level network manager. If the plan calls for upgrading the local area networks in the public terminal spaces at the college, imposing a decision upon the network manager by choosing a new LAN and telling him or her to install it cannot be considered involvement. Rather, this manager should have been brought into the process as early as possible and should have had considerable input in the choice of the new equipment and software. In that way, he or she would feel a commitment to the choice and have greater motivation to ensure its success.

The Role of Evaluation in Planning

Evaluation of past and current performance in the light of the relevant plans is an essential aspect of the entire planning process. Here, we will consider evaluation as part of the planning process; analysis of progress, success, and failure; the impact on the institution of implementation of the plan; adjusting objectives to new or revised missions; and documenting success or failure.

Evaluation as Part of the Planning Process. Liberal arts colleges, like all colleges, pride themselves on their planning ability in delineating goals and objectives for future development. Too few colleges, however, include evaluation of the outcomes of earlier planning and ongoing implementation of a plan into the current planning process. In other words, *Have the objectives of the plan been met, or are they being met?* Whether or not the objectives were met or are being met, this information is very valuable to the planning process. Successfully meeting goals allows the planner to propose actions that build upon those successes and strengthen the program under scrutiny. The inability to meet earlier goals forces a reassessment of the original objectives and resources, and may ultimately result in a set of more achievable outcomes. It may also bring into sharp focus any planning assumptions that are incorrect or that have been overlooked.

For example, many liberal arts computing organizations have had the experience of planning for a campus-wide network and producing operational plans for the network's implementation. After completing the basic hardware and software installation, however, they discovered that the system required daily management and trouble-shooting and that no one on the staff had the necessary expertise to take on this role. The failure to deliver the desired network services on schedule forced the institutions to reassess carefully the relationship between new technologies and the level of expertise (and the size) of their computing staff.

Analysis of Progress, Success, and Failure. What goals of the current plan have been completed successfully and why? What goals have failed and why? Among the techniques available for analysis of progress with respect to a plan are tracking, monitoring resource utilization, evaluating survey results, and interviewing users. Each of these relatively simple methods can be used to produce data that can contribute to the success or failure of planned goals.

Tracking is the process of maintaining detailed records of the efforts of staff members. Records, such as those collected by Williams College, can include information regarding types of projects being undertaken, time devoted to various activities relevant to the projects, resources (software, hardware) employed, expenditures entailed, and persons consulted. A standardized reporting format for tracking can greatly facilitate analysis and increase the usability of the data.

In parallel with tracking, some information technology groups use commercial software packages to monitor the utilization of computer systems. This software can record every use of the hardware and software and provide summary tables and statistics. Similar monitoring can be achieved manually for consulting and other user services as well as for hardware, software, and other resource utilization. Monitoring can be as simple as a periodic check of how many people are present in a laboratory and what they are doing, or it can be much more detailed, depending on what is needed to evaluate attainment of planned goals.

In some instances, it may be appropriate to survey users with a formal evaluation questionnaire designed to elicit information on the extent to which particular goals have been achieved. Such surveys should be created as carefully as possible following standard practices for questionnaire development that are outlined in the extensive literature on this subject. Data gathered from such a survey will provide evidence of the degree to which objectives are being met and where further efforts might be appropriate. At some colleges, the information technology group prepares an evaluation survey to be administered at the end of each semester in every class that made significant use of the facilities.

Care should be taken, however, to avoid overuse of the survey technique. Survey research is so much a part of our everyday lives, that many people suffer "survey burnout" and are reluctant to fill out yet another questionnaire. A negative consequence of either a large nonresponse or a selective response to a survey might be data that will misrepresent the issues and problems under examination.

One way to avoid survey burnout is to interview a selected sample of people on a rotating basis. For example, rather than surveying all the faculty in the college, it might be useful to survey a random sample or to rotate survey activities from department to department over a period of years. While it is normally not necessary to create a rigidly structured interview agenda, it is helpful to have several specific questions prepared so the data that are gathered will be consistent and easier to analyze. In addition, brief informal friendly discussions with users can provide valuable information.

The Impact on the Institution of Implementing the Plan. Another major aspect of evaluating a plan is to determine what impact implementation of the plan has had on the institution. For example, if a major goal of the prospective plan was to install a fiber optic network backbone on campus, what impact has the installation had on the college to date? Are administrative offices beginning to communicate via electronic mail? If so, has this form of communication had beneficial results? Have the faculty members in the chemistry department been able to access their number-crunching or molecular modeling programs from their offices? Has this helped their research efforts?

It is also important to determine how the institution is reacting to the implications of progress or lack of progress in achieving the planned goals and any consequent modifications in the plans and resultant actions. Using the same example, suppose that the plan called for pulling cable through existing conduits. However, it was found by the subcontractor that the conduits were already full of telephone cables that had been installed by the campus communications office but not recorded on the master plan kept by the physical plant department. This discovery would require a modification of both the operational and the budget plans. It would be necessary to plan for the installation of new conduit (most likely with additional trenching), with consequent modifications to time schedules and increases in expenditures.

What is needed at this point is flexibility on the part of the institution in dealing with adjustments to previous plans. The information technology group should try to establish a close working relationship with the higher administrative officers who are empowered to implement changes in schedules and budgets. At the very least, such a relationship will ensure that the appropriate parties are notified immediately of such serious difficulties. At best, it will provide for the appropriate flexible response that will enable the project to return to schedule. Whenever possible this close working relationship with higher levels within the college should be maintained and utilized.

Documenting Success or Failure. An annual report provides a "plan-versus-actual" summary, enumerating accomplishments achieved, evaluating progress and objectives, and fine-tuning future directions. This is a popular technique that is commonly employed in many colleges. In some institutions, unfortunately, such reports are little more than a formality — written, filed, and forgotten. But this need not be the case. In addition to their traditional reporting function, annual reports can serve as very powerful planning documents.

Annual reports are a formal vehicle for communicating with the rest of the college and for transmitting appropriate messages. The annual report provides an opportunity to present a written evaluation of the degree to which the objectives of current operational and budget plans have been achieved and to suggest any appropriate modifications. At some institutions, a summary report covering anywhere from three to five years may also be written. Such a report summarizes the annual reports for that period and is more oriented toward evaluation of the prospective plan.

These reports are, in effect, mirror images of plans, providing an assessment of progress and achievements relative to each goal. An information technology annual report might include sections on personnel, programmatic developments, hardware and general software (acquisition, maintenance, upgrades, obsolescence), courseware (acquisition, development, integration), administrative software (acquisition, installation, upgrades), and facilities, describing each of these topics in terms of the goals of the overall plan.

For example, at one college, the 1990 annual report for academic computing services provided an opportunity to discuss progress and problems associated with the transition from one main computer system to another. The report also included suggestions for modifications in schedule and expenditures for campus networking. Such details would not be appropriate for a summary report; in that document a much broader overview would be included.

The Role of Consultants

Believe one who has proved it. Believe an expert.

Virgil (70–19 B.C.) *Aeneid,* book XI, line 283

No one knows a college better than those who are employed there and devote their efforts to its day-to-day operation and improvement. But sometimes they can be too close to the institution; a broader perspective may be helpful. Furthermore, in the political atmosphere surrounding certain topics or actions, discussions or plans that relate to somewhat controversial subjects can be misperceived as self-serving rather than the sound advice they really are intended to be. It is sometimes necessary to rely on outside expertise, even though appropriate solutions to problems and suitable plans might be available in-house. Here, we will discuss the benefits of consultants, how to choose consultants, the cost of consultants, what to expect of consultants, and how to use the consultants' report in the planning process.

Benefits of Consultants.   Impartial, knowledgeable, experienced outside consultants can provide various benefits to an institution in the planning process. First, such consultants can avoid petty political and personality conflicts in their consideration of appropriate alternatives for the college. Skilled consultants interview parties and review materials relating to many aspects of the problems at hand before preparing their report. Second, consultants bring experience from similar campuses to bear on the problem under consideration. For example, obsolescence of staff training and skills is a common problem in the rapidly changing information technology field. Experienced consultants will have knowledge of how this problem has been addressed at various other colleges, and can make recommendations that are appropriate for a given institution.

A third benefit of outside consultants is that they are aware of the most recent developments in the field of higher education information technology. It is possible that no person on a particular campus possesses expertise in the area of concern. For example, it would be unusual to find someone experienced in installing fiber optic cable at a college that has not yet begun such networking. Also, it is likely that any experts on a controversial subject in question on a campus will be too closely involved in the problem or the implementation of the plan to be perceived at the college as being able to provide an unbiased proposal. The time and expense required for anyone else on the campus to develop the requisite expertise might be prohibitive (assuming someone could be found who was capable of and willing to undertake such an effort).

Fourth, consultants are paid to prepare a report and do so away from the campus that is the subject of the report. The combination of remuneration and distance from the day-to-day interference of those who may seek to influence the outcome enhances the consultant's ability to produce a timely, objective assessment. Normally, consultants return to their home bases after they have collected their information, and can be expected to produce a report within several weeks, probably faster than the job could be done by an in-house committee.

Finally, precisely because of their physical and emotional distance from the college, consultants can afford to make recommendations in their report that may be logical, sound, and appropriate, yet politically unpopular on the campus. The consultant will not have to live and work with those who will be affected by the recommendations, and can therefore afford to be candid in the appraisal of sensitive campus issues. This last benefit may be the most important of all, because it allows for impartial judgments on the part of consultants, untainted by politics, personalities, or self-interest.

Choosing Consultants. Several different types of consulting are commonly employed at colleges. They include visiting committees, independent consultants, and teams from professional consulting firms. Visiting committees normally consist of several persons considered knowledgeable in the field in question, who have been assembled ad hoc for a particular assignment. Visiting committees are sometimes formed with the assistance of a professional organization, such as an accreditation agency, for the purpose of evaluating a particular aspect of the college. Independent consultants have recognized expertise in a specialized area, but consulting is not their primary means of livelihood. Independent consultants are usually employed at colleges in positions that give them experience with the subject at hand. Professional consulting firms provide teams of experts whose primary occupation is consulting. Such professional firms are usually much better prepared to consult on administrative applications of information technology and related matters than on academic computing.

One definition of a consultant is "someone who has to take an airplane to get to the campus." This somewhat facetious characterization captures the perception of the consultant as distant or removed from the day-to-day politics of the college, above the petty jealousies and in-fighting, and thus able to render "pure" suggestions. This perception can be entirely erroneous, however, if the consultant has been selected by one faction in an internal controversy and is sympathetic to that faction's viewpoint. Mere physical distance from a campus does not ensure impartiality.

Whether selected by a committee wrestling with a particularly difficult new plan or imposed by administrative authorities upon a planning group having serious problems, consultants should be chosen on the basis of their expertise and reputation. There are several good ways to locate potential consultants. It is a common practice to search for a consultant by contacting friends and acquaintances at other colleges to ask for suggestions. Other good sources of potential consultants are professional meetings and the professional literature. While listening to the presentations at such conferences or reading the literature, you may encounter someone who appears to have had in-depth experience with the very problems you are dealing with. Another excellent source for potential consultants is provided by professional organizations—such as CLAC, EDUCOM and CAUSE— who maintain lists of qualified consultants.

No matter how they are located, potential consultants should be carefully screened before they are hired. A department would not consider hiring any other personnel without a thorough check of their background, vita, and references. Such a check is at least as important for a consultant. It is reasonable to expect potential consultants to furnish references from previous contracts and to supply sample portions of previous reports to demonstrate what may fairly be expected as the result of contracting with them. Potential consultants should provide complete resumes and a proposed schedule for completing the assignment, including the report, and a statement of the fee for the service.

The Cost of Consultants. Consultants may at first appear to be an expensive luxury. The cost for a two-day visit by a team of three consultants, plus their report and recommendations, will probably be $9,000 or more. Rather than considering this amount in absolute terms, measure it against the likely cost—in dollars, frustrations, and wasted time—of training an existing staff member to a level of expertise comparable to that of a consultant, or of making a serious mistake through ignorance or biased decision making.

Although it is difficult to assess the potential savings that can be realized through the use of qualified consultants, it is common for institutions—especially small colleges with comparatively little in-house expertise—to avoid expenditures reaching into six figures by investing in consultancies which rarely exceed $10,000. Even the most successful computing organizations acknowledge that the cost of a good consultant is generally recouped many times over.

What to Expect from Consultants. For consultants to be of value in the planning process, they must produce a report containing an evaluation of the current status of the area of concern, together with proposed goals and recommendations for the future. It is not good practice to hire consultants to write plans for the department with whom they are consulting. For a plan to be appropriate and acceptable to the department, it should be the product of the persons who are affected by it. However, the input and suggestions from the consultants' report can form an important part of the foundation on which the plan is built. This is especially true when problems exist or controversial choices must be made.

There is no fixed, agreed upon format for consultants' reports. They vary with the problems under consideration, the institution involved, the objectives of the institution in hiring the consultants, and the style of the consultants. (This last variable is a reason for examining a sample of the consultants' previous reports before entering into a contract.) The contract should include specific expected outcomes of the consultation. It is appropriate for the college or department to specify in advance exactly what questions are to be addressed and in what form the answers and recommendations are to be given. Furthermore, it is customary to withhold final payment until a satisfactory report has been submitted.

The one thing that it is not appropriate to expect or demand of consultants is endorsement of predefined results or recommendations. Preconceived outcomes do not require a consultant for confirmation. If they have been arrived at through legitimate planning procedures, they should be acceptable and should stand on their own merit. If they have been developed otherwise, perhaps through some political or biased process, no reputable consultant should be willing merely to endorse them, nor will any such endorsement make them any more attractive or likely to succeed.

How to Use the Consultants' Report. What is contained in the consultants' report is not necessarily what the department or college would *like* to hear. Sometimes consultants' reports contain some very unpalatable truths. The report should be treated with respect, but remember that it is not necessarily gospel. Except for individual personnel recommendations (which should be subject to the confidentiality accorded all personnel matters), the contents of the consultants' report should be made available to all affected parties.

The section of the report that assesses the current situation can provide a check on the accuracy of the department's own appraisal of its state of affairs, both in its annual reports and in its preparation for the current planning activities. In addition, the report can provide suggestions for possible goals to be incorporated in the plan under development. Each proposal in the consultants' report should be carefully considered by the planners, and not automatically incorporated just because the consultants are assumed to know best.

Consultants, no matter how skilled and experienced, cannot incorporate all of the local knowledge available to the planners. The consultants' report should serve as a major input to the thinking about a plan, but never as a substitute for the efforts of the local planners.

One other valuable use of the consultants' report is to lend credence and a stamp of authority to a plan that incorporates some or most of the report's recommendations. Such outside authority can be particularly valuable when a plan contains features that are unpopular. Outside endorsement may convince readers that the authors of the plan were not biased in their choices.

The Planning Cycle

Various authors have described different planning designs for different planning environments. In higher education, the design that is most commonly used is the *planning cycle*. The cycle consists of a definition of the mission, objectives, and assumptions of the institution, followed by institutional prioritization planning, department prospective planning, operational planning, budget planning, implementation, and evaluation. The cycle is then repeated.

Figure 1 is a schematic representation of the planning cycle. The outermost circle, encompassing all of the steps, is normally completed every three to five years. The inner path (dashed line) of operational and budget planning, followed by implementation and evaluation usually occurs once every academic or fiscal year. In some institutions where institutional prioritization planning has been successfully implemented and the infrastructure for information technology is in place, the inner planning cycle remains the focus of attention. In this instance, the institutional and prospective plans do not require significant modification unless the institutional objectives or mission change dramatically or unless a major shift occurs in technology.

Sometimes changes occur in institutional prioritizational planning that affect the plans of the information technology group. Such occurrences may be due to external forces (such as legislation or an unanticipated major gift), to a rethinking on the part of the top administration, or to a change in the president or provost. Several

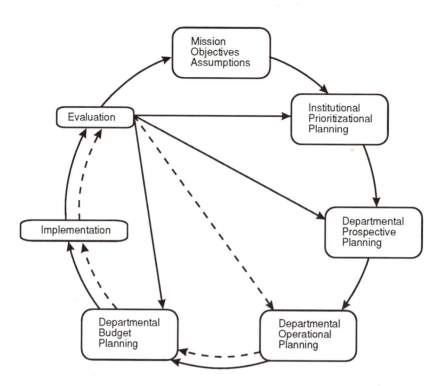

Figure 1: The Planning Cycle for Information Technology (from Chantico, p.12).

colleges report, for example, that their information technology groups had the full support of the administration for many years, making them leaders in computing among small liberal arts colleges. This continued until there was a change in the senior administration; the new administrations had different agendas they wished to promote, and thus the support the information technology groups had enjoyed was undermined. They were forced to adjust their objectives. Other colleges have experienced exactly the opposite result from a change in senior administration; fresh support for information technology goals suddenly enabled those goals to be realized. The degree to which the president, provost, or other top administrator can influence the prospective plan for information technology should not be overlooked or trivialized during the planning process.

The implication for departmental planning of the possibility of changes in institutional prioritizational planning is to reinforce the need for prospective planning to be an eclectic compromise between long-range and strategic planning. That is, departmental prospective plans, while providing specific goals to be attained and activities to be undertaken, should also contain built-in provisions for regular evaluation and reassessment with the possibility of modification.

Conclusion

> The best laid schemes o' mice and men
> Gang aft a-gley;
> An' lae'e us nought but grief and pain,
> For promis'd joy.
>
> Robert Burns, "To a Mouse" (1785)

In an ideal world, all plans are realistic and appropriate and institutions shape their courses accordingly, taking all requisite actions. Unfortunately, the world is not always ideal. Plans, no matter how realistic and appropriate, may be followed only in part or may even be ignored. If the normal practice at a college is to ignore plans once they are completed, there is probably little the information technology group can do to modify the institutional behavior. However, this does not mean that the group should stop planning; they should use their plans internally, and perhaps the institution will change its modus operandi when the benefits of planning are made obvious.

On the other hand, it is important to remember that over-planning— being completely focused on the planning *process*—can also be a detriment to action. Concentrating on the planning process alone may leave the planners with little energy left for implementation, resulting in brilliant plans that only gather dust. Perpetual planning— when the group never feels totally satisfied with the plan, is continually upgrading and updating it, and does not actually put a finished plan into action — is another potential pitfall to be avoided. Appropriate planning behavior follows the processes I have described: to obtain the very best information, to develop the most appropriate plan, and then to implement the plan.

For the information technology group to be responsive to the instructional, research, and administrative needs of a small liberal arts college, planning is essential. Good planning can be very successful; poor planning can be a detriment. The process of planning is not particularly complex and is available to any information technology group. The two biggest hurdles to overcome in order to reap the benefits of planning are the initial decision to plan and the commitment on the part of the group to the effort involved.

Acknowledgements

I have consulted many different sources in compiling these materials, and have discussed the issues with several of my colleagues. In particular, Robert S. Tannenbaum of Harvey Mudd College provided extensive assistance in the preparation of this chapter. Also, I would like to thank all of those who contributed their ideas, notes, planning reports, comments, and suggestions, especially Marty Ringle of Reed College, Bill Washburn of Colorado State University, Philip Cartwright of the University of California at Davis, Charles Staelin of Smith College, H. R. Gentry of Johnson County Community College, Edward Barboni of Allegheny College, and Everett Bull of Pomona College.

References

Baldridge, J. Victor, Janine Woodward Roberts, and Terri A. Weiner. 1984. *The campus and the microcomputer revolution: Practical advice for nontechnical decision makers*. New York: Macmillan.

Bergquist, William H., and Jack L. Armstrong. 1986. *Planning effectively for educational quality*. San Francisco: Jossey-Bass.

Chantico Technical Management Series. 1985. *Strategic and operational planning for information systems*. Wellesley, Mass.: QED Information Sciences.

Cope, Robert G. 1981. *Strategic planning, management, and decision making*. AAHE-ERIC/Higher Education Research Report no. 9. Washington, D.C.: American Association for Higher Education.

Keller, George. 1983. *Academic strategy: The management revolution in American higher education*. Baltimore: Johns Hopkins University Press.

League for Innovation in the Community College. 1989. *Planning guide for instructional computing*. Laguna Hills, Calif.

McLean, Ephraim R., and John V. Soden. 1977. *Strategic planning for MIS*. New York: John Wiley & Sons.

Naylor, Thomas H. 1979. *Corporate planning models*. Reading, Mass.: Addison-Wesley.

Reinharth, Leon, H. Jack Shapiro, and Ernest A. Kallman. 1981. *The practice of planning: Strategic, administrative, and operational*. New York: Van Nostrand Reinhold.

Shenson, Howard U. 1990. *How to select and manage consultants*. Lexington, Mass.: Lexington Books.

Chapter 3

The Cost of Computing: Shining a Light into the Black Hole

H. David Todd
Wesleyan University
and
Martin D. Ringle
Reed College

David Todd is director of university computing and adjunct associate professor of chemistry at Wesleyan University. He joined Wesleyan in 1971 and has held his present position since 1982, in which he is responsible for planning and management of academic and administrative information services and data communications. He teaches courses in computer science and chemistry. He holds a B.S. in chemistry from University of Illinois and a Ph.D. in theoretical chemistry from Johns Hopkins University. Except for a sabbatical at Stanford University during 1981–82, his professional career has been at Wesleyan.

Dr. Todd was active for many years in DECUS in a variety of roles including organizational development and as a board member for six years. Dr. Todd served as an ECG consultant for nine years and has been an institutional member of the EDUCOM board of trustees for three years.

Martin D. Ringle is the director of computing and information systems at Reed College in Portland, Oregon. He is responsible for academic computing, administrative computing, and campus-wide networking. Prior to coming to Reed in 1989, Dr. Ringle was coordinator of educational technology planning and chair of the department of computer science at Vassar College in Poughkeepsie, New York.

Dr. Ringle has served as a member of the EDUCOM Publications Advisory Committee, the EDUCOM Consulting Group, the Council Nominating Committee, and the EDUCOM board of trustees. He has also served on the board of directors of NorthWestNet and the InterUniversity Consortium for Educational Computing. He is currently the chair of the steering committee of the Consortium of Liberal Arts Colleges. Dr. Ringle has consulted for more than thirty-five liberal arts colleges and universities and has been an advisor to several dozen corporations and foundations involved in the support of computing in higher education.

Dr. Ringle received a doctorate in philosophy from the State University of New York at Binghamton in 1976. He has been a faculty member at Bennett College, Vassar College, and the University of Wisconsin and an invited scholar in philosophy, artificial intelligence, and cognitive science at the University of Chicago, Indiana University, the University of Florida, and elsewhere. A strong proponent of cross-disciplinary studies, Dr. Ringle is a member of the board of directors of the Cognitive Science Society and has been the executive editor of the international journal, Cognitive Science, *since 1987.*

> A billion here, a billion there—pretty soon it adds up to real money!
>
> —Everett Dirksen

Senator Dirksen's observation about federal spending could be applied—in spirit if not in actual amounts—to the attitude toward computer spending in higher education during the decade of the eighties. Major technology purchases of every sort, from microcomputers to supercomputers, flourished at colleges and universities throughout the country. For a while, it appeared that the only constant for computing budgets was the certainty that they would grow larger each year. Somewhere along the way, however, the gravy train jumped the tracks.

With the arrival of recession in 1990 and the demographic shortfall among prospective students, university administrators were suddenly forced to take austerity measures in their budgets, and information services became a favorite target for downsizing. Even schools that had enjoyed the most visible leadership roles in computing, from Dartmouth to Stanford, were forced to tighten their technology budgets.

Though the general retreat in technology spending has spread throughout higher education, the impact on liberal arts colleges has been considerably less severe than on universities. This is hardly cause for celebration, however, since the primary reason is that many of these budgets are already as small as they can possibly be.

Unlike universities, which require massive computing facilities for research, liberal arts colleges have rarely viewed computing as a key funding priority, hence their budgets for computing have never been particularly lavish.

During the past few years there has been slow but steady growth in information services at liberal arts colleges and an increasing awareness of computing as an integral tool for the instructional, research, and administrative activities of faculty and staff. The average size of the computing organization and its operating budget at liberal arts colleges has grown by nearly fifty percent since 1986, yet the demand for computing services has grown even faster. It may well be that the boom in computing that universities experienced in the eighties is simply late in arriving at liberal arts colleges and that the bust is yet to come.

Will the mid-nineties bring to liberal arts colleges the same cutbacks in computing already experienced by so many universities? Probably not. At institutions where growth in computing during the eighties was exceptionally robust a downturn may be inevitable. Most small colleges, however, have been very conservative in their funding for technology and they are likely to continue to be conservative throughout the next decade. Moreover, while it is true that many schools have used external grants to underwrite the cost of microcomputer acquisition, network installation, or mainframe replacement, the majority of liberal arts colleges have supported computing primarily through internal funds and this trend is increasing. By relying heavily on internal funding, liberal arts colleges have escaped much of the recent financial fluctuation experienced by so many universities (Gillespie 1989). The fact that most liberal arts colleges are private has also been a factor in maintaining budgetary stability, since the financial woes of state systems of higher education have had little or no direct impact on them.

Though there may not be a financial crisis looming for computing at liberal arts colleges, there are nonetheless many pressing budgetary issues that have yet to be resolved. The fact that computing is still so new at our colleges means that we cannot fall back on the time-honored practice of appealing to the "liberal arts tradition" for guidance. Nor can we look too closely at the approaches taken by universities, since their fiscal policies for computing do not always scale well to the organizational structure and culture of the small liberal arts college.

The financial models for colleges to follow—if indeed there are viable models—must be derived from the experiences of peer schools that share similar budgetary and staffing constraints, similar technical needs and limitations, and a similar curricular mission. The focus of our discussion in this chapter, therefore, is the liberal arts college perspective on three basic topics: funding sources, financial management, and funds allocation.

A word of caution to the reader. Models of any sort, and particularly financial models, should be viewed with some degree of skepticism. Although there are many similarities among small liberal arts colleges, there are many differences as well. Indeed, the differences are viewed with a great deal of pride, since they give each college its own distinctive personality. Ultimately, the approach taken to technology funding must be the result of each institution's unique blend of opportunities, priorities, and politics, not from a rigid adherence to national trends. Our discussion in this chapter is designed to provide a framework for considering a college's budgetary strategy and to provide comfort to those computer professionals, faculty members, and administrators charged with budgetary responsibility. It often helps to know that when you stare into the black hole of computer funding you are not alone.

Funding Sources

> Ere you consult your fancy, consult your purse.
>
> —Benjamin Franklin

At many universities, especially multicampus university systems, central computing services are viewed as revenue centers, and charge-back accounting is the rule. Though the university underwrites computing services to some extent, there are visible costs to end-users and the operating level of the central computing organization often depends upon the success of its revenue stream.

By contrast, liberal arts colleges tend to support their computing centers in the same way they support their libraries, through the general fund of the institutional operating budget. Charge-back accounting is minimal and the revenue from charge-backs to departments, faculty, or students is usually viewed as surplus income rather than as a fundamental component of the annual computing budget.

This model of funding is consistent with the belief that information services at liberal arts colleges are a necessary part of the institution's academic support infrastructure, rather than an income center or auxiliary enterprise, such as the bookstore. Since private liberal arts college tuition levels are often two to three times higher than tuition levels at other types of institutions, charging fees for basic academic services tends to be avoided as much as possible.

The dilemma many colleges face is that the demand for computing services is expanding faster than financial resources. Campus-wide networks are becoming more numerous and more complex, curricular uses of computing are increasing, administrative data processing is spreading to more offices, the number of college-owned and student-owned microcomputers is growing dramatically, and the level of expertise expected of computer center staff is rising sharply. Though computing budgets have been increasing at liberal arts colleges, the portion of the institutional operating budget devoted to computing has actually decreased, by approximately two-tenths of a percent during the past three years (Warlick 1989b, Henry 1990).

Even at colleges where the budget share for computing has risen, it is becoming increasingly difficult for information services to keep pace with the growth in users' demands and expectations. As a result, some schools are beginning to take a closer look at their approach to technology funding and to examine a variety of new strategies, including charge-back accounting. In the following sections we consider the funding and cost-containment methods liberal arts colleges have traditionally used to supplement ordinary operating funds. We then examine several methods that are likely to be used in the future.

Traditional Strategies	*Potential Future Strategies*
Capital campaigns	Microcomputer resale
Private donations	In-house maintenance
Government and foundation grants	Usage and training fees
Faculty research grants	
Consortial alliances	
Vendor grants and discounts	

Capital Campaigns

Colleges that define strategic plans for computing typically under-write the cost of major projects—such as providing all faculty members with a microcomputer, installing a campus-wide network, or replacing a mainframe—by raising funds within the framework of a capital campaign. Several campuses have discussed the idea of creating a restricted endowment for computing as part of a capital drive but, to the best of our knowledge, this strategy has never actually been pursued. The use of capital campaigns seems to be a declining strategy for funding technology at small colleges. This is partly a result of the decreasing cost of hardware and partly a tacit acknowledg-ment that computing costs are ongoing costs and should not be treated as one-time investments. Capital campaigns have a tendency to provide dollars for hardware and software, while ignoring the ongoing costs of maintenance and personnel. Such a campaign often produces a sudden increase in the availability and use of technology without a corresponding increase in staffing and other types of support.

Private Donations

Many liberal arts colleges are blessed with generous alumni and alumnae who have been eager to promote technological improve-ments at their former campuses. Some schools report that major strides in computing have been made as the result of a small number of former students, private donors, or trustees taking an avid interest in computing and translating that interest into personal donations or fund-raising activities. In addition, many graduates of liberal arts colleges are employed by major technology corporations that provide matching funds for cash donations. In some cases these corporations also provide equipment in lieu of cash at ratios as high as five to one.

Government and Foundation Grants

Though grants to small colleges for computing are not nearly as abundant as they are to research universities, there are some funds targeted specifically for this environment. The National Science Foundation Instructional Laboratory Improvement Grant Program (ILI) is a good example. Although the program requires the institution to provide half of the cost of a project, it is ideal for small schools since—as the program title implies—it focuses on facilities for instruction rather than research. For the past few years, the National Science Foundation has also had a grant program designed to help small colleges cover the costs of establishing an Internet connection. Private foundations, such as the Sloan Foundation, the Carnegie Corporation, the Pew Trust, the Annenberg/CPB Project, and others have made major contributions to the development of instructional technology at liberal arts colleges as well.

Unfortunately, technology grants from government agencies and private foundations reach only a small number of liberal arts colleges. Moreover, support for computing initiatives such as networking, library automation, and other basic resources, has diminished considerably in recent years. Attention has turned away from hardware and software acquisition to curricular uses of technology. In many cases, foundations and government agencies have come to question the long-range impact of disbursing grants for equipment unless such purchases are clearly part of a coherent and measurable strategy to improve the quality of education. Exploratory funding is still available, however, for projects that define new areas of application, particularly those on which computing has yet to have a significant impact, such as the arts and humanities.

Faculty Research Grants

Faculty research at liberal arts colleges is minimal in comparison to most universities, yet research activities do take place, and faculty members have sometimes been able to secure grants to underwrite the cost of equipment and technical support. As other types of grants disappear, colleges are looking harder at research grants from both public and private sources in order to obtain funding for projects that involve the purchase or enhancement of computing equipment.

When considering methods of raising funds for computing, we should also keep in mind special ways of cutting costs or acquiring equipment and services for free, since the net effect on the budget is the same. Two cost-containment strategies that have been extensively and effectively used are consortial alliances and vendor grants or discounts.

Consortial Alliances

Inter-college and college–university consortia can be especially effective ways to share major overhead expenses for facilities that do not need to be replicated on each campus. A good example of this approach is the joint support of library automation facilities by groups such as Connecticut–Wesleyan–Trinity, the Five College Exchange,[1] the CLIC group in Minneapolis–St. Paul, and others. Network piggy-backing has also been a popular form of consortial interaction. Schools that cannot afford the high cost of an Internet connection may be able to join with other schools to underwrite the cost of a single high-speed connection as well as the cost of the staff required for network management.

In addition to cutting operating costs for each school, consortial agreements are also good candidates for external funding. During the eighties, for example, Pew and other foundations actively supported college consortia and college–university alliances. Foundations and government agencies continue to be interested in projects that bring schools together in order to make better and more efficient use of technology.

---

1. See chapter 12 for further discussion.

Vendor Grants and Discounts

In some instances, computer vendors provide outright (cash) grants to colleges and universities for basic research or software-development activities, though few liberal arts colleges are in a position to take advantage of such grants (Green 1989). On the other hand, vendors are often willing to donate hardware and software or to discount their products steeply, even to colleges of less than a thousand students. Such grants and discounts, if used judiciously, can provide substantial relief to a tight computing budget. Private liberal arts colleges have had considerable success in obtaining grants and discounts by approaching vendors as local or regional groups. With so many vendors struggling to retain market share and profitability today, the climate for discounts and grants seems to favor those schools that aggressively seek out such opportunities, regardless of their size or annual budget.

A caveat with respect to vendor grants and discounts, however, is in order. During the past decade there have been numerous so-called discounts and grants that have ended up costing colleges a considerable amount of money. In some cases, the hidden charges for maintenance, network hardware, peripherals, expansion units, and so forth, cost more than the equipment itself. In other cases, the use of the equipment required the college to make a major investment in software in order to fit the technology into the existing computing environment. Though equipment grants and steep discounts may be offered with good intentions, and though in some instances they may provide a much-needed boost to an ailing budget, they should be scrutinized carefully with regard to long-term or hidden costs to the college.

While colleges will certainly take advantage of each of these funding or cost-containment measures if the opportunity arises, the areas of funding that have come under the greatest scrutiny as future sources of revenue are those that involve the sale of products or services to the college community. The three approaches we consider are: microcomputer resale, in-house maintenance, and usage or training fees.

Microcomputer Resale

During the early eighties there were extensive debates as to whether colleges and universities should require students to purchase microcomputers. When the dust finally settled it was apparent that only a handful of technical institutes and a few colleges and universities had actually implemented a policy of required ownership. The majority of schools decided to avoid such a heavy-handed approach, and some liberal arts colleges, going one step further, considered providing computers to students at no charge. Unfortunately, the cost of such an approach was—and continues to be—beyond the reach of even the wealthiest institutions.

While the debate about universal student access to institutionally owned microcomputers continues, most small colleges have opted for the more conservative approach of purchasing a limited number of machines and promoting voluntary student ownership. The principal virtue of this approach is that it keeps the college's ongoing investment in new computers to a minimum while it insures that students have access to the latest technology. The potential problem, of course, is that students may wind up being segregated into "haves" and "have-nots" and, as Dave Smallen points out in chapter 1, neither parents nor students would welcome the idea that owning a personal computer was a prerequisite for a college education. To avoid this situation, colleges must be careful to maintain a reasonable quantity of institutionally owned machines and must make private ownership as easy as possible.

Defining what constitutes a reasonable level of institutionally owned machines, however, is not an easy task. Among Liberal Arts I colleges, the mean ratio of students to college-owned computers is approximately 12 to 1 (Warlick 1989a). For a school of 2,000 students, therefore, a college might own about 170 public-access machines. But the acceptability of such a ratio depends heavily on the degree to which computing is integrated into the curriculum as well as on the level of private ownership among students. At many selective liberal arts colleges, such as Swarthmore, Williams, and Reed, the ratio of students to public access computers is less than 8 to 1 and the number of public-access machines frequently exceeds 250. Moreover, student ownership at these schools averages 34 percent, though at some schools, such as Wesleyan and Franklin and Marshall, the percentage may be as high as 70 percent.

Making it easy for students to own their own computers usually involves an on-campus computer store, generous discounts, convenient hardware and software support, low-interest or no-interest loans, and extended payment plans. Approximately 65 percent of liberal arts colleges have on-campus microcomputer sales facilities. While the markup for student purchases may range as high as 15 percent, the average markup is closer to 6 percent and nearly a quarter of these schools resell machines to students with no markup at all.

Though declining prices help to increase student ownership, they also tend to produce smaller profits for both manufacturers and campus resellers. This casts doubt on the viability of microcomputer sales as a future revenue center. If we allow resale prices to decrease and revenues to decline then campus computer stores may be unable to cover their own operating costs, much less provide any support for other computing activities. If we allow profit margins to increase, then we restrict student ownership and potentially drive campus stores out of business by making their prices less attractive than those of local retailers. Neither of these scenarios holds much promise for microcomputer resale as a potential revenue source.

What might change this equation is the possibility that students and faculty will develop a greater appetite for higher-priced items such as laser printers, high-resolution monitors, and UNIX workstations. As students and faculty become more sophisticated in their use of computers there may be a trend in the direction of "upscale" ownership, with the possibility of higher margins and increased revenues for the campus resale operation. Another potential factor is an increase in the sale of portable and pen-based computers. Many market analysts are predicting that the new generation of notebook and pen-based machines will produce dramatic growth in private computer ownership on campuses, and that falling margins will be offset by rising volumes.

Whether either of these factors will actually help to stabilize campus resale operations remains to be seen. For the immediate future, it appears that small colleges would be wise to view the proceeds of campus resale activities as excess funds rather than as a reliable revenue center for the computing operating budget.

In-House Maintenance

A far more stable funding source for computing, one that shows steady and solid growth, is that of in-house maintenance. During the mid-eighties, many colleges and universities discovered that when the installed base of microcomputers exceeded a few hundred machines, it became more cost-effective to hire technicians to perform in-house maintenance than it did to purchase annual maintenance contracts. What began as an attempt to reduce turnaround time and maintenance costs for college-owned equipment, however, quickly evolved into a means of acquiring revenue from members of the college community who owned their own machines. On-campus maintenance centers grew rapidly as students, faculty, and staff discovered that they were less expensive, more convenient, friendlier, and faster than off-site services.

While revenues from in-house maintenance operations may fluctuate from year to year, they generally tend toward stability and slow growth. Coupled with the cost savings for self-maintenance of college-owned equipment, they represent a solid funding source, even for small schools. The replacement of mainframes and minicomputers with powerful but modular workstations means that even centralized hosts may soon be candidates for self-maintenance. The potential budgetary impact of reducing or eliminating maintenance contracts for hosts is substantial and will be discussed in the section on funds allocation later in the chapter.

Usage and Training Fees

Should colleges levy fees for computer-related services such as printing? As we mentioned earlier, the traditional answer to this question—at least among liberal arts colleges—has been *no*. But the answer seems to be changing.

At many colleges, fees for letter-quality printing were originally established in order to restrict the usage of a scarce resource. In some cases, similar fees for non-curricular uses of laboratory computers were assessed for the same reason. Gradually, however, the scarcity of resources has declined. Yet the number of colleges that charge for laser printing and other services recently passed fifty percent and the number is continuing to grow. Though fees are generally modest, they are being applied to a wider variety of services, including:

- Laser and other specialty printing

- User manuals and help sheets

- Specialized user-training sessions

- File transfers between different types of microcomputers

- Home or dormitory rental of portables and other microcomputers

- Off-campus electronic mail

- Dormitory network connections

In most cases, user fees help to defray the cost of providing the service rather than cover it entirely. This is generally true for printing and documentation fees. In the case of specialized training and file transfers, fees are usually applied to labor costs for student or staff time and rarely cover more than a small portion of the cost. In some cases, however, revenues may be high enough to produce a substantial surplus that can be used to subsidize related computing operations, if local regulations permit. The last three items in the list are perhaps the best candidates for this type of funding.

The rental of desktop, portable, or notebook computers has been considered recently by several small colleges. At the rate of five dollars per day, the cost of an entry-level machine can be amortized in less than a year. More expensive machines may require two to three years. This is still far less than the general microcomputer replacement cycle (discussed later in the chapter) of seven to ten years. Since many students don't need continual access to computers, rental equipment may prove to be as economical for the student as it is for the college. At the end of the amortization period, the equipment may be sold to members of the community, thereby bringing in additional revenue for the purchase or upgrade of other college-owned hardware.

Off-campus electronic mail and other remote network services have generally been provided at no cost to students and faculty, since they offer a useful way of pursuing research with colleagues at other institutions. It is becoming increasingly obvious, however, that much of the e-mail traffic among colleges is purely social. Recognizing that colleges don't ordinarily subsidize personal long-distance telephone calls, some schools are now considering schemes to levy charges for long-distance e-mail and the use of various noncurricular database facilities. One strategy is to allow each student a certain "no-charge" limit—in order to encourage academic uses of the network—but to levy fees above the limit. Since the idea of levying off-campus e-mail charges is still relatively new, it remains to be seen how well this approach will work, especially at liberal arts colleges. It does appear to have significant potential as a revenue center.

Levying a fee for dormitory network access is an approach that has been implemented at a number of small colleges. Anecdotal evidence thus far suggests that it can be a highly successful source of revenue.[2] Network connection charges may be an alternative to off-campus e-mail charges or may be applied on top of network charges in much the same way that long-distance telephone charges are added to local telephone service charges.

The use of service fees to augment traditional funding sources for computing is clearly fraught with a variety of problems. In the end, some liberal arts colleges may simply decide that it is easier and safer to raise tuition. Yet service fees have the virtue of giving users some influence over the level of computing costs as well as the comfort of knowing that fees are assessed only for those members of the community who actually use a particular service. One thing is certain: If the growing demand for computing services is to be met, and if extramural funding sources continue to decline, colleges will have to re-evaluate the distribution of their institutional budgets or they will be forced to explore some of the cost-recovery strategies we described.

---

2. A discussion of this strategy is provided in chapter 9.

Financial Management

> The art of budgeting is to be able to convince yourself that the
> world will come to an end before the auditors arrive.
>
> —B. H. Snark

As anyone who has been involved in college administration knows, obtaining adequate levels of funding is only part of the battle. Deciding how to distribute and keep track of funds is as important— and often as difficult—as obtaining the funds in the first place. Not surprisingly, we've found that there are almost as many different approaches to financial management of computing funds as there are liberal arts colleges.

At some colleges, budget control for technology is in the hands of a single individual; in others it is reviewed and modified by a small army of faculty members, computing staff, and senior administrators. Some schools focus their attention on the competition of priorities within the computing budget, for example the cost of staff versus hardware, while others are primarily concerned with the way the computing budget competes with other budgets, such as those of the library or the physical plant.

There are many factors that influence the style and character of financial management for technology acquisition, including:

- The scope of responsibilities and reporting level of the person in charge of computing

- Whether academic and administrative computing are combined or separate

- Whether computing is combined with any other department, for example, telecommunications

- The degree to which technology planning efforts are coordinated with, or isolated from, technology budgeting procedures

- The degree to which budget management is influenced—or controlled—by user committees

• The degree to which faculty and staff actively
pursue information resources

• The level of support for technology by the president
and other senior administrators

The role each of these factors plays at a given institution indicates
the degree to which the institution considers computing to be a
strategic priority for the entire college rather than a tool to be
acquired and used at the discretion of individual departments. The set
of choices affects both budgeting and funding for technology and helps
to determine key financial management practices such as the organizational level at which information resources compete for funding.

There are at least three issues we would like to consider with
respect to the management of funds for technology:

1. How are technology purchasing decisions made?

2. How are funds for technology procurement distributed?

3. How do accounting practices affect technology
   purchases?

In order to address the first question we must distinguish between
major purchases that affect the whole college, such as the replacement of a central computing system, and minor purchases, such as
the acquisition of a microcomputer for a single department.

In the early days of computing at liberal arts colleges, minor
purchases—such as departmental minicomputers in the sciences—
were usually decided by the department themselves. Computers were
viewed as specialized pieces of equipment in the same category as
electron microscopes. By contrast, the purchase of central facilities,
such as mainframes, were frequently decided by a few administrators,
with little or no input from the community at large.

The situation at liberal arts colleges changed radically in the early
eighties with the proliferation of low-cost personal computers. Faculty awareness of computing intensified, academic computer centers
began to spring up, and everyone—faculty, staff, and students—felt
the need to be involved in purchasing decisions. Ironically, the
increased attention on computer purchasing affected the procedures
for major purchases and minor purchases differently. Major purchase

decisions, which had formerly been decided centrally by a small number of people, suddenly became the province of a broad cross-section of the community. On the other hand, decisions that had often been left exclusively to the departments themselves, gradually came under the purview of the computer center or of a centralized computing committee and became subject to institutional technology standards.

To highlight the character of technology decision procedures, we conducted a straw poll of the contributors to this volume and asked each to indicate the degree to which major purchase decisions, minor (departmental) purchase decisions, and technology standards decisions were centralized. The results, given in percentages of centralized decision making, are illustrated in Table 1.

School	Departmental Budgeting Decisions	Standards Decisions	Major Computing Purchase Decisions
Bryn Mawr	75%	95%	60%
Connecticut College	95%	100%	100%
Grinnell	95%	80%	70%
Hamilton	100%	100%	100%
Kenyon	100%	100%	100%
Mills	90%	80%	80%
Mount Holyoke	85%	75%	95%
Pomona	55%	75%	75%
Reed	95%	100%	95%
Smith	90%	90%	90%
Union	50%	90%	70%
Wesleyan	90%	95%	75%

Table 1: Centralization of Decision Making at Contributor Schools.

Note that standards decisions are highly centralized. This is in sharp contrast to university computing environments where standards for both hardware and software may be defined by individual departments and where any standards—institutional or departmental—may be ignored by researchers who are able to purchase equipment through discretionary grant funds.

Table 1 also illustrates the fact that decision making for departmental purchases is highly centralized. Though centralization may restrict a department's flexibility somewhat, it helps the institution as a whole to reduce its overall costs for maintenance, repair, software support, documentation, and network access. Central coordination of equipment acquisition insures that the people with the greatest technical expertise are part of the procurement process. It also allows the institution to realize economies of scale and thereby to negotiate better terms with vendors. Since standardization results in less technical diversity, it gives small schools the potential to create computing environments that are years ahead of their university counterparts, and to do so at a fraction of the cost.

With respect to major computing purchases, decision making among our sample group of colleges appears to be somewhat less centralized. Rather than leaving procurement decisions to the computer center or to a committee, some part of the college community is involved in the decision making process. Clearly, this is a reflection of the commonly held feeling that major technical decisions, such as the purchase of a central computer or the installation of a campus network, affect the entire institution and should therefore be undertaken with adequate representation from the faculty, staff, and students. Whether this trend is likely to continue in the future is an issue that we will return to in a moment.

The answer to our second question on financial management—How are funds for technology procurement distributed?—is closely linked to the first. In past years, computer purchases were large and infrequent, hence they fit well under the heading of *capital* or *special funds* allocation. At one point or another most liberal arts colleges have used capital allocations, restricted donations, extramural grants, bond issues, or other special methods to underwrite the costs of major technology procurements. Even the purchase of microcomputers, that in principle can be distributed over a period of several years, has frequently been paid for by this type of approach.

When we speak of "this type of approach" we are referring to one of four essential funding methods.

1. A college can tap its available funds and make a purchase outright (*capital expenditure*).

2. It can set aside funds over a period of years until a purchase becomes necessary (*reserve accumulation*).

3. It can borrow funds, internally or externally, make the purchase, and then pay off the cost gradually (*amortization* or *debt service*).

4. It can lease the equipment with an option to buy.

In terms of cash flow, the third and fourth approaches are essentially the same and can be treated as a single method.

When we questioned our sample group of colleges to determine which, if any, of these methods was the most popular for major purchases, we discovered that there was no clear winner. As illustrated in Table 2, methods vary widely from college to college. For departmental purchases there is a slight leaning toward the use of the operating budget.

The decision of whether to use reserve accumulation, amortization, or capital purchase seems to depend upon the financial well-being of the individual institution, its historical style of financial management, and the preferences of the person in charge of finances, rather than on any special feature of technology procurement. By contrast, the decision to use the operating budget rather than any other method seems to depend upon three technology factors: price, predictability, and scalability.

Price

The cost of certain major purchases has fallen dramatically during the past few years. The price of central timesharing systems, for example, has dropped from several hundred thousand dollars to as little as fifty thousand dollars. As prices for "big-ticket" items drop from six figures to five figures, the need to use funding strategies such as amortization or reserve accumulations diminishes. At some institutions, it may even be possible to dispense with central systems

School	Funding for Major Purchases	Funding for Departmental Purchases
Bryn Mawr	Reserve Accumulation	Operating Budget
Connecticut College	Amortization, Operating Budget	Operating Budget, Reserve Accumulation
Grinnel	Operating Budget	Operating Budget
Hamilton	Amortization, Operating Budget	Operating Budget
Kenyon	Capital Reserve, Budget	Capital Reserve, Budget
Mills	Reserve Accumulation	Reserve Accumulation
Mount Holyoke	Amortization, Operating Budget	Amortization, Operating Budget
Pomona	Reserve, Amortization, Operating Budget	Reserve Amortization Operating Budget
Reed	Capital Budget	Operating Budget
Smith	Capital Budget	Capital Budget
Union	Amortization, Operating Budget, Special Funds	Operating Budget, Special Funds
Wesleyan	Amortization, Capital Budget	Capital Budget, Grants

Table 2: Sample Funding Methods at Contributor Schools.

entirely and move completely in the direction of low-cost, networked microcomputers.[3]

Predictability

The relative newness of computing at liberal arts colleges and the dizzying pace at which technology has been changing have made it difficult for colleges to project future computing costs accurately. Until recently, most colleges have had no reliable data with which to predict the life span of most of their computing equipment, especially their microcomputers. Some colleges, however, are beginning to get a clearer picture of long-term costs and are therefore in a position to

---

3. See Ringle and Todd 1990.

include these costs as line items in their operating budgets. Better planning strategies, as discussed in the preceding two chapters, have helped colleges to avoid the "feast or famine" approach to equipment replacement and have allowed them to stretch the cost of equipment replacement smoothly over the years.

Scalability

Closely related to the last point is the fact that much of the newer technology is amenable to *scaled* rather than *all-or-nothing* implementation. In previous years, the reliance on central timesharing systems required infrequent but large expenditures. Today, much of the burden of central systems has been moved to distributed systems, which can be purchased individually or in small groups, thereby allowing procurement and installation to be spread across several years. The same is true of campus-wide networks. Though it may be necessary to plan the entire network at one time, it's possible to implement sections of the network sequentially, connecting one or two new buildings to the network during each funding cycle. Scaled technology implementation—together with lower prices and more reliable expense projections—allow an increasing number of colleges to fund major projects as line items in the operating budget, rather than as large one-time purchases.

There are, of course, still some exceptions to this trend. The purchase of an administrative computing package, for example, still tends to cost several hundred thousand dollars and though it may be predictable it is only marginally scalable. As technology evolves, however, even this type of purchase may one day become amenable to funding via the operating budget.

The answer to the third financial management question—How do accounting practices affect technology purchases?—involves more than just information technology. Many colleges and universities today face a serious *deferred maintenance* problem because they have avoided investing in the maintenance of the physical plant in favor of more pressing and immediate needs. In the past few years, the size of the problem has become a national concern. A major factor that led to the deferred maintenance problem was the routine practice among nonprofit organizations of not accounting for depreciation of capital

assets. Though auditing practices required accounting for depreciation in commercial firms, nonprofit organizations were not required
to do so.

In response to the alarming disregard for depreciation costs, the
Financial Standards Accounting Board (FASB) issued Statement 93
in 1987, *Recognition of Depreciation by Not-for-Profit Organizations*,
which requires recognition of depreciation on long-lived tangible
assets such as buildings, equipment, and similar items. The implementation was delayed by FASB Statement 99 to start with the fiscal years
beginning after January 1, 1990. FASB Statement 93 (as quoted in
Swieringa 1987) specifically states that:

> Not-for-profit organizations shall recognize the cost of using up
> the future economic benefits or service potentials of their long-
> lived tangible assets and shall disclose the following:
>
> 1. Depreciation expense for the period
>
> 2. Balance of major classes of depreciable assets
>
> 3. Accumulated depreciation, either by major classes of
>   depreciable assets or in total
>
> 4. A general description of the method or methods used
>   in computing with respect to major classes of depre-
>   ciable assets.

From the auditor's point of view, financial statements from nonprofit organizations will become more comparable to statements from
commercial organizations. From the point of view of institutions,
FASB will focus attention on the need to renew capital investments.
The FASB statement is not a requirement; institutions can choose
not to comply, but only at the risk of possibly receiving a qualified
opinion from auditors. In the long term, most private not-for-profits
are likely to comply.

The FASB statement is not very constraining, and colleges will be
able to account for depreciation in a number of ways. The easiest
method, and very possibly the first method to be used by a number of
schools, will permit depreciation to be lumped into physical plant
depreciation. FASB 93 does not require funding of depreciation or
distribution to cost centers, but many institutions may take the
opportunity forced on them by FASB 93 to account for depreciation

of capital assets in operating budgets. The result may well be that FASB 93 affects both capital and operating budgets for colleges and universities.

The problems schools face in replacing computing equipment are not as severe as those caused by deterioration of buildings and major pieces of equipment, but the solution to the latter may help solve problems with the former. Accurate accounting for the capital costs, lifetimes, and provision for replacement costs on a routine basis would help computing organizations tremendously. An immediate impact of this accounting change with respect to computing organizations is that it will require them to develop a comprehensive database of computing equipment to provide information about the identity, date of purchase, cost, expected lifetime, and so forth, of each piece of equipment in order to enable the chief financial officer to develop depreciation schedules. As schools begin to work out ways to account for depreciation in operating budgets, computer organizations may well see changes in their budgets.

In the longer term, FASB 93 may help to consolidate planning and budgeting for computing at higher levels of the college. The consolidation of accounting information about the actual investment in distributed computing systems will force institutions to realize the true scope of their investments. As competition for resources increases and as institutions refocus on primary missions over the next decade, FASB 93 may convince senior administrators and trustee boards that information resources are critical as well as pervasive elements on campus and that they require both high priority and long-term planning.

Looking Ahead

Each college can easily enumerate the ways in which its current financial management system for computing succeeds and fails. The complaints are well known: too little coordination of individual purchases or too much interference from the computer center, too much red tape in technology decisions or not enough input from the community. In many cases, the organizational structure, decision procedures, and budgeting practices of a college are the result of the idiosyncrasies of a single person or the collection of institutional quirks that we fondly refer to as the "liberal arts tradition." What can we expect from financial management for technology in the years ahead?

Turning back to the set of factors that influence financial management style, we can foresee the development of several trends. Separate academic and administrative computer centers are likely to evolve into coordinated organizations that report to a single administrator. Computing administrators, in turn, will carry more global responsibility for planning and budgeting and some colleges may raise the level of their positions accordingly, as Wellesley, Kenyon, Franklin and Marshall, Reed, and others have already done.

Technology planning will be more closely tied to the institutional mission and less isolated from budget planning. User committees are likely to be better informed and to become more involved in defining the goals for technology procurement, though they may exercise less influence over the selection of specific pieces of hardware. The actual selection, negotiation, and acquisition of technology will fall more and more to the central computing organization despite the fact that the computing resources themselves—microcomputers and workstations—will become less and less centralized. Institution-wide standards for hardware, software, and network connectivity will play a more prominent role in the selection of all forms of technology.

We can expect more of the burden for technology funding to move from capital and special allocations to the annual operating budget. Finally, though each college is bound to preserve its own idiosyncrasies when it comes to financial management, there probably will be a gradual increase in the standardization of accounting procedures, which will allow colleges to develop a better understanding of the scope of their investments in computing and a better sense of how to plan for future technology needs.

Funds Allocation: Spending and Saving Computing Dollars

Money is like manure. It doesn't do you any good unless you spread it around.

—Clint W. Murchison

Though there is a wealth of data on the allocation of computing dollars among colleges and universities, anyone who has examined these data knows that they differ substantially from one survey to another. The inconsistencies stem partly from the difficulty of keeping track of computing dollars that flow from different institutional sources and partly from the vagueness in the way that survey questionnaires are worded. It is often unclear to survey respondents whether or not benefits should be calculated into personnel costs, whether operating budget amounts should include contributions from departments or only funds assigned to the central organization, whether non–operating budget funds for hardware should include grants and equipment donations as well as capital allocations, and so forth. The problem of questionnaire interpretation is further exacerbated when the target population is a mixture of different segments of higher education including liberal arts colleges, two-year colleges, or research universities, rather than a single group.

Despite the differences and inconsistencies among survey results, however, there are some general points upon which they all seem to agree. With this in mind, we focus our attention on the rationale for allocation strategies rather than on formulas for slicing the pie chart. The key areas we consider are hardware and maintenance, personnel, software, and networking.

Hardware and Maintenance

During the late seventies and early eighties, discussions of technology funding nearly always focused on the most tangible aspect of computing, the equipment itself. Hardware acquisition constituted the largest expense item in small college computing budgets. In the past few years, however, hardware prices have dropped precipitously, inspiring hope among senior administrators, college trustees, and computing directors alike, that the expense drain for equipment will finally taper off. Is this a realistic expectation?

Most likely the answer is *no*. At least not to the degree that many would hope. Though decreases in unit hardware costs have been dramatic, they have not signaled corresponding decreases in overall computing budgets. We can identify two principal reasons for this: an increase in consumption of distributed resources and a shift in funds allocation from equipment purchase to support services.

When microcomputers began to enter the liberal arts college environment in large numbers during the mid-eighties, some believed that they would eventually make central systems obsolete. Some also felt that once microcomputer saturation was achieved, the days of expensive hardware procurement would finally come to an end. On most campuses, both of these beliefs have turned out to be false. Though platform size and cost have diminished substantially, most colleges still find it necessary to maintain central systems in order to support file serving, network operations, off-campus communications, and other tasks. Despite the fact that the future cost of central systems may drop as low as $25,000, they will still need to be upgraded and replaced periodically.

Much of the savings for central systems, however, has been shifted into the purchase of distributed microcomputers, workstations, and file servers. Colleges that began their microcomputer deployment early and that have already achieved effective saturation, are discovering that saturation does not mark the end of hardware procurement. Hardware failures, rising repair costs, and the inability to run new software on older machines eventually renders desktop computers obsolete and makes replacement necessary. Colleges that began their microcomputer distribution later or that have maintained less aggressive distribution policies are, nevertheless, going to run into the replacement problem within the next few years.

When we asked computer center directors how often they felt that college-owned microcomputers should be replaced, the most common response was five to seven years, an annual replacement rate of 14 to 20 percent of the installed base per year. When we looked at budgeting and acquisitions data, however, we discovered that the actual replacement rate was 10 to 13 percent, a seven- to ten-year cycle. Ironically, this is the same cycle that has traditionally been used for mainframe replacement. For a school of 2,000 students with an installed base of 110 college-owned machines, a total replacement would cost approximately $181,500, assuming an average price of $1,650 per unit.[4] It is worth noting that the decreasing cost of entry-level desktop systems is offset, to some extent, by the fact that schools are adding larger disk drives, color monitors, extra memory, and other options to their replacement units. As the sophistication of the user community grows, the desire to have more powerful and versatile computers grows as well.

A seven- to ten-year replacement cycle for both distributed and central equipment means that the long-term financial benefits of microcomputer saturation and decreasing hardware costs, though visible, will be modest. The downsizing and scalability of the newer technology, however, means that hardware costs can be smoothly distributed from year to year by the operating budget. More importantly, perhaps, it means that if budgetary pressure at liberal arts colleges increases, the replacement cycle can be stretched to accommodate it. The flexibility provided by distributed computing and newer host technology affords colleges a safety valve for cost-containment that can be opened and closed without triggering an immediate crisis in computing services.

Another factor that can influence the timing of hardware acquisition is the cost of maintenance. Up until the mid-eighties, nearly all maintenance work at small colleges was handled by external contract, usually from the principal equipment vendor. Since most maintenance contracts are pegged at 10 to 15 percent of the purchase price of the equipment—with occasional increments for inflation—the total cost of maintenance contracts accounted for a major portion of the annual operating budget. The decline in hardware prices in recent years has been accompanied by a corresponding drop in the price of maintenance contracts. For new machines, especially the RISC architecture platforms, contract prices are so low that the

---

4. The $1,650 figure is based on current median costs across both MS-DOS and Macintosh platforms. It includes essential software, memory, and disk options.

savings in maintenance costs can pay for the replacement machine within two to three years. In many cases, therefore, it makes sense to replace machines in less than the traditional seven- to ten-year cycle, even if a machine's performance is still adequate to meet the needs of the college.

The dollars saved on maintenance contracts can also be used to hire personnel for maintenance and repair of distributed equipment, thereby producing additional savings and, as discussed earlier, possibly providing a revenue stream to support other computing operations. The question of when it is appropriate to switch to in-house maintenance seems to be answered differently by each college. In principle, one need only add up the cost of maintenance contracts for all college-owned microcomputers, printers, and other peripherals to determine the funds that would be available for a staff position. In practice, there are subtle disagreements over the number of pieces of hardware that can be effectively maintained by a single individual and whether or not there are hidden staffing costs that must be included in the equation. The potential offsetting revenues from maintenance and repairs of privately owned machines also need to be taken into consideration. Anecdotal evidence indicates that more and more colleges are moving to self-maintenance and that schools that have established such programs have consistently found them to meet or exceed their savings expectations. At Reed, for example, doing in-house maintenance saved the college between $15,000 and $20,000 during the 1990–1991 fiscal year.

Personnel

Trading maintenance contract dollars for staff dollars, however, raises the larger issue of personnel costs. It is well worth noting that the primary rationale for hiring staff to do in-house maintenance is to save money. The irony in this, of course, is that in times of fiscal austerity many administrators focus on staff reduction as the preferred method of cost containment, little realizing that it may cost the college less to *maintain* staff size than to *decrease* it.

While budgetary benefits may be the most compelling reason for increasing staff size in certain areas of computing, there are others that are equally important. Over the past ten years, colleges and universities have come to recognize that technology cannot be effectively and efficiently used unless there is adequate support for both the computers and the people who use them. This recognition has come more slowly to liberal arts colleges than to other areas of higher education.

In 1987, the portion of the computing operating budget devoted to staff salaries[5] among liberal arts colleges was approximately 41 percent. By 1990, the median figure had risen to 51.5 percent, with many of the best organizations reporting figures of 60 percent or more. The area that received the greatest increase in personnel was user support. In many cases, the growth in the cost of staff salaries was accommodated by a commensurate decrease in funding for equipment acquisition and maintenance contracts.

This shift in emphasis from technology itself to human support for the technology is perhaps the most significant change in the liberal arts college computing environment of the current decade. Colleges have finally started to recognize that improvements in hardware, software, networking, or any other technical area, are pointless unless users are provided with adequate training, documentation, and consulting. This recognition has led to computing staff size increases at liberal arts colleges of more than 55 percent during the past four years.[6] It is not surprising to find that when users rate the overall quality of computing services at their institutions the (positive) correlation to staff size is much firmer than to the number or type of computers, the budget, or any other measure.

In sharp contrast to the situation at many large universities, few liberal arts colleges have experienced computing staff reductions in recent years. At the 1991 annual conference of the Consortium of Liberal Arts Colleges, for example, fewer than five percent indicated that cuts had occurred during 1990–1991 and more than a third indicated that new positions had been added. The remainder stated that staff size was stable, though a few added that hiring freezes were in effect. During the balance of this decade, we can expect that staff size at liberal arts colleges will fluctuate slightly and that schools

---

5. These figures are for academic computing only. They are drawn from the 1987 and the 1990 annual computing surveys of the Consortium of Liberal Arts Colleges (CLAC).

6. See chapter 5 for further discussion of staffing growth.

with increases may outnumber schools with decreases. The trend toward combined academic and administrative computing organizations will probably increase the number of full-time equivalents (FTEs) involved in user or technical services and reduce the number of FTEs involved in management and planning. The total FTE level will either remain unchanged or decrease marginally.

The general downturn in the economy has finally slowed the spiraling salary expectations in the technology arena, in higher education as well as in the private sector. The flattening of growth in staff size should therefore be accompanied by more predictable (and manageable) growth in salaries, hence the percentage of the computing operating budget devoted to personnel should show far less change in the next five years than it did in the past five years.

Before leaving the topic of personnel costs it is worth mentioning that small colleges have also been paying more attention recently to the issue of staff development. An examination of the funding level for staff training seminars, travel to professional conferences, visits to other campuses, and similar activities, reveals that amounts have doubled during the past four years, though on average they still constitute less than 2 percent of the computing operating budget. While such activities may appear to be extraneous to daily operations they can play a significant role in the long-term finances of the computing organization. Staff members who expand their knowledge and skills through off-site training events may become more effective in performing their duties and the time away from campus may serve to boost morale and thus decrease the rate of costly staff turnover. Development opportunities may be helpful during staff recruitment by making a position more attractive to a prospective candidate or by serving as part of an overall compensation package. Though travel and other staff development funds may be expendable in times of budget crisis, at other times they can be viewed as part of a long-term cost-containment strategy and should be assessed accordingly.

Software

While the price of hardware has been steadily dropping, the price of software has not. License fees for timesharing platforms have either remained constant or risen slightly in pace with inflation.

Some colleges have experienced initial decreases in software costs by moving from a host package to a desktop package, only to find the savings disappear as the number of desktop units multiplied. Though institutional site licenses are available for some packages, there are others that still require unit pricing. Quantity discounts that substantially lower license fees to large universities are frequently unavailable (or minimal) to small colleges. In addition, license fees for UNIX workstations, though lower than host fees, are two to five times higher than microcomputer fees.

Part of the overall software problem arises from the need to maintain costly licenses even if only one or two faculty members require the software. For example, a recent poll of liberal arts colleges (Price 1991) revealed that although many schools have acquired the SAS statistical processing package, virtually all of those schools continue to maintain older packages such as BMDP.

In the long run, however, several factors may contribute to an overall reduction in the amount of the budget to software. Increased student ownership of microcomputers will reduce the institution's obligation to purchase licenses for basic tools such as word processors, spreadsheets, and the like. Fewer and fewer of the older packages will be maintained on timesharing platforms. And as market pressure mounts, more software vendors will establish site license and network license options. Institutionwide standardization will allow colleges to strike better quantity purchase agreements, and the cost of non-standard packages is apt to move from the central computing budget to departmental budgets or possibly even to the personal funds of individual faculty members.

Networking

As mentioned earlier, campus-wide networking is an item that once appeared to require a major capital allocation but is now viewed as a scalable cost. While colleges in the eighties sometimes scheduled an entire network implementation for an eighteen-month period, colleges in the nineties are scheduling similar implementations for periods as long as seven or eight years. Schools have realized that not everyone needs network access, or the same level of network access, at the same time. They are also recognizing that the potential savings in labor costs afforded by implementing everything at once are offset by the savings in hardware costs of a scaled implementation. For small colleges the principal benefit of this new strategy is that networking projects that were previously out of reach due to the lack of capital funds can now be undertaken using the operating budget alone.

At the same time, however, colleges that completed the installation of campus-wide networks in the eighties have discovered that the cost of maintaining and upgrading them is higher than anticipated. As more computers and different types of computers are added to the network, hardware and software for gateways, bridges, repeaters, and other devices must be modified or replaced. The cost of a campus network, therefore, is an ongoing cost rather than a one-time expense, as was previously thought.

In addition to the expense of the campus-wide network, a growing number of small colleges must also cover the cost of inter-campus networking for BITNET or the Internet or both.[7] In the early eighties, networking accounted for such a small part of the college computing budget that data were rarely gathered on it; by 1990 liberal arts colleges were reporting that ongoing (internal and external) networking costs ranged from 3 percent to as much as 5 percent of their annual operating expenses.[8] As networking, both on-campus and off-campus, becomes more complex and more extensively used by members of the college community, we can expect to see its allocation in the operating budget grow, though scalability and declining prices should keep the growth modest.

Conclusion

Will the potential decrease in the cost of hardware and maintenance make up for probable increases in personnel and networking? Will potential revenues from in-house maintenance or dormitory networking offset the probable decline in other funding sources? Will

---

7. See chapter 7 for a discussion of inter-campus communications.
8. A poll of 20 liberal arts colleges indicated that the average cost in 1990 for a connection to the Internet was approximately $8,650. BITNET costs were 75 percent to 85 percent less than Internet costs for small colleges (Ringle 1990).

colleges truly escape the financial woes that university computing organizations now face? It is hoped the answers to each of these questions is *yes*. Given the number of factors involved, the uncertainty of future economic and demographic trends, and the uniqueness of each liberal arts college, however, it would be prudent for us to consider the alternatives. As we plan and budget for computing during the remainder of this decade those of us at liberal arts colleges should diligently monitor our expenses and economize whenever possible.

A recent issue of the *Edutech Report* offers the following ways of containing costs (Fleit 1990):

- Using videotape to supplement training done by staff members

- Purchasing off-the-shelf software rather than building it in-house

- Cutting down on unnecessary report generation and other data-processing activities

- Automating labor-intensive tasks (such as daily backups)

- Selling assets such as unused hardware and software

- Postponing filling open positions for as long as possible

- Using more students to compensate for small staff size

These are each valuable strategies, though they may not be appropriate or practicable under all circumstances. Postponing recruitments for an open position may help an organization to reassess the value of that position, but it may also trigger a support crisis. Using more students may help compensate for small staff size but excessive reliance on student workers may result in service problems. Judicious use of these and other strategies, however, can clearly help to contain costs and to make the entire information services organization more valuable to the college. Whether or not a computing organization encounters a fiscal crisis—and regardless of the availability of alternative funding sources—consideration of Fleit's suggestions should be at the top of everyone's agendas.

Liberal arts colleges have evolved a bewildering profusion of methods for funding and allocating information resources on campus. As competition for faculty and students increases over the next decade, schools are likely to focus more carefully on the factors that will help them be successful in that competition. Information resources will be one of those factors. Planning for information resources will benefit from exploration of alternate sources of funding or partial funding that can be generated from within the institutional community, from changes in accounting practices that recognize depreciation, from allocation processes that acknowledge the pervasive use of information resources throughout the campus, and from aggressive efforts to reduce operating costs wherever possible.

As the decade progresses it will become increasingly clear that information tools at liberal arts colleges are acquired in order to support institutional missions rather than as goals in themselves. In these environments, the officers in charge of computing must work as partners with financial officers, faculty, and other members of the community to anticipate the evolution of technology and to plan for replacement of computing facilities in the most cost-effective manner.

References

Augustson, J. Gary. 1989. Strategies for financial planning. In *Organizing and Managing Information Resources on Campus,* Brian L. Hawkins, ed. Reading, Mass.: Addison-Wesley.

Fleit, Linda. 1990. Hunkering down: Cost consciousness for computing. *Edutech Report,* November.

Gillespie, Robert G. 1989. Chargeback revisited. In *Organizing and Managing Information Resources on Campus,* Brian L. Hawkins, ed. Reading, Mass.: Addison-Wesley.

Green, Kenneth C. 1989. A perspective on vendor relationships: A study of symbiosis. In *Organizing and Managing Information Resources on Campus,* Brian L. Hawkins, ed. Reading, Mass.: Addison-Wesley.

Henry, Carl. 1990. *CLAC Annual Survey of Computing,* Consortium of Liberal Arts Colleges.

Price, Janet. 1991. Mini-survey on statistical software usage, *Consortium of Liberal Arts Colleges Newsletter,* 3:2.

Ringle, Martin D. 1990. CLAC electronic mini-survey on inter-campus data communications costs.

Ringle, Martin and H. David Todd. 1990. Innovative academic computing: An ECG case study. *EDUCOM Review,* 25:3.

Swieringa, Robert J. 1987. Issues in depreciation accounting and accounting for contributions, *NACUBO Business Officer*.

Warlick, Charles H. 1989a. Financial planning for information resources on campus: Baseline information and budget ratios. In *Organizing and Managing Information Resources on Campus,* Brian L. Hawkins, ed. Reading, Mass.: Addison-Wesley.

Warlick, Charles H. 1989b. *Directory of computing facilities in higher education.* Austin: University of Texas.

Part Two

Organizational Issues

The Organization of Computing Services

Thomas A. Warger
Bryn Mawr College

*Thomas A. Warger is director of computing services at Bryn Mawr College in
Pennsylvania. His scope of responsibilities includes academic and administrative computing services, audio-visual services, and technical advisement
for the Language Learning Center and the college's Office of Telephone
Services. Prior to coming to Bryn Mawr in 1986, he was assistant to the vice
president for academic affairs at Union College, Schenectady, New York.
While at Union he was also acting director of computing services.*

*Dr. Warger holds a Ph.D. in French studies and taught French on the
faculties of Gettysburg and Union colleges before switching to administrative
work. His original interest and experience in computing were in programming
computer-aided instruction modules for modern languages teaching.*

Among the first questions newly acquainted computing services
directors ask each other is inevitably: "And how is computing service
organized at your college?" The responses fall into several predictable
categories, but the listener attentive to the qualifications that
accompany most of these answers also learns that there is little
agreement on the definition of a good or appropriate organization.
Larger institutions have spawned network services groups, information centers, applications programming centers, and departmentally
based support services to respond to changes in how and where
computing is done. While the scope of operations is drastically
smaller at liberal arts colleges, the same impetus to re-examine the
support organizations that have carried us for a decade or more is a
current concern.

This chapter begins with a discussion of issues in computing support that are specific to liberal arts colleges. It surveys the common organizational structures, including reporting lines and advisory groups, found at colleges. Budgetary implications of organizational choices are discussed. Relations among computing and other campus groups are explored in order to situate computing services in the life of the campus. The conclusion suggests ways of framing sensible answers to the often-asked question about what form to give those services.

Issues That Shape Computing at Liberal Arts Colleges

Liberal arts colleges have not been in the forefront of technology. Having neither the resources of a university nor the vocational focus of a community college or technical institute, the liberal arts college has generally had neither the means nor the compulsion to be technology driven. For several reasons colleges have held back, watching computing developments and trying to decide upon the right moment to adopt a promising technology. There are several kinds of constraints on technological currency at these schools, expressions of an innate conservatism that most often relegates computing to a supporting role.

One of the strongest traits of the liberal arts college is the primacy of the traditional curriculum. Virtually all discussions of policy and money invoke this curriculum at some point, often to restrain some other purpose. The curriculum dominates faculty position allocations, construction projects, and college efforts in fundraising. It is defended against shifting ideological currents and societal pressure for vocational training, and is sometimes held to be threatened by pressure to adapt to changes in technology. Within these constraints, the case for computing services proceeds with conspicuous deference to the established goals of the curriculum. Thus, computers are touted to help scientists get on with the task of making up our national shortcomings in science learning or to help train the ears of music students. By passing the case for computers through the screen of the standard disciplines, the liberal arts college assures itself that the curriculum will not be jostled too severely. At Bryn Mawr, and many other colleges, the search to find a "home" for study in computer science has been a lesson in how the established disciplines filter the new technology through the test of the curriculum.

By the same token, methods of instruction are cited as defining qualities of the liberal arts college. The various tools of pedagogy—lecture, the laboratory session, seminar, tutored study—while found in different proportions at different schools, are given special attention by liberal arts colleges. Instruction is an exchange between faculty and students with minimal mediation by the apparatus of mass communications, or anything thought likely to diminish the importance of human contact. So the replacement of class-contact hours or office visits by computer-mediated instruction has never been a goal at these schools. Computing is instead seen as an aid to traditional pedagogy, another tool at the pedagogue's disposal. At Bryn Mawr, the greatest growth in academic computing usage has been the addition of "computing labs" to existing courses. History students spend a week approaching demographics through a computing assignment and students of Russian practice verbs through computer-based drills or interactive computer-video programs. But these new enhancements do not fundamentally alter teaching methods. The computer's effects on pedagogy have been generally gradual and modest.

Budget, too, leads these colleges to use caution in moving toward more computing. Unlike the commercial enterprise or the decentralized (and sometimes balkanized) world of the university, the liberal arts college is reluctant to identify "winners and losers" among its parts. A program in Greek, astronomy, or dance may have only three majors per year but the institution is proud not to discontinue it. Student counseling services grow each year. The residential campus must be attractive, not just adequately functional. The internal economy of the college is based on an understanding that all the competing projects will have their turn at a share of the funding, even though their costs and values are often not rigorously assessed. The worthy needs are many, the funding never adequate to all, and the imperative to do something for each of them all but irresistible.

In contrast to most universities, Bryn Mawr and nearly all other liberal arts colleges do not charge computing services back to the students, faculty, or departments who use them. The net effect is to spread around the available funding, providing a modest capability in computing across all disciplines, with some points of strength here and there. The resource is diluted; its development is held to a pace that will not leave behind any identifiable segment of the clientele; narrowly specialized projects are only funded if the principal faculty participant can secure grant funding (usually in competition against university researchers).

The liberal arts college has also been resistant to demographic trends. The idea of community has not evolved as fast as the changes that have brought more older, commuting students and a rising proportion of women and minorities into higher education in general. Consequently, academic facilities and support services at these schools have not felt the same pressure to adapt as have so many universities and community colleges. Computing support services at liberal arts colleges are still keyed to a resident student population that is nearly homogeneous in skills and needs. At Bryn Mawr, which is almost entirely residential at the undergraduate level, all students are presumed able to complete course computing assignments in the public-access labs. Only in the Graduate School of Social Work and Social Research, where most students are commuters, does the support of people working on computers at home and over modems become a significant concern.

For all these reasons, the computing environment at liberal arts colleges is less varied and less technologically intensive than at other kinds of schools, even where the per capita expenditure is comparable. A small support staff acquires and installs computing technology that has become an off-the-shelf commodity. Campus-standard hardware, networks, and software contribute to ease of support. Those needing to deviate from campus-wide prescriptions must fend for themselves. The central support group, meanwhile, seems always just short of offering the outreach services and the depth and diversity of technical knowledge everyone agrees would be ideal.

Academic computing is one of the last outposts of management by generalists. Former professors turned directors and statisticians turned programmers are more often the rule than the exception. They find themselves in computing at the liberal arts college because that community feels comfortable with staff whose credentials testify to their participation in the spirit of the place. The technical demands they face are eased by reliance on mainstream technologies and off-the-shelf products. By keeping a prudent distance behind the latest technological advances, these colleges do not need computer scientists and engineers to choose, install, and operate their computing systems. A kind of standard model for computing has emerged.

Common Organizational Structures

Various approaches to organizing computing services have emerged at points in the entwined codevelopment of technology and campus governance (Ryland, 1989). The three most common structures today are (1) a single department for academic and administrative computing, (2) separate departments for the two functions, and (3) a three-part scheme with academic and administrative applications support groups mediated by an operations or networks group. Other structures tend to be variations on these three basic themes.

The combined computing center is the oldest of these models and is still the most widely used among liberal arts colleges, especially smaller colleges. When the campus first acquired a mainframe computer, probably to do payroll and student records, it also accommodated a few academic needs as well. The programmers and keypunchers, who were the only ones capable of operating the beast, served a mixed community consisting of a few automation-minded administrators and several faculty members from the sciences and social sciences. The essential conditions for the success of this structure were that the clientele was small and that third-generation programming languages served all purposes equally, whether well or ill. The clients' reliance on the expertise of the computing staff is a defining trait of this model of organization—very few are able to program their own applications.

As advances in technology have diversified computing, the combined center has adapted by expanding and specializing its staff. Database programmers are now a breed distinct from those writing scientific algorithms in FORTRAN. Microcomputer support specialists, network installers and trouble-shooters, training specialists, documentation writers, and end-user service providers have all come to populate the central staff.

The downfall of the combined center comes when it is judged unable (or unwilling) to give one of its two client groups adequate service. In the majority of cases, the faculty find that the administrative needs of the college crowd them off the computing staff's agenda. In some cases, the faculty exercise sufficient influence to divert computing resources into teaching and research that might otherwise be used to support innovative administrative applications. A few such instances, if gracelessly handled, suffice to set a paradigm of inequality. Worse yet is to have each camp—academic and administrative—believe that the other is getting unwarranted attention at its expense. Whether the perceived inequity is unilateral or bilateral, someone inevitably suggests that the computing organization be split into two centers in an effort to improve the resource and services levels for both sides of the house.

The successful combined center diversifies its support services and seeks ways to lessen the differences between the two client groups. The rise of microcomputing, networking, and end-user driven computing has forced computer centers to develop support strategies that are more broadly focused than the simple software aids provided in the past.

The origin of most separate computing centers on college campuses can be traced to the fission of a combined center. The tensions leading to a split are usually felt on both sides. For administrators, contention for programmers' attention threatens the stability of operations. For faculty, the intensification of computing support required by the administration to accomplish its work threatens to relegate faculty needs to low priority. As the schism develops, technology evolves to give end-users enough local control and self-confidence to escape complete dependence on the central staff. Improvements to mainframe computer operating systems during the 1970s made the power of computers more accessible to those who were willing to invest the time to learn to program. Among faculty, a willingness emerged to become more involved with computers, to be more than passive clients. Some faculty members who became deeply involved with the operation and control of computers during this period went on to make careers in computer management, often heading newly created academic computing centers.

In this model, the technological bases of the separate centers are essentially still the same. Both use mainframes or time-shared minicomputers and find they must balance central resources against the clamor from the clientele for more localized and personalized service. The choice to segregate academic and administrative support has consequences that ill prepare the latter camp for technological changes. While faculty bring to computing an ethic of self-sufficiency that promotes lessened dependence on computer professionals, administrative staff typically deepen that dependence—particularly as it becomes necessary to develop (or acquire) large database applications that integrate many administrative functions.

In some cases, separate academic and administrative computing centers derive from observance of strict segregation of business functions from academic support and administration. In this situation, the administrative computing center may be the stepchild of the business office. Concern for confidentiality and security are common rationales for maintaining the separation. When the department is cast in this low-profile role, the virtual invisibility of administrative computing in the eyes of the campus community actually helps to promote better security. At the same time, however, it may also promote misunderstanding and a certain degree of mistrust.

Causes of discontent under the regime of separate centers stem from the very features that made separation seem so attractive. Academic computing escapes direct competition with administrative computing needs, but as a separate entity finds its equipment and staff needs difficult to fund in isolation from its twin center. The division weakens it financially by separating it from its natural ally and by absence of any other politically effective unit on campus—the few major faculty customers of computing being scattered throughout several academic departments that may have no other experience of collective budgetary cooperation.

A perennial problem in administrative computing, when separated from academic computing, is often that its clients' demands for maximal stability and minimal service interruptions strongly discourage the technological innovation necessary to provide serious improvements in service. The whole enterprise may be overtaken by a dogged incrementalism and may fall farther and farther behind an accumulating backlog of service requests. Under these conditions, it is not unusual for administrative offices to seek alternative solutions in microcomputing, only to find that the administrative computing center disavows any intention to support or even recognize locally developed office systems. The support deficit may then draw the academic computing center into the situation, to the chagrin of both the academic *and* the administrative computing centers.

The campus that has opted for separate centers and later changed its mind has several alternatives.

- A combined academic/administrative center

- Separate centers reporting to a single chief information officer

- Separate groups for application programming and user support combined with unified departments to address common needs such as networking

- Variations on one of these three models

A return to a combined department is practical only when a common base of operations can be established, for example, a single computer operating system and data network. Carleton College is an example of a campus that has followed this course. The main advantage in this fusion is that the new organization has more technical depth because it concentrates its human resources on a unified computing environment.

Constituting a new quasi-independent department for operations or networking leaves the tasks that are specific to the unique needs of each client group in the hands of separate academic and administrative computing departments. Computer systems operations, microcomputer support, and data networking are situated in the new group. This model of organization is quite common, existing in many similar variations. It has the virtue of spanning the differences between the separate centers without needing to resolve them. It also serves as an intermediate step to an eventual reunification in a single department without committing anyone to that decision in advance. One potential drawback is the awkwardness of having three (or more) computing organizations that need to cooperate to be effective. Another is that contention for the services of the operations group can be a new source of tension.

A campus interested in limited reintegration of separate computing departments can consolidate their management under one director. In this model, the two departments retain most of their autonomy, particularly in staff-to-client relations and in budget—issues that are likely to be sensitive in an environment where separation is well established. Coordination between the departments can proceed without disturbing relations within the constituencies. Institutional planning activities are well served by this fusion of management. The most obvious disadvantage is absence of savings from staffing consolidation and common operations. Bryn Mawr College has adopted this model because it saw a benefit in consolidated management and planning but has very different hardware, software, and networking environments in academic and administrative computing. Interdepartmental collaboration in microcomputer support and network development have been the main operational gains realized to date. From the college administration's view, computing services are virtually merged because there is one director and a single reporting assignment.

Yet another variation on the unification of computing support is proposed as an ideal by David Smallen at Hamilton College (1989), where staff specialists are assigned to projects that might be in either academic or administrative domains or that can cross both. The theory behind this organizational plan is that the appropriate structure is predicated on the types of services provided. The traditional classification of computing applications into academic and administrative functions or by the kind of technology used is accordingly de-emphasized.

The organizational options (and they may well be more diverse and numerous than those discussed here) appear generally correlated to stages in the development of computing technology and practice. The single-shop model had its origins in the mainframe era, and to the extent that it survives it has evolved to emphasize the integration of services. The separate-shops model reflects the economic facts of the minicomputer era. The prospect of affording two timesharing systems on campus made the organizational division possible. By the same token, the shake-out in the minicomputer industry has led some campuses to select a single vendor and operating system standard for the campus at the time of major equipment replacement, thereby increasing their options for consolidation in operations and organization.

The rise of microcomputers, networking, and end-user self-reliance shift support priorities from applications programming to the establishment of flexible and easy-to-use computing resources. The organizational consequence appears to be renewed interest in central service and coordination.

The pace of change is not everywhere equal. Nor is there necessarily a single line of development. Using the "eras of computing" in the history of technology as an index of technological change is useful, but the experience of technology at small schools is often discontinuous. Combined, separate, and hybrid types of organization exist on college campuses today. How appropriate each is to its setting is not solely determined by technology, but is influenced by other important criteria as well.[1]

Reporting Options

One of the most basic issues in organizational matters is determining a job title for computer department reporting. More than symbolism is at stake; this detail can determine the role of a computing department (and its director) as much as it reflects campus values.

Titles vary considerably. The most narrow and restrictive is *director of the academic (or administrative) computer center,* indicating custodianship of a central facility and saying nothing of any wider expectations. *director of computing* or *director of computing services* suggests more scope of responsibility and denotes either a single shop or some kind of unified management. A vice-president or vice-provost title usually indicates a position of higher rank in the organization

---

1. It is interesting to note, however, that among the members of the Consortium of Liberal A... s Colleges there has been a clear trend toward coordinated centers that report to a single director. In 1987, the percentage of schools that had separate centers was approximately 49 percent; by 1990 that percentage had dropped to approximately 33 percent.

chart than that occupied by a director, though in some cases a director may in fact report to the president. The more elevated title may also indicate a higher priority for computing at that institution. The inclusion of phrases such as "information systems," "telecommunications," or "instructional technology" in the title most likely points to responsibility for telephone service, audio-visual service, printing services, language lab, or some combination of them. In a few cases, small-campus computing directors also have formal involvement in institutional planning (perhaps because the statistical grist for planning research resides in the computers).

The reporting lines are also instructive about the way computing is viewed at a school. Most computing officers report to the chief academic officer below the president, generally a dean, provost, or vice-president for academic affairs. Some computing officers hold positions that are permanent administrative appointments; others are recruited from among the faculty to serve a specific term, with the presumption that they will return to the ranks afterward.[2] While the rotating faculty approach generally falls to someone with less technical and administrative expertise, those appointees are frequently in a better position to understand the computing needs of the faculty and students, hence they may be better able to identify appropriate technical goals. The optimal appointee may be someone who has held a faculty appointment at a liberal arts college but who has since decided to pursue computing administration on a full-time basis. Not surprisingly, many liberal arts colleges have focused their recruiting efforts in this direction.[3]

When the academic computing director has an administrative computing counterpart, that other person is likely to report to the chief financial officer, the vice-president for administration, or someone in a similar position. In a few cases, the director of a combined computing shop reports to the chief financial officer, but that arrangement raises the difficulty of debating policy with faculty in an administrative context which may be unfamiliar as well as inhospitable.

---

2. Franklin and Marshall and Swarthmore are among the colleges that appoint faculty members on a rotating basis to supervise academic computing.

3. Among the contributors to this volume, for example, nine out of fourteen hold a terminal degree and have held full-time or part-time teaching positions at liberal arts colleges.

Some top computing positions report to the president. While unquestionably a more prestigious assignment, it can have its disadvantages, too. The president might be interested and personally involved in computing, in which case the working relationship with the computing head is likely to be substantial. For many presidents, however, computing remains a somewhat mysterious domain and they are content to have the director of computing one step lower in the organizational structure.

An administrative position common to large commercial corporations and to universities but rarely used at small colleges until recently is that of the *chief information officer (CIO)*. A *vice president (or provost) for information services* typically has a wider mandate than that given to computing directors, including those who have responsibility for several electronic technologies. The key idea embodied by the CIO concept is that there is an information enterprise that includes computers, data, audio-visual technology, telephones, printing, and post offices, but which is more than just the aggregate of their operations. In this view the various means of handling words, numbers, charts, graphics, and so on, which are the tokens of information, are seen to be converging into a new discipline. The CIO is asked to assess how the institution might alter the way seemingly disparate tasks are done so as to gain new benefits from the coordination of technologies. An administrator with this charge might, for example, investigate the whole range of printing needs on campus, weighing the value of commercial typesetting services against training and equipping college staff to do more of this work themselves. The analysis is more than an exercise in applying a new technology; consideration must be given to the goals, working methods, and skills of officers and individuals who probably see themselves only minimally as users of electronic technology. The CIO must have the experience and credibility to work in a field much wider than that of the computing director.

Crossing administrative boundaries to reorganize work can provoke turf battles and other forms of resistance to change. Consequently, a chief information officer should have the highest level of institutional authorization and support. Anxiety about high technology is still quite general and persistent throughout the workforce, making efforts to infuse it into the skill base a sensitive task. The main focus of the CIO is to promote change across the boundaries of organizational units, to address issues more extensive than those subsumed by computing and telecommunications management.

The principal argument for a CIO position is the central focus, high visibility, and recognition it affords the information interests on campus. The influence of this administrator is bound to be stronger than that of computing services directors, who may find themselves reporting to this person. Strength in advocacy is balanced by increased accountability, better opportunity for cost control, and greater efficiency through avoidance of duplication in services in the affected departments.

Power concentrated in a CIO might threaten other campus groups, including competitors vying for budget priority, customers fearing loss of leverage with a newly expanded and diversified support organization, and those faculty, students, trustees, and other administrators who question the expansion of administrative structure.[4] The consolidation of several service organizations into a single more powerful organization carries an inherent risk of losing sensitivity to the needs of small constituent groups. Centralization of administrative control and responsibility in a time of decentralization and diversification in computing and information services can be a delicate proposition. The creation of a new position in the upper reaches of campus administration may be proportionally more difficult at smaller schools.

Whether a CIO is appropriate for any particular college depends on several criteria. The willingness of the president to include this interest in the highest circle of administrative representation is obviously critical. The commitment of the institution to sustain a stronger role for information technology on campus seems no less important. The campus community's acceptance of centrally coordinated planning is important, as is their acceptance of standards for equipment, software, and networks. An institution's readiness to work across traditional lines of organization is another indication

---

4. For a good discussion of problems posed by the growth of administrative services, see "The lattice and the ratchet," in *Policy Perspectives,* June 1990, vol. 2, No. 4, a publication of the Pew Higher Education Research Program, sponsored by the Pew Charitable Trusts.

that favors creating a CIO position. A final test may be in public relations. How will this concentration of interest coexist with that of the library,[5] and will the faculty, student, and staff constituencies see it as a benefit or merely an administrative convenience?

In the context of campus administrative style, reporting options take on different qualities. Where responsibility is strictly delegated and observed, the lines of reporting take on added importance. When access to other administrative officers is constrained, political difficulties tend to arise resulting from sensitivity to turf issues. However, such a system allows a greater degree of managerial autonomy.

When there is more consultation among top administrators, the lines of reporting are probably less critical. The reporting relationship tends to be embedded in the interaction of the members of the top administrative group in an environment where major decisions come from collective deliberations. When relations are harmonious and policy directions are known, the consultative style helps to build consensus and support. When disputes or unclarity prevail, this style can be slow and cumbersome.

Decentralization brings other issues into play. A college with semi-autonomous programs or schools (such as a music conservatory or an engineering division) brings to the matter of computing responsibility the whole complex of tensions between central academic and administrative authority and local rule. The computing director, regardless of reporting option, must participate in the context of cooperation and contention that accompanies decentralization. Although not normally in the director's job description, the ability to navigate those currents is essential in order to work with decentralized constituents. By and large, liberal arts colleges face far less of this type of negotiation than universities. At some colleges, however,

---

5. Stanford University has revived conjecture about the relationship of library and academic technical support organizations through the creation (in September of 1990) of a vice-presidency for libraries and information resources. This type of reorganization is beginning to appear at more and more colleges and universities which view it as a means to improve coordination, planning, staffing, and budgeting among all information services. It is also seen as a way to reduce or ameliorate competition for resources between the library and the academic computing facility. Franklin and Marshall, Hampshire, and other liberal arts colleges have recently followed Stanford's lead.

individual departments (or curricular divisions) have been known to exert an exceptionally heavy influence on computing decisions that affect the entire institution.

Access to other reporting forums can do much to relieve the shortcomings of any single reporting assignment. The opportunity to participate in a meeting at which other administrative heads share news and concerns can help a computing director stay attuned to the tenor of the institution. While most of the discussion in such a group is not directly germane to computing, it gives all present a better sense of the state of the community.

Occasions to present reports and plans to the board of trustees can also be valuable, particularly if the board likes to hear first-hand accounts from operating officers of the college. At some schools such access is rare and tightly controlled by top campus administrators. At others it is part of the normal flow of information. Any attempt to appeal over the head of the reporting official would naturally not be well regarded. But it can be a valuable opportunity to present plans with very technical components and to answer the questions of trustees who may be either very knowledgeable about computers or very fearful of them.

Faculty committees are another helpful supplement to the computing director's contact with decision makers and influence wielders. Meetings of department chairs, project supervision committees, and the general run of faculty self-governance activities are places where computing interests can join the range of concerns addressed by faculty. The astute director will know not to launch plans for a major capital project in a year in which faculty are preoccupied with some other expensive issue, like salary catch-up. Priority setting is a collective exercise and computing administrators need to participate in the process if they are to cultivate the support they need.

At Bryn Mawr, the director of computing services reports to the provost. But because the administrative style is very consultative, a close working relationship with the treasurer and easy access to various deans are comfortably available. The director participates in the treasurer's reporting group, the Group for Academic Administration and Planning, the Administrative Planning Group, and the Administrative Heads meetings. The frequency and degree of involvement of the director of computing services in each of these forums is different, ranging from weekly to semiannually. The amount of time devoted to them is not prohibitively large; the benefits in information are substantial.

Advisory Groups

Most colleges have *steering committees* that advise the director on policy and sit in a watchdog role as well. When academic and administrative computing are separate there are typically two committees, one from the faculty and the other consisting of heads of major computer-using offices. When there is one computing organization there might still be two committees or a single committee with mixed representation. In the latter case, the committee may have problems setting an agenda of interest to all. Topics may be too general or abstract, or alternatively too narrow in focus to engage all members. The prime usefulness of the steering committee is to help the director plan in accordance with the needs of the stakeholders and to warn when service is departing from expectations.

Another common type of committee is the *operational coordination group*. Perhaps more common where administrative computing involves closely scheduled batch and print processing and shared databases raise issues like data de-duplication, these committees can be valuable for securing interoffice cooperation among the clients. In their absence, the computing center becomes the unilateral arbiter and goad for these activities and earns no friends in the process. Often of a more ad hoc nature on the academic side, where faculty generally prefer to leave management to managers—only speaking up when they are displeased—advisory groups are charged to assist in the allocation of microcomputers to faculty or to prioritize network installations.

A necessary but unfortunate committee type is the *crisis task force*. One of these might be formed if the normal management and advisement mechanisms break down or if a policy decision overwhelms the standing advisory system. Worse still, if the constituents' confidence in the director sags badly such a group might be formed. In the case of a disaster, such as a flood or a fire, a crisis group would also be in order.

A kindred ad hoc group of the extraordinary type is the *request for proposal* or *RFP group,* assembled to advise in the selection of major equipment or software. This kind of committee is often poorly understood and managed. Few on campus have regular contact with the commercial world and many are ill prepared to sift through the kinds and amounts of information that vendors supply. The temptation to skip over the important step of setting criteria for selection in order to wade into the proposals overcomes many RFP groups. The declining novelty of computerization, the increased ability of computing staff to make professional procurement decisions, and the growing emphasis among users on functionality rather than underlying "bits and bytes," have diminished the need for RFP groups. RFP groups that do form now are motivated less by politics than by pragmatics.

Faculty and administrators bring quite different organizational values to committees. Faculty tend to insist on democracy and self-governance. Junior faculty are often accorded equal participation on committees with senior colleagues. Particularly where a major and infrequent kind of decision is before them, faculty may be as attentive to the legitimacy of their decision-making process as they are to the outcome of their deliberations. By contrast, administrators are often more conscious of organizational hierarchy, of organizational turf infringement issues, and of the reporting lines attached to each member of the group.

Administrative representation presents its own complexities. Steering committees require the participation of office heads or other staff members of sufficient authority to represent the views of their office and to deliver compliance with the policies that are decided. Too often the head of a computer-dependent office is insufficiently interested or knowledgeable to be the representative. On the other hand, if a low-level staffer, whose enthusiasm about computing exceeds his or her credibility in the office, is appointed, that representation might be useless. Operational committees typically have at least one high-level administrator who handles all computing assignments for an office, through failure to delegate appropriately and to understand the difference between steering and operating.

The success or failure of an advisory committee can turn on any of several causes.

• Nature of the charge

- Leadership

- Committee composition

- Resources

- Campus climate towards the committee

The essential, but often neglected starting point for success is a well-framed and well-understood charge. It is entirely possible for a committee to waste a whole year of meetings because the purpose is unclear. The chair of the committee is best situated to insure that all members understand the charge, and to provide clarification when they do not. Moreover, the charge must be sensible within the context of other institutional goals and the institution's governance structure. In the case of technology initiatives, a charge that is vaguely formulated, that conflicts or competes with other curricular, fiscal, or strategic goals, or that ignores organizational or political realities, may render the committee ineffectual before it even begins its work.

As with any college committee, leadership is a crucial factor in determining whether the work of a technology advisory committee will be useful or not. Unlike other college committees, technical advisory committees require leadership by someone who has as much technical familiarity as possible and who is broadly respected by the various constituencies represented on the committee. In small liberal arts colleges, it is often quite difficult to find individuals who meet these qualifications. As a result, technological advisory committees sometimes take on the character of special interest groups composed of individuals who simply lobby for their personal or departmental computing needs, rather than for the general needs of the college.

It follows that the right committee participants need to be selected. Too often on small campuses the same players are reconvened for advisory committees. Other interested but less experienced persons are deprived of the opportunity to learn and, in turn, to become good contributors. Still others do not get the chance to develop an interest when the usual champions are always appointed to the committees. In fairness, it is also not good practice to select only those who meet the computing director's approval or who will defer, through inexperience, to that person's judgment.

It is also important that the issues in question be solvable by average mortals. Obvious as it might seem, committees can fail—or at least give poor advice—if the issues just defy solution. Technical uncertainty, shortage of money, incompetent computing staff, or lack of campus consensus on computing goals and plans can singly or in combination doom to failure a committee and any decision makers who depend on it.

To be sure, the computing director can and should take steps to help an advisory committee be successful. Assistance in identifying the right issues for the agenda will generally be welcomed by the committee chair. Because the membership of faculty advisory committees changes considerably from year to year, the director might furnish the best thread of continuity. Realistic expectations about the amount of work, particularly writing, that a committee will actually accomplish would be wise also. Most members are willing to contribute to an outline or a list of topics and to read drafts written by someone else, but few will agree to write substantial parts of a planning document, and of those still fewer will be able to complete that work on a reasonable schedule. But the director who tries to dominate the committee can in fact provoke a backlash.

Regardless of the form of organization in computing services at any institution, appropriate and effective advisory committees appear to be important to good management. The successful committee provides good representation of its constituents' needs and views. And it carries back to colleagues an assessment of whether the services are being well managed. Committees can fail if their purpose is unclear, if they have the wrong members, if they are not given adequate information, if they are not valued by the director, or it they have the bad luck to be convened in a year when the issues defy solution or will take longer to sort out properly.

Budget and Organization

Financial considerations, not surprisingly, weigh heavily in decisions on appropriate organization. While it is not clear that separate, combined, or any other grouping of academic and administrative computing support is clearly advantageous from a budgetary perspective, there are aspects of fiscal practice that affect the suitability of each of these options.

A college with a unified computing organization, with one director, is potentially able to spend a larger percentage of available salary funding on technical positions than one with two or more departments, each with its own managing administrator. But the proposition might not be true if each of those head positions is filled by a person combining good administrative and technical skills—not at all a common conjunction. Consequently, a decision of whether to change from combined to separated centers, or vice versa, might be appropriately influenced by how the institution views its need for managers versus technical workers. A campus that finds its computing services in disarray due to inability to hire and retain good managers might opt to recruit or promote one manager under whose authority it could combine formerly separate departments. Elimination of one or more head positions would save funds or free them for reallocation.

Where computing hardware and operating systems can be managed by one organization rather than two or more, there is clearly an opportunity for consolidation of staffing. As campuses build full-service networks, they acquire increased staffing needs and therefore face an incentive to develop a single network (or set of network standards), even where academic and administrative computing still use different computer systems. In any event, signs are clear that data network support is the primary contributor to pressure for more staff in computing operations. Allowing that growth to occur in more than one department is probably beyond the financial capability of most liberal arts colleges.

The costs of management and operations are relatively accessible in the budgets of the departments in question. When conditions permit, consolidation promises to be more economical than maintenance of parallel services in two or more departments. But there are also computing-related costs in staffing, equipment, and supplies hidden or scattered in many budgets on campus. The organizational issue raised by this sector of expenditures is whether greater centralization and control would be beneficial. From a strictly financial view the answer would appear to be *yes*. But the trend to decentralization in computing is strong and has complex ramifications. It is unclear, for example, whether moving more of the responsibility for computing support into departments formerly dependent on the central organizations actually saves staffing or even reduces the pressure for new central staffing. The cost of time spent by those acquiring the new local responsibility for support is not usually captured by budget and control measures.

Yet as central organizations press their administrations for additional staff positions they are likely to encounter opposition suggesting that the support be absorbed instead by the client offices. In one sense, this approach merely disperses and conceals the cost of that work. In another, it could enforce the discipline of prioritization on the clients who press for more service: If they need to divert staff to new computing activities then they must weigh those wishes against all of their needs. But they only face that choice when the resource is allocated locally. The budgetary dimension of decentralization is not yet well understood, though the computing press reports a strong trend in this direction among large commercial organizations. The implications for smaller organizations are even less clear.

The experience at Bryn Mawr has been quite mixed, though college policy is moving towards decentralization in equipment allocation and applications development. Some departments, both academic and administrative, have resisted pressure to assume more responsibility for computing in their domain, fully aware that it would require reallocation of resources internally. Others find reliance on central services less satisfactory than handling local needs themselves. The net result is a certain degree of confusion as to where the delineation of responsibility falls, and how quickly or slowly it should move toward the client departments.

Measures of need and value are not identical in the academic and administrative computing spheres. One unpleasant illustration of the problems posed by this difference is that administrative clerks often have less difficulty securing computing equipment than do faculty. The case for word processing as an aid to productivity seems easier to make for secretaries than for faculty. Admissions and fund-raising offices have "bottom-line" rationales to support their budget cases. Unless the college has adopted a policy of universal entitlement—a microcomputer on every desk—faculty find themselves competing for available equipment allocations or being asked to pursue grant opportunities for it. The exigencies of running a business are difficult to square with the criteria that prevail in the evaluation of academic program needs, even where an institution's total budgetary scope indicates adequate support for academic programs.

It is not at all clear that a single channel for equipment and service requests, with a single set of criteria, can be established, even where there is one central computing organization. Budget awards for college departments depend on lines of reporting and the fortunes of administrative heads in the contention for institutional funds.

Budgetary accountability comes into play as an organizational issue on the question of whether combined or separate computing centers are better. In the latter case, the accountability is clearer, though the facts for each might not be known by both client groups. Where there are separate centers, it is not common that administrative offices know the budget of the academic center and vice versa. Where there is a single or combined center, questions commonly arise as to whether the departmental budget is equitably shared by both client groups. It can be difficult even to account for how much of the microcomputer support staff time went to administrative offices, as opposed to academic users. Few college-scale computing centers keep detailed time records on the partition of their services. As mentioned earlier, charge-back policies for service, though quite common at universities, are rare at colleges. While they are not feasible for a number of financial and "cultural" reasons, their absence leaves open questions about how central funds are really allocated.

The analysis of cost and benefit within small educational institutions is still largely uncharted terrain. Computing raises special problems of analysis because the service rendered crosses the departmental lines that shape the understanding of responsibility and budget. Still, a better grasp of the economy of computing, even where the scale is small, is required in order to evaluate organizational choices in computing support services.

Computing and Other Campus and Inter-Campus Organizations

As computing spreads through academic life it connects with a variety of other organizations. Increasingly, consideration of the best approach to managing computing service will need to include relations with kindred support departments and with new client groups.

Other electronic technologies are converging with computing. Audiovisual services deal with video display monitors, signal distribution networks and switches, switching devices, optical media, and computer-based control systems. Telephone technology grows closer to digital data as PBXs become more sophisticated. FAX technology spans computers, copiers, and telephones. Satellite broadcast and reception systems also combine equipment and disciplines shared by computing. The managerial knowledge needed to evaluate, acquire, and operate these devices is essentially the same. Most colleges have learned to watch the pace of development in high technology fields and to decide when performance, cost, reliability, and ease of operation come into line with their criteria. The technical staff required to operate them are able and willing to cross-train, which brings opportunities for better depth of support coverage.

The physical plant department finds itself drawn into higher technology as well. Their heating and ventilation equipment is increasingly computer controlled. Buildings are being retrofitted with remote-monitored sensors for temperature, smoke and fire, water flow, and intruder alarms. Support of this equipment has required their personnel to learn many skills used in the computing departments. Staff positions for "low-voltage electricians" are now common. Workers who once installed electrical wiring now also do sensor and alarm systems, telephone cabling, and data wiring. One of the keys to bringing down the very high costs of campus data wiring is to explore the extent to which physical plant workers can be employed to install data lines. Short of their direct involvement, contractors retained by the physical plant are likely to have moved into data network installation and are often the very firms to which computer vendors subcontract their campus wiring work. The mutual benefits of closer relations between computing services and the physical plant department are becoming increasingly obvious.

As libraries automate their catalogue, circulation, and acquisitions systems they become major consumers of computing technology. Access to these on-line services may rival the advent of word processing a decade ago as a promoter of computer usage. Many of those who discovered word processing and were sure they had exhaustively exploited the usefulness of computing are now finding telecommunications and database searching indispensable tools in teaching, research, and departmental administrative activities. The technical services departments of libraries are well-suited to add computer operations to their list of skills and will find natural allies in the computing departments once initial misgivings about turf invasion subside.[6]

Departmental computing facilities, some of which were formed in reaction to frustration with the inadequacy of central services, have now grown in size and complexity so as to need expert help. The proliferation of networks has also done much to lead break-away computing facilities back into communication not just with the computing center but with peer sites on campus and at other institutions. The central computing service might re-establish good relations with these units by offering consulting help and by not threatening local independence.

Inter-campus consortia are emerging as good resources for colleges. Several multi-college library automation projects are now well established. High-speed telecommunications makes sharing a single host computer technically feasible, and the advantage of access to the combined holdings of cooperating libraries is a substantial aid to scholars. The same data communications links used by the library service can connect general academic and administrative computing functions among campuses, forming an aggregate of resources no single campus could otherwise obtain.

As student governments and newspapers make use of computer-based communications and printing they help to bring computing firmly into the mainstream of campus life. Through the national data networks, these organizations are communicating to an extent never practiced before. BITNET and Internet connections are becoming

---

6. See chapter 12 for further discussion of computing and library automation.

significant channels for informal instruction and mutual assistance. At the same time, new variations on ethical dilemmas are presented to honor boards, student conduct committees, and deans. Many of these find the problems sometimes encountered on electronic bulletin boards and in virus epidemics quite unsettling. They turn to their computing centers for help in understanding the technology, the ethical issues, and the range of possible responses.

To pay for the growth in services, computing departments need to work with the faculty and institutional grants offices and to be included in the priorities submitted for capital campaigns. As colleges reach the end of the life span of the first major investments in computing, they have begun to realize that the costs are ongoing and that they must be included in long-range planning. While many computers were acquired from grants or through special capital projects, their replacement is very unlikely to attract the same extraordinary funding. Planning the timely retirement of aging and obsolete equipment and sustaining the growth necessary to keep up with the deepening importance of computers in nearly all academic disciplines are among the biggest challenges facing schools of all sizes and budgets.

Another group essential to the health of computing services is the board of trustees. The high costs of scientific equipment and college computing services compete for their attention with the costs of salaries, buildings and grounds maintenance, and insurance premiums. Board members generally no longer need to be convinced that computing is important, but many ask how much is necessary and by what means can it be had for less. They, along with top campus administrators, will require long-range plans that make the case for the kinds of technology and the levels of expenditure appropriate for their institution. Plans that propose purchases of equipment without a full discussion of what is accomplished by such purchases, at what continuing cost, and to what larger aim will not pass scrutiny. Computing directors, advisory committees, and administrators need to develop regular processes of planning and assessment.

As computers have spread from the computer center through the campus, the number and sensitivity of contacts with other organizations has grown. The work of shaping good support services is also more complicated than before. Directors must be effective leaders, well in touch with the whole range of activities on campus. Those who remain interested in liaison only with their traditionally important clients are finding themselves alienated and increasingly ineffective. The integration of computing organizations into wider campus forums for liaison and planning is a critical need that goes beyond the narrow question of how to organize the service.

Conclusion

Finding the right administrative structure for computing services is a matter for each campus to decide according to the many criteria that apply. In the past, stages of technological development spawned models that were widely adopted: large, timesharing systems created the computer center; minicomputers made subdivision possible and started the movement toward decentralization that was eventually accelerated by the microcomputer and the attendant revolt against the central monolith. The choice is no longer between two models, but among many considerations, beginning with values and practices particular to the campus.

Some principles for evaluating choices in administrative organization in computing can be derived from the history of computing on smaller campuses. The main question stated in its most basic form is, *Should my institution have a centralized form of computing administration, or would it be better served by a departmental or other decentralized model?* The first form favors centrally sponsored initiatives, the second local autonomy and the pre-eminence of the end-user's perspective. All too often colleges have been operating under a pendulum effect, where a crisis under one form leads to reorganization under the other. A centralized department that grows complacent or loses touch with its clientele becomes ripe for overthrow in favor of separate computing centers with closer focus on their customers' concerns. Alternatively, when the efforts of two or more computing support centers appear wastefully uncoordinated, fusion appears to be a solution.

The best proposition is to start with a good assessment of the facts pertinent to the college in question. While recent administrative history will exert some influence on thinking about change, an examination of the college's view of technology in the context of all that happens on campus is probably the best starting place for a sound decision on the proper form of administration. A consensus that electronic information technologies represent an expensive diversion from the main activities of the college tends to tip the balance toward decentralization, under which separate computing support units, close support of client applications, and no "computing czar" pressing for technological advancement per se characterize the administrative organization. Alternatively, if there is agreement that the institution wants to increase emphasis on electronic technology and give it a higher priority and more visibility, then the benefits of stronger advocacy give the centralized approach more weight. Separate units become consolidated and more emphasis is put on merging technologies and support for them.

These predispositions are most strongly influenced by the degree of technical sophistication in the campus community. Where word processing and data entry are the norms for computing proficiency, the larger realm of technology must appear distant and threatening. By the same token, an awareness of the potential in shared electronic information will lead to impatience with the isolation imposed by unconnected computing systems, no matter how well each appears to serve within its limited domain.

Colleges of roughly comparable size and degree of organizational complexity make different choices. A 1990 survey of liberal arts colleges found that the ratio of schools with combined computing centers to those with separate academic and administrative computing centers was approximately two to one (Henry, 1990). The same survey shows that schools with combined centers tend to have slightly fewer staff FTEs in computing, though the difference is fairly small, as indicated in the following table.

Organization Type	Academic	Administrative	Total Computing Staff
Combined center	6.25	7.77	14.02
Separate centers	7.38	7.92	15.30

What this binary classification conceals is interesting diversity in organization. Bryn Mawr's consolidation of management over separate departments has elements of separate and combined centers management. Kenyon College has a vice-president for information and computing services (a CIO position) over directors for academic, administrative, and networks/systems/technical services—with the third of these having as many staff as the first two combined. Reed College divides computing services along traditional academic/administrative lines for some operations, but combines hardware, networking, and user services into unified departments that serve the entire college. Hamilton College makes no distinction between academic and administrative computing in the titles of its support staff. They are classed by the type of function they meet: applications development, systems, or user services. The lessons in these cases are not that the organizational chart can be drawn differently, but that organizations can and should be re-arranged to serve the purposes of the college.

There is a temptation at small institutions to question whether structure or personalities ultimately have the greatest impact. The quandary is misdirected: It is essential that the choice of administrative structure be based on a good understanding of the interaction of computing with the interests of all. Too often, choices made earlier in the career of computing continue past the expiration of whatever validity they had.

If the lesson of the past two decades in computing has been that the pace of change can accelerate faster than can be absorbed by the tradition-bound academy, the implication for the future appears to be that decisions taken now on organization should be open to change. A willingness to reassess (and even rescind) past choices is probably as important as the merits of any given solution. Bryn Mawr's single management of separate departments, the tripartite combinations of academic, operational, and administrative computing, and the diversified single shop all provide more flexibility than the older pair of alternatives.

References

Henry, Carl. 1990. Status report on computing at CLAC schools: 1989–90. Consortium of Liberal Arts Colleges.

Ryland, Jane. 1989. Organizing and managing information technology in higher education: A historical perspective. In *Organizing and managing information resources on campus*, ed. Brian L. Hawkins. Reading, Mass.: Addison-Wesley.

Smallen, David L. 1989. Computing on campus: A small college perspective. In *Organizing and managing information resources on campus,* ed. Brian L. Hawkins. Reading, Mass.: Addison-Wesley.

Chapter 5

Staffing the Liberal Arts Computing Organization

Paul Dobosh
Mount Holyoke College

Paul A. Dobosh is director of computing and information systems at Mount Holyoke College. He received his Ph.D. in theoretical chemistry from Carnegie-Mellon University in 1969 and came to Mount Holyoke to teach chemistry in 1971. His background in computational chemistry led him to teach computer science courses and to become actively involved with the academic computing program. He was instrumental in establishing many of the college's computing facilities over the years, including its connections to the University of Massachusetts Cyber computer, the first microcomputer labs, the first VAX, and the creation of the campus-wide academic network.

In 1986, the academic computing program was formally divided into a computer science program and an academic computing organization. Dr. Dobosh assumed the newly created position of director of academic computing. Two years later, as Mount Holyoke began upgrading its administrative software systems and installing a campus-wide network, he was appointed to the position he currently holds, director of the newly organized Computing and Information Systems, combining administrative computing, academic computing, and networking. As professor of chemistry and computer science, Dr. Dobosh still teaches computer science courses on a regular basis. He is currently on the Board of Trustees of NERComp as well as a member of the American Chemical Society and the Association for Computing Machinery.

From 1960 to 1980, college computing developed along a relatively straight path based on timesharing systems of varying complexity. If it had continued on that path, staffing issues today would be limited to questions of how many programmers, systems analysts, operators, and consultants were needed and could be afforded. Most of the staff would be graduates of computer training programs or computer science programs and the barriers between the "priesthood" and the clients would be as firm as the glass walls of the computer room. The microcomputer and networking revolutions of the eighties threw that simple model out the window. We went through the last decade learning how to address a vastly increased breadth of computing needs, dealing with computers not under the direct control of the computer center, supporting clients whose familiarity with a particular machine might be better than our own, and hiring staff who have never seen a mainframe computer and might have no knowledge of programming at all.

The last decade saw incredible changes and growth in the demand for services from computer centers and an influx of staff with a variety of backgrounds. The coming decade may not see any lessening in the pace of technological developments but, in many ways, the growth in computing services and resources at liberal arts colleges may be leveling off. A large portion of administrative offices now have all the microcomputers and central services they need, computing staff levels will probably remain fairly constant for the next few years, and computing in general may be superseded by more pressing institutional concerns. Despite this, however, a large number of computer center staffing issues are lined up and waiting for action.

In the early days, colleges had computer *centers* and the emphasis was on daily management; now, we have computing *organizations* and the emphasis, more and more, is on making the organization a vital contributor to the academic mission of the college and its administrative efficiency. The machines are becoming almost incidental while the staff is gradually becoming the most crucial factor in computing activities. When we discuss issues of computer centers now, we are speaking more about the relationship of staff to their clients and to one another than about the relationship of the staff to the main computer. It is time we took a careful look at what we've built in the way of a computing organization. Do we have the people we really need to face the issues of the next decade? How do we find and retain excellent staff members? How can we fine tune the organization and its staff in order to provide a level of support that is consistent with the high standards of private liberal arts colleges?

Any one person's view of staffing a computing organization in a liberal arts college must by its nature be idiosyncratic. The size, composition, and organization of staff depend crucially on what the college sees as the role of computing in the institution, and each college has its own unique perspective. We all face very different problems relating to staff, from trying to eke out a few more full-time equivalents (FTEs) for an obviously undersized organization, to being forced to cut back on an obviously oversized one; from competing for trained individuals in a high technology community to searching for staff in a rural area; from doing nationwide searches for key individuals to retraining staff from other departments to staff the computer center. Although the wide diversity of liberal arts colleges makes any single model of staffing impossible, we can nevertheless discuss the factors that shape our different experiences. Conversations with colleagues reveal similarities as well as diversities in our positions.

In this chapter, I address a range of staffing questions that all liberal arts colleges face:

- How big should a computing organization be?

- Where do the staff come from and what does the technology demand in terms of staff background?

- How does organizational structure affect staffing?

- How do staff members grow (and go)?

- What kind of person should manage them?

While it may not be possible to define an ideal staffing model, this discussion should help identify key staffing issues of the next decade. I hope the discussion also sheds some light on ways of addressing these issues.

What Is the Optimal Size of a Computing Organization?

This question can't be seriously discussed unless we add a number of qualifications. The size of the computing organization depends critically on what the college sees as the role computing plays in the curricular and administrative functions of the institution. The ultimate goals of computing are set by the community, whether that involves faculty, administration, or both, and the key issue is how well the computing organization and its director can translate the goals set by the college into the specific service and support needs implied by those goals (and consequently into the appropriate level of staffing). This is not an easy translation, especially when one takes into account the fact that the players are continually changing and the goals of the institution may be changing as well. The agenda of a new president or chief academic officer can have a drastic impact on short-term institutional priorities and a dramatic effect on the size of the computing organization. On the other hand, while many presidents, deans, and other senior members of the college community may be uneasy about leaving the determination of required staffing levels entirely in the hands of the technical experts they may be forced to do so in order to avoid the pitfalls of micromanagement.

The history of computing at the college and its relationship to the history of the college itself also play a large part in determining the level of support expected of the computing organization. Those institutions with aging software systems often find themselves allocating an inordinate amount of staff to software maintenance. While conversion to newer systems may promise a reduction in staff size, it may require increased staffing in both the computing department and end-user departments during the conversion. Temporary staff can be very useful during a training or development push but many institutions seem curiously unwilling to make use of temporary staff, and the management of temporary staff creates problems of its own.

A third factor is whether the computing organization is intended to be primarily *reactive* or *proactive*. Few liberal arts college computing centers have been content to be primarily reactive service organizations, designed only to serve the customers' felt needs. Rather the computing department has evolved into an agent of change, responsible for helping the college move forward in its administrative and academic ventures. A proactive organization is more likely to bump into many of the service areas that now take advantage of computing, such as library, audio-visual, electronic publishing, and stenographic services. It is also likely to require a larger and more varied staff, one roughly proportionate to the pace of change the college wishes to maintain.

One needs, therefore, to distinguish between the minimum staff required to run any sort of computer operation and the critical mass necessary to have real forward progress in computing. Below a certain staffing level, the staff is running hard just to stay in place.

The culture of the institution also has an important impact on staffing. Some college computing operations exist in an atmosphere of great user independence, in which case such things as micro-computer support, data analysis, the establishment of computer labs, and the development of courseware may occur with little participation on the part of the central computer staff. In other colleges, computing may have been pressed on the faculty or on departments not quite ready for the computer age, or the community may be accustomed to an environment of total support. Users may demand help for the most trivial operations, easily overwhelming a staff whose size is based on a different set of specific projects and duties. And it is a difficult thing indeed to avoid a vicious circle of dependence in which well-intended helpfulness turns into user entitlement. The question of user independence becomes a key issue in staff size.

User independence, however, is a double-edged sword. Users who can handle almost all their own computing problems are a blessing; users who independently decide to move their departments off in new hardware and software directions, though laudably innovative, can create chaos for the institution and massive headaches for its computing organization. Even as basic a function as word processing begins to require more central support and coordination than it once did due to the increasing complexity of microcomputer operating systems and the growing need to electronically transfer and merge documents from different computing environments.

On the other hand, when users are dependent the massive training required to foster greater independence may be beyond the capabilities of a computing staff struggling to keep up with day-to-day demands. It often takes staff to save staff. That is to say, more computer staff may help to reduce staff in other offices by training them in computer methods designed to increase efficiency. Conversely, a decrease in computer center staff may result in the need for more staff members in other administrative departments and a higher overall cost to the college. It is important, therefore, when assessing the size of a computer organization, that you consider the potential increase or decrease in staff size in other departments that may result from computer center staff size changes.

In any discussion of staff size, we must recognize that no two colleges count exactly the same thing when they speak of their technology support staff. Are audio-visual services counted as part of computing staff size or not? Is there an electronics technician doing microcomputer repair and, if so, is that person part of the computer organization or of some other campus department? Are there programmers or user support staff spread out among administrative departments or are all the support staff concentrated in the central computing organization?

To assist us in understanding the relationship between the size of a computer organization and the services it performs, let us enumerate, in a general way, the range of technical support positions that can occur in liberal arts colleges. The list should include at least the following:

Director of computing
   Clerical and administrative assistants

Administrative computing director (or manager)
   Database administrator
   Database programmer/analysts
   Database report writers
   User support consultants (mainframe/mini/micro)
   System manager
   Computer operators
      Data entry clerks

Academic computing director (or manager)
   User support consultants (mainframe/mini/micro)
   Academic applications consultant
   Courseware developers/consultant
   Computer lab manager/programmer
      Student assistants

Technical services director (or manager)

Hardware (microcomputer) repair personnel
Network manager
Network technicians

Telecommunications manager

Telecommunications technicians

Audio-visual technicians

Library Automation Specialist

Library system manager

Each of these positions can involve people not normally considered part of the central computing organization. The list doesn't discriminate among academic, administrative, library, or departmental computing. Personnel in audio-visual services, telecommunications, and library automation, typically belong to departments other than the computer center, though recent head counts of technical support staff sometimes overlook this fact. One computing organization might assign half of a system manager position to management of the library computer while another organization might belong to a consortium and have a library (or other) computer system managed by staff at another campus. Some responsibilities may be *outsourced,* that is, handled on a contract basis with organizations outside the college. Telecommunications and hardware repairs are two areas in which outsourcing has been extensively used.

If we count only those positions in the list that clearly fall within computing (and networking), and if we modestly fill each category with only one person, the organization (not counting students) would still consist of at least 19 FTEs. This is considerably more than the 13.67 FTEs reported in 1990 as the mean computing staff size by the members of the Consortium of Liberal Arts Colleges (CLAC).[1]

---

1. Much of the statistical and anecdotal data used in this chapter are drawn from the 1989–1990 *CLAC Annual Survey of Computing* (Carl Henry, Consortium of Liberal Arts Colleges, 1990) and from conversations with the computing directors and other staff members of those institutions. A list of CLAC schools is provided in the Introduction.

In fact, less than 20 percent of the CLAC schools have computing organizations with 19 or more FTEs, and virtually all of those schools have more than 2,000 students to support.

The discrepancy between the number of FTEs suggested by our list and the actual size of liberal arts college computer organizations arises from several sources. For one thing, some personnel, such as microcomputer repair technicians, network staff, and courseware development specialists are not considered vital to the computing operation by many schools and those positions simply don't exist. At many schools, tasks such as data entry and various aspects of user support are left to the users' departments, hence there are no (or few) personnel in central computing to cover these jobs. In small schools or schools with single computer centers and very tight budgets there is one director who oversees all of academic computing, administrative computing, and networking, assuming that a network exists.

Looking at peer institutions is a common, though problematic, way of deciding on standards for staff size. The data from the CLAC survey provide some interesting numbers. For example, if we look for correlations between computing FTEs and measures such as number of students, faculty, staff, and budget, it appears that the best correlation we can find is a .75 correlation between total computing FTEs and total college operating budget. A simple straight-line fit between the two indicates that for each $2.5 million of budget, computing has 1 FTE. That means a staff of 20 for a $50 million budget. Inverting the calculation yields 0.4 FTE per million of budget, which breaks into about 0.17 academic computing FTE and 0.23 administrative computing FTE.[2]

Such numbers are interesting, but they may conceal more than they reveal. For example, while staff size seems to correlate well with overall institutional operating budget, it doesn't produce a high correlation with the size of the computing operating budget, the percent of the institutional operating budget devoted to computing, or the ratio between the portion of the computing budget devoted to staff salaries and the total computing budget. In other words, there

---

2. Mount Holyoke's staff of about 20 and budget of about $50 million puts it right at the mean; an enrollment of 1900 places it close to another commonly held watermark, which is 1 FTE per 100 students.

are institutions that may spend more on computing (in terms of actual dollars or percentage of operating budget) and have fewer staff members than a neighboring school that spends less.

Calculations of computing staff size that depend on a student-to-staff ratio—generally assumed to fall between 100 to one and 150 to one for liberal arts colleges—also tend to muddy the waters, since enrollment size does not always correlate well with faculty or staff size. Nor does it shed any light on who the computing staff members are. If there are a dozen FTEs in administrative computing and only three or four in academic computing, enrollment size may be virtually irrelevant to the issue of computer center staff size. Using peer schools as a basis for determining appropriate staffing size must be done with a careful eye to all of the relevant resource constraints and service requirements. Though liberal arts colleges have much in common, the disparities in enrollments, operating budgets, faculty and staff size, and computer service expectations, make it extremely difficult to determine meaningful targets for staffing levels for the entire set of schools that think of themselves as part of this community.

It would be interesting to develop a model of staffing, based on the provision of essential services, to create a common, transplantable organization that could be dropped into a college to support its basic computing needs. Unfortunately, such an exercise falls prey to the problems mentioned earlier. For example, if college administration is handled exclusively by manual or microcomputer operations, then systems management in the traditional sense of the term is simply irrelevant. The best we can offer here is a very rough outline of essential types of services, based on observations drawn from Mount Holyoke and approximately fifty other liberal arts colleges. Though this constitutes a sample of less than 10 percent of all liberal arts colleges, it can, nevertheless, provide a useful perspective from which to consider the issue of staff size.

Suppose we ask the question, Which staff members do you need regardless of how small you make your computer operation? This is another way of asking, What are the minimal essential computing services or functions found in liberal arts colleges? The answer to the first question follows logically from the answer to the second.

At a minimum, each college appears to support the following computing functions:

- System management and related technical support

- Database management and software support
  (programming)

- Training, consulting, documentation, and other user
  support

- Operations, clerical, and secretarial support

- Needs assessment, planning, purchasing, and
  administrative oversight

Even among the smallest liberal arts colleges, where there is
generally only one computing organization to handle the needs of the
entire college, these five basic functions are usually addressed.
Although the distinctions between the roles sometimes blur—and a
single individual may play more than one role—the five functions are
easy to distinguish and are frequently handled by five or more
different individuals.[3]

If we take these five functions as a set of essential "core" services,
then it seems that at a bare minimum we need a system manager, an
administrative programmer (or database administrator), a user
consultant, an operator (or secretary), and a director who may do a
little of everything besides being ultimately responsible for all
computing activities. Colleges with as few as 500 or as many as 1,000
undergraduates appear to require at least this many people (or FTEs)
to handle the essential operations. Institutions with fewer than five
FTEs in computing often operate in a state of continual crisis in which
innovation is virtually impossible and user support is a daily struggle
to avoid catastrophe. In rare instances, at very small institutions, a
smaller staff of truly exceptional individuals may be able to cover all
the tasks listed, but the loss of even a single staff member in that
environment often spells disaster for the entire computer center.

---

3. Fewer than 6 percent of the liberal arts colleges that participated in the
   1989–1990 survey of computing conducted by CLAC have computer centers with
   less than five full-time equivalent staff members.

Even if we view five FTEs as the smallest viable staff size for a liberal arts computing organization—remember, this is at best only a rough approximation—the actual minimum size for any particular college depends crucially upon a complex set of variables. Among these variables are the following:

1. The size and sophistication of the database operations. If departments handle their own records on microcomputers or workstations, fewer programmers will be needed.

2. The degree of automation of administrative and clerical operations. How many microcomputers and different software packages need to be supported? When the number is small, the support might be zero if only highly motivated users put microcomputers in their offices and can support themselves. As microcomputer deployment approaches saturation, the need for support may increase in a nonlinear fashion as those who are least computer literate are pressed into using them. (Attrition of workers not comfortable with computers may eventually lower the demand for support.)

3. The level of standardization on hardware and software. Less standardization requires more people to handle the diversity of support, maintenance, and repair activities.

4. The number of faculty who want to use computers in their courses in a substantial way and the number who want to be involved in the development of sophisticated courseware.

5. The number of students who have their own computers on campus.

6. The number of computers supplied for student use and the degree to which academic computing lab facilities are distributed around the campus.

7. The presence of a campus-wide network and the
   degree of complexity of campus networking.

8. The existence of a charge-back for computing services.
   It is common knowledge among computing support
   professionals that the demand for free services tends
   to grow indefinitely, therefore clients tend to become
   dissatisfied with services eventually. Unless there
   are some restrictions on user requests, the computing
   staff may never be large enough to meet the demands.

In addition to considering these eight factors, it is also useful to
distinguish between *goal-driven staffing* and *cost-driven staffing*.
Goal-driven staffing refers to staff positions that are required to
provide a service, such as system management. Cost-driven staffing,
on the other hand, refers to positions that are not essential, but that
provide a cost savings to the college, such as in-house microcomputer
repair. A case for staffing made on cost savings is the best kind,
especially if the cost savings produce additional benefits. A microcomputer repair shop, for example, might save the college enough on
maintenance contracts to pay for itself while at the same time
providing a faster and more reliable means of repairing college-owned
computers. In addition, revenues from the repair of student-owned
microcomputers might be used to support other computing operations.

Perhaps one of the biggest challenges for computing directors in
the future will be to justify administrative and user services staff on
a cost basis rather than a need basis. When departments across the
college are being scrutinized for possible nonreplacement of staff
(reduction by attrition), administrative computing may be able to
retain and possibly increase its staff by using careful systems analysis,
not just applications programming, to show departments how to take
full advantage of the computer power that has already been built on
the campus. (Directors should also be alert, however, to the reverse-
cost opportunity in which it might pay to farm out an entire operation
rather than pay internal staff and operating costs. Outsourced payroll
processing is a good example of this type of opportunity.)

Finally there is the question of whether separate versus combined
academic and administrative departments have an impact on the

total number of computing staff at the college. This is a difficult question to answer with any precision but it appears that the effect is minimal and may be mitigated in any event by historical accidents that force a combined organization to be physically separated.[4] If there is insufficient room to house the entire computing staff in one location, the fact that there is a single reporting structure may not eliminate the need to have duplicate positions in clerical support, operations, and possibly some technical areas as well.

In cases where two separate centers have merged in one location other problems can arise. For example, one of the frustrations sometimes felt by faculty occurs when they see a pool of programmers in the administrative shop who are unavailable for courseware projects because their programming skills don't transfer to academic projects or because the need for administrative program development is too high. Administrative programmers often are not trained to do the kinds of Pascal, C, or LISP programming needed by faculty members, though their skills may become more important in the future as administrative information becomes more of a faculty concern.

Administrative computer centers often have *operators* while academic centers have only *system managers*, so combining the organizations rarely eliminates an operator. On the other hand, microcomputer support for both academic and administrative computing can often be combined or at least placed in physical proximity to one another so that both sides of computing can share the staffing of a help desk. Even if both sides provide microcomputer support, a combined organization would probably require the same total number of FTEs since user consulting staff size is generally proportional to the number of software packages and the size of the client community.

This conclusion about combined organizations may change as we see the development of truly integrated organizations, where all of the systems, for example, are based on the same operating system and where the database demands of the library and other information

---

4. The 1989–1990 CLAC survey of computing, for example, indicated that the average size of combined computer centers was lower than that of separate computing centers by less than 1.3 FTE. In many cases, however, schools with combined computer centers actually had a *larger* staff size (per capita) than those with separate computer centers.

providers equal those of the administrative users. Whether one combined organization director can eliminate the need for separate managers or associate directors for administrative and academic computing or other areas is an issue I discuss later in the chapter.

Where Do Staff Members Come From?

All questions involving computing have the added wrinkle that the field of computing changes rapidly enough that last year's answers may not apply this year. It may be particularly true in terms of the kind of staff we need to hire. Staff in college computing organizations vary enormously in where they come from, where they want to go, and what their educational backgrounds are, both in and out of computing. The historical accidents of who happened to be where when a particular position came open seem to have had an unusually profound effect on computing organizations—probably because the field is so new, job descriptions are hard to pin down, and jacks-of-all-trades are not only accepted but necessary. We may now be approaching a somewhat more stable environment as job definitions are refined, more colleges standardize their hiring practices, and tighter budgets make it necessary to fill particular positions with individuals whose experience and/or training is specifically suited to the demands of the job.

A look at the range of backgrounds and sources of staff shows what impact past staffing factors have had on organizations and what implications they hold for the future. Several factors seem important:

- Computer training and programming ability

- National versus local outlook

- Business versus academic perspective

- Professional versus amateur status

Computer Training and Programming Ability. A very large number of staff members may actually have little or no specific computer training in any formal degree programs. In the more technical areas of administrative computing, some staff members may hold associate's degrees, certificates from vendor-sponsored training programs, or business degrees. In user services and many areas of academic computing, skills may be based solely on experience gained on the job. This is likely to be true of the director as well. The number of computing directors, especially directors of academic computing, who have moved over from faculty positions is surprisingly large at liberal arts colleges. In these positions, faculty perspective may matter as much as technical skills.

Many computing staff members, including directors, have now been in their positions for so long that their perspective and level of knowledge actually contribute to the definition of the profession—at least within the liberal arts college environment. In the past, the recruitment of staff members in computing has often been so difficult that any knowledge of computing, combined with the desire and ability to learn, were the critical qualifications. Very rarely did one see a job announcement for a position in either academic computing or administrative computing (with the exception of the director's position) that included a bachelor's (or other formal) degree as a requirement. As a result, the staff in computer centers were sometimes viewed as less "professional" than the staff in other administrative areas—such as the library—where degrees are required.

In recent years, there has been a growing emphasis on credentials and an increasing likelihood that staff members will come to the computer organization with an undergraduate degree in computer science or information systems. Computer science graduates are more common, with many of them coming from small colleges. They thus have an appreciation of the potential for computer use in this environment. They may decide that the flexibility and diversity of computing in the college environment are more attractive than the higher-paying but more confining environment of a high technology company. Sometimes these people are our own graduates who want to remain associated with the college or are graduates of other nearby institutions who simply want to remain in the neighborhood.

Staff members with graduate degrees in computer science are also starting to appear. These may be the same self-taught individuals mentioned earlier, who have decided that formal credentials and rounded-out knowledge have become prerequisites to advancement.

In addition to those with undergraduate and graduate degrees in computer science and information systems, there is also a growing population of support specialists—primarily in academic computing—with degrees in education or instructional technology. Such people may enter the college through the library, the audio-visual services department, or an academic department, as well as through the computer organization itself. Regardless of where they wind up, however, they often help to bring a broader and more sophisticated perspective to the whole area of academic computing.

While the number of potential staff members with formal credentials is increasing, the need for staff members who can program may actually be decreasing. There are two reasons for the decrease: first, there is a growing trend in liberal arts college computing organizations to add staff for such areas as user support, training, and documentation. It has become evident at many schools that the biggest obstacles to the efficient use of technology are the lack of proper training, consulting, and trouble-shooting, not a lack of technical resources. The second reason for the decrease is that colleges are using more canned programs and requiring less actual programming support. As programming languages, tools, authoring environments, and object libraries become more sophisticated, program development time may be drastically reduced, and the need for programmers may be somewhat reduced. Though we are still a very long way from dispensing with programmers altogether, the percentage of total staff time spent on programming—at least at small colleges—has changed somewhat in the last few years.

National versus Local Perspective. An interesting distinction that may be of increasing concern is where staff members view their employment market. The concern becomes acute when one has the opportunity to hire and has to decide whether a position merits local, regional, or national exposure. In the past, the majority of staff members were recruited locally, often within the college itself. Within the past few years, the search for directors, associate directors, and highly specialized staff members such as network managers has frequently been conducted on a national level. While national recruitment has brought with it the benefit of a larger candidate pool, it has also created problems such as delays in filling staff positions, complex screening procedures, and difficult salary comparisons. Despite these problems, the mobility of computing staff seems to be rising steadily and the employment market is becoming increasingly wide.

Business versus Academic Perspective. While staff members in academic computing frequently come from academic backgrounds, staff in administrative computing just as often come from the private sector. In hiring, the distinction between the two cultures is pointed out in cover letters and resumes, in which candidates from the private or government sectors reveal a profound ignorance of the difference between academic computing and administrative computing environments. Experience in corporate computing centers or small businesses, however, can be very useful. Individuals who are used to working with firm deadlines, cost-conscious limitations, stressful office conditions, outmoded equipment, and so on, are ideally trained to work in many small college computing organizations. For example, one of Mount Holyoke's very best microcomputer consultants came from a computer store where she was accustomed to doing everything under immense time and money pressure. She found our "hectic" collegiate atmosphere to be soothing by comparison. That different perspective can give an organization a boost and explode a few of the myths about its work style.

Those who have moved between the private sector and higher education know that many of the daily activities of a computing organization are the same in both worlds. Installing and managing a network, upgrading an operating system, performing system diagnostics, trouble-shooting software and hardware problems, developing software in response to user requests, and so on, all tend to be differentiated more by the technical environment in which they occur than by the prevailing organizational environment. Nevertheless, there are substantial cultural differences between academia and the business world which show up in the way people interact with one another, the terms they use, and the overall mission of the computing organization. Recruiting staff members from sources outside higher education should be done with some sensitivity to such cultural differences, especially if the position to be filled involves direct user support.

It is important to note, however, that even within higher education there are significant cultural differences. Computing professionals from large universities or community college systems may find the liberal arts computing environment less familiar than a corporate computing environment. Despite this, however, there has been considerable staff movement among different types of colleges and universities and this trend is likely to continue.

Professional versus Amateur Status. The question of whether we hire professionals or create them from eager amateurs is an interesting one. Computing organizations in colleges, and elsewhere for that matter, seem to have an inordinate number of people who have come from other fields and learned their jobs on the fly. Is there something about the nature of computing that makes it special in this regard? The answer is a firm yes—and no.

The *yes* part of the answer is reasoned as follows: First, the whole field of computing is still very young. Thirty years ago, almost everyone entering computing had to be an amateur, so administrative computing in the 1960s was populated chiefly by staff who had come to it from other fields. In the late sixties and early seventies, as separate academic computing enterprises were launched, the technology and style of academic computing differed so much from administrative computing that once again amateurs—primarily faculty members and students—were pulled in to build the organizations. Often those amateurs were skilled programmers, so the transition was relatively easy, but a major achievement nonetheless. Just as that group of professionals was beginning to stabilize, microcomputers appeared.

The microcomputer created another opportunity for many staff members outside of the computing center to become computer professionals without having made a commitment earlier in life to pursue a career in computing. With much of the early software and hardware used in academic computing, a typical user could not only become adept at using a particular package, but could really search out all of its workings to the point of being an expert. Often, in fact, the users had more time to explore the details of a particular software package than the professionals in the computer center. Some of these staff members gradually migrated to the computer center as they decided that user support was of greater interest than the work they had been doing originally. Today's liberal arts computing centers are heavily populated with former chemists, physicists, philosophers, and representatives of a host of other campus departments.

The era of computer organizations built by amateurs may have passed. For all the friendliness of graphical user interfaces, the newer operating systems and software packages are becoming increasingly complex, and users seem to require more assistance than ever before. Perhaps this is due to the vast array of available software options, or perhaps it is simply because we expect more people to do more complicated things with computers than ever before. In any case, we are back to needing a professional computer support staff.

Having said that, let me back up and give the *no* part of the answer. Computer organizations still have room for beginners and amateurs, but in the common way that all fields have room for such workers. Beginners can be brought into an existing professional structure and trained, as they are in other fields. The more appropriate their backgrounds the better, but, as in any department, we can't always hire individuals with three to five years' experience. Very talented individuals interested in computing can also take advantage of the fact that computing is still a fairly young field and in many instances it is acceptable, indeed, even admirable, to be self-taught. A background in a different field, particularly a liberal arts discipline, is still considered an asset for someone entering a liberal arts computing organization.

Ultimately, all of these varieties of experience, training, outlook, and so on, come down to two essential criteria for deciding if a candidate is going to be a useful staff member: How good is the individual at solving technical problems in computing and how well can that individual communicate with colleagues and clients. The problems that need solving can range from the standard headaches of designing and debugging a piece of software to dealing with a panic-stricken user on the phone. The job can involve learning how an entirely new computer works, or having to decide what technical or cognitive problem has a student stumped. The problems tend to be those in which the logic of the computer and the physical constraints of an electronic system provide the ground rules upon which any solution has to be based.

More and more, however, computer staff are forced to deal with human problems rather than computer problems. The microcomputer has demystified computing to the point that users will not tolerate mumbo jumbo from the high priests. Though there may still be individuals in remote corners of the computer center who spend most of their working hours communing with software or hardware, an increasing number of staff professionals are being selected for their ability to understand people as well as their ability to understand computers. Being personable, sensitive, and approachable are traits that carry as much weight as technical skills in the selection of many new staff members. Computing organizations are finally beginning to recognize that user support is as vital to the success of the enterprise as hardware or software support.

How Do We Recruit the Best Staff in a Tight Budget Environment?

Although personnel costs are discussed in chapter 3, there are a few observations worth making here. The first is that many colleges seem to have difficulty placing a value on technical expertise. Pay scales and job classification schemes are structured based on clerical help, professional administrative staff, and upper-level management. A first-rate computer consultant can be inappropriately assigned the same level as clerical help on the basis of supervisory and decision-making responsibilities. A careful case may be needed to determine the proper level for computer staff. Once such levels are internally defined, a director may still be faced with the problem of salary comparisons with other colleges or with non-academic computing organizations. At this point, coordination with the personnel office must be undertaken to define the real extent of the applicant pool and whether the salary levels for particular staff positions are "market impacted." Market impact can change dramatically with time. Several years ago, during the job boom in the Northeast, there were great opportunities for computer professionals throughout the region; today there are not. It is impossible to predict what the job situation will be like five years from now. Ignoring market data, however, frequently produces unrealistic salary ranges and may force an institution to conduct long and fruitless searches or hire staff members who are not really qualified for their jobs. Despite fluctuations in market pressures, it is still fairly common for colleges to experience "sticker shock" when they try to hire a computing professional, especially if the position has previously been held for a long time by someone who entered the field with a non-computing background and started at a relatively modest salary. Given the uncertainties of the market and the certainty that staff salary budgets will never be as large as we would like, how can we make the best use of our financial resources when it comes to staffing?

An approach taken by nearly all liberal arts colleges is to supplement professional staff positions with student labor. A student work force can be used in several ways. Almost all colleges employ students as consultants and monitors in public-access laboratories. At Amherst, students can be hired for individual tutoring by faculty, staff, or students in word processing and other computer skills. This lessens the need for a large professional training staff at the same time that it encourages offices to be less dependent on the computing organization for microcomputer support. At Bowdoin, students are the core of an ambitious program to bring the computer into three or four classes per semester—students become part of a software and instructional development team that contracts to develop computer-related materials for particular courses. At Smith, students work on database projects for a variety of administrative offices. At Reed, students are trained in microcomputer maintenance and repair. The roles that students can play in the computing activities of a college are as varied as the colleges themselves.

Despite the potential budget savings, however, there is a negative side to the use of student labor. During the academic year, students are usually limited in the number of hours they can work each week. At midterms, finals, and other busy times of the year, student workers have a tendency to evaporate, despite the fact that these may be the times when their services are needed the most. Just when students become really knowledgeable and proficient at their jobs they graduate, or they may decide to transfer or spend a year at another institution, taking all their experience and skills with them. Problems with continuity, consistency, reliability, and commitment are fairly standard when it comes to student labor. On the other hand, most of us have had very good experiences with student workers and would not want to do without them, even if we could. With careful selection, proper training, and sufficient guidance, a student labor force can serve as an extremely effective complement to the professional computing staff.

Some of the problems encountered with student workers can be addressed by hiring new or recent graduates of the school as interns. Since internships are defined as temporary positions lasting a year or two, they may be viewed as training opportunities as much as they are viewed as gainful employment. Consequently, the salaries paid to interns can be far lower than those paid to experienced professionals. Because they know the school well and have probably worked in the computing organization while they were students, interns tend to learn quickly, communicate well, pursue their jobs with great zeal, and generally make excellent workers. The potential drawback of interns is that they may have difficulty redefining their relationship to the faculty, and, like student workers, they tend to leave just as they have become masters of their trade.

A final choice that must be made in filling professional staff positions is whether it is more cost effective to hire *generalists* or *specialists*. In the past, colleges tended to hire generalists because they were often the only people available. Today, there is a growing number of professionals who specialize exclusively in such areas as database administration, courseware development, or user documentation. As a result of their focused credentials or experience, specialists tend to require less training than generalists, their performance is usually of very high quality, and their salary requirements are often a major burden on the budget. Are these the people we need in the liberal arts computing organization? Can we afford them?

In larger organizations, with perhaps twenty or more staff professionals, specialists may not only be cost effective, they may be essential. For example, at colleges with complex campus networks, such as Carleton, Franklin and Marshall, Kenyon, Wesleyan, Reed, and others, network specialists are needed to design, install, manage, and maintain all of the devices and software that make up the network. A generalist assigned to handle system administration on host systems, UNIX workstations, and other platforms, in addition to campus networking, would be likely to collapse under the workload. The cost justification for such specialists is simple: Without them we would not be able to maintain the network services that students, faculty, and staff have come to rely on. Specialists in other areas, such as database administration, may be equally crucial to the success of those operations.

Despite these examples, there are still good reasons to be partial to generalists. In small organizations it is important for everyone to know a little about everything in order to avoid major problems if a staff member leaves the college or is out of the office for an extended period of time. With a staff of less than ten, it is vital for people to share information, expertise, and creative ideas. Moreover, generalists are in a better position to adapt quickly to the rapid changes in hardware and software technology that we continue to experience. Specialists tend to be more conservative because their knowledge investment in a particular strategy or, in some cases, a particular product, is so much greater than a generalist's would be. As a result, specialists can inhibit change and lead a computing organization to cling to older technologies, even when the technologies are less desirable and less cost effective than newer technologies. In addition, high salaries for specialists do have a way of driving up personnel costs. Thus, while certain specialists may be necessary, a bias toward generalists is still a wise staffing practice, especially for smaller computing organizations.

How Does Organizational Structure Affect Staffing?

In a presentation on the reorganization of the Indiana University computing organization made at an EDUCOM conference a few years back, a comment was made that schools reorganize computing on the average of every 18 months, and, despite some laughter, no one seemed to take the comment as a joke. These are exciting times in computing when more and more of the success of our institutions may rest on how well our organizations work. It is no surprise that we need to think constantly about who our staff members are, what they know, and how they work together.

The preceding chapter discussed the ways small college computing services are organized and examined some of the consequences of various models for reporting and planning. Here, I'd like to consider some of the implications that different organizational structures have on the nature of staffing.

As mentioned earlier, there is little evidence to show that combining all computing services into one organization substantially reduces the number of FTEs in computing, though it does seem to result in modest savings. On the other hand, the unification of different service groups can have a dramatic impact on the positions that are encompassed by the organization, and possibly on the quality of support as well.

As suggested in chapter 4, there are essentially three models of computing organizations at liberal arts colleges, though variations on these models are abundant. The models, illustrated in Figure 1, are: (1) a single department for academic and administrative computing, (2) separate departments for each area, and (3) a multigroup organization in which campus-wide services such as networking are combined, while services specific to academic computing or administrative computing are handled by separate groups. (In the third model, all computing groups may report to a single administrator or there may be several reporting lines.)

Let us reconsider the list of core computing services defined earlier. It is apparent that certain tasks, such as needs assessment, planning, purchasing, and administrative oversight, are handled by the same person (or persons) in the first and third models but are ordinarily handled by different individuals in the second model. The advantage of the second model, quite naturally, is that each group feels that it is able to focus more effectively on its own agenda. Indeed, as pointed out in chapter 4, this is the primary reason that many colleges establish separate computing centers in the first place.

However, in terms of staffing, the separation of academic and administrative computing organizations usually requires some duplication in management positions. If total staff size remains roughly constant, it means that more staff are devoted to management and planning and fewer staff are available for technical or user support in the second model than in either of the other models. Given the small size of most separate computer centers at liberal arts

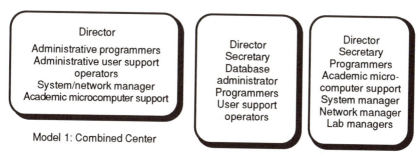

Model 1: Combined Center

Model 2: Separate Centers

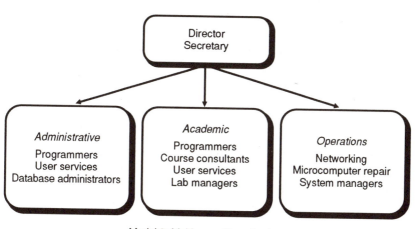

Model 3: Multigroup Organization

Figure 1: Three Models of Computing Organizations.

colleges—generally seven FTEs or less—it isn't clear that the duplication of management positions really helps the college at all. While
planning and needs assessment may indeed benefit from the diversity
of two perspectives, that may have more to do with the personalities
of the individual directors and the quirks of history than with the
organizational structures.

Comparable arguments can be made for several other types of
positions, such as secretarial and clerical support, microcomputer
hardware repair, system management, and network management. In
each of these cases, staff members may be performing similar or

identical tasks, regardless of their side of the house or their "clientele." Merging or pooling the people who fill these roles can help to reduce staff size or at least improve the quality of support and services if staff size is held constant.

In light of this, one might reasonably ask why any college should maintain separate computer centers or, for that matter, why there should be any organizational separation between computing support personnel. There are at least two answers to these questions, one technical and one cultural. The technical answer is relatively simple; although there are tasks that are indifferent to the distinction between academic computing and administrative computing, there are other tasks that clearly are not. For example, user support in administrative computing may involve training, consulting, or trouble-shooting for database operations in financial aid, gift processing, recruitment, business operations, and so forth. In order for a user services specialist to be of any value, he or she must be knowledgeable and proficient in these areas. A user-support specialist in academic computing, on the other hand, might be obliged to help faculty members develop course materials involving on-line data collection, data reduction, statistical analysis, and so on. The gulf between these two types of applications software is sufficiently wide that it is unusual to find individuals with comparable levels of expertise in both areas.

The same tends to be true of the people who provide application programming services. The terms and ideas of administrative computing differ markedly from those of academic computing. Some-one who is highly skilled at producing COBOL code for generating complicated financial reports may be entirely ignorant of the tech-niques for preparing a good simulation in population biology. And vice versa. Neither side of the house is necessarily more sophisticated than the other in terms of its user- or technical-support requirements; they are simply very different.

The second reason for splitting at least some aspects of the organi-zation is cultural. The students and faculty who make up the academic computing clientele are different in many respects from the staff members on the administrative side of the house. Differences in scheduling priorities, attitudes towards privacy and security, even dress codes, are cultural differences between the two sides of the house that can affect the nature of support personnel in computing. For example, in small, combined computing centers, it is often the case that staff members are hired primarily with administrative needs in mind. As a result, the center may have difficulty communicating with faculty and students, difficulty understanding their priorities, and be less able to support academic computing needs. Under these circumstances, faculty members frequently militate for the addition of support personnel who have academic backgrounds or for the creation of separate academic computing centers.

Schools that established separate computing centers during the seventies or eighties have often fared better in academic computing than those who stayed with small, combined centers. The price those schools paid, however, was more than the duplication of some staff positions and a larger personnel budget; they faced the problem of getting two specialized and autonomous groups to cooperate with one another on issues such as campus-wide networking, electronic-mail exchange, and long-range planning. In these arenas, the cultural differences between the two groups often produced serious headaches for everyone.

The compromise approach, illustrated by the third model, seeks to maximize the strengths of the other two models. While it integrates management, planning, clerical, and some technical areas (such as networking and microcomputer repair) it maintains a separation between certain client-specific services, such as programming and user support. In this type of organization, some of the technical and cultural distinctions of earlier organizational models are preserved, but there is also an opportunity for technical and cultural crossover. Establishing a multigroup organization (with a single chief administrator) by fusing together separate centers and then redrawing departmental lines is often very stressful on existing personnel. Small colleges that have taken this route during the past few years have typically encountered a significant restaffing problem. Nevertheless, it has generally been true that after the dust has settled, the resulting organization tends to be more productive, more cost effective, and more flexible. Multigroup organizations similar to the one depicted in model 3, make better use of technical expertise and are able to adapt more easily to changes in both technology and users' needs. As a general rule, the people who work—or work best—in this type of computing organization acquire a more global understanding of both the academic and the administrative uses of technology in the liberal arts college environment.

How Do Staff Members Grow (and Go)?

During the latter part of the eighties, one of the biggest staffing problems faced by college and university computer centers was the extremely high rate of staff turnover. It was not uncommon for programmers, system managers, and other technical staff members to leave an organization after less than six months. The weakening of the economy at the end of the eighties reduced the rate of turnover somewhat, but it continues to be a serious problem for many schools, especially for those with very small computing organizations.

Other administrative offices also have problems with staff turnover. Why should computing be any different from the admissions office or the development office? The simplest answer is that sophisticated technical skills transfer easily from one environment to another, thus allowing computing professionals to move relatively freely among academia, business, government, nonprofit agencies, and research organizations. This puts a great deal of pressure on the small college computing organization to provide an environment in which its computing staff will want to stay, at least for a reasonable period of time.

Some of the reasons computing staff members commonly give for leaving an institution include:

- Higher salary (benefits, perquisites)

- Higher status

- New challenge

- More supportive environment

- Burnout

- Geography

In any job change, a staff member tends to leave when there is a sufficiently high level of dissatisfaction with the current job coupled with a sufficiently high attraction to a new job. A good job offer by itself may not prompt a staff member to quit, if the current environment is extremely satisfying. Conversely, the absence of a good offer may not keep a staff member from quitting, if the current environment is sufficiently bad. Let's consider the items in the list in terms of what can and can't be done in the context of the small liberal arts computing organization.

Salaries

While salary issues arise in all administrative departments, they are particularly problematic for computing departments because of the contrast between academic and non-academic salaries. To what extent should a liberal arts computing organization attempt to be competitive with the private sector?

Though this is an extremely difficult question to answer, many computer center directors seem to feel that it is impractical and unwise to bow to market pressures outside of academia, unless there is no other alternative. If salary is the primary consideration in a staff member's decision to enter or remain in a small college, the college is bound to lose the contest to the private sector. Moreover, unless the computing organization maintains some internal equity among salaries, a concession to one or two staff members could easily provoke salary comparison problems among its own staff members and precipitate a budgetary crisis in the whole department.

On the other hand, some external comparisons may be impossible to avoid. Ignoring the realities of external market pressure altogether frequently leads to the loss of valuable staff members, fruitless searches, or the recruitment of unqualified individuals. If the local market for computing staff is extremely tight, the college may have no choice but to acknowledge external market pressure. In addition, with more and more computing professionals considering positions on a regional or even a national basis, it has become common for salaries to be compared across colleges. In computing, such comparisons often seem to carry more weight than comparisons between computing staff members and other administrative staff members within the institution.

The plain fact is that small liberal arts colleges cannot match the salary levels of the private sector nor, in many cases, even the levels found in universities. Trying to do so may cause as many problems as it solves. If salary comparisons are unavoidable, the salaries paid at small college computing organizations probably constitute the best reference framework, regardless of geographic differences in cost of living. If the local market cannot supply the needed staff members at the required salary levels, then a regional or national search may be advisable. The cost of the recruitment and relocation of the new staff member is likely to be considerably less than the cost of trying to match salary levels with those of local corporations.

Colleges facing ever-tightening budgets need to explore other ways of compensating staff members. Sometimes an extra week of vacation—time off for good behavior—can prove to be a low-cost, high-return method of keeping staff members happy. Special travel allocations (see discussion of Geography), off-site training opportunities, a better work environment, or even a new color monitor (or coffee machine!) can be used to offset some of the negative aspects of a lower-than-desired salary. In the past, colleges have devoted remarkably little attention to the issue of staff compensation, beyond basic salary comparisons. With budget dollars shrinking at many institutions, it behooves us to look for creative ways to make computing positions in small college settings as desirable as possible.

Status

Most small college computing organizations tend to be "flat" rather than hierarchical. As a result, there is frequently no way to promote a staff member to a position with higher status, causing some individuals to feel that they are languishing in dead-end jobs. In many cases, the only way to achieve a "promotion" is to quit and find a higher-status position at another institution.

A flat organization chart, however, doesn't mean that promotion is impossible, just that it must be tied to experience, training, and responsibilities, rather than to supervisory functions. For example, in lieu of having the single position of *user services consultant,* an organization can list positions of *consultant, senior consultant, lead consultant,* and *manager,* which can have degree and/or experience requirements, as well as different levels of independence built into the job description. An employee can be promoted from one level to another as a result of accumulated experience and increased responsibility, rather than a change in reporting structure.

Challenge

Closely related to the problem of status is the problem of boredom or lack of challenge. Many staff members, especially those who are the brightest and most creative, may become bored after they have mastered the technical details of their jobs. One way to address this problem is to periodically initiate projects that require staff members to learn new concepts or acquire new skills. Another way to deal with the problem is to have staff members swap some of their responsibilities with one another from time to time. A third way to address the problem is to insure that staff members have an opportunity to learn about and to help implement new technologies and new departmental practices. Professional growth can be achieved through training seminars, formal classes, conferences, colloquia, and a variety of other means. Though some of these may be expensive the cost should be viewed as an investment in the development of greater expertise within the computing organization and in increased staff satisfaction.

Supportive Environment

One of the complaints sometimes voiced by staff members who seek positions at other institutions—particularly staff involved in user services—is that they do not feel appreciated for their work. User services personnel often work long hours, deal with repetitive routines, and are confronted with insecure, frustrated, or angry clients. Phone calls at home in the middle of the night for help on a major project are not exactly what most user-support personnel view as a reasonable part of the job. Yet most of us recognize that computing organizations are sometimes treated like hospital emergency rooms, on call 24 hours a day.

Despite their dedication, support staff may become the targets of abuse by members of the college community. They are blamed for everything from the selection of the "wrong" word processor, to the sudden and untimely death of a disk drive. Stress from co-workers, end-users, and supervisors can contribute to a staff member's feeling of being unsupported or unappreciated.

It is important, therefore, to maintain an environment in which staff members can preserve their sanity, dignity, and self-respect. Directors, managers, and other supervisory personnel need to do more than just set agendas and insure that the work gets done on time. They need to be attentive to problems faced by computing personnel, and they need to help their staff members find solutions to those problems. Perhaps because of their technical concerns, computing organization directors and managers seem to be better at diagnosing and debugging software problems than they are at recognizing when a staff member is about to explode.

Burnout

It is well known that computing in the liberal arts college environment has expanded tremendously during the past few years. Less well known—or at least less acknowledged—is the fact that, in general, staff size has not kept pace with the increasing demand for services. As a result, many organizations are stretched to the limit and beyond, and staff members are often confronted with overload or burnout. At some campuses, staff burnout in the computer center is simply treated as an inescapable fact of life. The key to avoiding burnout lies in the magic word *no*. Computing organization directors (and their staffs) need to maintain a realistic attitude toward job scheduling, and they need to be able to communicate their limitations to users. Trying to satisfy the endless appetites of users may result in burnout, failure, or—when the demands are actually met—a signal to users that they should ask for even more.

Unfortunately, simply saying no to users can be dangerous as well as counterproductive. It is the responsibility of the director to help the faculty, staff, and student constituencies understand the limitations of the computing organization and prompt them to set priorities to control their expectations as well as their requests.

Geography

Many liberal arts colleges are fortunate to have beautiful campuses nestled in rural settings around the country. Unfortunately, this results in a certain amount of isolation. In order for staff members to learn and to grow, they need the opportunity to meet with counterparts from other institutions at conferences, seminars, and site visits to other campuses. Schools that are located in urban settings or that enjoy the company of other nearby schools may still suffer from isolation if staff members are not encouraged and enabled to interact with colleagues from other institutions.

The solution to the isolation problem is to provide the time, travel funds, and encouragement necessary to permit staff members to attend meetings and undertake site visits to other campuses. All too often, the line items for travel and training in the computing operating budget are small or nonexistent. Travel to conferences or visits to other colleges are viewed as unnecessary "icing on the cake," for all but the most senior staff members. Yet, in the long run, the learning and growth that results from staff interaction with colleagues at other institutions more than pays for the costs. Not only do staff members gain new and better perspectives on how to do their jobs, they also receive a morale boost, which can dramatically reduce the dangers of both burnout and boredom. Interactions with vendors can also be helpful and may incur no cost to the college. Mount Holyoke, for example, has collaborated with the other members of the Five Colleges (Smith, Hampshire, Amherst, and the University of Massachusetts) to host vendor-sponsored technical workshops. A related opportunity for training involves having staff deal directly with particular vendors. Such relationships can give staff members quick access to new announcements and access to sources of expertise that can help staff members stay at the cutting edge of hardware or software developments.

Training and travel costs should be viewed as investments in productivity and retention. When weighed against the costs in both time and money of workers whose productivity is steadily declining or, worse still, the costs of replacing staff who quit as a result of boredom or burnout, the costs of training and travel may begin to look like a bargain.

Does the Director Need to Walk on Water?

The past few years have seen an increasing number of advertisements for directors of computing at small liberal arts colleges, that
read something like this:[5]

> Applications are invited for Director of Computing at Babbling
> Brook College. Responsibilities include supervision of academic
> computing, administrative computing, and the computer net-
> work. The position reports to the Dean of the College. Desired
> qualifications include: a doctorate or other terminal degree in a
> liberal arts discipline, teaching experience in a liberal arts
> college, experience with the CHAOS™ administrative computing
> package for student and financial applications, experience with
> the GREED™ package for alumni/development, and knowledge
> of VAX/VMS, HP 3000/MPE, DOS, Macintosh, Novell Netware,
> COBOL, FORTRAN, Pascal, LISP, and UNIX. Prior experience
> in computer center management at a small college is desirable.

In all likelihood, advertisements of this sort are jointly drafted by
staff members in academic computing and administrative computing,
a faculty computing advisory committee, and possibly several administrators. Is the group looking for someone who will provide oversight,
leadership, and planning abilities? Or someone who will understand
faculty and student computing needs? Or someone who will be able
to provide training and consultation to administrative users? Or
someone who will stay up late at night writing and debugging programs for academic, administrative, and network applications? The
answer to all these questions is a simple yes. Do such persons exist?
Not very often.

Many liberal arts colleges feel that the director of computing, or at
least the person in charge of academic computing, needs to hold a
doctorate in a liberal arts discipline and to have at least some teaching
experience in a small liberal arts college. Are these qualifications
really necessary or even desirable in a computer center director? The

---

5. Linda Fleit makes a similar point using a similar "job listing" in her article, The
   Myth of the Computer Czar—Revisited, which appeared in Organizing and
   Managing Information Resources on Campus, ed. Brian Hawkins, 191,
   McKinney, Texas: Academic Computing Publications, Inc., 1989.

question is especially interesting, since so many current directors hold doctorates and have formerly held teaching positions. In fact, many directors are appointed with faculty status and are expected to do some teaching in addition to their administrative duties.

There is no denying that someone who has had teaching and research experience in a small college will be in a better position to understand faculty and student needs in computing. There is also no denying that someone with a terminal degree and teaching experience may command more respect from faculty members and be able to communicate more easily with members of the academic side of the house. These traits do not, however, insure that the individual is technically proficient or adept at managing an administrative department. In some respects, administrative skills run counter to the skills associated with good teaching and research. Moreover, it may well be the case that individuals with a faculty background are handicapped in their ability to appreciate the perspective of staff members and co-workers in administrative computing and other administrative departments. In short, it is safe to say that there are liabilities as well as benefits to selecting computing administrators with faculty backgrounds.

But this raises the next question: If these people *don't* come from faculty backgrounds, where *should* they come from? Unlike librarians, who can obtain master's or doctoral-level credentials in information science, there are (thus far) no real graduate degree programs for computing administration. Should we search for computing administrators with graduate or terminal degrees in computer science or information systems? Most likely the answer is *no*. Individuals with degrees in these disciplines tend to be trained for software development, theory building, research, teaching, systems analysis, or other areas of applied data processing. In general, they are neither trained nor particularly well qualified for departmental administration, especially in the context of a small liberal arts college computing organization.

We are left with very few choices. If we don't recruit former faculty members, we can either promote technical staff members to director positions, hire managers from outside academia, or rotate current faculty members into temporary director positions. Promoting technical staff members to director positions is a common practice but the people who are best at solving software problems often have difficulty when it comes to staff management, faculty needs assessment, or long-range planning. Their lack of academic credentials may also prove a hindrance in their relations with faculty members and senior administrators of the college.

Recruiting computing managers from nonacademic fields is also a common practice, but it too has potential problems. While information specialists with industrial or government experience frequently perform well in the administrative computing environment, they may be unaccustomed to the style of operations in academic computing, unfamiliar with the nature of applications software for teaching and research, and new to the concepts of campus and intercampus networking.

The practice of rotating directorships among faculty members has been used at Smith, Swarthmore, and many other liberal arts colleges. In view of the high-quality service organizations we are trying to develop, however, I am increasingly skeptical that the director of computing can be a rotating or part-time position for a faculty member. Conceivably, in a combined organization, the director of *academic* computing could be a rotated or part-time position. The required degree of interaction with the user community, the time necessary to watch developments in the rest of the computing world, the service orientation of the department, and, most important, the constant need to keep shaping and developing the staff to respond to the changing nature of the enterprise, make the director of computing position more like that of the head librarian and less like that of an academic dean. All of computing, including academic computing, is now more a service organization and less an academic enterprise than it once was. Service organizations respond more to the growth of skills, including management skills, of their members than from the infusion of new intellectual blood that is implied in rotating and part-time faculty leadership. Indeed, many schools (such as Smith) that traditionally maintained a rotating director of academic computing have since moved away from the practice.

Perhaps the most desirable solution is to establish graduate degree programs in computer-center management that could provide individuals with appropriate expertise and credentials. Like librarians, holders of such degrees would not be limited to colleges but could pursue computing positions in business or in secondary schools. Another possible solution might be an apprenticeship program, which could allow staff members to mix university courses with on-the-job experience in a computing organization. Unless and until such programs appear, however, recruiting directors who have academic credentials may still be the best choice among a limited set of alternatives.

A related question to consider is what the status of the director should be. At liberal arts colleges, computing directors may supervise as few as one FTE or as many as 32. They may handle only one department, such as academic computing, or they may handle many departments, including academic and administrative computing, library computing, networking, audio-visual services, telecommunications, microcomputer resale, stenographic services, and even institutional research. Computer directors at liberal arts colleges have reporting responsibilities ranging from associate dean to as high as president. This degree of variability in status is unusual among administrative positions, even in a community as idiosyncratic as that of liberal arts colleges. The explanation for such a high degree of variability is primarily that computing is a very new administrative service at liberal arts colleges; its importance has varied considerably from college to college, and until recently there have been few paradigms for schools to follow.

While it's difficult to say what status computing directors *should* have, some recent trends suggest the status they *will* have in the future. First, as pointed out in chapter 4, there has been a noticeable shift in the past few years from separate computing centers with separate directors to multigroup organizations or merged centers with a single director. More and more directors are now charged with the task of supervising both academic and administrative computing, campus networking, and microcomputer resale and repair. Second, as a result of this broadening of responsibilities, directors have seen staff sizes increase by much as 100 percent between 1985 and 1991. Third, with an increase in responsibilities and greater involvement in both curricular and administrative activities, directors have been assigned to report to more senior officers of the college.

If these trends continue, it is likely that the status of computing directors will become increasingly similar to that of head librarians, registrars, and other mid-level, professional administrators. The possibility that these positions will evolve any higher, into *chief information officers* as they exist at universities for example, is small, though a few liberal arts colleges are currently experimenting with that approach. The politics and organizational history of small colleges militate against the creation of this type of position. On the other hand, an argument in favor of such a position is that it consolidates related planning, budgetary, and management endeavors at the same time that it concentrates technical expertise under one roof. Since such consolidation can yield substantial cost savings and staff size reductions, it may become increasingly attractive to schools that face severe budgetary problems. The crystal ball is cloudy on this issue, so we're just going to have to wait and see what happens.

One thing is clear, however. The past few years have been a time of intense transition for computing organizations and their directors. In the three-year period from 1987 to 1990, more than half of the directorships among the 55 members of the Consortium for Liberal Arts Colleges changed hands. Many of them also changed definition along the way. The trend seems to be toward directors who are more professional, more people oriented, who have more sophisticated managerial skills, better academic credentials, and who command dramatically higher salaries.

Conclusion

The past decade has been tough on computing personnel. I'm tempted to speculate that if staffs survived the last decade, the future is a snap. Nevertheless, we still face a broad set of problems ranging from burnout to boredom. The status of computing directors and organizations is increasing, but so are the pressures to keep up with the relentless changes in technology and the ever-growing demands of our users. As Jonas Salk once said, however, " . . . the greatest reward for doing is the opportunity to do more." With that kind of philosophy he would have been an ideal candidate for our computing staff!

Chapter 6

The Role of Administrative Computing at Liberal Arts Colleges

David Cossey
Union College
and
Martin Ringle
Reed College

David V. Cossey has been director of computer services, with responsibility for academic and administrative computing, at Union College since 1986. Before coming to Union he was director of computing and instructional technology at the Wharton School of the University of Pennsylvania (1979–86). From 1968–79 he was at Barrington College in Rhode Island, where he taught mathematics and computer science and was director of computer services from 1976–79. Mr. Cossey has a B.A. degree from the King's College (New York), an M.A. from Lehigh University, and an M.S. from the University of Rhode Island.

Mr. Cossey has been president of the Association of Small Computer Users in Education (ASCUE), a member of the DECUS Symposium Committee, a member of the DECUS VAX Special Interest Group's Executive Committee, and Chairperson of the DECUS Refereed Papers Committee. He has made presentations at DECUS, ASCUE, EDUCOM, and the National Education Computing Conference.

(Note: Martin Ringle's biographical summary appears at the beginning of chapter 3, on page 69.)

In many circles of higher education, the world of administrative computing has been looked upon as a necessary evil, a poor cousin to the exciting world of technology found within the precincts of academic and research computing. The very stability required of administrative computing—a stability that is closely akin to that of data processing in the business world—is the reason it bears the reputation of being resistant to change and inherently less exciting than academic computing.

As computers become easier to operate and easier to purchase, however, their use in the administrative area is becoming more diverse and pervasive. Much of the mystery of the computer—and many of the "technical gurus" who guarded that mystique—are now disappearing. Anyone who has done word processing, used a spreadsheet, or purchased a computer for home use has had to assume the combined roles of operations manager, software mechanic, and technician. Despite this demystification, administrative computing software has lagged behind personal computing software in terms of innovations such as friendly user interfaces, networking, and so on. Much administrative computing software is still not user friendly, and a good deal of it is clearly user hostile, as many administrative staff members will hasten to point out. The situation, however, is beginning to change as more vendors adopt new software technologies.

A major factor in the evolution of administrative computing is the changing face of higher education itself. As colleges seek to remain competitive in a shrinking marketplace, the use of technology in the administrative area is increasingly being viewed as an underutilized resource. Colleges are facing the challenges of a dwindling number of high school graduates, rising costs, and tougher competition for endowment dollars. Many schools are pursuing major capital campaigns in a furious effort to bolster endowments, meet often deferred maintenance needs, and introduce new curricular, faculty, and physical resources designed to make the institution more attractive to potential students. This is also a time when private institutions are locked in a real struggle for public dollars with state and local institutions. Federal financial aid funding is decreasing in actual, if not in current dollars, and this trend is likely to continue.

Businesses have always had to worry about attracting and retaining customers, controlling costs, and reinvesting to provide for growth in the marketplace. In the business world, using information to gain competitive advantage is often taken for granted. Many colleges and universities are just beginning to recognize the role that information systems can play in key areas. It has become increasingly apparent that, in addition to improving administrative operations, administrative computing technology can be used to assist in attracting and retaining good faculty members, attracting potential donor dollars, and managing spiraling costs. It can also be an invaluable asset to institutional planning, resource management, and executive decision making. While the use of information technology cannot in itself solve major problems nor insure the survival of a failing college, it can, nevertheless, make college administration more effective as well as more efficient.

The purpose of this chapter is to identify some of the current and future issues in administrative computing as they relate to the small liberal arts college. At many institutions it is common to hear that the real benefits of administrative computing lie just around the corner, "after the next system upgrade." One goal of this chapter is to peek around the corner a bit and see if those benefits are any closer to being realized than they were a decade ago. We highlight some of the problems that liberal arts colleges face in defining strategies for administrative computing and consider the ways in which technology, organization, staffing, and finances affect strategic decisions.

Putting Administrative Computing into Perspective

In the early sixties, many small colleges began the process of transferring their daily administrative operations from manual records to computerized databases. A small staff of computer professionals—including programmers, data-entry operators, machine operators, and a manager—were hired to handle all the administrative computing needs of the college. The computer center was the hub of all computing activity and users had to travel to the center to submit data and programming requests or to retrieve printed reports. For the most part, programs to suit the institution's specific administrative procedures were written in COBOL, FORTRAN, or assembly language by staff programmers. In some cases, colleges shared their software with other schools, thus providing the option of program modification in lieu of pure programming.

During the sixties and seventies, the size of administrative computing staffs grew as colleges expanded their data-processing operations and became more dependent on in-house program development. Although academic computing centers at liberal arts colleges were almost nonexistent in the early seventies, administrative computing staff size frequently grew from one or two positions to as many as half a dozen. Among the larger and wealthier colleges, staff size sometimes expanded to ten or more positions.

The growing complexity, expense, and size of administrative computing, coupled with rapid changes in computer technology, posed several challenges for administrative computer centers. Unlike large universities, which could maintain a staff of twenty, thirty, or even fifty full-time programmer-analysts, small colleges were generally restricted to not more than three programmers. Keeping up with changing demands and changing technology grew increasingly difficult. Integrating all the different databases and programs became a full-time and often frustrating task. By the early seventies, many colleges looking for relief found a solution to their problems in the form of off-the-shelf or *turn-key* packages.

Turn-key administrative computing packages were touted as the answer to uncontrolled growth in administrative computing. Although the scope of the early packages was fairly narrow, they typically included a student record system, a course registration system, and a financial system for billing, accounting, and so forth. Some of the more innovative packages included special modules for admissions, alumni, and event scheduling. Among the advertised benefits of these packages were:

- Improved (though far from complete) integration of data processing for different administrative functions (such as student registration and billing)

- Vendor-based software support (with the suggestion that internal staff size could be held in check)

- Commercial quality software that would run better and faster than "home-grown" software

- Automatic upgrades and bug-fixes from the vendor

- In many cases, a single support organization to handle both hardware and software

For small colleges, turn-key computing packages provided an attractive way to deal with administrative computing.[1] Yet less than a third of all liberal arts colleges availed themselves of these systems during the seventies. Why? There are at least three reasons.

- Probably most important was *cost.* Even in the seventies, the cost of purchasing a complete, turn-key system ranged from several hundred thousand dollars to more than a million dollars. Furthermore, the software maintenance costs could run as high as fifty to a hundred thousand dollars annually. Many small colleges simply lacked the financial resources necessary for the purchase and ongoing support of a good commercial package.

- Despite all claims to the contrary, there was no evidence that purchasing a turn-key system actually helped to reduce the size of the administrative computing staff. In fact, staff size typically increased after the installation of a new system.

- The administrative practices of many liberal arts colleges varied to such a degree that off-the-shelf software had to be extensively (and expensively) modified to fit the institution—or the institution had to change its practices to accommodate the system. Neither choice was particularly attractive.

Despite these problems, however, a substantial number of small colleges did purchase administrative packages (or parts of packages) in the seventies and the number increased steadily during the eighties.

---

1. By contrast, larger universities often found that the complexity of their operations made it more cost-effective to develop and maintain their own administrative systems.

By 1989, approximately half of all liberal arts colleges had acquired or experimented with some off-the-shelf administrative software.[2] The remaining colleges continued to use home-grown software, modified software obtained from other colleges or universities, general purpose microcomputer packages (such as spreadsheets and personal databases) or, in some cases, external data-processing support purchased from a nearby university or a commercial firm.

Although administrative computing continued to enjoy a high degree of decision-making autonomy, the proliferation of microcomputers in the 1980s shattered the monopoly of computing expertise traditionally enjoyed by professionals. As academic computing grew, administrative computing centers found their mandate shifting from one of totally centralized control to one of dispersed services.

We are now at a stage where most administrative computer center employees are seen as facilitators of computer use rather than as the sole practitioners of computing. End-users are taking more direct control over their information-processing needs, and increasingly the job of the computer center staff is to guide users through the programs and databases they need while insuring that those programs and databases function properly.

Where We Are Today

Many colleges are now approaching a turning point in administrative computing. Schools that have been using home-grown software are exploring commercial software packages and schools that adopted turn-key packages in the seventies and eighties are now seeking to acquire more advanced software and hardware to help them streamline and enhance their data-processing operations.

Companies that marketed products written in BASIC, COBOL, FORTRAN, and other third-generation languages, are aggressively switching to newer systems using fourth-generation (4GL) languages and tools. These new programming tools make it possible for colleges

---

2. In many cases, however, the software consisted of a single module—such as a module for alumni/development applications—rather than an integrated system for all administrative applications.

to modify their systems quickly and easily with a minimal investment in staff time and energy. Not only does this help to decrease the institution's dependence on the vendor but it allows the vendor to devote more time to the complex tasks of extending and improving the overall system rather than customizing small parts of the system for each client. For example, development time for new reports—for both users and vendors—is now measured in hours or days, rather than weeks or months. These technical changes have significant consequences for both the size and effectiveness of administrative computer center staffing.

The key goal in administrative computing has changed little over the past decade. In the most general terms, it is: to provide easy-to-use, readily available, and flexible computing resources to accommodate institutional operations, departmental operations, strategic planning, archiving of institutional records, and decision support for college administrators. Recently, however, there has been an increased emphasis on specific goals.

In today's administrative computing environment there is a growing trend towards the promotion of user independence from the computer center. Such activities as conducting database inquiries, requesting and printing reports, and modifying screen presentation formats, once under the total control of the computer center, are slowly migrating out to the users themselves. The goal of the computer center now is primarily to insure that users are well trained in the methods for dealing with the system and that both technical and operational standards are followed throughout the institution.

A second goal is to promote and facilitate the sharing of data among departments, thereby minimizing the duplication of data-collection and management activities. During the seventies and eighties it was common for each administrative department to develop its own data-collection procedures, its own databases, and its own method of accessing and using data. The proliferation of databases created problems such as time delays between "rolling over" information from one database to another, inconsistencies in the data held in two related databases, and incompatibilities among the data-processing procedures of different offices. The divergence in data handling among administrative offices often created a nightmare for adminis-

trative computing staff members. The current move toward convergence, data sharing, and standardized procedures helps to minimize
duplication of effort while lowering the risk of data inconsistencies.

The three watchwords of administrative computing have always
been *stability, reliability,* and *security.* Random or inconsistent
performance, frequent system modifications, unscheduled down-time,
or unauthorized access are simply unacceptable in an administrative
computing environment. The nature of stability, reliability, and security, however, have taken on new dimensions in recent years. With
technical improvements coming at a dizzying pace, the administrative computing staff is constantly forced to weigh the benefits of
adding or modifying a system feature against the dangers of upsetting
the system's stability. As so many users know, the most dreaded word
in the administrative computing environment is *upgrade.* Yet it is
essential to conduct regular evaluations of system capabilities and to
upgrade both software and hardware in order to take advantage of bug
fixes, optimizations, or innovative features.

Reliability has also changed its complexion. In the early seventies,
when most administrative computing was done in batch mode, users
became frustrated if it took more than a few days to retrieve their
data. Today, users become frustrated if it takes more than a few
minutes. By the mid-nineties, the frustration threshold may be
reduced to a matter of seconds. Administrative users expect their
computing systems to function with the same reliability as their
telephones. When you pick up the telephone receiver, you expect to
hear a dial tone. When you press a button on your keyboard, you
expect to see a response on the screen. As one director of computing
recently put it, "95 percent system reliability is just another way of
saying that you have a 5 percent window for total disaster."
Administrative operations that have become dependent on computer
support can be severely crippled by software or hardware failures
lasting more than a few hours. Liberal arts colleges, which were far
behind universities a few years ago in their use of computing for
administration, have now introduced computing into nearly every
aspect of their operations. The option of returning to paper and pencil
when the computer fails may no longer be a viable one for many of
our administrative activities.

With the vast increase in on-line access to the administrative computing environment, security has also become a far more complex issue. Simple password protection to an administrative host has gone the way of punch cards. Today, users often require access to specific fields of information within specific records. Multilevel passwording, elaborate audit trails, locking keyboards, and a variety of other measures are part of the burgeoning field of administrative data security. Despite all these measures, however, there are growing concerns that technical innovations such as networking and distributed computing, policy changes that allow faculty members to access administrative databases, and intentional disruptions from off-campus hackers or computer viruses, will make security one of the top priorities of the coming decade. Thus far, liberal arts colleges have had relatively few security problems in contrast to large universities. It is still unclear whether or not this will continue to hold true.

The Trend toward Industry Standards

Until very recently, commercial packages for administrative computing were built upon proprietary databases, proprietary operating systems, and proprietary hardware. The advantage of such turn-key systems was—and is—that there is only one vendor to call when trouble arises or when the system needs to be upgraded. Turn-key vendors often guarantee results rather than products, and many administrative computing departments, especially those of small colleges, are less interested in the sophistication of the underlying technology than they are in the overall reliability of the system.

One problem with this approach is that it often forces the institution to make decisions about software on the basis of a database or an operating system or, worse still, on the basis of a specific hardware constraint. Software decisions should be based on such key factors as functionality, reliability, and security. A second problem is that, if the desired administrative package runs on a proprietary operating system and/or hardware platform, the institution is forced to purchase the hardware at whatever price is quoted. Negotiating separately with the hardware vendor and the software vendor may help, but both types of vendors can take advantage of the lack of competition to keep prices as high as possible.

The solution to both of these problems lies in the trend toward hardware and software standards. The two most significant developments in this area have been the growth of *structured query language* (SQL), relational databases and the increasing acceptance of nonproprietary operating systems as a foundation for administrative applications.

Relational database products using SQL[3] have been extremely successful during the past few years because they provide more flexibility and are more powerful than other technologies, such as hierarchical databases. They simplify the development of application software, and they provide a standard that dramatically improves software portability and intersystem communication.

Nonproprietary operating systems (primarily UNIX) have entered the administrative computing environment at a slower pace than SQL relational databases. Past weaknesses in the user interface and the general lack of security features have led many administrative computer centers to avoid the UNIX operating system. Recently, however, there has been a shift toward UNIX, due to the introduction of rigorous security features and the addition of friendlier user interfaces. The underlying motivation for the movement towards UNIX is twofold:

- *Price-performance.* The use of RISC architectures for UNIX machines has produced a price-performance ratio that is far superior to the ratio for traditional CISC architectures.

- *Portability.* UNIX is the first open system that is supported on hardware from virtually every major vendor and that cuts across every level of machine from microcomputer to supercomputer.

---

3. The dominant SQL relational database products in the liberal arts college market today come from Oracle, Inges, Sybase, and Informix. In addition, each major hardware vendor typically has its own relational database product.

Although the first motivation may lose strength as vendors move proprietary systems to RISC architectures or find ways to improve CISC architecture performance, the second motivation is likely to remain. Standardizing on an open operating system like UNIX allows organizations to reduce their hardware costs substantially through vendor competitiveness. Because all the major hardware vendors[4] offer machines that support UNIX, colleges can negotiate lower price-points for hardware purchases while still being able to select the vendor of their choice. The same is true of all major SQL relational database systems, since they are compatible with UNIX and will run on the platforms of each of the major hardware vendors.

Since most implementations of UNIX still lack the sophistication of many proprietary operating systems, work is underway to replace UNIX with an equally generic but more robust successor. The Open Software Foundation (OSF) has defined a UNIX descendant which provides improved functionality, security, and efficiency. The alliance between Apple and IBM to cooperate on UNIX (AIX and AUX) development may also change the future of proprietary systems in a dramatic way.

Interest in UNIX and other open operating systems has been growing steadily among administrative computing specialists; although the majority of software vendors continue to focus their products on proprietary platforms, a growing number of them are moving in the direction of SQL relational databases and open operating systems. As they do so, the market will become increasingly competitive, prices are likely to moderate, and colleges will find it easier to focus their software purchases on functionality rather than on hardware compatibility or other incidental constraints.

Meeting the Goals of Administrative Computing

The first issue raised by many schools in determining their administrative computing strategies is whether to procure a commercial package or to develop (or redevelop) the software themselves. There are actually several options to consider. An institution can:

---

4. For example, IBM, DEC, Hewlett-Packard, SUN, Sequent, Apple, AT&T/NCR.

1. Purchase a total administrative computing environment and rely heavily on the vendor for support and
   modifications

2. Purchase a total administrative computing environment and perform in-house modifications and support

3. Purchase several commercial packages and link
   them together internally

4. Purchase some commercial packages and link them
   to some internally developed software

5. Develop all the software internally

The principal advantages of the first option are that staff size may
be kept to a minimum, the software is of professional quality, there
is a vendor and (usually) a group of fellow schools to turn to for
assistance, and upgrades are produced on a fairly regular basis. The
disadvantages of the first option are that a certain amount of tailoring
and accommodation may be necessary in order to get the software to
match the needs of the institution, the cost of acquiring and maintaining a commercial product may be quite high, and the institution
may become dependent on a commercial vendor over which it has
little or no control. This option is often facilitated by powerful report
writers and query languages that are delivered with the package.

The principal advantages of the fifth option are that software may
be tailored precisely to fit the needs of the institution and software
maintenance costs can be held to a minimum. The disadvantages are
that the system can become difficult to enhance (or even to maintain)
without a major commitment to staff size; knowledge of the system
is often in the hands of one or two individuals whose departure from
the institution may result in potential disaster, and the software itself
may be far less sophisticated than a commercial-quality package. The
introduction of powerful 4GL development tools, relational database
packages, and other technical advances are clearly improving an
institution's ability to undertake successfully its own software development. Unfortunately, the complexity of demands on administrative
computing are growing at the same time, making in-house development a very problematic endeavor.

Options 3 and 4 provide an institution with greater flexibility to mix and match software to meet its specific needs but they both tend to create complexities that in the long run make an environment difficult to support. However, even with a movement towards hardware and software standardization, it is still extremely difficult and time consuming to integrate and maintain different software packages within a single administrative environment.

The second option, to purchase a comprehensive package but not rely exclusively on the vendor to make modifications, is gaining acceptance among small schools since it combines the virtues of commercial quality software and vendor support with the flexibility of internal tailoring using powerful 4GL tools. The critical question to ask with respect to this option is: How much utility is provided by the predefined commercial package and how much must (or can) be added by the institution itself? If a great deal of internal work is required, option 2 becomes indistinguishable from option 5; if too little internal work is permitted, option 2 becomes indistinguishable from option 1. Only a handful of commercial vendors provide truly robust software packages that are at the same time amenable to easy institutional modification.

More and more small colleges are moving in the direction of the first and second options in order to take advantage of user groups, vendor support, and high quality software, while preserving their ability to "tweak" the software or develop add-ons that don't substantially interfere with vendor-supplied upgrades, bug fixes, or enhancements.

The Need for Better User Interfaces

While administrative computing vendors have paid a great deal of attention to the need for improving the functionality of their software, relatively little attention has been paid to improving the end-user interface until recently. Even with the most sophisticated administrative packages on the market today, most users are forced to memorize arcane codes and character sequences, to navigate complex layered menus, and to struggle with procedures for down-loading portions of their databases to desktop tools such as word processors and spreadsheets. While many vendors would argue that there have been steady improvements in screen layouts and the design of menu structures, the fact remains that most character-based user interfaces are a generation behind the graphical interface that is now available on most desktop machines, including Macintoshes, MS-DOS machines, and UNIX workstations.

The virtues of bringing a consistent "point-and-click" environment to the administrative user interface are many: The learning curve for new users or new employees is minimized; usage of system features is enhanced; productivity is increased, and errors, fatigue, and frustration are substantially reduced. What sometimes appears as a need for additional system functionality is really a need for improved user access to data. In many cases, the interface including user access methods is closely intertwined with the perceived functionality of the system itself.

Better interfaces help to empower users, to put more control into their hands and to make them less dependent on the programming and support staff of the administrative computer center. This manifests itself in at least two ways. First, with a sufficiently friendly interface users are able to design new report formats themselves rather than turning to a programmer when changes are necessary. Second, the transparency and intuitiveness of a friendly interface means that support staff are required to devote less time to training and assisting users with common procedures and can therefore spend more time working on especially difficult problems. Since the demand on administrative computing staff constitutes one of the most critical problems facing small colleges today, anything that can help reduce the staff burden is extremely valuable.

Many software vendors who specialize in administrative and business applications are beginning to acknowledge that the graphical user interface (GUI), popularized in the academic computing environment of the 1980s by the Macintosh, represents a major step forward for administrative computing. Despite the inherent resistance to change within this environment, momentum is building to create friendly GUI front-ends for existing software packages and to design new packages that take full advantage of graphical interfaces.

As a first step toward a full-featured GUI, several vendors have begun to develop and market windowing environments that allow some concurrent processes, some basic cutting and pasting across windows, and other features that are clear advances over the traditional character-based interface. There are already several products on proprietary platforms, such as Oracle's *Oracle Card*™, that provide basic point-and-click functional access to databases from a microcomputer or workstation. Interest in GUIs based on nonproprietary platforms, such as X-Windows, is also growing, although it is doubtful that this approach will find a large market within administrative computing.

Graphical user interfaces may be the most promising next step for accessing administrative databases, but there are other approaches that are likely to grow in significance during the next ten years. Among these are natural language interfaces and pen-based interfaces. Natural language interfaces allow users to formulate queries and commands in ordinary English, without prior knowledge of the internal structure of the database. Ideally, they permit users to begin working with a system with very little training. The growth of natural language interfaces has been slow during the past two decades due to technical limitations and high costs. Gradually, many of the technical problems are being solved and pricing has become more aggressive. We can expect to see more of these systems and higher levels of acceptance in the latter part of the nineties.

Pen-based systems utilize drawing and hand-printed data entry in lieu of keystrokes or mouse movements. Within the framework of college administrative systems, pen-based technology holds great potential for various types of users, such as admissions recruiters, fund raisers, and senior administrators, who require access to databases while they are traveling. The commercial development of pen-based interfaces is still fairly new and widespread usage within the administrative computing environment is likely to grow slowly. Nevertheless, like graphical and natural language interfaces, pen-based interfaces represent significant improvements in the usability of administrative computing systems, and once the technology becomes stable and the price-point is low enough, acceptance of pen-based systems may rise abruptly.

Administrative Computing and End-Users

Though questions of technology tend to be at the forefront of most discussions of administrative computing, anyone who has been involved in providing computing services to administrative staff members knows that technical problems generally take a back seat to human problems. Among the primary issues that play an important role in defining the relationship between administrative computing and end-users are these:

- *Agenda setting.* Who determines priorities for administrative computing activities?

- *Communication.* How is information exchanged between end-users and the administrative computer staff?

- *Hardware and software standards.* How does the college coordinate the potentially divergent technical strategies of different offices and individuals?

- *User support.* How should administrative computer groups determine the nature and appropriate levels of user support?

Agenda Setting

A commonly voiced complaint made by end-users is that the administrative computing group is not meeting their needs because it is working on other priorities. In many cases the complaint is fully justified. The central question that must be answered is, Where do these priorities come from?

Accepted wisdom says that there are two major categories of agenda setting, those made by an individual and those made by a group. Individual agenda setting for administrative computing may come from the director, the director's supervisor, or someone higher on the administrative ladder, up to and including the president. It may be the result of heavy influence by a single trustee, administrator, or faculty member. At some institutions, the state of computing at peer schools—as interpreted by a single computer advocate—may play an inordinately high role in setting agendas as well.

Group decisions, on the other hand, may issue from the administrative computing staff, an administrative computing user or advisory committee, a group of senior administrators, or an ugly mob. Unfortunately, the latter has had more influence on the shape of computing decisions at liberal arts colleges than one would like to admit. A long-range, committee-authored planning document prepared in response to the needs of many different administrative staff members may also play an important role in group agenda setting for computing.

There are at least three advantages to having the agenda set by an individual. First, it is likely to represent a more focused and coherent set of priorities than would result from a group effort; second, the agenda is likely to be more technically sophisticated; and third, it may be more sensitive to pragmatic issues, such as staffing and budgeting.

A major disadvantage of having an individual set the agenda is that it may serve to disenfranchise the very people who are most directly affected by it. If those people are unable to determine—or at least to influence—the prioritization process, they may become hostile toward computer center initiatives and severely limit the center's effectiveness. This alone argues that agenda setting must be done through a community process.

Agenda setting in administrative computing is one of those phenomena peculiar to the liberal arts college culture that has an enormous impact on the operation of the college and yet is rarely discussed or modified unless there is a major upheaval, such as the abrupt departure of a director or a disaster in user support.

Observations of agenda-setting activities at a variety of liberal arts colleges suggest several practices that contribute to a healthy relationship between the computer center and its clients:

- End-users play a clear role in the process of setting priorities

- Senior administrators are aware of and endorse the priority list

- The completed agenda is circulated to all concerned parties

• The computer center director is allowed to exercise
leadership and to apply his or her expertise to the
process of setting priorities.

It should be noted that these practices represent a synthesis of
individual and group priority-setting strategies. While the specific mechanisms for implementing these practices may differ from institution
to institution,[5] the inclusion of senior administrators and end-users
in the decision-making process, guided by the leadership of the
computer center itself, seems to be the common formula for success.

Communication

We often assume that in a small liberal arts college, communication
among staff is far easier than in a large university. It is a reasonable
assumption, yet the facts often suggest otherwise. At many small
colleges the primary channel for information (and misinformation)
about computing initiatives is by word of mouth—the ever-present
rumor mill. To minimize the frustration and confusion that can result
from poor communication, small colleges have resorted to a variety
of strategies, including electronic mail, newsletters, meetings, reports,
and standing committees.

An approach that has been successful at a growing number of
colleges is to designate a computing *liaison* in each administrative
office. The liaison is the person who attends meetings, receives and
disseminates computer center memos, and alerts the computer center
to local computing problems or needs. Explicitly placing responsibility
for communication between users and the computer center in the

---

5. At Union College, for example, the Administrative Computing Policy Advisory
   Committee is charged with recommending policy, including the development of
   long-range plans for administrative computing. This group is organized into a
   representative body, with an executive committee of seven members, including
   two members of the Computer Services Group in an advisory capacity. There is
   also a larger and more representative group composed of representatives from
   most administrative offices on campus. The executive committee consists of
   representatives of some of the larger and more computer-intensive offices on
   campus. At Reed College, there is an Administrative Users Group which
   provides input to the Computer Center on both policies and procedures; it
   consists of a representative from each administrative office.

hands of an individual helps to minimize the proliferation of rumors and to promote a good rapport between the center and its clients.

Electronic mail has also had a beneficial effect on the exchange of information. Reed College, which conducts an annual needs assessment among end-users for administrative computing improvements, has begun collecting requests and distributing the priority list via electronic mail. The annotated database of programming projects, moreover, is available to both users and administrators on an open file server. This allows all members of the executive and administrative staff to see the status of current and future changes to the computing environment.

Hardware and Software Standards

During the decades of centralized timesharing, the administrative computer group exercised nearly absolute control over the selection and use of both hardware and software. With the proliferation of microcomputers and the evolution of distributed networks, some administrative departments—like their academic counterparts—have assumed responsibility for their own hardware and software acquisitions. In some cases, this movement towards localization has resulted from dissatisfaction with the choices made by the computer center; in other instances, however, individuals or departments have departed from the norm in order to take advantage of a special pricing option, a particularly friendly piece of software, or a desire to use hardware or software that is used at other institutions (or which they themselves used elsewhere).

The advantage to such diversity is that each office (or individual) can acquire the technical platform that is most satisfying or most appropriate to the particular task at hand. Unfortunately, diversity has a price. For example, purchasing by individual departments may prevent the institution from negotiating quantity discounts and thereby reducing overall computing costs to the college. The lack of centralized coordination may also mean that the technical expertise of the computer center—especially with respect to hardware purchases—is excluded from the procurement process. While the end-users within an administrative department may be in a better position to identify the most ideal software package to meet their needs, their selection may ignore important technical, financial, or long-term support issues.

There are other problems with diversity as well. Network services—such as shared printing, electronic mail, automatic backup, and archiving—may be extremely difficult to provide in a heterogeneous computing environment, especially in light of the resource restrictions found at most small colleges. The same holds true for maintenance, upgrades, and user support. When the size of the computing staff is small and the dollars are tight, adherence to collegewide hardware and software standards may be the only way to insure an adequate level of administrative computing support.

Diversity and decentralization bring with it a far more serious problem involving the data maintained by the institution. Much of these data have relevance and use beyond a single office. However, when data are maintained on a single-user personal computer system, they become inaccessible to others who need access to them. For a small college, keeping centralized data still makes sense—they are accessible by several users (although only one office may update them). If we decentralize access to data, we are in danger of creating a new class of experts, and users may lose the convenience of generating reports on demand from the comfort of their offices. From the point of view of operating costs it also makes sense to keep data in a central location. While machine costs keep going down, personnel costs continue to rise; and the cost of several people keeping redundant data cannot be justified.

Establishing and maintaining standards, even in a very small college, may prove difficult unless it is made clear to everyone that the advantages of standardization outweigh the benefits of diversity. The administrative computer center must be prepared to identify specific areas of savings to the college that can accrue from standardization and be able to articulate this message to both the end-users and to the senior administrators. Moreover, decision makers in individual departments must be provided with appropriate incentives to make the movement toward standardization attractive to them. Improved responsiveness and increased resources are generally the most effective "carrots" which the computer center has to offer. An administrative computing advisory committee can also play a crucial role in enlisting end-user cooperation in the development of and adherence to technical standards.

User Support

As it does for hardware and software, the computer center must define standards for end-user support. In many respects, the quality of user support is the principal measure of the success or failure of computer center operation. Put another way, when users perceive that the computer center staff is responsive to their needs, they generally rate administrative computing highly, regardless of the state of the technical environment; conversely, when they feel that computer center staff do not respond to their questions and requests, they tend to rate the center lower, even if the technical environment is quite sophisticated.[6]

Setting user-support standards simply means codifying and clarifying the types of services the computer center can effectively provide, given its human resources. It involves the effort to bring the user's support *expectations* in line with the computer center's support *capacity*. End-users must be informed if the center is understaffed, undertrained, or otherwise lacking in institutional resources, in order for them to understand why deficiencies in support levels exist.

If the technical environment for administrative computing is heterogeneous, the computer center must differentiate the levels of user support. For example, the computer center may prepare documentation, offer tutorials, and provide immediate consultation for its own software, but it may be able to do little more than arrange a phone call to a vendor or another college in order to obtain assistance with a software package purchased independently by a department or an individual.

The disparity between the highest and the lowest levels of user support can produce some very undesirable situations. At many liberal arts colleges with small administrative computing staffs, one occasionally finds "data specialists" in various administrative departments. The role of these specialists may include hardware and software procurement, system administration, data-entry operator supervision, and even programming. Their primary role, however, is end-user support. While such individuals generally provide important

---

6. This observation is based on consulting interviews by one of the authors with administrative staff members at more than thirty liberal arts colleges.

services to their departments, the overall benefit to the institution may be questionable, especially in very small colleges.

Addressing the problem of insufficient centralized user-support levels by adding staff to individual departments leaves the underlying problem intact and promotes further expansion of staff within departments. This may drive up the institutional cost of computing, however obscurely. That is, cost accounting for personnel (and technology) distributed among individual departments may be difficult or impossible to track in comparison with cost accounting for the computer center itself. On the other hand, in colleges where budgetary or staff size constraints on computing are not severe—or where it is politically prudent to distribute user-support personnel—defining user support positions for individual departments may indeed be the most viable approach.

Access to the Administrative Computing Environment

With the growing sophistication of computer users on campus, there is a new unrest as many nontraditional administrative users want to have access to selected portions of the institution's administrative data. These new users include senior administrators, administrative staff members who have previously avoided the computer, and faculty members. Access for faculty members poses a host of complex problems, some technical and others political in nature.

While there are clearly applications for which access must be carefully restricted—such as payroll records, alumni giving records, and accounts receivable—there are specific areas of information that are clearly relevant to the activities of faculty members and faculty chairs within academic departments.

For example, academic advising can be facilitated by allowing faculty members to have on-line access to the most up-to-date records for student advisees. Simple programs can be used to handle tasks such as prerequisite checking, listing of required courses, course sequencing, and schedule conflict identification. Freed of many of the mechanical aspects of advising, faculty members can devote more of their attention to substantive issues of course selection based on content and student interests.

A second example lies in the area of budget control. At most small colleges, department chairs are expected to balance their expenditure records against monthly statements from the comptroller's office. With this method, unfortunately, discrepancies sometimes take months to discover and may be difficult to resolve. Occasionally, purchases must be delayed while the department tries to determine whether or not it really has sufficient funds left in its budget. By providing on-line access to budget control information, account reconciliation can be done continuously, discrepancies can be spotted immediately, and the entire purchasing process can be rendered more efficient.

A third example involves faculty committees charged with reviews of programs or self-study needs. These require access to data that were previously unavailable or available only to the office of institutional research. Whether for an accreditation review, for a required report, or for internal use, many faculty committees need access to the institution's current and historical data. These data must be readily available, convenient to use, and secure from unauthorized access.

The primary political issues of faculty access to administrative data revolve around the fear—justifiable or not—that access to administrative data by anyone other than administrative staff members will result in a lower level of security and that privacy and confidentiality of institutional information will be compromised. Many colleges have simply avoided addressing the key questions of who should have access to administrative data and under what conditions such access should be provided. In some cases, the political issue is hindered by technical barriers between incompatible administrative and academic computing environments.

To a great extent, however, most technical barriers are beginning to melt away with the growth of campus-wide networks. Machines from different vendors can be linked to one another via a network, and data stored on the administrative host in one format can be transferred to an academic host (or desktop machine) in a different format.

Security concerns are both receding and increasing in the face of new technologies. With the more robust administrative software packages, it is possible to specify access privileges as high as the system level or as low as the field and value level. Multilevel passwording and other software barriers can be established for dealing with sensitive data at virtually any level of storage. In addition, network routing hardware makes it possible to constrain administrative database access to specific network nodes, thus providing an extra level of access control. On the other hand, easy access to data, especially over networks, increases the possibility that confidentiality and privacy can be breached.

An alternative to allowing faculty members access to the administrative database itself is to provide automatic, one-way down-loads of information from the administrative to the academic environment, thereby eliminating the possibility of any tampering with the database by users on the academic side of the house. Privacy can be enhanced by encrypting all such information and requiring double passwording.

While the issues of security and confidentiality are important issues—and the steps that must be taken to address them are not trivial—they may be solved using current technology. The policy question of who should have access to administrative databases ought not be obscured by rhetoric about whether or not such access is technically possible.

In addition to faculty members, there is another constituency that needs to be addressed. Senior administrators, who traditionally kept their distance from computers or, at most, used them for word processing, are beginning to develop an interest in decision-support and personal-productivity tools such as spreadsheets, graphics packages, modeling programs, inter-campus electronic mail systems, and so forth. More and more we are seeing deans, provosts, vice-presidents, and occasionally even presidents who demand some degree of direct access to portions of the administrative database.

The problem of access by senior administrators is that most administrative computing environments are still relatively inhospitable. The senior administrator who wants immediate access to data in order to polish up a memorandum to the faculty or a report to the trustees, has neither the desire nor the time to learn a complex query language or wade through a convoluted menu structure. Many software vendors are striving to address this problem by creating executive information systems (EISs), which consist of focused, flexible, and extremely friendly interfaces for administrative database access and decision support. EIS tools include robust *natural language* or *graphical* query methods with which the user is able to perform searching, sorting, list generation, and other basic data retrieval operations with virtually no prior training nor any knowledge of the structure of the database. Thus, for example, a provost or dean might enter a natural language request such as "List the percentage of tenured faculty in all departments during the past ten years" and receive the relevant information immediately in display or print format. Graphical query methods are slightly more cumbersome than natural language methods, though they are potentially more powerful and still far easier to use than any traditional query languages.

Administrators who have been exposed to advanced EIS tools generally react with enthusiasm. In the time that it currently takes to describe the nature of a data request to an assistant or to a staff member in administrative computing, a senior administrator can enter the request directly and retrieve the desired information. In addition to time savings, the EIS approach also adds a degree of confidentiality in data retrieval not previously possible. Administrators at liberal arts colleges, however, have received less exposure to EIS tools than their university counterparts and the adoption of EIS environments at small colleges is likely to move at a slower pace.

The Relationship between Academic and Administrative Computing

No discussion of administrative computing in liberal arts colleges would be complete without some observations on the relationship between administrative computing and academic computing. Although the issue has been raised and discussed in the two previous chapters, a few remarks are in order.

In the earliest days of computing at liberal arts colleges there was generally only one computer center. Most—if not all—of its activity was dedicated to administrative computing. The development of academic computing in the seventies led colleges down one of two roads: (1) the expansion of computer center staffing and facilities to strike a balance between academic and administrative computing resources or (2) the creation of a separate center for academic computing. Many colleges have experienced lengthy internal debates about whether separate centers or combined centers were preferable. The answer, in virtually every case, depends on the specific resources and needs of the college.

The advent of microcomputers, the implementation of campus-wide networks, the adherence to hardware and software standards, and the need to conserve financial and human resources have all contributed to a growing sense that academic and administrative computing needs to be *coordinated*, if not actually combined. At some colleges, coordination results in shared technology, shared space, shared budgets, and shared staff members. This, more or less, is the traditional model of a single computer center, which serves both sides of the house. At colleges where academic and administrative computing have previously been separated, coordination may take the form of joint supervision by a single director or vice-president, with some resources being shared and others remaining separate.

Computer services at both Union and Reed College follow the second model. For example, while some staff members are assigned exclusively to one side of the house, other members, in areas such as technical and network services, provide support to both sides of the house. This permits the computer center to define staff assignments by content rather than by user groups served. Where content and user group are uniquely related—for example, in administrative application programming—staff assignments may conform to the earlier distinction between academic and administrative computing. Where content and user groups overlap—for example, in network services—the distinction between academic and administrative computing effectively disappears. The same holds true for hardware, software, space, and other resources; some may be shared by both sides of the house and some may be kept separate, depending upon the pragmatics and the politics of each situation.

The overriding element of coordination in this type of environment is that of administrative unity—a single director who supervises planning, budgeting, staff management, and technology decisions for all aspects of computing. By having a single administrator in charge of all computing operations, incompatibilities between technical approaches, competition for computing funds, and unnecessary duplication of staff assignments may be eliminated. At the same time, however, a lower-level division of resources allows the computer center to acknowledge and address the fact that the needs of the two sides of the house frequently differ in significant ways.

It is worth emphasizing this last point. Many institutions have had difficulty in establishing communication links, joint policies, and joint technology standards across the academic/administrative gulf. The differences in the types of computing activities that take place on each side of the house mirror the deeper distinctions that exist between faculty (and students) and administrative staff members. Each side of the house speaks a slightly different language, operates on a different timetable, and has different goals and different measures of success. For faculty and students, computing may be a framework for research, innovation, and an object of study in itself; for administrative staff members, computing is a basic tool of the trade. The term "user friendly" may have a radically different meaning for each side of the house. Given the cultural differences between academic and administrative members of the college community, it can be extremely helpful to have someone in computing at the executive level who can provide a bridge in the areas of resource allocation, long-range planning, technology standardization, and so forth. In the long term, separate academic and administrative computing operations that lack such a bridge are more likely to wind up wasting some portion of the institution's resources.

Where Do We Go from Here?

As new hardware and software technology becomes more available and more affordable, administrative computing will become increasingly innovative in its vision, scope, and application. The traditional areas of admissions finance, registration, financial aid, alumni/development, personnel, and so forth, are already being complemented by new software for:

- Point-of-sale cash registers in the bookstore

- Universal student/faculty access cards for bookstore purchases, meal plans, library, and so forth

- Campus security, access/control/alarm systems

- Energy management for physical plant operations

- Student services, community calendar, electronic bulletin boards

- Off-campus (telephone) access to on-campus computing—for remote registration, for example

What effects will this next wave of administration applications produce? In many areas, this software will help colleges streamline their administrative operations, offer a wider range of services, and make better use of existing resources. As the competition for students and dollars escalates, so will the need to make better use of information and technology. Advanced software packages—sometimes called *expert systems*—may find applications at the reference desk of the library and at help desks in the computer center. Systems will become available to assist in student advising for registration, career counseling, and other areas. The forces that will drive the acceptance of these and other new technologies will be the cost, the ease of use, and the added value of the applications developed. Since very few small colleges will have the resources to develop and apply these new technologies themselves, there is likely to be an increasing reliance on universities, college consortia, and administrative software vendors to provide the technology and guidance necessary to make advanced systems feasible at liberal arts colleges.

As we look ahead to the future, we realize that administrative computing will continue to evolve into new areas of functionality, applicability, and ease of use. The notion that administrative operations—and the applications of computers to these operations—is a fixed, known quantity is gradually disappearing. Change may come more slowly to administrative than to academic computing, but it is just as inevitable. Colleges most likely to prosper in the coming years are those most willing to move to new technologies when their needs are not being met or when they are not being met on a cost-effective basis with existing technology.

The commitment to provide adequate computing resources requires a long-range and continuous commitment of college resources. The purchase of microcomputers and workstations is no more a one-time event than is the purchase of a central computing system. Hardware must be upgraded and replaced, software must be modified and constantly re-evaluated, and staffing must be maintained at a level commensurate with the training and support needs of the staff.

The future is exciting for anyone involved with administrative computing—it is also frightening for people who are uncomfortable with change. The pathways to the future need to be built now, and administrative computing groups need to keep their collective eyes on the changes in technology, organization, and services. While the ideal administrative computing may still be a long way off, many of the individual promises regarding ease of use, convenient access to broad amounts of information, consistent system reliability, and so forth, are no longer far-fetched ideas. They are already at our doorstep and will find their way into the small liberal arts college environment at an increasing pace during the next few years.

Part Three

Networks, Distributed Computing, and Telecommunications

Networks and Distributed Computing: Where Are We Going?

William Francis
Grinnell College

William Francis is director of computing at Grinnell College. His responsibilities include the oversight of academic computing, administrative computing, and telecommunications. Dr. Francis came to Grinnell in 1987 from Georgetown University, where he was assistant director of academic computing. He was appointed to the director's position in September 1988, after serving as associate director for software for one year.

Prior to working at Georgetown Dr. Francis was an assistant professor of psychology at Lawrence University in Appleton, Wisconsin, for four years. He has a Ph.D. in psychology from the University of Pittsburgh and a B.A. in psychology from S.U.N.Y. at Binghamton, New York. He has served as chair of the IITF (Iowa Internet Task Force), a group of computer service individuals from public and private institutions, collaborating to establish a statewide data network in Iowa. He has presented papers at Snowmass, the Consortium of Liberal Arts Colleges, and other educational computing gatherings.

There are a number of significant computing questions facing small colleges and universities as they move through the 1990s. What are the different ways colleges can provide computing power to their constituencies? Is there a best way to connect micro- to minicomputers? Are cost savings realized through the sharing of software applications, printers, and other equipment, or does the cost of providing networking expertise and technology absorb any potential savings? The common thread that runs through all of these issues is the question of networking.

How should computing resources that are distributed throughout a campus—and across different campuses—be connected to each other?

At Grinnell College, a great deal of effort and expense is directed toward minicomputer, microcomputer, and workstation networking. For the past several years we have tried to keep abreast of the progress made in networking at other small colleges and universities in order to guide activities at Grinnell. In this chapter I will try to identify some of the key issues in campus networking that are particularly relevant to small liberal arts colleges and universities. The perspective taken will be a combination of the experiences acquired first-hand at Grinnell and the experiences of the fifty-five member schools of the Consortium of Liberal Arts Colleges (CLAC), as presented in their 1989 report on administrative and academic central systems, microcomputers, networks, dormitory connections, network access in faculty and staff offices, and the campus-wide availability of computerized library systems.

Although Grinnell and the other CLAC schools have a great deal in common,[1] the report reveals that they have taken a wide variety of approaches to networking. While a comprehensive review of these approaches is beyond the scope of this chapter, I will try to highlight the major trends and discuss some of the reasons why networking strategies have converged on different campuses. Where possible, the pros and cons of the different approaches will be weighed. The intent of the discussion, however, is more descriptive than prescriptive; the factors that contribute to the adoption of a particular network strategy vary considerably from campus to campus. If anything, the purpose of this chapter is to raise questions, not to solve them. There is, at least thus far, no ideal approach to networking at small colleges. In the end, each institution must assess its own needs and resources and reach its own decisions about networking and distributed computing.

---

1. The schools represented in the 1989 report ranged in undergraduate enrollments from 600 to 4,000 with a mean of approximately 1,900. Computing support staff for all operations, including academic, administrative, and networking, averaged approximately 14 FTE. Total annual computing operating budgets averaged approximately $700,000. The size of support staff and operating budgets at these schools is somewhat higher than those of the majority of private liberal arts colleges.

Local Access to Central Computing: The Data Switch Model

It is impossible to describe small colleges' current attempts to provide networked computing resources to campus users without some mention of their points of departure. Current equipment and the residue of previous attempts to provide computing access color each school's computing efforts, despite the attempt to plan and install equipment that will best serve in the future.

Historically, many institutions of higher education have relied upon computing equipment located at a central site on campus ("the glass house"). In many cases the first demands for more local-access computing came in the mid to late 1970s from a contingent of administrators and faculty who wanted access to the central systems from their offices. It is not surprising that these users wanted to minimize the number of trips to the central computing site. Indeed, "minimizing the walk" may have been the principal force that motivated the creation of the first campus-wide networks at many colleges and universities.

In the late seventies and early eighties, computer center staff at many colleges moved toward a relatively economical method to provide remote, that is, interbuilding, connections—the data switch. The data switch (or combined voice and data switch) was economical because it could use existing telephone wire to connect the central computer to terminals throughout the campus. A combination of data-over-voice and multiplexer equipment was used to carry the RS-232–based data signals to the switch, which was usually located in or near the computer center. Though comparatively slow by today's standards, data communications via a switch were considered to be extremely fast in the seventies and early eighties, and the convenience of access from one's own office or a public terminal cluster made the $800 to $1,000 cost[2] per connection well worth the investment.

---

2. This cost includes active network devices but not the cost of the terminal or other desktop devices.

At the same time that many small schools were distributing computing via data switches and RS-232 wiring, some were beginning to
install true, high-speed Ethernet networks using coaxial cable as the
physical medium. Initially, this type of network was used to connect
two or more machines into a loosely coupled *cluster* in one room.
Such connections allowed the central systems to share disk, printing,
and tape resources with one another. Though the use of networking
was often geographically limited, its impact on campus thinking was
significant. At the least, it represented another layer of software to
manage, and at some sites this first experience with networking
colored computer staff and users' expectations for all types of
networks to come.

The trend toward campus-wide access to computing continues to
grow at small and large institutions alike. For example, approximately half of the small colleges that provide access to central
computing across the campus still rely on a data switch or combined
voice-and-data switch, even though they may use more sophisticated
forms of access at the same time.[3] In the last five years, many small
schools have rewired their campuses to allow students to have telephones in their residence hall rooms. During the rewiring, central
computer access was often improved as well, sometimes by making
better use of an existing data switch and sometimes by moving to a
different technology altogether.

Most schools have placed student laboratories with switch-
connected systems around campus and at many schools extensive
twisted-pair, terminal-oriented networks have evolved. A small number
of colleges now offer terminal service in nearly all (more than 85 percent)
of their dorm rooms. Perhaps as much as a quarter of all liberal arts
colleges provide every faculty and staff member with low-speed
desktop access to the central computing site using switch technology.

The combination of a switch and one or more central computers has
many advantages. It allows faculty, students, and staff to access

---

3. These figures are based on projections from computer surveys of liberal arts
   colleges conducted by Martin Ringle (Reed College) and Carl Henry (Carleton
   College) during the period 1985–1990. Similar estimates of installed technology
   at small colleges that appear throughout the chapter are based on the same
   sources.

centrally stored software (for example, word processors, compilers, spreadsheets, and statistical packages) and data resources (for example, administrative databases); to communicate with one another easily using a central electronic mail system; and to share printers. Many users appreciate the assured data backup and the fact that they do not need to install or manage their own software.

Switches allow easy access to on-line card catalogue systems, as well as communication and file transfer with other colleges and universities. Although less than half of all liberal arts colleges have installed automated catalogue systems, a substantial number of the ones that have been installed utilize a data switch as a means of campus-wide connectivity.

By and large, data-switch technology has worked well and it is mature. It is relatively stable, its costs are predictable, and its performance is reliable. Computer center staff understand the technology well and can maintain it easily.

Many smaller colleges that have very limited central computing facilities seek to provide more computing power across campus. Should these schools consider the addition of a central computing system and a data switch? The answer, of course, depends on the goals, current equipment, and resources of each college. Yet we can make some general observations that may be of use to schools that are re-evaluating their computing environment or considering the development of a network.

Central computers provide a strong anchoring point for administrative database applications, connections to external networks, and access to applications that demand considerable CPU power and file storage (such as statistical packages). It is hard to beat central systems when it comes to transparency of access to applications, printers, and files. These computers, however, are expensive to purchase and maintain. Given the increasing power, flexibility, and ease of use of current microcomputers, it is probably better not to try to have all academic users rely upon central CPUs for their main processing power. In addition, unless the college already owns a voice PBX that can be upgraded to carry data, I would argue against investing in a data switch. As described in the following discussion, economic and technical forces point in the direction of high-speed networks and terminal servers to provide the bulk of the connections needed within the main academic buildings. For those out-of-the-way sites that need just a few connections, it may be feasible to acquire one of the new generation of inexpensive, desktop-sized switches. Schools that are primarily interested in enhancing interpersonal communications, rather than general computer services, might look into the economics and features of voice mail as well.[4]

Several difficulties face colleges relying on data switches. They relate both to technical limitations of the low-speed connections and to the cost of increasing the number of connections and the load upon central computing systems.

Many schools that installed telephone switches during the sixties or seventies are now facing a shortage of spare lines around the campus for extra telephone connections, FAX lines, energy control or security lines, and answering machines, as well as computer terminals. Consequently, some portion of faculty or staff are forced to forgo some types of communication services. While colleges can usually add trunk lines of twisted-pair wire to selected spots, this alternative can be expensive. At Grinnell College, for example, a 600-line cable from the switchroom to a renovated academic building 600 feet away cost $17,000. Unlike the newer network technologies discussed later in the chapter, the cabling required for data switches cannot allow for unit-by-unit expansion. If an additional ten lines are needed to a particular location, the labor costs for trenching, conduit installation, interior rewiring, and so on, make the additions prohibitively expensive. Yet, the installation of a new trunk, with several hundred lines, may be unwarranted and financially unjustifiable. The result is that certain locations are forced simply to do without the desired communications line for an indefinite period of time.

At some schools the data switch is beginning to show its age. Grinnell College, for example, has received notification from Micom, Inc., that manufacture of the existing switch, installed in 1983, has been discontinued. Over the next several years, the college will face increasing difficulty in getting parts and service or will need to

---

4. See M. Robbins, *The voice mail reference manual and buyers guide,* Riverdale, N.Y.: Robbins Press, 1989.

consider the purchase of a new switch. While it is possible to purchase a new switch, it is unlikely that Grinnell will do so. Alternative modes of connection are more cost effective, provide greater bandwidth and higher speed, allow more flexible resource sharing, and permit easier methods for unit expansion.

Despite an increasing trend toward newer network technologies, many small private colleges have a substantial investment in the hundreds of connections provided via the data switch. The simplicity of the data switch model, its general reliability, and its low cost of maintenance, contribute to its endurance. Colleges that have not experienced a dramatic increase in requests for communications lines, that make only modest use of computers, or that operate under severe budget constraints may find that it will be many years before data switch technology is finally abandoned. On the other hand, schools that have experienced significant growth in computer use during the past few years and that can afford the initial investment of moving to a newer technology, are likely to phase out their data switches if they haven't already done so.

Microcomputers and Distributed Computing

Many colleges began the 1980s with a sprinkling of stand-alone microcomputers and a variety of other machines (such as DEC PDP/11 minicomputers) scattered around such departments as mathematics, education, and psychology. By the end of the 1980s a very different situation had evolved. By 1990, the average liberal arts college owned more than a hundred and fifty microcomputers and— at least among the wealthier colleges—student ownership of microcomputers exceeded thirty percent and ranged as high as eighty percent. Nearly half of those schools actively supported personal computer ownership by opening a facility to resell microcomputers to students, faculty, and staff.

The proliferation of personal computers brought the term *distributed computing* into the vocabulary of liberal arts college computing environments. In its most basic sense, distributed computing simply means that computations occur on a number of different processors, rather than on a single processor. More specifically, it refers to the *distribution* of processors across a campus (or other type of organization) rather than the *concentration* of processors in a single location, that is, a computer center.

The term distributed computing has come to acquire other, more complex meanings within different contexts. In some instances, for example, it refers to the decomposition of a single computing job into several components, each of which is run (in parallel) on its own processor. "Parallel distributed computing" requires a sophisticated means of connecting processors to one another in a high speed network. This is very different from the simple placement of a number of microcomputers around a campus, each with its own printing, storage, and other resources.

The first experiments in distributed computing at liberal arts colleges involved the acquisition of stand-alone microcomputers for a handful of faculty and administrative offices. Interestingly, the purchase, installation, maintenance, and support of these machines often fell outside the purview of the traditional computer center. Faculty and staff at most colleges were extremely pleased with their microcomputers and the quality and diversity of microcomputer software. This new form of computing was especially well received by faculty in foreign languages, arts, humanities, and other areas that were traditionally untouched by (and sometimes hostile towards) mainframe computing. The addition of stand-alone microcomputers allowed colleges to increase their overall computing power at a much lower cost than was possible by upgrading a centralized machine. There were, however, drawbacks as well as advantages to microcomputing.

From the perspective of many users, the installation of microcomputer software is difficult and time consuming. The user is presented with a variety of choices pertaining to graphics cards, communication ports, and other configuration details. Many users do not have the expertise to answer these questions or the inclination to learn about file systems, communications protocols, diagnostic routines, and other technical tidbits required for the "care and feeding" of a personal computer. Surveys indicate that most users don't back up their data files, are oblivious to the concept of archiving, and frequently experience panic when their data suddenly vanish from the screen or diskette. While a user typically enjoys the freedom of making software choices (such as a word processing program), that user may find that a colleague with whom he or she hoped to collaborate has made a different choice. File conversions, frustration, and flights to computer center experts soon follow.

Grinnell College tried to avoid placing stand-alone microcomputers for a number of reasons:

- The time needed to manage software for stand-alone microcomputers in terms of the update cycle

- The potential for software theft by a few campus users

- The difficulty of assisting users of unconnected systems over the telephone

- The difficulty of providing laser printing in a convenient yet economical manner

- The time needed to assist users with file transfers across different types of unconnected microcomputers

Within a few years of the introduction of microcomputers to liberal arts college campuses, the shortcomings became apparent. To circumvent some of the problems, microcomputers were wired to central computers and pressed into duty as "intelligent terminals." By redefining the personal computer as a part-time terminal, schools were able to combine some of the benefits of central computing with the benefits of distributed computing. Users could run programs and access files on the central machine with all the confidence and security of the traditional timesharing environment, but they could also download data to a microcomputer where it could be fed into word processors, spreadsheets, statistical packages, and other microcomputer productivity software. The hardwired connections between microcomputers and central machines also allowed for electronic mail, a limited amount of resource sharing, and other benefits, while still preserving much of the freedom of working with a personal computer.

The hardwire, terminal emulation approach to microcomputer–mainframe connectivity solves some of the problems associated with distributed computing but it falls short in some other areas, particularly in terms of communication speed, unit expansion, and resource sharing among users at remote locations from the computer center, among others. The next phase in campus computing strategies, therefore, was to combine the strong points of central and distributed computing by means of a high speed, flexible local area network.

The Local Area Network and Distributed Computing

In order to reduce the magnitude of problems engendered by stand-alone microcomputers, many colleges have connected small clusters of microcomputers through local area networks (LANs). Typically these systems allow for print serving and file transfer within the LAN. In some cases special purpose servers also allow for file serving, mail serving, application serving, and centralized data storage and management. In many cases, LANs have helped to solve nearly all of the problems that have resulted from the proliferation of stand-alone microcomputers or microcomputers that have been hardwired to a mainframe. Some LANs also allow such problems as software theft, data security, and viruses to be addressed because of the control that the LAN administrator can exercise over program images.

By 1990, more than half of all liberal arts colleges had either installed or planned the installation of at least one LAN. Installed LANs range from pure microcomputer environments, such as AppleTalk for Macintoshes, or token-ring for IBM PCs and clones, to a variety of more sophisticated technologies for linking minicomputers, microcomputers, workstations, and a wide variety of peripheral resources to one another.[5] The most common type of LAN in 1989 was the AppleTalk network, perhaps because of its low cost and ease of installation.

---

5. The most common LANs for PC compatibles are Novell NetWare, IBM Token-Ring, AT&T StarLAN, Corvus, 3Com, and Banyan Vines. The most common LANs for Macintosh computers are AppleTalk over LocalTalk, AppleTalk over PhoneNET, and TOPS.

Despite the trend towards total connectivity, many liberal arts colleges have LANs that do not communicate with the central computing systems on campus. Nearly half of the CLAC schools surveyed in 1989 reported that their LANs had no connection to the central computers or any campus backbone network. In most cases such LANs are confined to one building or two adjacent buildings. Although these LANs are not connected to either a campus backbone or a central computer system, some of the microcomputers that constitute the LAN have terminal emulation capability and a second (hardwired) connection to either a modem or a data switch. In these cases, integration between the microcomputers in the LAN and the campus-wide facilities is generally limited to terminal emulation and file transfer.

Why would a college install LANs that are not connected to the rest of the computing equipment on campus? There are at least two reasons. First, there are technical difficulties in getting a particular LAN protocol to communicate with another dissimilar protocol. This has been a major stumbling block to campus-wide networking and will be discussed in some detail presently. Second, there are circumstances under which it is desirable to limit or prevent communication between a particular set of users and other campus computer systems.

Grinnell has operated an AppleShare network for several years. When the college received the machines as a grant from Apple, a great deal of consideration was given to the intended functions of the LAN and how those functions might best be served. In the end, it was decided to take advantage of the special features of the Macintosh for curricular applications such as the music department's use of the Mac for teaching the rudiments of ear training, composition, and so on—software that cannot be offered on a minicomputer cluster. Faculty in chemistry and sociology were also enticed to tie the use of this equipment into some of their courses. A major concern of the faculty in these departments was freedom of access for students with computer-related assignments. It was decided jointly that the only way to ensure access to the students needing the special Mac–only software was to discourage other uses.

Grinnell has tried schemes to allocate priorities in computer use to specific functions and, for the most part, feels that the self-policing component of these schemes does not work well in practice. Accordingly, the Macintoshes were not connected to the rest of the campus computing system in any way, and no word processing software was installed on the Macintosh server. The official policy was to encourage word processing in other computer areas.

By and large the Mac laboratory has been a success. A wide variety of curricularly related software is used in association with specific classes taught at the college, and faculty interest in this sort of utilization of computers has increased. But the tradeoffs are significant. Because of the association between these machines and specific class assignments, the demand for a seat at one of the networked Macs is extremely variable. For two or three days after a computer-related class assignment the lab is jammed, but for long intervening periods the lab is empty and there are frequent complaints about "wasted space," "no software," "no access to the VAX," and so on.

There are other problems associated with LANs. First, there is the obvious issue of cost. The up-front cost of conduit and cable installation, network interface cards, and software can be significant, even when such work will result in lower expenditures over the long term. In some cases up-front networking costs have been covered, or partially covered, by hardware vendors who see the development of a network as an impetus for the college to purchase more of their computing equipment. During the 1980s, many liberal arts colleges received substantial grants to underwrite the cost of designing and implementing everything from small LANs to campus-wide networks. The long-term, hidden costs of networking, such as maintenance, monitoring, repairs, and upgrades, however, were generally overlooked by vendor or foundation grants, and many colleges entered the 1990s with a network infrastructure that demanded a good deal of attention and new budgeting. The availability of grant funding for networking, moreover, all but vanished as the novelty of campus networks waned.

Second, there is the sheer complexity of the LAN operating software, which may present a problem to small colleges that are already struggling to support multiple operating systems such as VMS, VM, Primos, MPE, or UNIX on their minicomputers and DOS, MacOS, or OS/2 on their microcomputers. While the complexity of network operating systems varies (for example, AppleShare versus NetWare), they are, in general, nearly as complicated as traditional multiuser operating systems and can require a substantial amount of a system manager's time for maintenance and trouble-shooting.

Even when technical issues have been set aside or solved, a number of political and policy questions remain on campus. Who pays for the network installation—the department using the network or the computer center? Who provides the long-term financial and technical support? If the academic or administrative users pay, do they get to hire their own support staff? Will political jealousies in the academic departments be exacerbated by the installation of a network system in just one department? Who gets to use the network—department members only, appropriate majors, or members of the college at large? Colleges have taken a variety of approaches in answering these questions. It appears that there is no best solution even among the relatively homogeneous group of private liberal arts colleges. Instead, local tradition and the character of the departments involved in networking have determined each college's response to these questions.

On some campuses the smaller LANs are managed by faculty or others not on the computer center staff. The manager may be responsible for system setup, software installation, data integrity, user support, and training. In many cases this arrangement works well, since the manager of the system knows the users and their needs very well and is well acquainted with the capabilities of the network. But this arrangement can also cause problems. When the faculty LAN expert goes on sabbatical, who is left with knowledge about the day-to-day operations of the department LAN? In many cases neither other faculty nor computer center staff have enough experience with the LAN to keep it running reliably. A campus that has become accustomed to having a reliable LAN for such things as e-mail, printing, and file serving, will experience a severe shock if the network is unavailable for an extended period of time. Anecdotal stories abound of crisis situations that have resulted from network expertise being concentrated in a single person who suddenly leaves the institution.

Workstations and Distributed Computing

At many research-oriented universities, the terms *networking* and *distributed computing* bring to mind the deployment of UNIX-based workstations and minicomputers. In the mid- and late-eighties some smaller colleges also began to purchase small numbers of work-stations to assist in the teaching of mathematics, computer science, physics, and so on. In 1989 nearly three quarters of the CLAC colleges, for example, reported having at least one UNIX workstation on campus and several of these schools had acquired ten, twenty, or more such machines. The systems represented a variety of offerings from vendors including Sun, Hewlett-Packard, Apollo, DEC, NeXT, and IBM, among others. In most cases these machines are configured in a high-speed, Ethernet LAN.

Typically, these systems offer a very high level of connectivity, including network access to software applications and printers, remote login (terminal emulation to other workstations or servers), distributed data storage, and even remote procedure calls on an as-needed basis. The systems usually communicate via TCP/IP, NCS, RPC or proprietary protocols such as DECnet. These networks allow CPU power and output bandwidth to be distributed, while disks, printers, and other resources can be shared and administered centrally. Cost and staff savings are realized thereby.

At most schools these machines are used heavily and with great success. They combine the advantages of a personal computer with the processing power of a mainframe. The use of large, bit-mapped displays and multitasking software allows students to undertake complex tasks, such as creating and debugging programs, on a system that is friendlier than the usual timesharing system. At the same time such systems relieve much of the load placed on central computing systems. In addition, workstations are in demand for use in a variety of classes aside from traditional programming classes. They are often used to run packages for symbolic manipulation, matrix algebra, statistics, group theory, and so on, and workstations are now beginning to be employed in non-science departments for applications in areas such as music composition and synthesis, multimedia presentation in the arts, theater design, and so forth.

What are the costs of this form of distributed computing? Can small colleges afford to manage, maintain, and upgrade these systems? There are at least three important issues small colleges must face if they intend to acquire UNIX workstations: purchase costs, the availability of software, and staff support and maintenance. Although workstation technology has started to filter into the liberal arts environment, many colleges are not yet in a position to answer these questions. The costs of workstations are dropping very rapidly—but these systems are still quite expensive, typically twice as expensive as middle-of-the-road microcomputers ($5000 versus $2500 each). Software and maintenance are also considerably more expensive as well. In most cases the file servers for these systems are about as expensive to maintain as a minicomputer, while the workstations themselves generally don't lend themselves to self-servicing in the same way microcomputers do. For example, there is often no second source for parts.

Though the variety of software available for these systems is quite good in the technical areas, many popular microcomputer packages are not available, or cost up to four times more than the microcomputer version. Friendly interfaces, integrated software packages, format transfer protocols, and so on, are rapidly being developed for UNIX workstations, but the overall software environment is still leaner and less hospitable than that of the microcomputer environment.

A networked UNIX system is also difficult and expensive to maintain. In some cases experienced UNIX system managers are difficult to find or train. The overall complexity of the system represents a significant obstacle to a small college struggling to maintain central systems, Macintoshes, PC compatibles, and small LANs. The difficulties of getting UNIX workstations to interact effectively with other non–UNIX machines are not trivial. At Grinnell, for example, one full time staff member is needed to maintain a network of fifty workstations and three servers.

These machines seem to have a short "half-life" of usability. For example, Grinnell's Sun 3/50s were purchased in 1987. In 1989 Sun decided to base their product line on SPARC processors rather than the Motorola processor that had been the company's mainstay. As Sun brings out a new version of its operating system new computers will be incompatible with the older Motorola–based Sun computers purchased by Grinnell and other colleges. Thus, the long-term prospects for the Sun systems are uncertain, and Grinnell College will face the hefty costs of a complete change in processors much sooner than originally anticipated. Similar problems face schools that have purchased Apollo, DEC, and IBM workstations as well, since these vendors have also rolled out new product lines that are only partially compatible with their older model lines.

Most of the administrative and political issues raised with regard to microcomputer LANs apply here too. For instance, at Grinnell, faculty and staff are grappling with questions about computing approaches in statistics classes. Should the college requirements in statistics be taught using workstations or should they remain on timesharing hosts? Certainly the excellent graphics of workstations could help make statistics instruction easier and more interesting, but is the college in a position to acquire and deploy workstations to every department that currently teaches statistics? If not, then how does the college decide to allocate scarce resources and how does it justify supporting one statistics course with advanced workstations while another struggles along with character-based terminals linked to a timesharing computer?

What should small colleges that seek workstation-level capabilities do? Does the purchase of UNIX based systems make sense? In cases where the needed software is available only on a workstation, such purchases may be justified. However, in many cases, high-end microcomputers may be an acceptable, cost-effective alternative. The required software may now be available for microcomputers. The power-to-cost ratio of microcomputers is increasing each year. Microcomputer displays are increasing in resolution. Small schools that are considering the acquisition of UNIX workstations as a supplement or an alternative to centralized computing need to address each of the three issues mentioned; in particular they should perform a careful study of long-term costs comparing microcomputer to workstation solutions.

The Future of Academic Computing: High-Speed, Campus-wide Networking

Computing center staff on many campuses feel that the future of academic computing, and the solution to many of the problems mentioned, is a high-speed, campus-wide network—a backbone connecting all academic and administrative buildings. The main goal of many colleges' efforts to install a campus backbone is to combine the connectivity features of the switched central computer facility, the software options and low cost of the microcomputer, and the graphics and power of the UNIX workstation. While this approach has a great deal of appeal, is it possible? What are the costs that should be considered before embarking on this ambitious path?

The most difficult technical questions and issues concern connectivity between different types of LANs and hardware from different vendors. Among the questions that many small colleges have already faced are these: Which protocols facilitate LAN interconnections? Will other protocols be allowed on the backbone as well? How will electronic communication be provided both on campus and to other campuses? The task of simply providing a workable e-mail system, so easily answered with terminals and a minicomputer, is very difficult on campuses with a mixture of LANs.

Among the CLAC colleges, more than sixty percent had connected at least two buildings on a high-speed campus backbone by the summer of 1989. In the majority of cases the backbone is an Ethernet using fiber optic cable as the physical medium. Most of these schools provide connections between microcomputer LANs and the campus backbone directly, via a high-speed bridge, or through a lower-speed gateway or other protocol converter. Often, multiple protocols are run on the backbone simultaneously. However, since many of these schools connect the backbone to DEC systems, DECnet is the most frequently used protocol in this environment.

Typically, microcomputer LANs with low-speed gateways to a campus backbone allow for print serving, e-mail, and file transfer, both within the LAN and across the backbone to central systems. They also enable terminal emulation across the backbone and, in some cases, application serving and central data storage within the LAN. While AppleTalk networks connected to DECnet/Ethernet backbones are widespread among liberal arts colleges, there is a substantial number of IBM Token Ring networks and a rapidly growing number of low-cost microcomputer networks based on third-party software from companies such as Novell and Banyan.

For a price, there are technical solutions to the problems posed when different protocols run on the microcomputer LAN and the campus backbone. Unfortunately, gateways and protocol-interchange programs are sometimes unreliable, and although most systems can now communicate with one another, it should be recognized that managing multiple protocols is still a formidable task.

An alternative solution is to run a single protocol or a single suite of protocols across the backbone and all LANs. Some colleges have set up the backbone in a manner that allows microcomputers to sit directly on the campus network, or on a subnet with a high-speed bridge to the backbone. In these cases protocol conversion is not necessary. The goal of these systems is to allow application serving, print serving, central data storage, e-mail, file transfer, and terminal service across the entire campus network. Colleges have implemented a number of protocols with these functions in mind, including DEC's PCSA, Banyan's Vines, Novell's NetWare, 3Com (either 3+Share or 3+Open), Alisa Systems' AlisaShare, and various flavors of NFS and TCP/IP. In some cases the central computer systems run processes that perform a gateway function and thereby allow host-to-micro communication.[6] It should be noted, however, that this solution involves some of the most technically demanding software. A small school starting down this path will probably require at least one full-time staff member to monitor and manage the network system software.

Grinnell found out just how expensive it is to connect PCs, Macs, SUNs, and VAXes with a high level of transparency. Without going into an extended technical discussion, let's consider a few of the numerous small hurdles that were encountered, obstacles that stand

6. Examples are AlisaShare on a VAX to allow AppleTalk communication, NetWare/VMS to allow IPX communication, DEC's IPX Gateway, and various TCP/IP host-based products.

a little outside the usual stream of technical problems that most computer managers expect—such as software compatibility with the network. For example, let us consider just the DOS–based PC issues.

First, early in the planning process it became apparent that the net-connected PCs should be high-end, relatively powerful units. Two megabytes of memory per machine were required as a minimum. Some of the network operating system (NOS) loads into high memory and allows the DOS applications to use more of the 640K of conventional memory. A memory manager for each PC was purchased to allow pieces of the NOS to be installed where they were needed. It was decided that the DOS front-end, in combination with arcane NOS commands, was just too unfriendly for most users, so a menu system was purchased for each machine. The terminal emulation package that comes with the network is character based rather than graphics based; a third party program was purchased to enhance the machines in that regard. The college is still seeking third-party packages that will assist its attempts to keep commercial software from being copied from the network in order to help regulate the numbers and types of users of specific pieces of application software, and its attempts to serve microcomputer users from remote locations. The compatibility of the NOS with specialized PC peripherals (CD-ROM, data tablets, and so on) remains largely untested. The planners have confidence that the network will work well with the latest version of Microsoft Windows and OS/2 but have yet to validate this assumption. It is planned that departmental secretaries can be trained to assist in the management of shared areas, passwords, quotas, and access, but at the present they are still working on NOS basics. The network environment is shaping up well, but implementation has been much more difficult and expensive than expected back in the planning stages.

Does it make sense to try to connect UNIX workstations to the campus backbone? Certainly many schools are interested in trying to solve some of their computing problems by attempting to do so. Such connections might allow staff in the computer center to perform such system management tasks as account creation, network monitoring, and system backup, on a remotely located UNIX-based LAN. In addition, the campus backbone allows workstations to be distributed to remote sites on campus. For example, the Grinnell Mathematics

Assistance Center, which is located in an administrative building on campus, uses a diskless Sun workstation connected to the MathLAN network over the campus backbone. This type of distributed computing will prove to be of increasing value over the next few years, as more computing is done in the *client-server* mode.

The implementation of UNIX workstations on the backbone is not without its problems, however. For example, schools such as Grinnell that utilize central VAX systems often have a predisposition to use the DECnet protocol over the backbone. Since most UNIX workstations use the TCP/IP protocol, any efficiencies to be gained by connecting workstations to the backbone must be balanced against the real costs of managing the interface itself. At Grinnell both TCP/IP and DECnet protocols are used with some degree of success. In 1987 a Sun–engineered DECnet emulator and terminal emulator were installed to handle the file transfer and terminal emulation demands. These emulators use the proprietary CTERM protocol of DEC to transmit data packets. In 1989, when the computer center upgraded the operating system of the VAXes to VMS 5.1, this software began to generate errors during terminal emulation. The origin of the errors was tracked to a change in DEC's use of the CTERM protocol with the new version of the operating system. Either for technical reasons or because of a lack of interest, Sun has not (as of this writing) updated the emulator to eliminate this problem. A TCP/IP product for the VAXes was purchased in 1989 in order again to allow the SUN workstations to log in to the college VAXCluster as "VT100s." This appears to be working satisfactorily. However, a price is paid for this functionality inasmuch as computer services are now responsible for providing expertise in yet another protocol.

What level of connectivity should be sought between the workstations and the central systems on campus? Here too there is no pat answer. Total connectivity at the highest level might not be desirable. At the time of this writing, Grinnell is considering the purchase of a product that would increase the functionality of the SUNs as VAX terminals (that is, moving from the VT100 to the VT340 level). Certainly it would be nice to have those packages that currently run only on the VAXes (for example, Minitab) to be able to generate high-level graphics on the SUNs as needed. But what would this capability do to the utilization of the MathLAN workstations? Would they become clogged by VAX users who really could go elsewhere to do their computing? Would students interested in packages that run only on the SUNs be crowded out? These are specific questions that apply to Grinnell College alone. But they are typical of a class of questions that is of general concern—what functions should be allowed on special purpose LANs when they connect to the campus network?

Let us reconsider the advantages that a high-speed network offers to those who use terminals. Terminal servers on the net offer low-speed connections (up to 19,200 bits per second) with greater reliability and more features (for example, more intelligent load balancing of multiple hosts) than most data-switch connections. In sites where there are concentrations of terminals, the network/terminal server combination can be cheaper than the data switch. Grinnell College avoids the expense of placing more telephone trunk lines by reallocating twisted-pair lines when terminal servers are deployed. During the next few years a growing number of colleges will likely phase out their data switches or replace older, large switches with smaller switches to serve those locations that cannot access the high-speed connection.

Some important questions still remain in this area of terminal connections, however. Will colleges be able to provide the secure networked connections that administrators need, given that network economics favor shared data paths for all users? Currently, more than two-thirds of all liberal arts colleges have absolutely no connections between their academic and administrative systems. What are the costs of maintaining such a division at schools with high-speed backbones? Should small colleges run separate fiber lines for academic and administrative users despite the intermixing of faculty and administrative staff within buildings? Can bridges be relied on to provide security where the fiber is shared, or do we need to look to data encryption? What are the costs of encryption, both financially and in terms of CPU overhead for retranslation? The issues surrounding network security remain incompletely addressed and largely unresolved. For the most part, the major research institutions are still feeling their way toward solutions. It may be quite some time before clear-cut, economically feasible solutions are available for smaller schools.

There are a number of questions about the long-term future and physical bases of campus networking. Large research-oriented universities are just now devising strategies for the articulation of networks and emerging technologies such as fiber distributed data interface (FDDI), campus-wide video, and integrated services digital network (ISDN). Computer center directors wonder if they will be able to afford the expertise needed to manage and maintain emerging voice, data, and video networks. The solutions that eventually emerge at large universities or multi-campus community colleges, however, are not likely to scale well to the needs, goals, and resources, of small liberal arts colleges.

Finally, aside from the technical issues involved in inter-networking, there are other important questions that must be answered in the area of network policy and administration. Who decides which campus departments will receive networking and what type of network will be installed?[7] How restrictive should departmental networks be in terms of the choice of software applications, users permitted on the network, and quotas and access privileges?

The Future of Academic Computing: National and International Networking

In addition to seeing greatly increased on-campus networking, most computer center staffs see national and regional networking as increasing in importance. There are a number of international and national forces contributing to this perception. First, there is an increasing recognition that the economic health of the United States is influenced by changes occurring in other parts of the world; there is the westernization of eastern Europe, the movement of western Europe toward a unified economic and political system, the ever-increasing economic strength of Japan, and so on. Many policy makers on college and university campuses feel that it is crucial that their graduates be able to communicate internationally. In addition,

---

7. For a useful discussion, see G. Ricart, Slowing the big bang of networking, *Academic Computing*, 1989, pp. 28–29, 53–55.

the nation's commitment to a number of "big science" projects also influences our sense of the importance of campus-to-campus communications. The Human Genome project, the Superconducting Supercollider project, and other nationally funded projects require the collaboration of large numbers of scientists and students on a national basis. This collaboration will largely occur over computer networks via campus-to-campus remote logins, electronic mail, file transfers, and database and bulletin board interactions. One other driving factor should be mentioned here—the high and ever-increasing cost of journal subscriptions, library books, and classroom textbooks. In an effort to control costs while providing good access to a wide variety of materials many librarians, faculty, and campus administrators are pinning their hopes on on-demand electronic publishing, electronic distribution of scholarly papers, and increased sharing of the collections of major research universities. These technologies all rely upon increased inter-campus networking.

The CLAC schools are well connected to the national networks—nearly all of the schools are connected to either BITNET or the Internet.[8] Nationally, about 25 percent of small liberal arts colleges are connected to BITNET, while 10 to 12 percent are connected to the Internet. These numbers are likely to increase rapidly in the next few years. For the CLAC schools the national networking debate has turned to the question of BITNET versus the Internet. Which network makes better sense for a small school? Are both going to be needed in the future? Grinnell is struggling with these questions; it is currently on BITNET but not yet on the Internet. It has found the benefits of BITNET to be:

- Reliable e-mail communication with peer institutions

- Reliable file transfer to other schools

- Good access to a variety of national discussion
  groups and other network resources

---

8. As of June 1991, nineteen CLAC schools (approximately 34 percent of the membership) had established Internet connections. Many CLAC schools and other liberal arts colleges have pursued Internet connections with grant support from the National Science Foundation.

- Easy access for students, faculty, and staff

- Inexpensive membership charge

- The hardware needed to connect into it is relatively inexpensive given that a timesharing system is already in place on campus

- Relatively inexpensive line charges

- Relatively inexpensive software

- Minimal security considerations

- A relatively moderate CPU load on the campus timesharing system

Overall, Grinnell got onto BITNET for about $8,000 for hardware and software. Recurring charges are about $9,000 yearly (for membership fees, hardware and software maintenance, and line charges).

Grinnell is very interested in obtaining an Internet connection as well because it sees the Internet to be of increasing importance to small schools in the future. Currently, the Internet offers several services not available over BITNET. These services include remote login capability to national supercomputers, databases, and library catalogs. Other resources may eventually be available over the Internet but not BITNET. In addition, the Internet connects to more systems nationally and internationally than does BITNET, and there is greater variety in those sites (for example, government and commercial sites). The Internet may pose a number of problems to a small school though, so Grinnell is proceeding slowly. There are concerns that the Internet may:

- Be relatively less user friendly than BITNET

- Not allow easy interactive messaging

- Not allow easy sender-initiated file transfer

- Be more expensive than BITNET in terms of hardware, software, membership, and line charges

- Require support of TCP/IP on college microcomputers

- Pose a greater security risk to campus computing
  systems

- Be more technically demanding to manage than
  BITNET

- Not form a clean interface with existing campus
  mail systems

- Become a major load on existing timesharing CPUs

- Become a significant load on the campus backbone

Overall it is believed that the recurring costs of Internet access would be about twice those of participating in BITNET.

Many peer institutions are deliberating upon these same issues. There is no easy resolution that can be presented at this time since there are many shifting cost factors. Each institution will need to prepare its own cost-benefit matrix in order to make a decision. Overall, however, I believe that some form of national network access will be crucial by mid-decade for most small schools.

Conclusion

The computing history of small colleges and universities reveals that in the space of only ten years, a variety of forces have acted to produce heterogeneous and complex computing environments at most schools. In this environment the diversity and sophistication of tools for users has increased tremendously. When all systems are working well, the convenience of computing still astonishes many faculty and staff. The darker side of distributed computing and system diversity is also showing up—especially in terms of hardware and software costs, staff size, and training.

Incremental networking during a period of changing network technology has led to the adoption of a variety of new systems that utilize different operating systems, different network protocols, different physical distribution media, and different management strategies. At the same time, large investments lead many colleges to maintain older technologies such as data switches, even when such new technologies as terminal servers on Ethernet have been shown to be more cost-effective in the long run.

The need for more diverse and sophisticated software, which is often platform specific, has led to the proliferation of a growing mixture of PC compatibles, Macintoshes, UNIX workstations, and minicomputers from at least half a dozen different vendors. Since support costs are as much related to diversity in equipment as they are to the sheer number of devices, these costs have skyrocketed.

In the case of microcomputer LANs and workstations, good connectivity has been provided—within each LAN. While each LAN provides reasonably good connectivity for a small cluster of machines within a single building, the sharing of data, printers, and file servers across LANs on a campus-wide basis has remained a problem. The issues of connecting LANs to other LANs across campus haven't been resolved at most small schools.

The networking solutions that have emerged and will continue to emerge at research universities and community college systems do not scale well to the small liberal arts college environment. The lesson to be learned from this is that we must pursue our own initiatives, take our own risks, and find our own solutions. Although the discussion in this chapter may raise more questions than it answers, I hope it will help network planners identify critical issues to be considered. It should also help them place their own concerns into the context of networking experiences at schools that are similar in size, resources, and institutional goals.

Chapter 8

Network Technology: Designing and Building the Infrastructure

Thomas F. Moberg
Kenyon College

Thomas F. Moberg is vice-president for information and computing services at Kenyon College in Gambier, Ohio. His duties include oversight of all information technologies, including academic computing, administrative computing, campus networking, information systems, office automation, and library automation. In addition, Dr. Moberg participates in general college management through service on the president's Senior Staff, and is involved in planning activities related to the telephone system and printing and audio-visual services.

Dr. Moberg holds a Ph.D. in mathematical statistics from the University of Iowa. Between 1975 and 1987, he served as director of academic computing and resident statistician at Grinnell College. He has taught mathematics at the University of Minnesota in Duluth and statistics at Grinnell College.

Dr. Moberg has been a member of the EDUCOM Council Membership committee, a board member of the Consortium for Computing in Small Colleges, a member of an ACM SIGUCCS Peer Review Team, Statistics Series editor for CONDUIT, and president of the Iowa section of the American Statistical Association.

The transmission of information—followed, one hopes, by the conversion of that information into knowledge and wisdom—is a fundamental component of the liberal arts college mission. An electronic network that links faculty, students, and staff to each other and to information resources both on and off campus is rapidly becoming a necessity. Accordingly, virtually every liberal arts college is now in the process, sometimes only at an embryonic level, of developing its own unique information technology network. An information technology network is not only a collection of electronic devices and conduits for transmitting information; it is also a set of ideas and goals that provides a unifying concept for campus-wide integration of resources and services. Networks are like biological organisms that evolve rapidly into increasingly complex, unique, and ever-expanding forms.

In the previous chapter, William Francis outlined much of the history and major policy issues involved in campus-wide networking at liberal arts colleges. In this chapter, I address some of the more technical and pragmatic issues involved in designing and building networks. In particular, I will emphasize campus-wide networks that reach all places in which faculty, staff, and students carry on their academic work. The first section contains a discussion of the unique nature of liberal arts colleges and the context in which networks are developing in such institutions. The next two sections raise some of the issues related to the design and construction of networks. Finally, a few considerations about the management of networks in small colleges are noted. The appendix to this chapter contains examples of technical specifications related to building networks that may be useful to colleges that have yet to develop such standards of their own.

Liberal Arts Colleges and the Impact of Information Technology

Other chapters in this volume describe the major trends in information technology that are affecting liberal arts colleges today. Among these are rapid changes in technology that cause obsolescence of equipment; convergence of information technologies (computing, printing, FAX, library automation, audio/video resources, telecommunications); distributed computing; development of local, regional, national, and international networks. Coupled with these technology trends, or sometimes as consequences of them, are other changes in the college environment. For example, faculty, staff, and students are asking for more services of all kinds, including those related to information technologies. The needs and activities of academic and administrative computer users are blending as both groups make wide use of word processing, electronic communications, and databases. A campus-wide perspective on computing services requires an increased need for campus-wide planning and coordination. Finally, there is a growing recognition among college administrators of the importance of information as a strategic resource. All these forces are pushing colleges to develop comprehensive information technology strategies.

As discussed in the previous chapter, liberal arts colleges have their own unique characters and cultures, but they also have many inherent similarities, particularly in the information technology area. Most colleges provide computing resources to the campus with one or more timesharing minicomputers and a variety of microcomputers arranged in classroom or laboratory settings. On many campuses, academic computing needs have been centered around departmental concerns, resulting in the development of small local area networks (LANs), the main purpose of which is to support a particular department, program, or physical space. A few colleges have collections of high-end workstations connected together in LANs. Small colleges in the process of implementing high-speed, campus-wide networks, often continue to rely on the old wiring of their relatively primitive telephone systems for terminal connectivity because that is the only available cable plant. Most liberal arts colleges have started some form of library automation program and view it as a major component in their information technology future.

In the computing arena, the basic resource allocation strategy at small colleges is usually to concentrate scarce financial and staff resources on a minimum number of approaches so that adequate support can be provided. The heavy competition for resources generally dictates a limited number of network strategies, the imposition of standards, and an imperative to find comprehensive, campus-wide solutions to problems. The key questions that must be asked during resource allocation discussions are *How will this option improve undergraduate instruction?* and *What are the long-term implications for support and maintenance?* Diversity, usually a highly desirable characteristic of the college environment, is not always a desideratum in computing.

Although the volume of computing equipment at small colleges has grown dramatically over the past fifteen years, many curricular, cultural, and economic barriers have impaired the development of computing and networking. In truth, computing has not enhanced undergraduate instruction as much as it could or should. For example, at most small colleges the majority of computer use is limited to basic utilities such as electronic mail, word processing, and spreadsheet operation.[1]

The resources needed for technological developments have generally been inadequate at small colleges, probably because, unlike universities, most colleges have not had a curricular justification for building high-speed networks, acquiring large numbers of high-end workstations, or developing comprehensive delivery systems for audio-video instructional materials. The technology development dilemma is often a circular one. Resources for technology are not committed because the curriculum doesn't require the resources, but the curriculum can't change to use technology until the technology is available.

One of the obvious barriers to more effective use of computing in small colleges has been the lack of adequate networking capability and connectivity to central computing resources. Few colleges have had resident staff members with network expertise who could lead major implementation efforts. At this point, most faculty and staff don't feel a need for networks with blazing speeds, but they do need reliable, predictable connectivity to shared resources. Most colleges have now realized they need some type of campus-wide information technology network that provides full access to information resources, both on and off campus, to all areas where faculty, students, and staff work.

Information Technology Networks

The information technology network is increasingly viewed as a fundamental component of a college's infrastructure or utility system. The notion of a network, however, may be interpreted on several levels. There is the *physical entity,* composed of fiber and copper cabling, communication devices, and computing equipment. To

---

1. See chapters 10 and 11 for discussions of how software packages are actually
   used in liberal arts colleges.

control and manage the electronic information flow over the physical network, there are *software tools* such as DECnet and TCP/IP. The resources available to network users, such as computers, printers, and modems, are the dimension of the network called *services*. And at the highest level, the network is a *concept* that gives the institution a focus for planning, budgeting, and managing related information resources. In other words, the network provides both electronic and administrative linkages to create an institutional coherence that has not previously existed.

Some type of physical networking has been under development in most liberal arts colleges since timesharing minicomputers were introduced in the 1970s. The most common mode of networking is still just simple connectivity between asynchronous terminal devices and timesharing computers.

Many, perhaps most, small colleges use some portion of the college telephone system to provide low-speed, cross-campus connectivity for terminal devices. A whole spectrum of configurations exist. Some institutions rent spare cable pairs to use for direct or multiplexed connections between asynchronous devices and central computers. Another common approach is to use some variety of data-over-voice technology coupled with a voice/data switch to provide terminal connectivity. It is even possible to hire the telephone company to handle all details of data and voice communication over an integrated Centrex system.

On many campuses, there are serious difficulties to using the existing telephone plant for even low-speed terminal connections. One of the major drawbacks to piggy-backing data communications on the telephone system is that the telephone cable plant is often inadequate in size, reliability, or signal carrying capability. Over the years, computer center staff members at many colleges have spent huge amounts of time trying to establish workable terminal connections over old twisted-pair telephone wiring that was never designed to support data communications. Consequently, most colleges decide to install some cabling of their own.

Often the first stage of installing a campus network, driven by the frustration of trying unsuccessfully to use existing telephone cabling, is the installation of new twisted-pair copper cable as home runs from wall jacks to satellite equipment rooms within buildings. Although this type of wiring has often been installed merely to provide low-speed terminal connectivity, it is becoming increasingly easy to incorporate this cabling as an intrinsic part of a high-speed campus network.

Since the early 1980s, colleges have been installing pieces of high speed networks, generally based on Ethernet backbones using standard transmission protocols such as DECnet or TCP/IP. Fiber optic cable has become the medium of choice for the high-bandwidth, high-speed, cross-campus component of Ethernet backbones. Often, coaxial cable is also used as part of the campus backbone within buildings.

For most colleges, network evolution is the most significant (and costly) part of the development of their information technology systems. The network itself comprises the whole gamut of information resources, including sub-networks, large computers, specialized output devices, computer-based laboratory equipment, modem pools, library resources, FAX systems, video and audio resources, and of increasing importance, linkages to off-campus networks. Network services continue to grow in power and complexity, presenting major new management challenges for traditional computer center staffs. Each college tends to develop its own idiosyncratic network from a unique collection of existing hardware devices, data transmission paths, financial and human resources, ideas, opportunities, and goals.

Design Issues and the Importance of a Full Campus Network

Liberal arts colleges find themselves pushed toward increased use of information technologies by curricular and societal trends as well as the desire to provide a high-quality academic environment that will attract students and faculty in a competitive marketplace. There are myriad ways to design appropriate pathways for moving digital packets that represent text, data, graphics, voice, and video information.

Good teaching, close interaction between faculty and students, and strong dependence on information resources are dominant character-istics of undergraduate education in liberal arts colleges. Faculty and students interact in offices, laboratories, classrooms, libraries, lounges, gymnasiums, bookstores, and residential areas. If transmis-sion of information is a key part of the educational process, then it seems obvious that an information technology network should cover the entire campus.

A fundamental tenet of academic computing in many liberal arts colleges is that the institution should provide the computing resources needed by students to carry out their educational tasks. The tradi-tional mode of providing student access to computing has been to construct terminal clusters and microcomputer labs in public areas. These sites give students access to sharable computing resources such as word processing, statistical packages, programming lan-guages, electronic mail, databases, printers and plotters. For many colleges, such clusters will continue to play an important role in the computing environment as both individual and group learning sites. The campus network design obviously must include these areas.

Library automation projects are major driving forces behind campus network development on many campuses.[2] The library is probably changing more rapidly than any other aspect of the liberal arts college environment. Over the next decade, virtually all small college libraries will be automating some aspects of their operations. Further, resource-sharing linkages are developing between libraries at the regional, state, national, and international level as wide area net-works develop. Library applications alone justify the installation of a full network at most small colleges. Any network design should assume that all members of the campus community will want to have access to library resources from all instructional and study areas.

Few colleges have adequate facilities to permit the use of modern instructional technologies in classrooms. Rarely do classrooms have the necessary ready-to-use combination of computing devices and display equipment suitable for using computer-based materials as a regular component of courses. Faculty members almost have to be

---

2. See chapter 12 for further discussion.

electrical engineers to assemble and operate the equipment required
to do simple computer terminal projection in a classroom. Partly
because of this lack of appropriate facilities, few faculty members
have developed teaching styles that incorporate classroom access to
computing. Since audio, video, and computer-related instruction
are becoming increasingly important in undergraduate instruction,
a campus network design should provide for access at every
instructional location.

Laboratories and studios, like classrooms, must be considered
when a campus network is being designed. Providing computing and
network access in laboratories and studios can be difficult. Not only
are there the problems related to network connections and video
display capabilities that affect classroom computing, but college
policies and procedures for purchasing, installing, and maintaining
laboratory and studio equipment may be unclear. Labs and studios
are usually the closely guarded territory of individual departments,
who may want particular services from the academic computing
department but don't want to relinquish control or to share budgets.
It is unusual to find a campus that has a comprehensive, coordinated
plan for developing and administering laboratory and studio computing
applications. Viewing these activities as part of the network development can clarify and unify the process.

Student ownership of personal computers is increasing, even
though mandatory ownership requirements are virtually nonexistent
at liberal arts colleges.[3] The trend toward student ownership has
implications for many aspects of the liberal arts college environment.
Colleges are being challenged to find ways to help students use their
personal machines for creative, productive activities in conjunction
with curricular programs.

One obvious strategy by which a college can integrate student-
owned computers into the overall college computing program is to
provide an interface between personal computers and the college

---

3. Current estimates for student ownership at liberal arts colleges range from 15
   percent to as high as 80 percent. As the price of computers continues to drop and
   the use of general software packages for word processing, electronic mail, and so
   on, continues to grow, the percentage of student-owned machines is likely to
   increase.

network facilities. Many liberal arts colleges stress their residential nature as a key component of their identity. The learning that takes place in student living areas is considered to be as important as that which occurs in structured classroom settings. Students often do a significant portion of their studying in their dormitory rooms and lounges. Thus it will be imperative to consider network access from student residences in designing a full campus network. This type of access will increasingly be seen as not only desirable, but absolutely necessary. For example, in a May 1990 stratified random sample of 133 Kenyon College students, 88 percent said that, if they owned a computer, they would want network access from their dormitory rooms, while 5 percent said they would not, and 7 percent were undecided.

A network design that incorporates student residences may require new cabling for data, voice, and video distribution channels to every room, along with extension of high-speed, cross-campus pathways (that is, the backbone) to all residential buildings. By extending the campus backbone to the student residence areas and by wiring the rooms, it is easy to provide access from each room to the campus network. As they are to faculty and staff, low-speed asynchronous connections are much more important to students at this time than Ethernet speeds. As network traffic increases, however, this is likely to change.

One possible connection strategy for dorm rooms, assuming that appropriate in-building wiring and cross-campus backbones exist, is to provide terminal server ports for each residence room. Terminal servers are now widely available for less than $100 per port, making them very economical. Another approach is to install a small LAN in a dormitory, with some type of connection to a campus backbone. Students with personal computers can then connect to the dormitory LAN and share local resources such as printers and mail and connect to the larger campus network as well.

A strategy being used by some institutions is to tie dormitory network access closely to the telephone system. Students increasingly expect to have telephone access from every dorm room, and colleges, to remain competitive, feel obliged to facilitate that service. If new telephone cable has to be installed, this can obviously be tied to the installation of network cabling. In fact, these could easily be combined in the same system. Telephone companies are happy to sell combined Centrex switching for voice and data using their own cable plant, connected at some point to the rest of the campus network. One advantage of this strategy is that it provides a method for monitoring and controlling the volume of use. A disadvantage of this approach, however, is that mixed voice/data technology is several years behind the technology for data-only networking.

Colleges might find it useful to finance both construction and operating costs for dormitory connections by some value-added billing policy. For example, terminal server ports could be rented to students on a yearly basis, an approach that some students find appealing. In the Kenyon College student poll noted above, 52 percent of the 133 randomly chosen respondents said they would be willing to pay for such a connection, while 24 percent said they would not, and 24 percent were undecided. Another cost-recovery strategy used by some colleges is to sell telephone services to students and use the proceeds to fund computing and network projects.[4]

One major decision point for colleges as they design their networks is whether or not to connect the academic and administrative computing spheres. On a small campus, there are very persuasive arguments for linking the two areas. Anyone familiar with academic politics understands that colleges typically need improved communication between the faculty and the administration. These groups have many similar tasks (such as planning, budget management, personnel decisions, and acquisition of supplies and equipment) and can benefit from the use of shared software tools. While electronic linkages are not the only component of better campus cooperation, they can help significantly.

There are several design issues to consider in the linking of academic and administrative areas. While it isn't absolutely necessary to have the same or identical networks for administrative and academic computing, high compatibility will greatly simplify management, resource sharing, and construction. Colleges with separate academic

---

4. Chapter 9 provides a thorough discussion of an approach to telephone resale and its relationship to data and video networking.

and administrative networks will eventually find it necessary to develop clear policies for cross-network access, have some mechanism for overall coordination of both nets, define and resolve budget issues, and establish ongoing procedures for planning, development, and maintenance.

Linkages between academic and administrative networks must have good security measures. Hardware, software, and management procedures all contribute to the security picture. For example, with the types of Ethernet backbone networks in use at many colleges, security can be provided at the terminal server level (for example, by controlling the service options at each port), at the connection level (by authorizing only certain users to communicate across a bridge between the administrative and academic backbones), and at the machine level (by assigning accounts and passwords only to authorized users).

When a college's information technology network is viewed as one of the college's utilities, it is easy to see relationships to other utilities such as fire detection, security monitoring, and electrical power systems. Each of these areas should be considered when a campus network is designed. For example, cable installations for both fire detection and security monitor systems can be tied to network cabling projects. And while electrical feeder systems don't run over data network cables, it may be possible to carry out joint construction tasks such as using common trenches for both electrical feed lines and fiber optic cables for data. The college's maintenance department staff should be closely involved in the design discussions and the college's maintenance buildings should be incorporated into the network plan.

Backbone Design Issues

A fundamental assumption running throughout this chapter is that most liberal arts colleges will find it highly beneficial, if not absolutely necessary, to design and build a full campus information technology network. There are many possible ways the physical network can be built, but at this stage in the technological development of networks, most colleges will have a network that consists of high-bandwidth, high-speed pathways between concentration points (for example, buildings and small LANs) and both high-speed and low-speed pathways within the concentration points.

Small colleges may find it beneficial to retain an engineering consultant to develop and document an appropriate campus network design and prepare cost estimates. Consultants are available both individually, for example, through organizations such as EDUCOM or CLAC, or through engineering firms that specialize in telecommunications and networking. Before actually hiring a consultant, it is generally prudent to request and check references from other similar institutions for which the consultant has worked. Many consultants come from large universities, where the problems and available solutions may be significantly different from those at small colleges.

Some firms, including IBM, AT&T, Bell Atlantic, and Digital Equipment Corporation, will sell complete network design, construction, and management services. For most small colleges, the cost of this approach is prohibitive. Instead, small colleges will probably find it more cost effective to build their networks slowly, relying heavily on college computing and maintenance staff for support and expertise. There are many advantages that tend to outweigh the slowness of the "slow but steady" approach to network construction. This point is discussed in more detail later in the chapter.

Each campus has to develop its own unique topology for installing the major cross-campus transmission pathways. The physical transmission modes may include coaxial cable, fiber optic cable, and even microwave devices, although the latter are rarely used on small campuses. Fiber optic cable is the favorite medium for campus backbones. Affordable technology will eventually be available to allow fiber to be used for complete pathways throughout the entire network ("fiber to the desk"). By careful planning and installation of redundant cable pairs, colleges will be able to reconfigure the pathways into almost any reasonable topology that may be required in the future.

Fiber optic cable is very versatile; it is relatively inexpensive, comes in a wide variety of types and sizes, and provides complete protection from electromagnetic interference. It can be used for asynchronous terminal communications, multiplexed asynchronous signals, high-speed and high-bandwidth digital signaling (for example, Ethernet networks), connections to PC LANs, audio and video transmission, monitor systems, and so forth.

At present, very high speed fiber optic cable networks are based on the fiber distributed data interface (FDDI) standard, a suite of ANSI–developed rules specifying digital data transmission at 100 megabits per second. An FDDI LAN is logically designed as two counter-rotating rings, a primary ring and a backup ring. One common use for FDDI LANs is as backbones to connect other LANs, often Ethernets. Devices connected to the FDDI LAN, such as concentrators serving as network hubs or routers and bridges used to attach other LANs to a concentrator or the FDDI LAN itself, repeat the signals they pass, thus maintaining the high transmission rate.

Few small college applications require the transmission speeds available with FDDI devices at this time, but it seems quite likely that the bandwidth and speed available on Ethernet systems will eventually be inadequate. Some applications can choke the network, requiring colleges to increase bandwidth substantially. For example, as scanners for creating image data files become common and as image data becomes more extensively used for instructional purposes, the network's capacity to carry the traffic may become problematic. Also, as on-campus networks carrying data, voice, and video information become part of regional, national, and international networks, the high bandwidth and high speed of the FDDI devices will be required. Even backbones that connect a variety of small microcomputer LANs may become overloaded by routine traffic among the LANs. By anticipating the FDDI ring topology when a campus fiber optic cable network is being designed, it will be possible to convert all or part of the network to the FDDI standard when appropriate.

One of the most common of the many varieties of fiber optic cable available, one that seems to provide wide flexibility for future applications, is the 62.5 micron, multi-mode, graded-index type. This style is widely used in today's Ethernet systems with 10-megabit-per-second transmission speeds and can handle the 100-megabit-per-second speeds of the FDDI standard.

Prudent installation of the right kind of fiber cable now will ensure that the cable plant will handle FDDI speeds when they are perceived to be necessary. Some designers believe it is important to include both multi-mode and single-mode fiber in their network plans to allow for possible future needs. While the use of thinner, single-mode fiber will eventually allow FDDI rings of very large size, an FDDI ring based on multi-mode fiber can support up to 500 nodes in a maximum ring circumference of 100 kilometers. Thus multi-mode fiber should be more than adequate for most small college networks.

In-Building Wiring Issues

Both thin-wire and thick-wire coaxial cable is widely used within buildings both as part of an overall campus backbone and to serve as a LAN backbone. It is less common for coaxial cable to be used outside buildings since fiber optic cable, with its imperviousness to interference, serves so well for that purpose. Coaxial cable is typically used as part of the network backbone in satellite equipment rooms (that is, wiring closets). Using transceivers attached with "vampire" taps to the coaxial cable, it is easy to attach devices such as terminal servers, remote repeaters, active star couplers, and routers to the backbone as active network components.

Most colleges rely on twisted-pair cabling as a basic connectivity medium. Up until recently, this type of wiring was only used for low-speed asynchronous transmission. Many manufacturers now produce devices that allow data transmission at Ethernet speeds over twisted-pair wiring, thus allowing the twisted-pair cable plant to carry Ethernet traffic. Existing telephone cabling often consists of just two pairs of barely twisted, heavily spliced wire sheathed in anything from lead to cloth, so many colleges have found it necessary to install new twisted-pair cable as part of their network design.

There are no industrywide standards for the installation of twisted-pair wires although the IEEE 802.3 committee is developing 10BaseT guidelines to specify standards for wiring and equipment that will be used for Ethernet transmission over unshielded, twisted-pair copper cable. Many vendors recommend installation of at least two sets of separately sheathed, 4-pair cables, one for computer wiring and one for voice transmission, to every work location. (It is important to provide separate sheathing on the two cables to prevent crosstalk interference.) Although there may be some initial redundancy when this much cable is installed, the cost of cable is very inexpensive compared to the installation cost.

There are different opinions about the use of shielded and unshielded twisted-pair cabling. Some network designers prefer shielded cable to provide greater protection from electromagnetic interference, while others prefer to risk the interference to gain a longer signal path (less attenuation). Most of the cable currently installed for telephone use is unshielded. Vendors of equipment that supports broadband communication (such as Ethernet) over twisted-pair cables usually recommend unshielded cable but this doesn't seem to be a firm requirement.

Even though twisted-pair cabling will support Ethernet devices (and eventually, FDDI devices), some colleges have chosen to install coaxial cable to support LAN installations and video transmission. As networking has become commonplace, vendors have begun to market special cables that incorporate twisted-pair, coaxial, and fiber optic cable all in one sheath, designed to be pulled directly to the face plates. This type of cable, while expensive, provides great flexibility for present and future network configurations. Twisted-pair wiring remains popular, however, because it is economical, easy to maintain, supports most types of simple LAN designs, and is easy to connect to network devices such as terminal servers. Also, it is simple enough for local contractors and maintenance departments to understand and install.

Connecting Sub-nets and Campus Networks

Many liberal arts colleges already have small special-purpose LANs, frequently managed in some ad hoc fashion by faculty or students, and often not connected to an all-campus network. While such LANs can and do serve many specific needs and even extend the lifetime of more expensive network services such as timesharing computers, it is nearly always desirable to include links among campus networks as part of the overall network design. Academic computing concerns are rapidly becoming less provincial, extending to other departments, other campuses, and other countries, so self-contained LANs will be too limited for many purposes.

Theoretically, almost any networks that have grown up on college campuses can be connected using bridges, gateways, protocol converters, and so on. As new products appear on the market (for example, equipment to allow communication between token-ring networks and DECnet), network linkage strategies should become simpler. But at this point such connections can be frustrating, confusing, time-consuming, highly technical tasks, particularly for understaffed, overburdened computing centers. Here, as in many other aspects of computing, diversity may be a wonderful attribute, but the cost in money and staff may be higher than small colleges can afford.

In addition to linkages between LANs and a wider campus network, there are many hardware/software combinations that allow individual microcomputers to be attached directly to campus networks. For example, microcomputers with add-on Ethernet cards can act like full nodes on an Ethernet network. Such connections raise significant security and management issues on a broadcast network such as Ethernet and must be considered during the design stage of network development.

Standards in Network Design

It would be foolhardy to begin building a campus-wide network without articulating the standards that will guide the development. Clear specifications are needed for every detail of the network. Some of the items that need standards, and examples of each, are the following:

Technology	Options
Cable plant	Type of twisted-pair cable; type of fiber optic cable
Wiring installation	Maximum length of cable runs; minimum distance from interference sources
Cable terminations	Punch down pattern for twisted-pair wiring, connector type for fiber cable; face-plate style; punch-block type
Names	Face-plate names; terminal-server names; building names

One key part of the standards is the design for in-building twisted-pair wiring and the associated face plates (or jacks). In many cases, this design includes the installation of both voice and computer cabling at the same time, with both cables terminated in one integrated jack. It is possible to purchase modular cabling systems that include wall jacks, plugs, patch cables, racks, cross connect systems, and so on. Such systems tend to be somewhat more expensive than generic equipment purchased from cable vendors, but the ease of installation and maintainability of the modular systems make them a good investment.

It is also valuable to work out early in the network development project general principles or standards that will govern such issues as network access, connection procedures, and level of support for applications. Even with a clearly stated set of college standards, it can be quite difficult to adhere strictly to the standards at all times. Some untidiness is bound to exist. Small college computing staffs are unlikely to have time to do all the labeling, managing, and monitoring necessary to have a totally documented and consistent system.

Construction Issues in Building Information Technology Networks

The previous section discussed a number of issues related to the design of a campus network. After the network design issues have been settled, many other questions about the actual construction arise. For example: How fast will the network be built? Who will do the actual construction? How and where should cable be installed? How will the network be documented? As it does with the design, each college must answer these questions in its own unique fashion. This section offers some possible answers to such questions. Of course, these suggestions are not right for every college, but should at least provide a perspective for evaluation.

Few colleges have the resources to build a complete campus network over a summer vacation. Instead, campus networks grow slowly over several years as additional buildings are wired, more fiber is installed across campus, small LANs are connected, and most importantly, as financial resources become available. There are many advantages to this incremental approach. The computing center staff is able to learn as the project develops and to profit from early mistakes. A slow development pace allows the campus to digest the idea of the network more easily. Library automation projects, often closely related to network development, usually take years to complete. New technologies can be exploited as they develop. Costs of cabling and network devices tend to decrease, sometimes very dramatically, over a one- or two-year time span. For example, terminal server costs have dropped more than 400 percent between 1989 and 1991.

Telecommunications Contractors versus Internal Maintenance Staff

It is natural to think about hiring network specialists to help build a network. The telecommunications field is replete with companies that offer full network installation services. Some large firms, such as computer vendors and telephone companies, will bid on a job, but then contract the actual work out to small sub-contractors who may have very limited experience and resources. The highly knowledgeable person who negotiates the bid and inspires confidence in the company is not necessarily going to be the supervisor on the job. The quality of the job, and whether or not the work adheres to the college standards, finally depends on the lowest-paid apprentice who actually pulls the cable. Even companies that have extensive experience in telephone wiring may have difficulty understanding that data wiring standards and protocols are different. The rule with telecommunications companies is the same as with any other major purchase: *caveat emptor.*

For some colleges, a simple way to avoid the risk of hiring an unknown outside contractor is to have the campus maintenance staff do the work. College maintenance crews often have highly competent electricians and carpenters who can carry out such network development tasks as pulling cable, installing faceplates, building satellite equipment rooms, grounding coaxial cables, and burying conduit. In most cases, it costs more to have outside contractors do such work, and the contractors would still need the cooperation of the maintenance staff.

The college maintenance staff can either be a network developer's strongest ally or worst enemy. Maintenance people are the traditional managers of campus electrical systems, equipment rooms, steam tunnels, conduits, blue prints, storage areas, and sometimes telephone systems, all items that are intrinsically involved in network development. While some maintenance staff may initially be resistant to a network developer's wild vision of the new information age, it is well worth the time and effort to help the maintenance staff understand what is planned and needed.

Treating the network as a utility is one way to help maintenance staff become a part of the development project and to see the project as an important college priority and opportunity instead of a threat. For example, the maintenance crew may find it convenient to acquire special tools such as core drills or special cable pullers, which they can use for other jobs as well. Regardless of who does the actual network construction, it is very important to specify the requirements precisely and clearly.

Relating Network Development to Other Construction Projects

The installation of a fiber optic cable plant can often be tied to other construction projects and technology needs, both on campus and in the surrounding area. For example, some institutions are converting their electrical feeder plants by constructing new 12,000-volt transmission loops, often putting the cabling in buried, concrete covered conduit systems. Since fiber optic cable is impervious to electrical interference, the fiber cable and the high-voltage cable can be placed in adjacent conduits in the same trench, thus saving considerable construction costs. As another example, a city or utility company project near the campus might provide an opportunity to bury some conduit for college network use. Other examples include the installation of cable to be used for telephone, fire detection, and cable television systems. In each case, it may be possible to link the installation of one type of transmission system to the campus data network development program.

New building projects and building renovations on campus also provide useful network construction opportunities. By working closely with college maintenance staff, it is often possible to have in-building wiring installed as a routine part of every building and renovation project, the kinds of activities that go on constantly on college campuses. Side benefits from such projects include the chance to get additional funds for the network development and an opportunity to raise campus consciousness about the importance of the network.

Installation and Documentation of the Cable Plant

Installing network cable is much the same as installing electrical or telephone wire, except that there are more constraints on construction details such as bend radii, proximity to EMI and RFI sources, and cable testing. Colleges typically use any and all available installation pathways for network cables, such as plenum spaces, building conduits, and buried conduits.

The common sense rules about general cable installations apply also to network cable installations. For example: *Install extra conduit and leave pull cords in it. Use sub-duct wherever possible. Don't direct bury any network cables if it can be avoided. Stay as far as possible from cable installations or buried pipes controlled by utility companies.*

Fiber optic cable requires somewhat more care than copper cable during installation. Colleges that are building their networks mainly with local staff may want college electricians to install fiber as well as copper cable. While maintenance staff members generally have little or no experience pulling fiber, it can be useful and cost-effective to have them learn how to do it, perhaps by first observing an outside contractor do part of the project.

One of the most crucial parts of fiber optic cable installation is termination of the strands, a rather delicate task that basically involves polishing the ends and gluing on connectors. It is quite easy to hire electrical or telecommunications firms to do just the fiber terminations on a per strand basis. Outside contractors will also have specialized equipment such as fiber cable time domain reflectometers needed to test and measure the fiber strands. Alternatively, some colleges may find it useful to have a maintenance or computer center staff member learn how to do fiber terminations to reduce costs. Since most fiber installations involve more strands than are needed initially, another way to save money is to leave some strands unterminated until they are actually needed. The downside of this cost-saving strategy is that the fiber pulls cannot be tested until they are finally terminated.

It is extremely difficult to manage a complex network without having good records and maps for the system. A key part of network construction is to assign unique, systematic names for everything: buildings, rooms, face plates, satellite equipment rooms, star hubs, bridges, routers, fiber optic repeaters, transceivers, terminal servers, terminal server ports, computers, printers, and so on. The network design should specify naming conventions for all components of the network. For devices like routers and repeaters that are attached to one end of a fiber run, the device name should indicate the location of the device and the location of the other end of the cable. A good rule of thumb is, *Anything that can be labeled should be.* All names should be recorded (and updated) using a good data management package. Good network maps, both geographic and logical, should be created on a CAD system.

Like the banks of a fast moving river, the network will be constantly changing. A system for monitoring and updating the network maps and records should be a key part of the network management activities.

Conditioning Electrical Power

There is wide empirical evidence that suggests that electrical power quality and reliability are poor (and getting worse) in many locations. Since all active network components run on electricity, the entire network can be affected by power sags, surges, or spikes in even a small part of the campus electrical grid. These power anomalies not only cause momentary disruptions, but over time, can cause serious problems with electrically driven equipment.

Since there is little that colleges can do about electrical disturbances that originate at the power source, the only solution to power problems is to install power conditioning equipment at the point of use. At a minimum, power conditioners providing protection against surges, sags, spikes, as well as radio frequency (RFI) and electromagnetic interference (EMI), and have a rapid clamping time, should be installed on all network and computer equipment. If it is financially feasible, it is useful to install uninterruptible power sources (UPS) on active network components. Even a battery backup of a few seconds can sometimes be enough to keep the whole network from going down when power sags occur.

Adequate power conditioners currently cost at least $50 and small uninterruptible power sources cost at least $100. But since a college network can easily include hundreds of microcomputers and network devices, providing a power conditioner on each electrical device, while very important, can be prohibitively expensive.

Some Network Management Issues

Network management and administration is a developing area of responsibility at most small colleges. Colleges that have fully operational campus networks generally need the equivalent of one staff person to handle network construction and management. Many colleges also have a number of small microcomputer LANs in departments or buildings, each requiring some level of support and management. A wide variety of management strategies, ranging from completely centralized to completely distributed models, have evolved. For example, the small LANs may all be managed by a member of some central organization such as the computing services department, or each LAN may be independently managed by a faculty member or student.

Each college has to develop a LAN management strategy appropriate for its resources, style, and culture. Some institutions can afford substantial diversity in the type of networks installed, and thus allow entrepreneurial freedom to be the operating style of network development. Other colleges, seeking to conserve resources and focus support, suggest or mandate a very limited number of standard design options for small microcomputer LANs. Whatever the style, it is important to expect that each LAN will require some level of support and maintenance from someone. Subjective estimates from network personnel at various educational institutions suggest that it typically requires one-quarter to one-half of a full-time person's effort to support each individual microcomputer LAN.

This chapter has primarily been devoted to a discussion of campus-wide networks that touch many locations across the campus. Many colleges that have installed small microcomputer networks eventually want to connect those small nets to a larger campus backbone network in order to use an external network, access central computing resources, transfer files among the small networks, or use electronic mail across the entire campus. Devices now exist that allow almost any network to connect to any other one. However, the greater the variety of network designs and protocols in use, the greater the amount of work required to effect the connections. As with other management issues, small colleges with small staffs can optimize their limited support resources by limiting the variety allowed in network configurations and styles.

Network management is closely related to network design. If a network is well designed, it will certainly be easier to manage. Some key management decisions have to be made during the design stage of network development, particularly with campus networks. To start with, there has to be high-level administrative support for the notion of a campus-wide network. Then decisions have to be made about everything from broad concepts, such as what type of network to install, to more mundane details like finding spaces for constructing satellite equipment rooms.

Careful management is required during construction of a campus network. Even if the contractor is experienced and conscientious, the integrity of the network can be compromised by sloppy work from the lowest-paid cable puller. Common installation errors include excessively small bend radii in fiber cable, twisted-pair cable laid on top of fluorescent light fixtures or near other sources of electromagnetic interference, and twisted-pair cable runs that exceed maximum distance specifications. The network manager should monitor the construction regularly and carefully to ensure that design standards are met.

Once a campus network is essentially constructed, various types of management are required. The physical parts of the network (jacks, cables, network devices) have to be maintained and occasionally repaired. The physical and logical addresses of the network devices (bridges, routers, terminal servers) must be carefully recorded and maintained in a database. Wiring closets, especially those also used by janitorial or utility workers, have to be checked regularly to make sure that the wiring and network devices are not tampered with or jostled.

To manage a campus LAN properly, one individual will have to serve as a network administrator to configure network devices, assign addresses, maintain all appropriate data, enforce standards, monitor changes, and so forth. At small colleges, this same person may actually do the installation work as well as serve as LAN administrator. More and more, liberal arts colleges are finding it cost effective to employ at least one full-time staff member in computing whose responsibilities are devoted exclusively to network support.

Even with careful design, construction, and management, it is possible to have network problems that are beyond the capability of local staff to solve. Such problems can arise from construction errors (such as improperly installed cable), design errors (violating the "two repeater" rule in Ethernets), intermittent equipment failures, load problems, and so on. In such cases, it may be useful to retain a professional network consulting firm to assist in identifying and solving the problem. Such firms can also provide other useful services such as designing additions to a network, auditing an installed network, and creating CAD-based maps of the network.

Most liberal arts colleges now have or are in the process of installing connections to some outside network (generally BITNET or the Internet). Such a connection is often treated as an off-campus extension of an on-campus network, and as such, requires management. These connections generally involve installation and management of modems, routers, router software, and communication lines. Maintaining an external network connection through a nearby university, a common practice, requires regular communication with network people at the university. In order to keep the connection working properly, someone has to support and update the router software, monitor the impact of external network use on the server systems of the local network, occasionally upgrade the hardware and communication lines, and diagnose and solve problems. Then, to make effective use of the external connection, someone must identify and promote useful resources, provide user-oriented documentation, develop usage policies, and police violations of the policies. All in all, the management of an external network connection can occupy a significant amount of staff time.

Conclusion

This chapter has considered a variety of issues related to the design, construction, and management of campus networks. Such networks are rapidly becoming an essential part of the information technology environment at many, if not most, liberal arts colleges. As an information conduit, a campus network plays a key role in a college's ability to carry out the fundamental task of providing access to the world of information. Further, a campus network provides an integrating context for developing and managing information technology.

The construction of a campus network is a major decision for liberal arts colleges. Those who propose the construction of the campus network generally find that the project goes more smoothly if all relevant constituencies are involved in the decision process. The faculty want to see how the network will substantially enhance the teaching and learning environment at the college. Senior administrators, who generally make the final decision and allocate resources, have to be convinced that the network is a fiscally sound and manageable investment that is central to the mission of the institution. And if the college maintenance department is willing and able to play a major role in the project, the construction of the network can be substantially simplified.

Research on new network technologies that allow ever faster speeds is a continual process driven by the ubiquity of networks in business, industry, and education. Nevertheless, the basic technology has stabilized sufficiently that colleges can make the substantial investment in a campus network without fear of committing to either untested or obsolete networking equipment. For example, a very common design based on twisted-pair cabling within buildings and fiber optic cable between buildings is currently in use at hundreds of educational institutions.

As with any utility system, it is important to take care in planning and designing a network. Development of standards for every component part of the network will help ensure that the network works properly after it is constructed and will greatly simplify management of the network. Since networking technology and functions change over time, the network should be designed to be as flexible as possible. One way to build in flexibility is to install ample, even redundant, strands of fiber optic cable between buildings, and to install twisted-pair cable runs to every imaginable place anyone might work with information technology.

A network, like any complex system composed of active and passive components, requires ongoing support and management. If there is one mistake that experience with campus data networking has revealed to us during the past few years it is that networks cannot simply be installed and then forgotten. They require extensions, upgrades, modifications—in other words, a great deal of care and feeding. The better the planning, the more flexible the network will be; but even the best planning cannot yield a network that is maintenance free.

Appendix: Some Design Specifications for Computing and Data Communications Facilities

The following design guidelines are used at Kenyon College to inform contractors, technicians, and maintenance staff about the requirements for construction of network facilities. The rules are intended to cover installation and connection of network cables from the face plate to the satellite equipment room (SER). Some of these guidelines are based on industry standards, while others are unique to the Kenyon College environment. Other institutions may find it useful to develop their own set of design guidelines using this set as a model.

Specifications for In-Building Data Wiring

The following points apply to twisted-pair data cables and to coaxial cable, including regular and thin-wire Ethernet cables.

1. Twisted-pair cable must meet the published specifications of the IEEE 802.3 committee for 10BaseT communications. In particular, the cable must consist of four-pair, 24 AWG, twisted-pair, solid conductor cable with at least five twists per foot. The proper type of sheathing must be used for any environmental airspaces that may be present.

2. The maximum cable run from a face plate to the SER punch-down block is 90 meters (278 feet).

3. A 10-meter separation must be maintained between the cable and sources of high-level radiated energy (for example, radio transmitters and high-current switchgear).

4. A minimum of 3 meters separation (for twisted-pair cable) and 15 centimeters (for shielded coaxial cable) should be maintained between the cable and EMI sources (for example, power wiring, transformers, DC motor-generators, telephone cabling, and fluorescent lighting fixtures).

5. Installed cable should be supported every 3 meters (10 feet) or less by bar joists, J hooks, shelves, or similar support hardware.

6. Cables must not be laid on (nor supported by) pipes, conduit, other data cables, phone cables, or electrical wiring.

7. Cable support hardware must be mounted close to the SER racks. All cables routed into the SER must be supported by and fastened to this support hardware.

8. Cable must not be stretched, crimped, compressed, or crushed.

9. At least 1 meter of slack should be allowed per 10 meters of cable length.

10. If metal wall boxes are used, rubber or plastic grommets must be installed in the wallboxes to protect the cables.

11. Label every cable with wrap-on labels on both ends.

12. The minimum bend radius for 4-pair twisted-pair cable is 1 inch.

13. The minimum bend radius for standard Ethernet cable is 20 centimeters.

14. Cable should not be installed in an area where temperature varies outside the range 5°C to 50°C or humidity outside the range 10% to 95% relative humidity.

15. Any conduit used to penetrate walls and floors must be sized to provide 50% unused space for future use.

16. Leave 6 inches of extra cable in the wall box, to allow for future reconfiguration of the face plate connection.

17. All openings made for routing the cables through fire walls must be sealed with UL-listed fire barrier caulking or fire seal. Ensure compliance with fire codes.

18. When installed together, telephone cables and data cables should be separated as much as possible, using separate conduits where such pathways exist. In no case should telephone and data cables be intertwined or bound together.

Special Guidelines for Installing Ethernet Coaxial Cable

1. Use a volt-ohmmeter to check the center conductor and shield of every cable section for continuity, shorts, and/or opens before unreeling.

2. Start at either end of a segment and proceed on a section-by-section basis, installing and testing a section at a time until the entire segment is in place.

3. Use only standard-length factory-terminated cables.

4. Do not exceed pulling tension of 110 kilograms (242 pounds) on the pulling device.

5. Excess cable must be coiled with a diameter of not less that 75 centimeters (30 inches) and neatly stowed.

6. Provide extra cable at one end of each segment to allow the segment end to be brought to the floor for testing.

7. When installing the cable between floors, secure the cable within 18 inches of its entry and exit to each floor.

Specifications for Satellite Equipment Rooms

These guidelines should be followed in the design and construction of a satellite equipment room to hold computing and communications network components.

1. The SER should have dimensions at least 5 feet by 8 feet, with a ceiling at least 8 feet high.

2. The door should be lockable and labeled with a warning such as "Warning—Authorized Personnel Only."

3. The floor should be linoleum, tile, sealed concrete, or a similar nonporous surface and suitable for the placement of lag bolts that are used to attach the rack assembly to the floor.

4. Adequate incandescent lighting should be provided. Provide an emergency light that turns on when power is lost to the building.

5. The room should not be used for storage of any material or equipment not directly related to the cabling system, especially flammable material.

6. The room will generally contain two equipment racks, each of which will require a minimum clearance of 30 inches on the front and on at least one side.

7. The room may require supplementary heating and cooling capability to maintain stable conditions, but equipment such as fan coil units must not be placed close to cabling or equipment racks.

8. The SER should have two dedicated, grounded 20 amp electrical circuits installed, each terminating in a double duplex outlet box.

9. Strictly avoid the placement of any high-voltage sources or EMI sources in or near the room.

10. Keep cable in the room 18 inches from the floor. Keep cable installed within 48 inches of the floor in protective barriers to avoid damage from being bumped.

11. Cable should not interfere with heating or cooling ducts or the normal movement of anyone working in the room.

12. Follow building and fire codes.

13. Provide phone service in the room.

14. Try to design the room to locate Ethernet transceivers and other active network components in the room itself, rather than at other locations in the building.

Face Plate Guidelines

1. Place the face plate 12 to 36 inches above the floor.

2. Place the face plate within 3 feet of an electrical outlet. Both the face plate and the electrical outlet should be within 5 feet of the planned equipment to insure that the power and data cabling can both reach their intended outlets.

3. Ensure easy access to the face plate. Don't locate the face plate where it is likely to be blocked by furniture.

4. Make sure that each cable is properly and completely labeled at the face plate end and at the SER end.

Resale of Telecommunication Services at Four-Year Colleges

Thomas C. Makofske
Connecticut College

Thomas Makofske is director of computing and information services at Connecticut College. He is responsible for setting the direction for the use of information technologies in all areas of the college. In the last 12 years, he has managed three computing and telecommunications facilities, and established the systems and procedures needed for successful resale of telephone services both at Bryn Mawr College, where he was director of MIS and telecommunications from 1983 to 1988, and at Connecticut College.

Mr. Makofske's other professional activities include consulting with Harvard's Latin American Scholarship Program for American Universities (LASPAU) for the purpose of expanding, enhancing, and interconnecting telecommunications networks linking scholars and researchers in South America, Central America, and the Caribbean. He is an institutional representative to the Consortium of Liberal Arts Colleges and a trustee of New England Regional Computing Program.

This chapter discusses reselling telecommunication services as a method of partially supporting the construction and operation of a college's telecommunication systems and other information technologies. Since Connecticut College has recently undertaken a comprehensive resale program in conjunction with its implementation of a campus-wide network, the discussion draws freely on the results of that project. The purpose of the chapter, however, is not to provide a case history of Connecticut's experiences. Rather, it is to use the strategy pursued at Connecticut College as a framework for addressing the general issues of campus computing and telecommunications resale. To the extent that small, private, liberal arts colleges share a great many similarities, the Connecticut strategy may provide some guidance for schools that are contemplating this type of initiative. It should be kept in mind, however, that the success of the resale strategy described in this chapter depends upon a combination of factors including enrollment size, budget resources, local costs of materials and services, state laws, and campus culture, to name a few. These factors must be carefully weighed in determining whether a resale strategy will achieve its objectives on a particular campus.

Many liberal arts colleges approach the coordination of data, video, and voice incrementally—a part of the system here, a link between a few buildings, some local video there, and a variety of partial wiring and conduit schemes. Connecticut College, however, recently installed a full telecommunication system including a new conduit structure, fiber, coaxial, and twisted-pair wiring, digital PBX, voice messaging, and a campus-wide data network. From the outset, the college intended to support part of the construction and operation of that system from revenues collected from students through the resale of services.

In order to put the discussion of telecommunications resale into the sharpest possible focus, this chapter will consider specific answers—derived from experiences at Connecticut College—to some of the most commonly asked questions raised by colleagues at other liberal arts institutions.

1. Why would a liberal arts college undertake such a comprehensive and expensive project?

2. What is resale? What conditions make it possible?

3. Why should a college consider reselling telephone or other telecommunication services?

4. What kinds of products or services can be resold?

5. What are the legal, political, and tax issues related to resale of telecommunication services?

6. What kinds of billing systems are there?

7. What are some issues regarding the resale of video and CATV services?

8. What are the administrative and technical requirements for resale?

9. What are some of the administrative benefits of reselling telecommunication services?

10. What about the resale of other services?

11. What can the college do with any net operating profits?

12. What sorts of problems might come up after the resale system is installed?

13. What are some concerns various constituents will have about resale and how might they be addressed?

14. What are some of the policy issues?

An Overview of the Technology Deployed at Connecticut College

In order to provide comprehensive services and benefits to students and faculty—and to be able to collect revenues from those who would benefit most from the new system—it was necessary to install an *information port* in every dormitory room, faculty office, laboratory, classroom, common room, administrative office, auditorium, and other public rooms. This port contains eight unshielded twisted pairs divided into two four-pair cables connected to two separate RJ45 jacks—four pair for voice and four pair for data. Additionally, an F connector and coaxial cable are provided for video programming.

Each building on campus is connected by a distribution system that includes twisted-pair copper (primarily for voice service), coaxial cable (for video transmission), and at least twelve strands of multi-mode optical fiber. The campus is divided into two main telecommunication centers or nodes arranged in a double star topology. Each node includes a digital PBX connected by fiber and a fiber hub used for data transmission. The main nodes are connected by 72 strands of fiber to allow for growth, redundancy, and an easy progression to fiber distributed data interface (FDDI) ring topology or SONET.

At each information port a student, faculty member, or administrator can use a digital PBX capable of handling data and voice, a voice messaging system, discounted long distance and intrastate calling, an array of personal safety and security systems, access to a high-speed campus-wide LAN running over fiber, local and international data services, automated library services, BITNET and Internet, file servers, mainframe resources of the computing center, and other computing resources distributed across campus in several special-purpose labs. In addition to standard cable television programming, special educational programming received by the College's satellite antennas will be distributed to the common rooms, dormitory lounges, language laboratory, and the library.

Planning for the system began in March 1988; vendor selection, design, and competitive bidding took place during 1988–89; award of the project for construction and installation occurred in January 1990; construction began in March 1990; and cutover to the new system occurred, on schedule, in August 1990.

In the remainder of this chapter, the discussion answers specific questions concerning resale of telecommunication services to students. A useful place to begin, however, is with the general question of why this kind of project is undertaken in the first place.

Why Undertake Such a Project?

At Connecticut College this question was answered with the following points.

1. We wanted to change the nature of communications at our college. We thought this could best be done by using technological resources currently available for amplifying our students' ability to share and communicate information. We wanted to increase the ability of our students, faculty, and staff to communicate with each other and with their colleagues everywhere. We wanted to increase the forms of communication and the extent of communication, so we chose to provide voice mail, asynchronous data communications,

campus intercom, and local area dialing as part of
the basic communications services.

2. We wanted the scholar to be in the center of the information universe, connected to a world of information
and communication through his or her workstation
and the network.

3. We recognized that peripherals and protocols change
on a daily basis so we focused on the "roadway," or
the infrastructure that would connect those peripheral
systems and resources to one another and make
them available to scholars and administrators both
on and off the campus.

4. We saw that the demands for speed and bandwidth
by users and their applications would steadily grow,
hence the infrastructure had to be able to accommodate that growth.

5. We saw a great increase in the number of services
soon to be available from the telephone networks and
we wanted to position ourselves to be able to tap into
those resources.

6. Information comes in a variety of formats; by providing a network capable of supporting and coordinating the delivery of voice, video, and data services,
we would ensure that our students and faculty would
not be locked out of information presented in any of
those formats.

7. We saw an opportunity to divert a revenue stream
from an outside vendor, in this case the regional
telephone company, to support the creation and
operation of a network that would serve our own
purposes.

What Is Resale and What Conditions Make It Possible?

The concept of resale is a simple one. Basically, one buys something at a low cost and sells it for more than one paid for it. So, for instance, a college might purchase long-distance service in volume at a discount and resell that service to students and others at a somewhat higher price. The net or margin that accrues from this transaction can then be used to help defray the costs of putting in the infrastructure and equipment necessary to take advantage of the volume discounts. The goal in this example might be to resell the discounted long-distance service to students at a marked up price that is less than they would pay for the same calls made from a residential or public pay phone. In this way, both parties benefit: The college experiences significant discounts in the cost of long-distance calling and can reduce its administrative costs while students have access to discounted long-distance service.

Resale of services works best when there is a captive market—such as a large group of students living in dormitories who are interested in purchasing necessary or desirable services such as basic dial tone for local calling, discounted long distance, data services, emergency and cross-campus intercom capabilities. Another way of looking at resale of services is to see the college as a private phone company providing services to a village or small city. The college installs the central PBX or "switch," the wiring connecting each customer with the PBX, and the wiring connecting the PBX with the off-campus telephone network. A customer-service operation handles trouble calls, new installations, and disputed calls or charges. A billing system is installed along with revenue collection and accounting systems; a records database and a system for comparing costs with revenues are established.

When a college chooses to become the local phone company for its constituents, it has in fact replaced the regional Bell company or some other independent phone company as the supplier of services to those constituents. In doing so, it retrieves a sizable portion of revenue from the third-party vendor, that is, the regional phone company, and brings it back in-house where it can be applied toward the operation of its own telecommunication system.

Why Consider Reselling Telephone or Other Telecommunication Services?

Primarily, reselling services gives the college an opportunity to create a revenue stream to offset the administrative costs of providing phone and other services to students, faculty, and staff. This means that a cost center is offset with income and that can mean a net reduction in the costs a college must expend for the administrative support of its operations. The revenues generated from resale of services offsets the costs the college incurs in providing the systems, staff, and infrastructure needed to provide information technology. The costs are reduced because they are shared among those who most benefit from those services.

The acquisition, installation, and operation of modern information systems and technologies is an important measure of the seriousness and credibility of an institution of higher learning. The quality and extent of these technologies has a direct impact on the ongoing survival of the institution and thus are strategic in nature. In the increasingly competitive marketplace of the nineties, these technologies are essential in order to recruit and maintain first-rate faculty and students. Proper application and management of these technologies can lead to better administrative control of costs through the use of better reporting systems. Reselling telecommunication services helps defray the sizable outlays of capital required to install a comprehensive telecommunication system and makes available a steady stream of revenue for its operations, maintenance, and enhancement.

What Kinds of Products or Services Can Be Resold?

Services, features, hardware, and access to special networks or computing facilities can all be obtained at a discount and resold at a higher price. Some of these services and features may be combined to produce a basic package; others may more appropriately be offered as options. Hardware (including special phone sets, FAX systems, personal computers, or various add-on boards that let the user connect to high-speed data transmission lines) can be rented as well as sold.

Connecticut College has basic and optional features and services. Students pay a flat fee in two installments over the school year—once in August, and again in January. Upon paying this fee, they receive unlimited local dialing privileges, full campus intercom, emergency security system with calling number location displayed at the security console, voice messaging services, a personal identification number that allows students to make discounted long-distance calls, and free asynchronous PC connections to the campus network. The basic phone service includes the ability to make and receive calls and to have incoming calls routed to their voice mailbox.

There are many ways this basic package can be modified. For instance, some colleges charge a fee to cover the administrative overhead involved in giving a student a personal identification number, to replace a lost or forgotten number, or to change an extension number. Some colleges charge a monthly fee for the rental of voice mailboxes. Some larger universities provide to PC owners, free of charge, the add-on circuit boards required for connecting to high-speed networks; other universities rent or sell these boards to the users of the data network.

Connecticut College provides an optional set of special features such as conference calling, call waiting, and speed dialing for an additional monthly charge. Depending on the flexibility and capability of the institution's wiring scheme, it is possible to charge fees for connection to the campus network and to its mainframe computing facilities.

Sale of special "off-premise station" extension numbers to outside businesses, along with a voice mailbox or bulletin board, is an excellent way to generate additional revenue. For example, the college may approach a number of local pizza vendors and offer, to the highest bidder, an on-campus extension listed in the college phone directory. If voice mail is available, students could dial into the vendor's mailbox and leave their order. Voice mail allows the vendor to verify the extension number and name of the person who left the voice mail message, and provides the student with verification that the message was received by the pizza vendor. Also, the vendor could rent a mailbox that plays a message advertising specials or providing other information to prospective customers. Other kinds of vendors who might be interested in purchasing off-premise extensions include travel agencies, bookstores, clothing stores, theaters, and ticket agencies.

The off-premise extension coupled with a voice messaging system can make the college's telecommunications network an effective way for several kinds of businesses to be readily accessible to a concentration of several hundred to several thousand students. This arrangement can result in significant revenue to the college, excellent relations with local businesses, and the possibility of discounts being passed on to students. Other opportunities for revenue include a return in the form of a percentage of long distance tolls being returned to the college if students and employees use a particular long-distance carrier's calling card when they are off campus.

Resale of other information services including FAX transmissions, laser-quality printing, document scanning, file serving between sites on and off campus (for example, to printers or graphics vendors), and connect time to public databases, such as Dialog and the NYT Index, can be done at cost or with a margin added to the cost the college incurs in providing these services.

Some states permit the purchase and installation of college-owned or -leased pay phones, while others permit a third party to install and operate a pay phone while paying the college a percentage of all revenues collected from it. The latter service can represent a real saving in monthly telecommunications costs since a pay phone purchased from the regional phone company can cost several hundred dollars a year, not including the cost of installation and connection to the phone company's network. The royalties returned to the college from the use of the pay phone can be used to offset the monthly line charges required to support a pay phone.

If the college's infrastructure includes either single-mode fiber or coaxial cabling along with the appropriate connectors in student rooms, the resale of cable TV programming represents another opportunity to generate revenue. However, it should be noted that the issues surrounding the distribution and resale of video are complex and include legal, financial, and technical considerations as well as discussions of whether providing commercial television to each student's room will have a detrimental impact on the academic program or the intellectual life of the campus. (This issue is discussed later in the chapter.)

What Are the Legal, Political, and Tax Issues?

Telecommunication services often involve consideration of complex legal and political issues. Judge Greene's decisions notwithstanding, telecommunications is still a regulated industry and a college wishing to resell services may, depending on its location, have to deal with a growing number of state and local officials and regulations specifically concerned with telecommunications. Consequently, a college planning on resale must obtain legal advice reviewing whether or not a private entity may resell telephone services in the given setting.

States have different laws governing what may be done. Connecticut, for instance, specifically prohibits the resale of telephone services—except for colleges and hotels. The local Bell or independent phone company has several legally mandated tariffs—or products and services they are allowed to sell and for which they can set prices. Sometimes, a tariff defines what the regional phone company can provide as opposed to what a private phone facility can provide to its constituents; these tariffs may also specify the services the college can purchase from a third party and those services they are obliged to purchase from the regional phone company.

For instance, Pennsylvania law permits a private institution to purchase pay phones and related services from private vendors; Connecticut law stipulates that pay phones may only be purchased from and maintained by the regional phone company. However, even in the latter case, a portion of the revenues collected by the pay phone is returned to the college in the form of royalties. Furthermore, while a college may not be able to install or lease its own pay phone, it can choose any long-distance vendor to carry long-distance service from that pay phone and in doing so increase the royalties it receives from the use of that pay phone.

Another possibility for savings exists where several colleges can connect their PBXs together over dedicated lines and form what is often called a *bypass network*. The main advantage of such a network is that the participating colleges can use one another's PBX and trunking to provide local calling between colleges regardless of the actual distance between them. For instance, Connecticut College can connect its New London PBX with Trinity College's PBX in Hartford.

The distance between the two colleges is about fifty miles; by linking the two PBXs together, calls made from Connecticut College to the Hartford dialing area can be billed as local calls. Trinity's PBX receives the call from Connecticut College's PBX and then routes it to the local Hartford trunks. Trinity and Connecticut College both have unlimited local calling rates, so all calls to Hartford's local area from New London and all calls from Trinity to New London's local area are not treated as toll calls since they appear to the phone company as local calls dialed from the campus PBX. A monthly charge for local trunks is necessary anyway to provide local service, and the cost of the dedicated line between the two switches, which varies depending on the bandwidth and distance between the connections, may still be considerably less than either installing several foreign exchange (FX) lines or paying the metered costs.

Savings can be increased if other colleges are added to the bypass network. It is important to note that some regional and independent phone companies may frown on this practice and may have local tariffs that prevent a college from entering into a bypass network arrangement with another institution.

Considerations regarding taxes include the determination of who has to pay and how much, the collection of taxes, and the procedures for passing along collections to the tax collector. Once again these matters are governed by the state (and sometimes even the local jurisdiction) in which the college is situated. Private, four-year colleges are usually tax exempt. Often they are not required to pay taxes on their purchases nor to collect taxes for services or products directly related to their educational activities. However, in some states students may be required to pay a sales tax on the services provided or on the toll calls they make. If this is the case then it is relatively simple to add a surcharge to student bills and send it on to the tax collector. This requirement will vary according to the state and local jurisdiction and so each college will need to determine its own responsibility.

Recently, a variety of organizations representing small businesses successfully lobbied federal and state governing bodies and the Internal Revenue Service into agreeing that public revenues might be enhanced (at the expense of limited student budgets) if taxes are assessed against products or services sold by not-for-profit institutions when those products and services are deemed unrelated to education. The tax assessed, known as unrelated business income tax, (UBIT), is justified on the theory that for-profit businesses must pay taxes on the purchase of products as well as on net operating profit, and so are at a competitive disadvantage with a not-for-profit organization that takes advantage of its tax-exempt status to market products and services to its constituents at discounted prices. These businesses claim the discount is only possible because not-for-profit organizations aren't required to pay tax on the cost of the products or on any profit generated from the products or services resold at a discount to students and others.

Consequently, a college that wishes to benefit from resale of services must be able to show that income derived from resold services is related to its primary mission of instruction and research. Otherwise it may be liable to pay some sort of UBIT. The issue of determining the college's tax liability should be reviewed by its attorney, the college's legal and financial experts, and possibly local and state legislators. One method of avoiding taxes on revenues (practiced by a number of small businesses) is to ensure that the costs of providing services are at least as high as the revenues generated from resale of those services. So, it makes excellent fiscal as well as pedagogical sense to keep the college's networks and information technologies modern, extensive, and deeply integrated into the academic life of the institution. The changes and new directions in technology demand a reliable stream of capital required to purchase and pay for upgrades to these strategically important systems as well as related peripheral equipment and modifications to infrastructure and plant. Any revenues generated by the resale of information services can be put back into the operating budget of the college to provide for the ongoing financial support and enhancement of information technologies.

A college might use the following argument to reduce its liability to taxation on the revenues it receives from the resale of information services: Colleges are information intensive; they carry out their mission by effectively providing information to their students. Information technologies facilitate and amplify the ability of instructors to communicate information to students, and these same technologies also enhance the ability of students to access, collect, assemble, and communicate information back to faculty members and the world at large. To the extent that administrative savings are experienced "in kind" by the installation and operation of information systems, the college may be more efficiently administered and more effective in providing an administrative and physical environment conducive to the educational activity that takes place.

Consequently, it is vital that a steady, effective, and reliable stream of revenue be found to support the sharing of information between scholars and students. This revenue can be derived from the resale of services. A final reminder: Regardless of what argument a college makes to ensure that it is not taxed unfairly, each state and locality has different customs, laws, and practices; consequently, the college attorney's input and professional judgment will be necessary prior to any dealings with government regulatory or taxing agencies.

What Kinds of Billing Systems Are There?

Resale of telephone and long-distance services requires a reliable, accurate billing system that is easy to support and operate. The purpose of the billing system is to collect and store records of billable calls made by users of the campus phone system. It is crucial that this system be dependable and accurate since resale involves billing the users later for long-distance charges already paid for by the college to its long-distance carrier. If the system fails for any reason, the college stands to lose substantial revenue since the PBX will continue to place long-distance calls, but no record of those calls will be collected by the malfunctioning billing system.

The PBX keeps track of the number called, the time and date of a call, the duration, and the station from which the call was placed. Some systems can also provide trunk information and records about calls made between on-campus extensions. This station-to-station calling information is useful for documenting the duration, frequency, and destination of computer communications; also, nuisance calls placed from one phone to another on campus can easily be traced. The PBX outputs the call information usually through a serial port called a station message detail recorder (SMDR). This port is the usual interface to most billing systems.

Ideally, a billing system provides search capabilities for locating individual calls; detailed call information in the form of bills; records sorted by office account numbers, station numbers, time and date of call, or area-code location; and summary reports showing usage, costs, and traffic over a given period of time. There are two types of billing systems. One is installed on-site and includes the applications software, rate tables, and hardware necessary to calculate and produce bills and reports; the other type of system is located in a service bureau and collects call records, calculates bills, and produces reports for a fee. The service bureau also charges the college for any toll charges incurred in collecting data from the PBX. Some service bureaus also require that the college purchase or lease on-site collection equipment such as Pollcats or PCs in addition to the communications link between the bureau and the college.

There are advantages and disadvantages to each kind of billing system. The most important advantage to the in-house billing system is that the college doesn't pay an outside firm for this service. Also, bills are often available on demand—an important feature for those who want to resell services to summer students and conferees. However, staff are needed to administer the billing system and a reasonably powerful PC, workstation, or minicomputer, along with a production-level printer, is required since the calculation and printing of bills is a computer-intensive activity. Some of these activities include computer operations such as database backups, forms and paper ordering, printer operations and maintenance, sorting and mailing of the bills, revenue collection procedures, monitoring of unpaid accounts and accounts that have surpassed a preset spending limit on toll calls, possible liaison with the administrative computing staff and the controller's office, and disputed call handling and resolution.

There are disadvantages to operating an in-house billing system. The computing system, peripherals, power, and environmental conditions must be reliable. Furthermore, the computing system needs to be monitored frequently throughout the day or appropriately alarmed in the event the billing system or power supply fails. Suppose, for example, the billing system fails on a Friday evening and the failure is not discovered until Monday morning, resulting in a loss of several thousand dollars in uncollected call records. This represents lost revenue the college can't collect to defray the charges it will pay to its long-distance carrier for the calls made. In-house billing systems also need a set of regularly updated rate tables in order to assign costs to the call records. These tables exist for all the major long-distance carriers and updated tables can be obtained every few months if necessary. They are generally expensive to purchase and require several minutes of the billing system being taken off line to load the updates into the database. These rates are usually those that the user of the phone system will be required to pay.

Rate tables contain the carrier's "casual" (dial-1) rates which will be higher than the volume rates the college actually pays. The margin between the actual cost to the college and the amount charged to the user provides additional revenues for offsetting the cost of providing the services to those users. To make the use of the college's long-distance service more attractive, many colleges offer a discount on casual calling rates and pass that back to the users of the long-distance service.

The advantages to using a service bureau include the following: Fewer staff are needed to support the billing activity; the college has almost no capital outlay for computing hardware and software; the college can usually negotiate to have penalties paid to the college by the service bureau if the billing system fails and causes a loss of call records; rate tables are frequently updated. Time-consuming computer intensive activities are handled by the service bureau. Some bureaus will also mail the bills, collect the money, handle disputed calls and delinquent accounts, and, after taking their fees from the collected revenues, send the college a check once a month along with a statement of activity.

Their main disadvantage is that, depending on the kinds of services and the numbers of bills produced, service bureaus can be expensive. Generally, however, the costs will vary between two and three dollars per bill per month. Other disadvantages include the lack of flexibility in the format or content of the reports, the lack of certain summary calculations a specific college might want to see on a report, and difficulty in changing the frequency of the billing cycle. Also, during the summer, when many colleges rent rooms to conferees and summer students, some service bureaus cannot generate bills on demand.

These latter disadvantages can usually be overcome but often require expensive modifications to the service bureau's software to accommodate the specific needs of a given college.

An important feature of most billing systems is that they provide the college with the ability to monitor and reduce the abuse of its long-distance services by employees. Bills can be generated for any station or for any personal identification number, detailed bills can be sent to the individuals or their supervisor for review. Summary bills can be sent to budget officers charged with overseeing the fiscal expenditures of an office or department or to the controller for review. Once the cost of calls has been calculated, this information can be entered into the college's MIS database via a tape or diskette upload.

Furthermore, once the call-record data are available to the administrative system software, it should be possible to prepare a monthly bill summarizing the toll and other charges incurred by students in one line on a bill and payable to the cashier. Consequently, the detail of calls made and the specific charges are printed as a separate statement and sent by the telecommunications office to the student. The controller's office prepares the single summary charge for telecommunication services and sends it in the form of an invoice to the student.

Assuming the college has a central, integrated database-management system designed for college administration, it is possible to write software that flags delinquent accounts and prevents the registrar from issuing transcripts, enrolling the student in classes, issuing grade notices, or permitting graduation until bills are paid. Administratively, the summary costs of calls can be charged against the funds available to pay for telecommunication services allotted to the departments and offices in their yearly operating budgets. Deducting the costs of each office's or department's use of long-distance service from its operating budget may give the appropriate budget officer an incentive to begin reviewing the calls made by staff and faculty to determine if they are business related or personal. Finally, once the call record and cost information is part of the administrative database, reports may be produced relating the college's overall cost for the technology and services provided to the revenues garnered, thereby showing whether a net operating profit or loss occurs after these accounts are rectified.

What Are Issues Regarding the Resale of Video and CATV Services?

At the outset there are—as with telephones—technical, legal, and financial considerations. State and local laws often control the provision of cable TV services; therefore, it is necessary to research the legal limitations and statutes regarding the resale of these services. In Connecticut, for instance, a college (or anyone else for that matter) is permitted to "overbuild" and provide an alternative to the local cable TV franchise. Consequently, there are no legal limitations to a college developing its own cable TV facility and marketing this service to its students and others who live on the campus. Distributing services off campus, while not legally prohibited, would involve getting a number of rights of way and easements in order to place distribution cable outside the boundaries of the campus.

The resale method for video services works much the same as it does with telephone services: The college provides the distribution infrastructure and programming and then charges a fee to viewers. The distribution infrastructure includes a "head end" or source of programming. The *head end* contains the electronics for collecting video signals from satellite or other antennas, selecting the desired channels, and downloading the programming on those channels into the campus video distribution system. The distribution system from the head end to a given building is usually over coaxial cable; however, recent technological developments have made distribution over single mode optical fiber an attractive, though somewhat expensive, alternative.

There are several important considerations regarding the relative advantage of fiber over coaxial cable and the overall topology of a video cabling system that need to be addressed before a video resale system can be effectively implemented. The issues are highly technical and are outside the scope of this chapter; however, the college's audio-visual technicians, consultants, or the local cable TV franchise can provide the initial answers.

Should the college wish to avoid installing the electronics just described, it can purchase programming from the local cable TV company. The programming can be fed directly onto campus by the local company and distributed over the college's wiring. The operating requirements of the local franchise may require them to absorb the cost of installing the necessary distribution system to deliver programs to the users on campus and they may also have to turn that cable over to the college after a specified period of time. If the college chooses this latter course, it may not be able to add any margin to the cost the cable TV company charges the students for service, nor will it have as much control over the installation and use of the distribution system. Furthermore, the cable company may not consider the college's wishes with regard to the impact of its installation on existing conduit systems, building interiors, the natural environment of the campus, and the need to minimize disruption of campus life while the installation of the cable TV system takes place.

Ideally, cable TV systems are designed for the largest potential number of users in a given site rather than the actual number requiring service. This is because the types of electronics involved do not lend themselves to a partial or modular design approach. Finally, the Federal Communications Commission is about to propose new standards for controlling the leakage of radio signals from large-scale cable TV systems. This is to prevent interference with airport to airliner communications. The college will need to determine that the materials used in their video distribution system are in compliance with these new standards.

The method of charging can vary from a flat monthly fee to a per capita charge based on the number of people who have access to the programming. In addition to the capital costs involved in providing the electronics and wiring system, there are also ongoing charges for the programming, whether the college obtains it from the cable company or collects it from its own antenna. Other ongoing charges include those related to the maintenance and repair of electronics and cabling (if the campus elects not to purchase its programming from a cable company), installations and disconnects, administrative procedures related to billing and collection of revenues, and staffing. The care and maintenance of a coaxial video system with several cascading amplifiers include regular tuning and recalibration of amplifiers and other electronics and will have a significant impact on the cost of operating an in-house cable TV system.

The provision of video services to individual student rooms often provokes a discussion among deans and faculty as to the impact this may have on the intellectual and academic life of the college. Some see it as negative and interfering with the educational process, others see television as an important information resource and argue that this medium can provide a number of educational benefits as well as entertainment. For instance, the college can have its own channels with programming consisting of lectures, films, and course materials. Security bulletins and announcements about campus activities can be scrolled throughout the day on in-house information channels. Furthermore, the college can choose to air just those networks or programs that are determined to be consistent with the educational mission and values of the college. Restricting a student's access to television may be perceived by some as interfering with the rights and privileges of private individuals who are presumably old enough to be discerning about the quantity and quality of programming they consume.

Another potentially divisive issue can arise if the college is perceived as censoring and controlling the content of programming made available to students. Finally, because providing video services is costly, it may require a large customer base to generate enough revenue to offset the costs involved. Unlike telephones, which have an important role in enhancing personal safety, television may be seen only as a luxury, one that most students would expect to have the option not to purchase. To the extent it is optional, its educational benefits to the entire campus will be limited. Also, the cost of a television monitor or receiver and the monthly service charge may divide the campus into those who can afford educational programming and those who cannot.

Connecticut College has taken the middle ground and has placed public monitors in high traffic areas and provided a wide range of programming, including campus events, to common rooms and lounges. It is not the college's intention to resell video services at this time, although every student room has a video connector and cabling connecting it to the campus-wide coaxial and fiber backbones. Some programming is obtained from on-campus satellite antennas and other programs are purchased from the local cable TV franchise. A task force, established in 1989, was charged with studying the wider distribution of video and the creation of production facilities on campus, and it remains to be seen how long this middle course will be satisfactory to students and faculty.

What Are the Administrative and Technical Requirements for Resale?

Some of these requirements have been mentioned in passing; however, a brief summary follows.

- Student rooms need to be wired and connected to a campus-wide distribution system.

- A modern PBX with multiple user features, several classes of service options, data-handling capabilities, least-cost routing, T-carrier capabilities, and an SMDR is required.

- A jack must be installed in each room, providing a standard interface to the campus wiring system. A more sophisticated version of the simple phone jack, called an *information port,* facilitates connection to several services.

- A reliable, computerized billing system is needed that is capable of producing detailed bills based on rates selected by the college and summary reports of costs, usage, and network traffic. It must be able to off-load information in computer-readable form for transmission to the college's administrative or financial systems.

- Bill calculation and distribution functions must be separated from revenue collection and cash handling activities.

- Procedures must be established for comparing revenues against costs and pricing, and for documenting the college's fiscal experience.

- Procedures must be established for repairing and troubleshooting equipment, wiring, and software.

- Procedures for new service, disconnects, and blocking of long distance access must be established on an individual as well as on a large group basis. The former is a counter to delinquent accounts, the latter is a response to a failure in the billing system.

- Procedures for discovering and correcting credit card abuse and unauthorized use of a personal identification number to steal long-distance services must be established.

- A model, usually expressed in a spreadsheet, must show the current and projected costs of providing services along with current and projected revenues collected. At least one row of cells should show the net operating profit or loss after revenues are applied to expenses.

What Are Some of the Administrative Benefits?

The most obvious benefit is that resale of services provides a revenue stream to offset a cost center. Even if revenues are only equal to costs, the reduction of cost represents a net increase in funds available to the college for other purposes. Telephones, data communications, and so forth are usually supported out of several different operating budgets. The creation of the preliminary spreadsheet model comparing current expenses with expenses after resale revenue represents an excellent opportunity to draw together all expenses related to voice and data communications from across the institution into one model. This analytic process helps executives at the college understand the true cost of telephone and data communications.

In-kind benefits may accrue to the college from the installation of high-volume long-distance lines that allow the college to apply those savings to administrative and faculty toll calls as well. Increased reduction of the college's administrative overhead occurs because adding students to the college system increases the level of discount available to the college from long-distance carriers. With the larger volume of usage, the college experiences a net increase in the savings for long-distance service because the administrative users are pooled with the student users. Other services such as voice mail may be installed as a benefit or a product for students, but the valuable voice messaging services provided by such systems are also available to the administration and faculty for their use as well.

The college can use the billing system to reduce toll abuse by staff and faculty who might otherwise use the long-distance service for their personal benefit. The monitoring and control of toll abuse can represent a significant amount of money. Some estimates place this abuse at thirty percent of all calling on an unmonitored system. This control is possible because detail billing can be based either on the station number or on an account number.

Some institutions require that all administrators and faculty have a personal identification number that must be entered whenever a long-distance call is made, thereby associating all toll calls with a specific individual or account. While some consider the entry of an additional string of numbers a nuisance, others argue that it significantly and permanently reduces toll abuse and theft of services by employees. Many billing systems also summarize the total number of minutes each individual spends on the phone during the billing period. The total time spent on the phone is a useful indicator to supervisors whether or not an employee is spending more time on the phone, possibly transacting personal business, than would be required by his or her job assignment.

The collection of revenue generated by resale and the possibility of net operating profits creates a potential for funding expensive capital improvements and expansions in information technologies, infrastructure, and peripheral support equipment. The billing system required for resale may also permit the telecommunications office to assign a base monthly cost for equipment and service for each administrative and faculty extension and charge these back against the operating budgets of each department or office. Costs related to moves, adds, changes of wiring or station equipment, and negligent damage of equipment or wiring can also be charged back to the requesting office.

While the actual process is to transfer funds from one part of the organization to another, the effect is to make each user and each budget supervisor attentive to the costs associated with telecommunications. This attention may result in the reduction of costs to the college for purely aesthetic changes in wiring and equipment, and also represents a way for the college's fiscal administrators to absorb unexpended funds in individual operating budgets at year's end. (This is done, for example, by underfunding the costs for telecommunications in the operating budget and expecting costs to exceed available funds, then allowing transfers from other budget lines to make up the overrun in the telecommunications line.) Real costs are associated with the service, wiring, and equipment. Awareness of the costs involved can lead to better control of inventory, reduced damage to equipment, improved facilities management, and closer scrutiny of the quality and cost of services the college purchases from third-party vendors including the independent phone company.

What About the Resale of Other Services?

Some institutions charge fees for the use of some or all of the following: data networks, computing labs, printing facilities and materials, voice mailboxes, and so on. Others provide these services free of charge. The difficult issue of who can and who can't afford to pay for services that are integral to the educational mission of the college must be addressed. Particularly in the case of data networks and the use of computing systems, it may be inappropriate to allow for a situation in which some students might not be able to afford to use the campus computing system. For example, should a college charge a student a specific fee for time spent on the network accessing the college's automated library system?

Also, there are a variety of other services that can be resold including special boxes on the voice mail system for bulletin boards or advertising, the sale of off-premise stations to off-campus vendors, high-quality laser or offset printing, access to special outside services or entertainment via the data or video networks that are not directly related to the academic requirements of the college.

What Can the College Do with Any Net Operating Profits?

It is not likely that the college will have any net operating profits during the time it takes to pay off the lease or pay back the endowment with the capital required to install a full telecommunication system. If the college's costs are equal to or higher than the revenues taken in no difficulties regarding possible tax liabilities or charges of "gouging the students" are likely to occur. Consequently, it is important to try to keep costs higher than revenues; however, as the college begins to reduce its leasing or pay-back costs, more revenues are likely to become available. Most colleges are finding, however, that a steady stream of capital is required to keep up with changes in technology and in user requirements.

Significant upgrades to the PBX and data-transmission systems, including their eventual replacement, should be anticipated and funds set aside for those contingencies. Maintenance and repair expenses will increase as the hardware and cabling ages and inflation forces the yearly maintenance fees to increase. Some colleges provide the jack in the wall and the wiring to users for access to the campus's information resources. Others, because of their commitment to computing and data transmission services, consider their network services to include, at the college's expense, any add-on boards needed by a user's PC to allow that user to take advantage of high-speed data communications.

Revenues or profits, if they exist, can be distributed as a form of financial aid to ensure that no student is denied access to the college's information resources. For example, PCs could be provided to students who can't afford them, larger public facilities can be made available, add-on circuitry and software sharing services can be installed and maintained, or subsidies to faculty and students who wish to use public database resources could be provided. In short, there are nearly unlimited opportunities for obtaining dramatic results coming from the commitment of spare revenues or profits, ensuring that all students and faculty are given the tools they need to access and utilize the available resources. Finally, if the college chooses, it can lower the costs to students for services or increase the discount on long-distance usage.

What Sorts of Problems Might Arise?

The majority of problems come about if the college tends to treat the resale operation as just another administrative activity. It should not do so for two reasons. First, the college has become a vendor of a crucial service and it is charging customers for that service. Second, the college is paying for all long-distance tolls in advance of billing the students, hence efficient and accurate accounting and billing systems are essential.

Students will spend inordinate amounts of time arguing with overworked staff over relatively small amounts of money. Parents will also scrutinize bills and service charges. Therefore, it is necessary for staff to be able to respond accurately and promptly to questions regarding the college's charges, the quality and nature of its services, and its policies regarding services, unless it employs an outside billing service to handle disputed calls, billing, and collection of aging accounts. This is a highly visible business activity, and the importance of the need for the college to provide the necessary administrative support cannot be overstated. If the resale operation gets out of control, the college can stand to lose many thousands of dollars and important credibility with regard to its ability to manage its business operations. The good news is that since resale of services generates revenues, the costs of supporting these services can be documented and passed along to the users as the cost of doing business on their behalf.

Serious problems with the operation of a resale system are usually caused by inadequate staffing, vague or nonexistent administrative procedures, faulty accounting procedures, or unreliable technology. Problems that result from staffing are usually caused by inadequate training in the use of the systems and accounting procedures, understaffing for the amount of work that needs to be done, and poor or indifferent supervision. Training is required in the use of the software, data entry, administrative procedures for handling disputed calls, customer service and etiquette, and in recognizing when the billing system is not operating properly. It is essential that documented administrative procedures be established for processing calls, entering data, distributing bills, collecting revenues, updating the college's financial systems, and handling delinquent accounts or disputed calls. If these procedures are written down it makes it easier to refer to them later for clarification, publication, and training of new staff.

The departments charged with creating the bills should be organizationally separate from the departments charged with collecting the money. Furthermore, the college will need policies covering fees for students on financial aid and those who work in some capacity for the college or student government. Since the telecommunications office is providing services to these categories of students, it ought to receive some sort of payment or credit since it will initially incur the costs for the services those students receive. Some colleges approach this problem by allowing the telecommunications office to bill the financial aid office or the office of student services for tolls and basic service charges. There is much to recommend this approach since it may force other offices to set more realistic priorities on the allocation of their funds.

There are three kinds of technical problems, including failure of the computing systems, loss of the telecommunications link between the SMDR and the data-collecting devices, and problems with the interface between the PBX and the off-campus telephone network. Each of these problems represents a serious situation, since calls can be made and not recorded. The college will still be billed for the calls but will have no way of assigning the cost of a call to the party that made it. The usual kinds of failures in hardware include failure of some component (for example, a disk drive or a printer), or a failure in the electrical system that powers the computing and related equipment.

There are several ways to protect against problems resulting from hardware failure including redundant PCs simultaneously collecting the same data, *mirroring* disk systems, procedures for blocking long-distance calling while the computing systems are down, and, of course, regular backups of call records. To protect against failure of the power system, uninterruptible power sources using batteries or a portable generator should be installed. If possible, the billing system should be connected to the same power supply that provides battery backup power to the PBX. Additionally, suitable alarms notifying staff when failures have occurred in either the computing systems or the power systems should be installed so that immediate action can be taken to prevent the college's experiencing any loss of revenue from unrecorded calls.

Software-related problems are usually due to some aberration in the functioning of the hardware which may create a broken file structure in the database, a faulty restart of the program after a system has been rebooted, overflow of the disk space available for storing call records, or entry of incorrect information into one of the processing parameters.

The tables that permit the calculation and assignment of costs to calls need to be updated regularly in order to keep them consistent with the rates being charged by the college's vendor of long-distance service. Students and parents listen to the advertising claims made by the competing vendors of long-distance services and are not shy about letting the telecommunications office know about various sales promotions.

If the college uses a service bureau, most, if not all of these problems may be the responsibility of the service bureau to contend with. They have to demonstrate to the college how they will ensure that a minimum of loss will occur in the case of malfunctioning systems. If the college operates its own computing equipment, then considerable attention must be paid to the reliable and error-free operation of the computing systems. This may require employing staff with the appropriate technical skills or siting the computing system in the college's main computing center to ensure that it receives proper maintenance and supervision.

Failure in the communication between the PBX and the billing system may be due to conditions in the PBX or in the SMDR circuitry. These problems are identified through built-in alarms and diagnostic testing and should be referred to the individuals who repair the PBX. Failures in the collection devices have already been discussed. Failure in the communications lines between the SMDR and the collecting device may require a procedure for blocking all student long-distance calling until the line is repaired. Whether the line is on campus or installed by the regional phone company, it will still take time to locate and repair the problem. During that time, the college will be liable for any calls made and, until the communications link is restored, the college will have no method for assigning the costs for those calls to the parties who made them.

Problems that occur between the network and the college's PBX include those related to the way the network handles calls. Most of these problems come from "answer supervision" and tend to be more frequent on overseas calls. The systems that support the national phone network sense when a call has been completed and report this condition back to the long-distance carrier or the local central office which reports it to the PBX. Upon receiving notification that a call has been completed, the PBX reports the duration, date, and extension from the call dialed to the billing system via the SMDR. Unfortunately, the PBX has no way of determining whether the call dialed was answered or if a call resulted in a "reorder" or busy signal. Consequently, it is necessary to adjust the billing system so that all calls of less than a certain duration—usually 30 to 60 seconds—are not billed. This adjustment will significantly reduce the number of complaints regarding the billing for calls that the user contends were never completed.

Another odd billing situation often occurs with PBXs that allow a second dial tone to be initiated while the first line is still engaged. The following situation appears to happen most frequently with analog switches and overseas calls. A person dials an overseas number and gets a reorder signal, hits the switch-hook, but instead of disconnecting the first call, actually connects to a second trunk out of the PBX, redials and gets through to the overseas party. The disconnect signal, when returned by the network, terminates the second call, but the first attempt is left active until the PBX times out the line by default, usually several minutes later. The bill shows two calls made to the same number usually at the same time from the same extension. One of the charges is obviously incorrect and must be credited back to the student and backed out of the accounts-receivable system.

If a call is disputed, the college can verify the actual call by looking at the detail billing sent by the long-distance carrier. The student's detailed bill will list the date and time of the disputed call. The college's recourse is to try to locate the same call in the statement sent by the long-distance vendor and in this way verify whether or not the college was charged for the call. If the carrier's bill, detailing each call for which the college was charged, is sorted by date, time, and area code, it will be that much easier to determine if the disputed call was actually made. Also, note that the amount charged for that call may not reflect the amount actually billed to the office or student, so discretion in studying the bills is recommended. Keep in mind that, although the actual costs of providing service are passed back to the users of the service, the charges itemized on the carrier's detail bill reflect only a part of the cost of providing long-distance service to students.

The storage and archiving of vendor invoices, call records, payment records, copies of detailed bills, and summary reports requires organization and space. Some sort of policy for the retention of records needs to be developed in cooperation with the controller or other fiscal officer of the college. Many colleges write a copy of the month's billing detail to tape and send it out to be microfilmed. Other colleges choose to store the entire bill as a database on a computer disk so it can be accessed quickly in case of questions or disputes. Some policy of how long a given set of bills should be kept on-line, and how long archived bills and invoices should be kept needs to be determined. Additionally, the appropriate environment for the storage of computer tapes, fiche, and paper for at least a year needs to be provided. The size of the space depends on the size of the population being served. A documented floor plan and materials location map are necessary in order to retrieve specific information from the archive at a later date.

What Are Some Concerns Various Constituents Will Have?

Adding a margin to the cost of purchasing a service for another person does not necessarily result in a net profit because there are many costs involved in providing services in addition to the capital outlay for equipment and ongoing costs of purchasing of volume services. Staffing, environment (including power, heat, wiring, and furniture), paper and supplies, taxes, licenses, and fees must be included in the algorithm used to calculate the margin that is added to the basic cost of the service purchased. Nevertheless, the first concern that may be raised is that the college is "gouging" the students. The best counter to this claim, assuming it isn't true, is to show either that the amounts charged for the system are less than the phone company would charge and that expanded services are now available to the student, or that the overall student contribution in support of the system is equal to the number of students who use the system versus the number of college employees who are users of the system. That is, the administrator and student each pay their fair share.

For instance, if the total phone bill for service is $500,000 per year and students represent 65 percent of the total number of users of the phone system, their contribution to paying the bill should be $315,000. It is important that the students recognize that they have a legitimate stake in supporting a service that benefits them as much, if not more, than any of the other campus constituencies.

It may be necessary in a college with a smaller enrollment to require that all students purchase phone service in order to ensure that the student body makes a sufficient contribution toward the support of the overall telecommunication system. Some students and parents will object to the mandatory nature of this requirement, so it helps to remind them that the phones in their rooms are primarily "emergency safety devices." Their purpose is to give every student the ability to reach the campus security office in an emergency. Modern phone systems can be designed so that a sequence of numbers, such as one-one-one, causes the phone to ring in the campus safety office and to display the location of the phone making the emergency call to the dispatcher.

There are a number of other safety-related systems that can be installed once a telecommunication system serving the entire campus exists. A comprehensive security system is rapidly becoming a service colleges must provide for employees and students in order to conduct business. Such systems not only protect people, but may also lessen a college's liability in the event an incident occurs.

Some colleges may wish to set a limit on the amount of tolls that can be accumulated by a student before his or her bill is paid. This protects a student from running up high bills for long-distance calls and also keeps a reasonable ceiling on the amount of exposure the college has should the student for some reason not pay back the amount owed the college. Another option the college has is to require an up-front deposit equal to the amount of the toll limit. When the limit is exceeded, access to long-distance service is curtailed until the full amount of the bill is paid. Should the student default, the deposit is then used to reimburse the college for the amount it has already paid out to the long-distance carrier. Certain groups of students may object to the limit because they have special calling needs, for example, foreign students or students who have business or other concerns. In these cases, arrangements can be made, such as collecting a higher deposit or obtaining a credit-card number from the student and charging costs as they exceed the limit rather than accumulating a very large bill during the normal billing cycle. One additional note: Students on financial aid should have the cost for basic phone service included in the living-expense allocation; this is especially necessary if purchase of the telecommunication service is mandatory.

What Are Some of the Policy Issues?

A successfully implemented resale system will have clear policies to help guide decision making and operations. Some of the policy questions that may arise include:

- Should some individuals be subsidized while others pay the full amount of basic voice and data services? Will some individuals be excluded from the telecommunication and safety benefits made possible by such systems because they cannot afford the cost of the services?

- Will some services be basic and others optional? Which ones?

- What kinds of peripherals will be connected to the phone wiring? Devices designed to use phone wiring intended to support analog sets such as FAX machines, modems, and answering machines cannot be installed on circuits intended for digital phone sets.

- Will students or other members of the college community be allowed to use the system for commercial reasons not necessarily connected with their studies?

- Should entertainment calls, such as those provided by 900 and 976 exchanges be blocked?

- Will the college require every student to pay for basic phone services? How will prices be set? Will there be a formula based on the benefits students receive? Will discounts be passed along to students?

- How will excess revenues or profits be handled? Will they be passed back to the students or used to improve the college's information resources?

- To what extent will students be apprised of the financial assumptions and administrative operations underpinning the resale system?

- How many distribution lists will students be allowed to create? Which features of voice mail will be basic and which will be optional? How will voice mail be administered?

- How will complaints be handled and what dollar limits must be passed before the college will take valuable staff time to investigate a disputed call? One private university will not investigate any dispute under twenty-five dollars. If staff doesn't investigate, will the college then waive the disputed charge?

- How will delinquent accounts be handled? Who will notify the students and what pressures will be brought to bear? Should parents be notified if bills are not paid? Is it a violation of a student's privacy to send a copy of the detail bill to his or her parents for payment when the student account is delinquent?

- What mechanisms are in place for storing student records to keep call details and patterns of payment confidential? How long should archives be kept before

destruction? Is it appropriate to turn an uncollected
account over to a collection agency and file a report
with a credit bureau?

In conclusion, the issues surrounding the resale of telecommunication
services to students are numerous, often complex, and may involve
decisions that affect nearly all the individuals that make up the
college's community of scholars, administrators and students. Many
of the decisions will be politically sensitive; others hinge on passing
"points-of-no-return" in the direction a college takes with regard to
the selection and installation of information technologies. Even small
failures can be highly visible and real economic success of the resale
activity will only be revealed after all the costs (many of which are
not just monetary) and revenues are compared over a ten-year period.
However, few other capital projects undertaken at a liberal arts
college during the nineties will have as dramatic an impact on its
day-to-day operations as the task of providing its scholars, students,
and decision makers with comprehensive, well-integrated and
supportive information technologies.

Part Four

The Impact of Computing

Information Technology in the Liberal Arts Environment: Faculty Development Issues

Carol Lennox
Mills College

Carol Lennox is director of academic computing and campus networking at Mills College in Oakland, California. Her responsibilities include long-term planning for academic computing and campus networking, faculty and student training and support, and management of all academic computing resources. In addition to her administrative duties, Ms. Lennox is a lecturer in the department of mathematics and computer science, does thesis advising, and teaches two graduate courses in the Interdisciplinary Computer Science masters degree program. Prior to coming to Mills, Ms. Lennox worked for five years on a variety of computing projects for Stanford University.

Ms. Lennox has been a member of the EDUCOM Consulting Group and the Membership Committee, the EDUNET Task Force, and the ESI Project. She has served on the SAC board of trustees, the Microsoft Educational Advisory Board, and since 1988 has been a member of the EDUCOM board of trustees. In 1985 she was cochair of the Berkeley conference of the InterUniversity Consortium for Educational Computing. Ms. Lennox has lectured, written, and consulted extensively on all aspects of academic computing and networking, especially with respect to liberal arts colleges.

Institutional Missions and Information Technology

Over the last two decades the transition in the United States to an information-based, service-oriented economy has prompted those of us in higher education to examine the role information technology should play in the education of our students and how that affects our work. Higher education began its debate with issues concerning the quantity and quality of exposure to information technology needed by our students to deal both with the information explosion and with the increasing rate of change they face upon leaving our ivory towers. Today the debate has broadened significantly and resembles in many ways that held by corporate America during the eighties—what is the importance of information technology to us as "producers of education and research ideas" in enhancing our own creativity, teaching effectiveness, and productivity?

While many large research institutions have been able to garner the institutional resources and funding to provide faculty with desktop access to computing resources and to experiment with the development of comprehensive student learning systems based on technology, the efforts at most liberal arts colleges have been modest by comparison. With few exceptions, the infusion of information technology at liberal arts colleges has sprung up around the pioneering efforts of one faculty member or one discipline, inspired by the potential for enhancing students' learning experiences, rather than springing from an institutional commitment to explore the potential benefits of technology for faculty and students.

William H. Graves, director of the Institute for Academic Technology at the University of North Carolina at Chapel Hill, has provided one of the most comprehensive and insightful commentaries on the potential of affordable interactive technologies to add value to teaching, learning, and scholarship. As the editor of *Computing Across the Curriculum: Academic Perspectives,* recently published as part of the EDUCOM Strategies Series on Information Technology, Graves offers the following challenge.

> To view the investments of the individuals and institutions represented in this book as investments in technology would be shortsighted, for they are nothing less than investments in faculty development, curriculum development, and institutional development. Such investments are farsighted at a time when colleges and universities are competing vigorously for students and faculty and when the public's expectation is that technology can help solve many of the nation's problems, including its problems in education (1989).

If faculty are to be the primary source for student exposure to appropriate uses of and choices about information technology, and if they are to explore uses of technology for their teaching and scholarship in providing solutions to education's problems, institutional mission statements need clearly to reflect this expectation. In addition, institutional support of faculty development programs involving curricular and other scholarly uses of information technology should be high on priority lists when colleges make decisions about educational strategies that support their broadest institutional missions.

Faculty Development and Information Technology

While institutions grapple with the development of institutional strategic plans and resource allocation decisions crucial to these educational goals, many faculty share a fundamental set of concerns as researchers and teachers. Again, quoting from the introduction of *Computing Across the Curriculum: Academic Perspectives* (Graves 1989) these concerns are distilled most succinctly as follows:

- Those individual scholars whose accomplishments are reflected in all three parts of [this] book are dedicated to improving their teaching and their students' education. This, above all else, has motivated them to develop and use instructional technologies.

- Developing software requires an enormous commitment of a scholar's time, even with support. Without support from an institution, a vendor, or some combination of these and other sources, sustaining a project requires Herculean energy and persistence. Vendor support, in particular, has played a major role in progress to date.

- Evaluating the results of using instructional technologies is an important but difficult agenda that is seldom supported with institutional resources.

- Academic governance and reward structures are inhospitable to developing and using instructional technologies.

- The various vendor-specific flavors of technology and their constant changes present a moving, chaotic target for academe, which by its incremental nature and its budgeting mechanisms cannot allow change to dominate stability for very long in the curriculum. This and the high costs of the human talent behind technology-based curriculum development projects make it difficult to sustain such projects over time.

• Developing software that can be adapted to the individual instructional needs of others is difficult.

• Making software available to others across institutional boundaries is often difficult in today's review and distribution environments.

• The in-class use of technology is an important component of instructional computing. Because the associated costs of equipment and staff support are high, it is often an absent "luxury."

Faculty at liberal arts institutions who have taken the information technology plunge during the last ten to fifteen years share these concerns with a growing number of administrators. A brief review of the experiences and insights gained over the last two decades by liberal arts faculty involved in developing computer-based learning systems, in creating and using computer-based scholarship and research tools, and in collaborating electronically with colleagues in these efforts can assist us in assessing the appropriate curricular and institutional commitments for the future.

Faculty Development Efforts of the 1970s and 1980s

What can the last two decades tell us about preparing liberal arts faculty and students for intelligent uses of and appropriate choices concerning information technology? Not only have attitudes and accessibility to information technology changed drastically in the last twenty years but also the environments in which higher education has explored its uses have also changed.

The 1970s liberal arts computing environment was characteristically based primarily on centralized computing facilities using mainframe and minicomputer technology. Development tools for faculty were primarily those created for scientists and the commercial sector.

The 1980s liberal arts computing environment was characteristically an environment moving first toward distributed campus computing facilities brought about by the growing use of microcomputers and then to the interconnection of these facilities through campus-wide networks. The range of information technology tools available to students and faculty broadened significantly with the appearance of generic microcomputer applications such as word processors, databases, and spreadsheets. A growing appreciation of the power of graphical presentation of information for students and breakthroughs in digitization of images and sound have led to a corresponding interest from faculty for authoring tools allowing them easily to incorporate such multimedia materials into instructional computing efforts. Emerging studies from the cognitive sciences on visual thinking and on contextual exploratory learning have also increased the interest in interactive multimedia systems that link multiple sources of electronic information.

The 1990s liberal arts computing environment will undoubtedly follow, at least partially, the pattern of the larger universities in the 1980s, with slowly increasing investments in advanced workstation clusters, library automation, connections to national and international networks, access to supercomputing facilities through regional networks, and more intense experimentation with interactive multimedia computing materials.

An Example from the 1970s: The Mills Computer Literacy Project

For those unfamiliar with early liberal arts computing efforts, the following summary of a computer literacy project at Mills College typifies experiences at other colleges during the 1970s and early 1980s. Mills has an unusual history in computing, considering its small size. The college has offered courses in computing since 1960 and in 1974 became the first women's college in the United States to offer a bachelor of arts degree in computer science. These experiences led Mills to believe that the fastest way to achieve the integration of information technology into the curriculum in the 1970s was through a strong faculty development program in the uses of information technology. The expected outcome was that faculty would then pass on appropriate uses to their students within each discipline.

A formal faculty development program began in 1977 with funding from a National Science Foundation (NSF) CAUSE grant to establish a campus-wide computer literacy program and to augment on-campus minicomputing facilities. The program provided broad exposure to social issues surrounding computing and access to computing for all members of the community. It promoted hands-on computer training workshops for faculty in the social sciences, the physical sciences, and mathematics; it introduced students to computing at the introductory course level in all science disciplines; and it enhanced upper division courses in the sciences through exposure to discipline-specific computing applications. After gaining a working knowledge of computers through hands-on experience, faculty were given released time for course development and revision that included the integration of computing components. The grant period ended in June 1980, with more than 20 faculty and staff members (15 percent) having participated, and with 360 to 450 students (45 to 50 percent) using the computer center facilities in a classroom context during the academic year.

Outcomes of the Mills Computer Literacy Project. As the NSF CAUSE grant came to an end, the college responded to the success of the program with the development of a new series of strategic plans, calling for significant upgrades of existing minicomputing facilities, support for faculty research and curriculum development using computing, and exploration of applications of microcomputers in faculty research and teaching. Several of the strategies from the NSF CAUSE grant that faculty found most helpful continue to be useful today.

- Abundant opportunities, tailored to a variety of faculty schedules, were provided for learning about generic and discipline-specific applications—brownbag lunches, small 40-minute hands-on workshops, faculty development colloquia, intensive one-week workshops during breaks, demonstrations of existing computer-based learning materials, software checkout libraries, self-paced video- and audiocassette learning tools, and so on.

- A faculty-only center provided daily staff support, 24-hour access to special equipment, and an atmosphere conducive to informal exchanges with colleagues about research efforts, college events, interdisciplinary interests, and computing.

- Training and support programs were developed for academic secretaries through academic computing staff on the use of generic computing applications such as word processors, statistics programs, and spreadsheets so that faculty and support staff can seamlessly pass electronic information back and forth.

- Training and support programs for students were developed by academic computing staff on the use of generic computing applications such as word processors and spreadsheets so that faculty and class time were not used for teaching generic application skills.

- Common computing platforms and campus-wide software standards for generic applications enhanced technology transfer, cooperative help and trouble-shooting efforts, and development of a common set of computing skills across all tiers of the community.

- It was made economically feasible for faculty, staff, and students to purchase personal computer systems matching the systems and software supported by the college.

Other observations during the 1970s that still guide planning for the 1990s include the following.

- Faculty who embark on courseware development need clear information from the institution as to whether or not their curricular innovations will assist them in the promotion and tenure process, and how such efforts compare to the traditional measures of published research, teaching, and community service.

• While faculty have usually carefully thought out the teaching process for their courses, they often have no clear student learning model in mind and must take the time to articulate or develop one as a crucial step in designing effective computer-based learning materials.

• Faculty are not necessarily trained in design, graphics, and human-interface issues, adding an additional time factor to the generation of high-quality instructional computing materials.

• Faculty who may be interested in using information technology rarely sustain that interest if required to become computer programmers in order to create computer-based instructional materials.

• Faculty will not take full advantage of computing technology for any purpose if access to such technology means a trip to another building—away from office, phone, and work materials.

The Broader View

When asked how information technology might best support student learning and their specific teaching goals, liberal arts faculties in the 1970s often thought first of statistical analysis, simulations, and self-paced drill and practice applications. As is often true with new technologies, these old familiar tasks were the first to be tried with the new technology. The tools with which faculty developed statistics and simulation applications were drawn primarily from the pool of professional applications such as SPSS, SIMULA, SIMSCRIPT, and TSP running on mainframes and minicomputers. Other materials were developed using traditional programming languages such as ALGOL, BASIC, FORTRAN, and PASCAL, although programming languages such as SNOBOL and PILOT were developed specifically to address non-computational applications such as text analysis and the creation of drill and practice learning materials.

Computer-aided instruction (CAI) systems, often designed originally as electronic versions of pencil-and-paper drill and practice
sessions, were some of the first computational learning systems
developed within higher education. The early CAI systems eventually
led to dialogue-interactive systems allowing the learner to drive the
learning enterprise through questions posed to the system. The CAI
systems led to more extensive computer-based education (CBE) systems
and computer-managed instruction (CMI) systems incorporating
graphics, performance tracking, and performance analysis such as
that used in the PLATO system. In many ways the 1970s represented
an era of transferring self-paced learning systems from paper to
computer and exploring the available empowering uses of the technology, such as simulations, for student learning.

For those who persevered through the agonies and ecstasies of
successfully creating computer-based materials with these tools,
there was rarely a pot of gold at the end of the institutional rainbow.
Faculty usually discovered that they had spent one or more years
improving their courses in a significant but nontraditional way that
was not recognized by the institution's promotion and tenure policies.
For young, untenured faculty members, this was a bitter pill to swallow.

By the mid-1970s, CONDUIT, the first national center for the
review and dissemination of higher education classroom computing
materials, reported that higher education recognition and reward
systems were not adequate to allow faculty, tenured or nontenured,
to pursue the development of computer-based instructional materials
on a long-term basis. In large universities, as in small liberal arts
colleges, the criterion in the promotion and tenure process continued
to center on research results published in traditional printed form. It
did not acknowledge activities such as curriculum development using
information technology. Faculty developers reported apathy from
colleagues, lack of institutional support, and pressures to pursue
traditional research for the purposes of promotion and tenure. These
were major obstacles to early leaders in this area. Young faculty
members in tenure-track positions, those most likely to have become
familiar with information technology during their graduate studies,
were often the early leaders who found that they could not afford to
pursue potential uses of information technology in the classroom due

to the risk of being passed over in the tenure process. The lack of formal recognition for faculty developers of curriculum revision based on the incorporation of information technology was, and continues to be, a major bottleneck in the creation of a large pool of sharable software for higher education.

The Emergence of Microcomputing in Higher Education

With the spread of microcomputers in the early 1980s, individual faculty members at liberal arts colleges found it possible to purchase these computing systems for their departments, often without needing the usual institutional blessing for computing purchases and support. In a handful of disciplines such as education, computer science, and the natural sciences, computer-based classroom and laboratory materials were developed on this new platform. In other disciplines, faculty found that generic applications available on microcomputers, such as the spreadsheet and word processor, were extremely useful in their research and publication efforts and the use of such applications by students in the classroom began to grow.

Liberal arts institutions with broad curricular initiatives sometimes found agreement among their faculty about the potential of these generic computer applications to facilitate and encourage exploration by students in writing and analytic tasks. Such agreement often provided the foundation for an institution's first investment in information technology in direct support of its broadest educational goals.

As institutional investments increased, students, faculty, and academic support staff quickly learned the educational advantages of campus-wide standards. Students were able to leverage the time spent learning a word processor or spreadsheet for one class into an asset for many other classes. Similarly, faculty were able to use the same generic tools for class preparation, research, and departmental administration. And small academic computing support staffs could focus their support efforts more effectively in assisting an ever-growing user community. Economically, such standards also served as institutional cost-containment tools by making more efficient use of staff and by providing opportunities for volume discount purchases, despite small institutional size.

But perhaps the most important outcome at these institutions was the development of a familiarity with information technology for a much broader segment of the faculty. This direct experience with technology and its impact on their professional work created a new credibility in the minds of many faculty and administrators regarding the power of information technology to transform and enhance their daily work, whether extended to students or not. In addition, the faculty use of generic microcomputer applications often became the natural stepping stone to an interest in exploring discipline-specific tools to help students in the learning process. It is interesting that despite the effort required by faculty in revising their courses to incorporate these generic tools, such efforts did not seem significantly to raise faculty expectations about promotion and tenure rewards.

The Emergence of Graphical User Interfaces

As the mid-1980s approached, graphical user interfaces such as that of the Macintosh appeared. A handful of pioneering liberal arts institutions including Dartmouth, Reed, and Franklin and Marshal re-examined their institutional missions in light of society's transition into the information age. These institutions concluded that the importance of information technology in society as a whole, along with its potential for changing the nature of higher education learning experiences, should be formally reflected in their educational goal statements. Each made or renewed major institutional commitments to the curricular integration of information technology in all disciplines, extending far beyond the use of generic applications, and to the exposure of faculty to such technology for administrative and research uses.

These institutions initiated programs that provided extensive support for faculty interested in developing computer-based instructional materials and made large capital investments to provide the faculty-development and student-delivery platforms for use of such materials. These efforts were, and continue to be, very successful in unleashing creative faculty exploration of ways to transform student educational experiences through computer-based instructional materials.

In part this success stems from the excitement some educators have experienced in rethinking their models for student learning and in watching their students absorb concepts more quickly and in more depth than previously possible. Less tangible side benefits have also been cited by faculty at these institutions. They mention the unexpected but enjoyable collaboration with colleagues about computing and the occasional interdisciplinary fruits of such collaboration. And in part the success stems from institutions first expecting that all faculty learn about information technology and then providing the opportunity and resources to allow exploration of its impacts on society, on their disciplines, and in the classroom. Finally, this success must also be attributed to the formal acknowledgment in the promotion and tenure process at each of these institutions of the high value of such computer-based curricular innovations.

One common insight gleaned from the efforts of these institutions, and confirmed at the larger research and comprehensive institutions that have made similar commitments, was that the support needed by faculty to create high-quality teaching materials was inevitably more than had been anticipated. In addition, the time spans originally projected for such development were often underestimated, partially because the tools available for creating these materials were still based on traditional programming skills that many faculty found difficult to acquire.

While the majority of individual faculty members and departments in such institutions were convinced that the quality of student learning experiences was perceptibly enhanced or transformed in some significant way by the materials they created, the publication of results based on formal evaluation with evidence of actual cost benefit was, and still is, sparse. Evaluation efforts from a few large multiyear projects such as MIT's Athena project and Brown University's Intermedia project have been well documented. But at liberal arts institutions the projects supported have usually been much smaller and there has been nearly a total absence of professional evaluation.

Exploratory Learning, Merging Technologies, and Other "Speed Bumps"

In the mid-1980s, faculty and researchers began to explore new ways to support teaching and student learning with technology by involving students in exploratory modes of learning relying on graphic simulations, diverse visual and sound databases, and extensively interlinked reference materials—things that would not be possible without the technology. The ability to incorporate images and sound with text, to digitize slide collections and to build simple-to-use browsing tools for multimedia databases became technically viable for those who could afford the high cost of specialized equipment.

Studies performed in the cognitive sciences over the last fifteen to twenty years support the notion that certain types of materials are best grasped visually by human beings, regardless of dominant or preferred learning modes. Further, the lecture format and accompanying text materials traditionally adopted as the primary means for delivery of educational information in most disciplines in the western world is heavily biased in favor of those students most skilled in language and logic. The presentation of the same classroom materials simultaneously in oral, graphic, and printed versions is usually absorbed by more students or made more meaningful to all students because of the opportunity to exercise multiple cognitive skills rather than only one. The experiences of those developing and using extensively linked sets of related materials have transformed the adage, "a picture is worth a thousand words" to "a well-designed multimedia system is worth a thousand lectures." While few of us who consider ourselves educators would be in total agreement with this, it does suggest that teachers should perhaps pause to reconsider the manner in which they have traditionally provided their students with one- or two-dimensional learning experiences.

Although these more elegant possibilities were enticing, the steep learning curves required for preparing multimedia courseware quickly became apparent to those adventurous souls who leaped in. Faculty and academic computing support staff were faced not only with the need to develop new programming skills and tools specific to building learning materials, but also with the need to absorb new concepts resulting from the rapid integration of computing with publishing technology and digitized sound, text, and video materials.

Given the expense of developing multimedia materials, the need to develop rapid prototyping and formative evaluation methods early in the design cycle soon became apparent to many developers. These steps involved limited development of initial ideas, testing the effectiveness of the student learning model, exploratory navigation strategies, content cohesiveness, content clarity, visual design, and other learning approaches. Developers also found that long-term summative evaluations, although frequently not funded, were critical to establishing the effectiveness of their efforts in the eyes of colleagues, funding agencies, and their institutions. These two discoveries—the need for development of rapid prototyping and formative evaluation techniques and the need for summative evaluation efforts—were often among the major reasons for longer-than-expected development times.

As mentioned earlier, the high costs to the pioneering institutions in the exploratory learning and multimedia arenas were usually underestimated, both in terms of the amount of time and support required to allow faculty to develop such materials and the costs for high-performance equipment for interactive multimedia applications. An additional area of frustration often emerged when developers attempted to obtain copyright permissions for sound and graphic images to be included in such projects. The incorporation of non-print materials into computer-based systems was as new to higher education as it often was to the publishers of such materials. Industry agreements within the video and music communities are often inadequate, incomplete, or vague when considered as models for the educational computing environment. Delays in project time until copyright issues were resolved, as well as the additional expense of the copyrights and the legal expertise to obtain them, were almost universally overlooked in planning early multimedia projects.

Development Tools, Standards, and Technical Support

Coupled with the complications of merging technologies has been the lack of authoring tools that can buffer faculty and support staff from the many different, often incompatible, standards for hardware and data formats. The lack of uniform standards among computing vendors for digitized video, graphics, text, and sound data formats further complicated the learning process, perhaps even more than the limitations of the technologies themselves.

Early leaders in the multimedia arena found that they had to purchase an exotic collection of equipment to convert analog sound to digital formats acceptable to the specific programs they had chosen for authoring; this format often was not usable by other programs eventually needed to edit, enhance, or filter the original sounds, necessitating yet another layer of conversion by experts. Similarly, the capture of analog video signals for conversion to digital format for storage and later access in the computer required the installation of special analog-to-digital video boards to capture images in digital form. Once captured, the author was often forced to choose from and/or move among various computer-based graphic storage formats such as EPS, PICT, TIFF, or RIF, as the need to edit images or manipulate them arose. The collection of requisite image-manipulation programs and formats demanded not only knowing which program required which format, but learning two to five programs to achieve the desired results. And even if one became a wizard at such manipulations, the huge amounts of disk storage required for both sound and video images often became the limiting factor in the richness of the materials that could be assembled.

One solution for multimedia systems was the use of video disks to store long sounds and large images, thus avoiding the disk storage issue. While this path usually arrived at the desired results, it too was a complex series of new tasks for the uninitiated. For example, images are usually captured first on video tape and then edited professionally to create the desired frame sequences and the necessary control information, and to eliminate flutter and other evils that occur when moving from the primary medium of video tape to secondary storage media to be controlled by computer. Having created a reasonably professional video tape on three-quarter- or one-inch media, faculty then must create a *check disk* locally (if the proper equipment is available) or send the video tape to a professional studio for pressing. The editing and pressing process often is repeated several times before the final video disk is mastered and duplicated for distribution to computer labs and students. The process for creating a CD-ROM disk, an alternative high-storage medium, is even more complex, time consuming, and expensive. Fortunately, creating rich materials on these two media is becoming less expensive with the appearance of several inexpensive commercial services for mastering check disks, the emergence of programs that provide "one-stop" facilities for capturing and integrating graphics, video, and sound into courseware, and simplification of the user interface for the authors.

The heroic efforts of the handful of liberal arts educators who have persisted and produced outstanding classroom products tapping into the rich learning potential offered by these merged technologies have turned out to be expensive in terms of faculty time required, programming and design support needed, and institutional investments in hardware platforms to deliver these products to large numbers of students. On the other hand, authors are for the most part very enthusiastic about what they perceive to be significant changes in student learning, the stimulation of curiosity, and the more comprehensive grasp of a period, field, or principle after students use their systems. The most impressive potential long-term impact for students using new exploratory learning systems, such as the Brown Intermedia project, may lie in the model it gives students for doing traditional scholarly research—the exploration of multiple related sources of information to develop context as well as details about specific figures, events, and phenomena. With the recognition provided by recently developed award programs within disciplines and by the EDUCOM *Software Awards*, a handful of faculty authors of such systems say in their efforts are finally being acknowledged in the promotion and tenure process at their institutions.

Sharing the Wealth

While many liberal arts colleges have not yet developed the internal resources and expertise necessary to support faculty in the creation of computer-based learning materials, many faculty are nevertheless aware of their colleagues' efforts at other institutions. Attempts to participate in evaluation efforts or to import a colleague's computer-based learning materials for classroom use, however, are often frustrated by having to recreate the exact hardware and software platform used by the developer to run such materials. The lack of portability of programs, graphics, sounds, and data across hardware and software platforms still remains a major barrier to effective sharing of high-quality learning materials. And this barrier becomes even larger if one wishes to bring to one's home institution interactive multimedia materials that require special peripherals.

As indicated earlier, standards for graphic, video, and sound storage, color representation, and compression techniques are just now emerging. As the lack of portability for software applications across hardware platforms is a stumbling block, so the lack of computer industry standards for rich-text, sound, graphic, and video data presents another major barrier to sharing information. Currently, standards have emerged or are in the process of emerging for the following:

- CD-audio formats

- CD-ROM formats (ISO 9660 and High Sierra formats)

- Video disk formats (CAV and CLV)

- Still video formats (JPEG)

- Motion video (MPEG)

However, the fact that computer hardware and software vendors, the music industry, and the film and video communities have not adopted cohesive standards that incorporate digital audio, digital video, and compound document formats (combined graphics, text, sound) will continue to limit educators in their ability to exchange multimedia classroom computing systems and tools.

An additional barrier to easy sharing of wealth has been the lack of a national forum or collection point for the review and distribution of instructional computing products and research tools. While the review and distribution of printed research materials and textbooks have long been established through discipline-specific professional organizations and commercial publishers, few widely accepted national equivalents for review and distribution of faculty-developed computer-based learning materials have established themselves in the 1970s or 1980s. Given the high level of faculty effort and expense in developing quality computer-based learning materials, the distribution and sharing of such materials have now become major issues, along with the expense of the hardware platforms to deliver them, in liberal arts institutional efforts to integrate information technology with student learning.

The commercial publishing sector has been cautious in its approach to marketing computer-based instructional materials, although publishers such as Addison-Wesley and Wadsworth have ventured gently into the field of supplying higher education with textbook-software combinations in recent years. Already slim profit margins are further jeopardized by the lack of transportability across hardware platforms for each potential educational user of a given textbook-software package and by faculty desires to tailor instructional materials to their own style and sequences. Ongoing support and maintenance of the software for purchasers and users is also an issue that few faculty developers or publishers are prepared to cope with over the long term.

The problems of sharing classroom materials and research tools across multiple computing platforms with faculty at other institutions also raises a basic question of whether computing technology can truly have the revolutionary impact on higher education that many of us have long believed to be possible.

National Electronic Networks

The development of national electronic networks such as the Internet and BITNET has given many faculty at small institutions their first taste of instant information exchange and electronic dialogue with colleagues at other institutions. Flushed with the success of electronic mail, some faculty have attempted to pass programming, research information, and compound publications through the network only to find a daunting new level of complexity that only experts seem able to untangle for them.

Two instructors with the same personal computers and the same word-processing software on their desks who wish to share nothing more than formatted textual information though these electronic networks may be faced with format conversions for transfer over the network to retain the appearance of the document, compression and decompression techniques to reduce transmission times, and numerous other barriers. When graphic images, digitized sound, and executable binary programs are added to the equation, many faculty members simply abandon all thought of mastering the techniques currently necessary for successful electronic transmission of such items. The lack of uniform standards across vendors and networks for rich-text and compound documents, graphic images, digitized sound, and executable binary program images, coupled with a lack of tools to hide the complexities of the necessary transformations, have presented a major barrier to faculty who wish to share their work electronically. This barrier again raises the issue of cost effectiveness since it inhibits inexpensive electronic sharing of computer-based learning materials, research applications, and other scholarly tools

Milestones and Achievements of the 1970s and 1980s

Despite the expense and lack of hard, nonanecdotal data to convince skeptics of the effectiveness of information technology for enhancing student learning experiences, the academic, research, and corporate communities have made significant efforts to address these issues. Throughout the last two decades, many groups have made noticeable contributions, a sampling of which is described in the following sections.

In the early 1970s CONDUIT—an organization that provided faculty with a channel for evaluation and distribution of academic courseware—served as the first model for setting standards of documentation, for assuring some level of quality assurance for other faculty, and for serving as a central distribution site for faculty authors. This effort allowed faculty effectively to share their efforts with colleagues through an impartial low-cost mechanism. Nevertheless, faculty looking for classroom products often found that the very package that sounded most useful would run only on a hardware platform that was not available at their institutions.

We are still plagued by the same problems today. While software centers, such as ISAAC, WISC-WARE, AppleLink, DECUS, the

Software Clearing House at Iowa State University, Intellimation, and others have undertaken national software distribution efforts, each is geared primarily to one or two specific hardware platforms and none has achieved a sufficiently high level of acceptance to be considered a universal source.

An interesting trend that bears watching is the use of electronic bulletin boards for the distribution of software within higher education. Many of the largest electronic databases of software for the Macintosh and MS-DOS platforms are available through user groups located at or affiliated with large universities. The Boston Computer Society, the Berkeley Macintosh User Group, and the Stanford Macintosh User Group are only some of the major sources of such shareware and related information.

For those in the UNIX community, the use of electronic news groups such as "comp-sys-news" for dialogs about systems, applications, and development issues and of "ftp" sites (file transfer protocol) which house collections of software, object libraries, and related documentation serve a similar function. The encouragement by NeXT Computer of national ftp archive sites at three universities for the sharing of object libraries, programs, and documentation has been very successful in allowing members of the higher education community developing applications in the NeXTStep environment to take advantage of the work of others when developing their own applications.

Another approach to providing access to curricular materials can be seen in the EDUCOM efforts to establish a Distinguished Software Collection Lending Library. The purpose of this project is to provide faculty, librarians, and academic computing support staffs access to disciplinary and interdisciplinary collections of software that have already been evaluated by appropriate faculty peer groups and that can be used to demonstrate or experiment with various types of classroom learning materials. While the home institutions for the regional collections have only recently been identified and established, the expectations for this project are very high, particularly among academic computing support staff who are often charged with locating discipline-specific software for faculty evaluation.

Acknowledgment and Support of Faculty Development Efforts

The EDUCOM sponsored *Educational Uses of Information Technology* program known as EUIT—an outgrowth of the *Educational Software Initiative* (ESI)—has had a very significant impact in raising national awareness of faculty development efforts. EUIT/ESI established and administers the EDUCOM *Software Awards Program* as well as many other projects directly related to faculty use of information technology in the classroom and scholarly research.

The EDUCOM awards have provided a national focus for the review and recognition of outstanding software projects that support student learning. The awards are given high national visibility at the EDUCOM annual conference and also provide significant cash awards to faculty developers. While award winners indicate that the cash rewards do not begin to approach appropriate reimbursement for their efforts, many have cited the receipt of the award as a positive factor in the promotion and tenure process. In addition, the award-winning software packages provide other faculty developers with models and approaches to design issues that have been judged successful by instructional psychologists as well as peer faculty discipline experts.

The publication of *Ivory Towers, Silicon Basements* by the FIPSE Technology Study Group and seminar offerings of the same name provide a faculty perspective on the possible role of information technology in liberal arts learning (FIPSE 1988, 278). The EDUCOM/EUIT *Academic Software Directory Project* has not only compiled useful information about software sources but has also participated in a library project with the Online Computer Library Center to explore the possibility of developing cataloging standards for software product descriptions and reviews. In addition, disciplinary organizations in Europe are beginning to establish their own awards for innovative uses of technology in the classroom, such as Germany's Higher Education Software Awards, which are modeled after the EDUCOM awards program.

Progress toward Portability of Machine-Readable Educational Materials

A primary goal for the InterUniversity Consortium for Educational Computing (ICEC) formed in the early 1980s, was to convince hardware and operating-system vendors that there was a critical need within higher education for portability of software across different platforms as higher education prepared for the arrival of advanced workstations on campuses later in the decade. While ICEC activities have now been absorbed by EDUCOM, the impact of the group's efforts can be seen most visibly today in the vendor support of the UNIX family of operating systems on advanced workstations from all major workstation vendors in the United States. The porting of a software application from one UNIX system to another running on different hardware platforms with similar capacities is now frequently done with little or no change to the underlying source code.

With the growth of campus networks and the integration of multi-vendor hardware platforms, commercial software vendors of generic application products such as word processors, page-layout programs, spreadsheets, and graphics programs are providing users with a different portability path. These vendors are developing their products on two or more different hardware/operating-system platforms and then providing translators that allow the end user to move documents from one platform to another. Programs such as WordPerfect, PageMaker, WingZ, Word, Excel, FrameMaker, and several database products are now available for MS-DOS and Macintosh platforms, and often for UNIX platforms as well. While not completely transparent to the end user, this approach to portability has certainly made life easier for those institutions supporting multiple vendor platforms.

For groups who need to share documents and data without the convenience of a network for transmission, computer manufacturers such as Apple are beginning to take steps to make the exchange of rich-text documents as easy as using a word processor. The FDHD disk drives, now delivered as part of all Macintosh systems, can read either Macintosh or MS-DOS 3.5-inch diskettes directly. When used with the Apple File Exchange program included with the system software, or other commercial products such as MacLink Plus, the conversion of, for example, an MS-DOS WordPerfect or Lotus 1-2-3 document saved on a 3.5-inch diskette to a usable Macintosh Microsoft Word or Excel document is now a matter of a few mouse clicks. Similar compatibility and interoperability approaches are likely to emerge from the 1991 codevelopment agreement between Apple and IBM, the Advanced Computing Environment consortium which includes Microsoft, DEC, and others, as well as a variety of similar industry alliances.

As we venture into the 1990s, we are beginning to see products that have been designed with platform independence in mind. Any necessary conversions are hidden from the user. This type of transparent use of information is now being explored even by vendors of multimedia authoring environments. In the not too distant future, educators should be able to move a system created in one software environment to an alternate environment with relative ease, provided that the latter is of comparable capacity and is equipped with the necessary peripherals. Clearly, we are not yet at that stage but the fact that such strategies are being discussed as viable commercial choices indicates that attention is being focused on these issues by those who provide the applications needed to create complex learning systems for higher education.

National Disciplinary Adoption of Information Technology

Several professional discipline-oriented organizations, such as the Modern Language Association, have begun formal review processes for computer-based learning materials related to their disciplines. These reviews, which occasionally give a recommendation for specific software products, are printed in professional journals and other communications of scholarly associations.

The recognition of intellectual property rights in conjunction with electronic information is also being acted upon by various disciplinary groups. Groups such as the Society for Computing in Psychology and the Mathematical Association of America have formally adopted, as an integral part of their professional standards, the EDUCOM Code, a statement of principle about intellectual property and the legal and ethical use of software.

National Initiatives Supporting Institutional Curricular Goals and Technology

Major foundation, government, and corporate funding sources have also contributed significantly to the exploration of information technology uses in higher education. One example was the funding initiative for The New Liberal Arts program by the Sloan Foundation to encourage the examination and redesign of the traditional liberal arts curriculum to integrate discussions and uses of technology across the curriculum. The Annenberg/CPB Project has supported major projects for curricular innovation, both for the distance learner and for the liberal arts environment, while the Olin and PEW foundations have made significant contributions in the area of library automation and library sciences.

From the commercial sector, Apple Computer established the Apple University Consortium with publications such as *Wheels for the Mind* to disseminate information throughout higher education about classroom computing initiatives. IBM established the Advanced Education Program (AEP) which accomplishes much of the same purpose for the IBM development platform. The AEP includes the support of a number of educators as consulting scholars who travel throughout the United States for one or more years providing insight and guidance to those who are interested in developing computer-based materials.

Another effort undertaken by various higher education organizations is the offering of one- or two-day seminars for college presidents, provosts, and vice-presidents on information-technology issues, institutional strategic planning for information technology, and organizational approaches to planning, managing, and delivering information-technology services on their campuses. Organizations such ACE, AAHE, and EDUCOM/CAUSE have offered such seminars in the past, and the Seminars for Academic Computing held in Snowmass, Colorado, each August continue to offer such one-day programs for college officers.

National Initiatives Supporting Electronic Information Sharing and Access

Another broad national initiative of the 1980s can be seen in the establishment by the National Science Foundation of supercomputer centers for higher education and of the NSFNET linking these centers. The supercomputer centers and NSFNET give faculty from all over the nation access to computing resources that small institutions, such as liberal arts colleges, would not otherwise be able to provide. This access, along with the explosion in the use of electronic mail and file transfers among researchers, faculty, and students, has led to the expansion of NSFNET into NREN (National Research and Education Network). NREN will play a critical role in the exchange of information and tools among those in higher education and their corporate partners in research, both within the United States and around the world.

Support for the establishment of gateways to interconnect different national networks and for the provision of a standardized name service for routing information across networks continues to grow. In the last four years, regional networks such as SURNET and BARRNET have been developed around the country as links to NSFNET and the Internet as well as for regional communications. The recent merger of BITNET and CSNET, two other prominent networks within higher education, into the CREN network is also evidence of the progress being made to provide a more cohesive network infrastructure within the United States.

An early electronic access project, focusing not on infrastructure but on information passed across the network, was also sponsored by NSF. Although no longer active, the EXPRESS project set out to explore standards and technologies needed for the transmission of compound documents across the various electronic networks used in higher education, as a means of electronically exchanging formal research publications and proposals. It was undertaken jointly by Carnegie-Mellon University and the University of Michigan.

A more recent effort by NSF to provide information access services to the academic community is the newly launched Science and Technology Information System (STIS). STIS provides a publications database, available over the Internet or through dial-up service, that includes descriptions of NSF programs, guidelines, and policies on preparing proposals for research projects, descriptions of research funded by NSF, studies and papers sponsored by NSF, and reports prepared by NSF's Division of International Programs on basic science and technology trends, developments, policies, and resource allocations in selected foreign countries.

Another recently initiated project, the Coalition on Networked Information (CNI), also focuses on the access to information over national networks rather than on the infrastructure to deliver it. CNI brings together the interests of research librarians and traditional academic computing groups to lead the way in the effective use of the national networks to enrich intellectual productivity and scholarship. CNI is an outgrowth of the converging interests of the Association of Research Libraries, EDUCOM, and CAUSE to establish standards for information retrieval, protection of intellectual property rights, access over national networks to commercial information resources along with higher education and government services now available, and governance issues of information transfer over national, regional, and local networks.

Vendor Contributions to Institutional Technology Goals

Vendors of hardware and software have contributed in essential and indisputable ways to faculty development efforts involving information technology. Academic pricing and packaging agreements offered by major hardware and software vendors, while serving each vendor's own goals, have also allowed higher education effectively to share the financial burden of making technology available on a massive scale on most campuses. These discount purchasing agreements have also helped smaller institutions contain support costs by providing an economically feasible path for the adoption of campus-wide support for a limited number of high-quality software products.

Several of the large development efforts mentioned in this chapter would not have been possible without vendor contributions. While most vendor initiatives in the past have involved large research universities, recent efforts by DEC, Apple, SUN, and others have specifically focused on liberal arts colleges and consortia such as the Consortium for Liberal Arts Colleges. These vendor efforts to support the liberal arts community have included grants, discounts, software codevelopment projects, and other forms of support.

Vendors continue to show interest in supporting higher education through participation in various forums and higher-education organizations. For example, EDUCOM provides a Corporate Associate Program (CAP) for vendors that wish to participate in EDUCOM activities. CAP members provide funding for the EDUCOM Software Awards, participate in the EDUCOM annual conference, serve on the steering committee of EUIT, carry on dialogs with faculty and staff participants at the annual EUIT conference on topics such as network licensing, make special discounts for software and hardware products available to EDUCOM members, and, most importantly, share their vision of the role higher education can play in creating graduates who are prepared to use information technology when they enter the workforce.

New Horizons for the 1990s

Is there any reason to believe that the hurdles and barriers faced by faculty in the last two decades of experiments with computer-based instruction, research, and electronic sharing of information will be lowered or disappear? Is there anything on the horizon that allows us to hope that our institutional investments in information technology will begin to show uniformly noteworthy returns across the curriculum, beyond the productivity and attitude shifts brought about through word processing and network communications by the first wave of technology adoption on our campuses?

Certainly the past experiences of liberal arts institutions—such as Dartmouth, Franklin and Marshall, Reed, Mills, and others— that ventured into these curricular arenas during the 1970s and 1980s with heavy investments in technology and ambitious faculty-development programs have made us much more realistic about the professional support levels, the faculty time, and the development tools needed by faculty to create the high quality learning materials that have a significant empowering effect on students. There are also insights learned from larger institutions—such as Stanford, MIT,

Brown, and the University of Michigan—that support professional programming staff, graphics designers, human-interface specialists, and legal counsel to resolve copyright issues. Other major developments are also underway that provide some justification for continuing to invest in information technology for our institutions and our students.

Design Guidelines and Effective Classroom Models for Faculty

Literature from instructional design specialists and cognitive scientists on student learning models, on memory organization models for retention and retrieval, and on the power of visual thinking and learning is only now becoming available in a form accessible to those who are not experts in these fields. The availability of such literature should produce enormous time savings for faculty venturing out on their first efforts in developing instructional materials. The accumulated set of award-winning programs that can serve as inspiration and as models for new development efforts has also reached a critical mass and level of availability. Faculty developers who are exposed to such models are spared the need to "reinvent the wheel"; they reduce their design and development time and create more effective software for their students than faculty who are not exposed to such models.

Similarly, interdisciplinary literature on the relationships between graphic design, human-interface issues, navigation strategies, and student learning is also appearing in a form that can be pragmatically applied and experimented with by those whose expertise is outside these fields. Particularly in liberal arts environments, where specialists in these areas are least likely to be available for consultation, such literature can now be used by support staff and faculty to lay the groundwork necessary for effective design. Again, some of the time spent in the past on trial-and-error experimentation can be saved by using this growing body of literature and by taking advantage of pragmatic materials written to help those new to desktop publishing and the design of computer-based presentation materials.

Authoring Tools and Environments

Powerful software authoring tools for faculty that provide easy-to-use methods for incorporating simulations, graphic images, video-disk materials, CD-ROM materials, and sound have recently appeared in the marketplace on a variety of hardware platforms. Examples of such tools for the Macintosh platform include Intermedia, Course of Action, Course Builder, MacroMind Director, and Mentor; for developers using IBM platforms, InfoWindows, NeXTStep, and Intermedia; and for NeXT developers NeXTStep, the Interface Builder, Media Station, and Diagram. These authoring environments provide most of the important functions needed to create effective multimedia materials and will significantly reduce the time spent by faculty in learning and accomplishing the steps necessary in assembling their creations.

The trend in corporate America to move to object-oriented environments to obtain cost savings in software development is receiving serious consideration in the academic community. Witness the growing adoption of development languages and environments such as C++, Objective C, SmallTalk, Actor, MacApp, MPW, and the Interface Builder with its object kits for various application areas. In addition, tools for creating and maintaining libraries of reusable objects such as those offered by Course of Action, Think Pascal, and Think C for the Macintosh and by NeXT and other third-party vendors for the NeXTStep environment are becoming a major attraction to the academic community. These environments hold the potential for significant cost reductions in development time by allowing faculty to pick and choose from previously developed objects, while still having the tools for easily creating their own custom objects. Such an environment should aid in the quick creation of classroom and research tools for student learning and research efforts. The availability of a library of commonly needed generic and discipline-specific objects developed with uniform messaging standards for even two or three of the most common development environments has the potential for drastically cutting development time and the programming expertise needed by faculty to create effective materials.

Vendors are also providing advanced workstation platforms with built-in hardware and software that can ease the process of creating

highly interactive, multimedia learning materials. The incorporation
of high-performance chips to manage digital signal processing and
real-time video capture and compression into most new workstation
products will reduce the need to purchase, configure, and program
special-purpose boards and boxes. The newer high-end workstations
come with the ability to do real-time capture and playback of high-
quality sounds and high-resolution color video. The power of today's
workstations' new compression techniques that allow dynamic
compression and decompression of large sound and image files also
begins to accommodate the vast storage requirements for large
multimedia archival systems. The incorporation of these technologies
in off-the-shelf workstations is going to eliminate many of the time-
consuming tasks that used to be faced by faculty authors trying to
create rich instructional and research systems.

Portability

Major software vendors of generic tools are rapidly acknowledging
the importance of moving their products to multiple hardware/
operating-system platforms—vendors such as Adobe, Aldus, Frame
Technologies, Informix, Lotus, Oracle, Sybase, Wolfram, and
WordPerfect have made commitments to bring their products to the
UNIX marketplace in addition to their traditional DOS, Macintosh
OS, and proprietary mainframe platforms. The availability of a given
product across many platforms will greatly enhance the ability to
share certain types of data and classroom materials developed by
faculty at one institution with colleagues at another, despite the use
of different hardware and operating systems.

Libraries and Electronic Information Sharing

With the automation of many liberal arts libraries in progress or
completed, the library community is now actively engaged in debate
and exploration of the impact that unlimited electronic access to their
archives will bring to scholarship and the traditional ways of organizing
and providing access to information. The multitude of academic and
research networks and the gateways among these networks that have
created such a fertile ground for electronic mail at a national level

are now being re-examined by groups such as NREN and CNI. They hope to lead the way for higher education, not only in assuring that the networking infrastructure for research and scholarship will be vastly improved, but in shaping the national dialogue about the issues of transportability of software, exchange of compound documents and other resources, and the governance and protection of individual and corporate intellectual property rights.

If national support for networking and information sharing is sustained or increased, then individual faculty members and librarians will also have to reassess the manner and sources which students will draw upon in their work. Faculty will need to adapt assignments for students who will have access to materials far beyond those volumes on the home library's shelves with which they are most familiar. Librarians will need to respond to student questions about electronic searching strategies for a large number of on-line resources outside the domain and control of the home institution. In their probing of available on-line resources, students may stumble across information with which neither librarians nor faculty are yet acquainted. Open access by all members of the academic community to vast on-line resources will surely entice most educators to reconsider both the content and the format of their courses.

The Unremitting Pace of Change

What are the ongoing and potential new speed bumps that liberal arts and other higher-education institutions face for the 1990s? The list includes at least the following:

- The limited lifespan of classroom and research tools, as hardware and software platforms continue to evolve and what that means for the faculty developer.

- The ongoing cost and unremitting pace of change in hardware and software platforms, especially as the multimedia market matures and becomes more affordable for higher education.

- The financial constraints on further major capital investments to support multimedia classroom delivery platforms and the need for careful, selective choices with respect to workstation technology investment.

- The clarification of intellectual property rights as digitized sound, video, and photographic images become available on national and institutional electronic networks.

- Further improvement of authoring environments and tools for faculty development of teaching and research materials.

- Continued development of standards for exchange of compound documents, binary images, digitized sound, video, and graphics across networks, hardware platforms, and vendors.

While universal solutions to these concerns are not yet at hand, the experiences of liberal arts and other colleges that invested early in information technology should help all liberal arts colleges sort through the issues as they plan for their futures. For example, we are now beginning to appreciate the hard-to-measure costs of *not* adopting information technology, not only for our students but for the long-term goals and viability of our institutions. As we improve our understanding of the magnitude of the long-term costs in adopting information technology, we are better prepared to analyze the economic tradeoffs between information technology investments and other programmatic thrusts or institutional needs that draw significantly on liberal arts institutional resources.

Liberal arts colleges need to continue to build the body of research on the impact of computer-based systems on faculty vitality and student learning in the liberal arts environment. There are many positive indicators that higher education and its partners in the commercial and government communities have not only learned a great deal over the last decade but are responding constructively to the challenges uncovered, at a national as well as an institutional level.

Perhaps most importantly, liberal arts colleges must consider the impact of the availability of vast amounts of information through national and international networks on their faculty, students and staff. This electronic availability is having, and will continue to have, a transforming effect on large numbers of faculty in their research, in their communication with colleagues, and eventually in how they structure homework and research assignments for their students.

Liberal arts colleges need to make sure their voices are heard in the various national forums addressing global electronic information access issues. These forums include federal legislation debates to create and sustain a national network as well as the standard-setting activities of groups such as CNI. While liberal arts colleges are initially participating primarily as end-users of the national network, we eventually will serve also as providers of information, electronically distributing research results produced by our faculty and even our students. We cannot afford to leave the resolution of the network standards and access issues, usually addressed only by the large research universities building the infrastructure for such information access and exchange, in the hands of others with very different goals and needs.

References

Graves, William H. (Ed.). 1989. *Computing across the curriculum: Academic perspectives.* Reading, Mass.: Addison-Wesley.

FIPSE Technology Study Group, Diane P. Balestri, Chair. 1988. *Ivory towers, silicon basements: Learner-centered computing in postsecondary education.* Reading, Mass.: Addison-Wesley in association with EDUCOM.

Chapter 11

Computers for Teaching and Learning

Marianne M. Colgrove
Reed College

Marianne M. Colgrove is the associate director of computing and information systems at Reed College. She is responsible for coordinating the day-to-day operations of Reed's computing departments, planning for and providing computing resources in both academic and administrative departments, and managing the hardware services department. She is also responsible for solving bizarre little problems for people and making decisions that require knowledge of "the way we've always done it."

Upon completing her B.A. in psychology in 1984 at Reed, Ms. Colgrove began her work with instructional computing as a technical writer and interface designer in Reed's Academic Software Development Lab. Prior to her current position, she managed Reed's Five-Year Technology Plan, a special project to integrate computing into all aspects of the academic environment.

Ms. Colgrove is an active contributor to the Consortium of Liberal Arts Colleges, both as a conference speaker and past member of the Vendor Relations committee. She has served as a member of the Apple University Consortium Executive Board, an institutional representative to the InterUniversity Consortium for Educational Computing, and the coordinator of conferences on campus-wide networking and computing in the liberal arts, both hosted at Reed.

While the eighties were a time for significant growth and experimentation in educational computing, in retrospect computers have not promoted the sort of widespread educational reform originally anticipated. Even at large universities, which have the resources to support curricular innovation and creative uses of technology, the impact of computers on the curriculum has been modest. At small colleges, which do not have such institutional resources, the curricular impact of computers has been even smaller.

There are many fundamental challenges that face higher education in the nineties. Overall college enrollments are expected to decline and with the national economy in retreat, many institutions are suffering funding cutbacks—and academic computing is a prime target. In an era when the entire educational system is being investigated for its apparent inability to meet basic needs, computing may be seen as a frill. In this difficult environment, the need for more focused, less exploratory approaches to educational computing is increasingly urgent. This is especially true for small colleges, which must be particularly careful with their resources. The educational advantages of computerization over traditional methods need to be stated as explicitly as possible. We must take care that the use of computers in higher education is driven by educational needs, rather than solely by product innovations or technical issues.

The bulk of the literature on educational computing in the eighties wholeheartedly welcomed computers into the instructional arena. In numerous books, articles, and conferences, enthusiastic educators extolled the many virtues of computers. Of course there were detractors as well, with equally strong opinions. This chapter seeks to offer a balanced view of instructional computing. It begins with a discussion of the problems encountered during the eighties in developing and using courseware—problems that were particularly difficult for small colleges to overcome. With these lessons of the eighties in mind, I then describe the educational goals common to liberal arts colleges and examine the ways in which computers might be expected to support these goals. Finally I examine a variety of ways that computers can have a positive effect on teaching and learning in liberal arts colleges. A word of caution: The reader may be surprised to find that the chapter offers many critical remarks about computing. Let me hasten to point out that for those of us who are truly convinced that computers can bring about valuable changes in higher education, an open-minded assessment of our goals, illusions, and former failures is a vital ingredient to achieving our future successes.

Academic Software in the Eighties

Academic computing grew explosively in the eighties. Fueled by the availability of increasingly powerful microcomputers and decreasing prices, colleges and universities of all sizes committed new resources to computer technology. The investment in hardware was tremendous as institutions deployed computers for faculty, students, and administrators; installed networking and communications equipment; automated library systems; and updated aging central computing systems. We began to build the support infrastructure required to move computers into all realms of college life and to exploit the promise offered by all our new machinery. The decade was characterized by enthusiasm for computers and anticipation for the revolutionary changes the technology would bring to higher education.

Most of the available microcomputer programs were general use productivity packages—word processors, spreadsheets, databases, and communications programs. These programs were, and are, quite useful to students and faculty. Productivity software makes it more convenient to do many necessary day-to-day chores. Many enthusiasts predicted that the increased efficiency and productivity afforded by generic software would free students and faculty from mundane, repetitive tasks, leaving more time for thinking. Early planning documents at Reed, for example, predicted that by using computers for word processing, students would be able to spend more time on rewriting and improving their papers and thus would become better writers. Increases in convenience and efficiency, in other words, could lead to qualitative improvements in learning.

Of course for every preacher of the faith, there is a computing skeptic. "Computers will not really improve education." "Computers will cause more trouble than they're worth." "Students will hole up in their rooms like the prisoners in Plato's cave." The slogans are now familiar. And indeed, it soon became apparent that hardware and generic software alone were not going to have the promised effect unless accompanied by a concerted effort to integrate computers into the curriculum. The technology could not live up to its potential as long as it was just tacked onto existing courses. Productivity software and information tools, without guidance in their use, would not improve learning.

Courseware became the buzzword for a new breed of educational software. Unlike generic software tools, courseware is not just an information management tool. It has an educational content specific to an academic discipline or a particular course. Faculty on many campuses developed software that was intended to explore the possibilities afforded by the emerging technologies. Sometimes this prompted the development of new courses, or course segments, designed around a new instructional application. Computer manufacturers with a stake in the higher education market supported faculty development projects with equipment grants. The 1980s were an era of experimentation with rapidly evolving technology and new instructional methods.

In many respects the experiment has paid off. Numerous examples of excellent and innovative academic software emerged during the eighties. Over the last four years, 91 EDUCOM/NCRIPTAL awards have been granted to developers of exemplary courseware projects (NCRIPTAL 1990). Of these, about 85 percent explore subjects in humanities, social sciences, and natural sciences that are relevant to undergraduate liberal arts education. A variety of successful computing projects in the arts and humanities have demonstrated conclusively that the sciences are no longer the sole domain of computers.

For small colleges, experiments with instructional computing have had mixed results. Successes like those mentioned have been very scattered and have almost exclusively been within the domain of large universities. At most small colleges, the explosion of quality educational applications we had hoped for has not really materialized. Fewer than eight of the 91 EDUCOM/NCRIPTAL award winners are from small undergraduate institutions. Small colleges are generally underrepresented in vendor-sponsored consortia like the Apple University Consortium (AUC) and IBM's Advanced Educational Projects (AEP) program. Only two of the original 21 members of the InterUniversity Consortium for Educational Computing were small liberal arts colleges.

The Challenge of Courseware Development

Developing one's own courseware can be an attractive proposition. As a faculty developer, one has complete control over the content and format of the software and can thereby insure that the materials are well integrated into each class. Unfortunately, software development is an endeavor fraught with difficulties.

Academic software development is resource intensive, both for faculty developers and for the institution. By all accounts, courseware development is unimaginably time consuming. According to one EDUCOM/NCRIPTAL award winner, "Software development requires a thirty-six-hour day" (Meiss 1989, 43). The friendly graphical user interfaces that make personal computers so accessible to students require a programming effort that vastly increases demands on developers. Many faculty who choose to develop academic software must secure released time in order to avoid cutting into the time they spend on their own research.

Along with the investment in time, there is of course the investment in hardware. Since there are few tangible incentives for courseware development, many schools rely on new equipment to encourage faculty involvement. Grants from hardware vendors have helped many schools to defray the costs of providing exciting new equipment. Unfortunately, the schools that are most in need of equipment grants—small colleges just beginning to invest in technology— are often the ones least able to acquire them. In addition, computing equipment is usually not a one-time cost. Developers often need to take advantage of better features offered by evolving hardware platforms, operating systems, and development software. Equipment sometimes needs to be replaced or upgraded on an annual basis.

And hardware is just the beginning. Institutional culture and availability of human resources are even more important. At universities, faculty engaged in development projects often work with a team of programmers and curriculum design specialists. Many of the projects highlighted in *Computing across the Curriculum: Academic Perspectives* (Graves 1989) hail from universities that offer a variety of support for instructional innovation, from project planning to programming and video production services. The University of California at Santa Barbara, which has a thriving academic software

development program, has a long history of support for new instructional technology. Computer-based teaching tools are just a natural
extension of that effort (Marcus, Nicholson and Phillips 1990).
Through similar strategies, many other universities have been able
to support a culture that is conducive to experimentation with
educational software.

In addition to the resources required, academic software development is simply hard to do. The energy spent actually coding the
software is the least of the effort. Many different components must
be pulled together to create a cohesive, complete package. Developers
must plan the overall format of the program, design the user interface, incorporate the academic content, identify and fix bugs, and
create documentation. Anyone interested enough in programming to
undertake a development project is often a lot less interested in other
project components. This is particularly true if one is forced to rely
on student programmers. In the Academic Software Development
Lab at Reed College, for example, student programmers work with
extraordinary zeal until all the interesting coding problems are
solved. After the first few intense weeks, the project might drag out
for months while the program and documentation are polished up
enough for classroom use, lending support to the adage that the last
ten percent of a software project takes ninety percent of the time.
Once this Herculean effort is complete, few people in an academic
environment have the enthusiasm to make design improvements and
bug fixes, or to meet the ongoing need for updates and enhancements.

Authoring tools such as *Course of Action*™ and *HyperCard*™ have
eliminated some of the problems associated with programming
courseware. However, since much of the difficulty in creating a
successful piece of software is not the programming itself, authoring
tools have not really solved the problem for faculty developers. Even
if the mechanics of programming can be eliminated, a good academic
program still requires attention to design and planning of the academic content and its presentation. According to Bruce Sherwood,
developer of the *CMU Tutor* authoring environment, better
development tools do not decrease the time required to develop
software. Rather, they improve the expectations of the developer and
ultimately the quality of the application (Cavalier 1990). Increased

quality is obviously desirable, but we shouldn't fool ourselves into believing that authoring systems necessarily save time.

Since a development effort has so many varied components, one of the difficulties lies in defining the most appropriate role for the faculty member. Should a would-be courseware developer acquire the skills to complete the project alone? Or is it better to work with a team in which every member has a different type of expertise to offer? There is a real dynamic tension between the desire of many professors to control the creation of their course materials and the time and expertise required to undertake an entire development project independently. Many full-time teaching faculty simply cannot dedicate the additional energy required to develop their own programs. In some cases the professor functions as little more than a content expert. On the other hand, the team approach risks the same types of problems that plague many academic committees—poor communication and an inability to work efficiently.

The desired educational outcome of instructional computing projects is not always clearly defined or understood. All too often, instructional software development is driven by new developments in technology. The emphasis on experimentation with computing causes many people to focus on what computers can do, rather than on what is needed from them. Dependence on vendors for equipment support exacerbates this tendency, since computer companies naturally promote projects that highlight their technical innovations or fall within one of their target markets. Also, because of the difficulties already mentioned, faculty often become focused on the technology itself, or the mechanics of the development process, rather than on the pedagogical value of the software.

If the development effort eclipses the reasons for the development, the instructional outcome can be lost. This makes it very difficult to evaluate whether or not the software works well, and the process of evaluating the success of the work and identifying positive results may be completely ignored. Because educational results are often intangible, it is also difficult to evaluate the quality of a faculty development project. This is one reason why professional rewards for faculty are low—a particular irony given the enormous dedication and skill required by faculty who develop courseware.

If there is anything to be learned from a decade of experimentation, the lesson is that courseware development is tough work with no guaranteed return. In general, our pool of knowledge about the elements of high-quality courseware is quite limited—there is no recipe for success. It is difficult to tell what approach will work in a particular discipline. In short, while courseware development can be tremendously satisfying, it is a high-risk proposition.

Unfortunately, small colleges are particularly susceptible to these risks. Small colleges are rarely able to offer the variety of technical support services that universities offer through their instructional service organizations and academic computing departments. Even if a small college can provide some technical consultants to help faculty developers, they often lack the level of sophistication found in larger institutions. Many institutions identify equipment donations and cash grants as critical elements of a successful instructional computing initiative. But without the technical support infrastructure and culture that encourages technical innovation, liberal arts colleges have a much harder time attracting external support. If large universities, with resources like those described earlier, cannot reliably produce high-quality courseware, then what chance has a small college with limited resources?

The Failure of Trickle-Down

Those projects that have been successful in the large university environment rarely trickle down to small liberal arts colleges or comprehensive universities. The failure of the trickle-down notion typically results from the limitations of the courseware itself. Often, courseware is too simplistic to really enrich a course. When the program doesn't offer obvious instructional benefits, it isn't worth the time and expense to work it into the class. In many cases the problem is simply that the concept of courseware as it has traditionally been approached— drill and practice, tutorials, quizzes—is too limited for college-level use. Or, in the words of Milton Glick, the provost at Iowa State University, "so much of the available software has nothing to do with reality" (Glick 1990, 37). Too expensive to buy, or too cheap to want, it runs on the wrong platform, the documentation isn't clear, the program structure doesn't seem logical. Courseware often just isn't quite right.

Personal and unique teaching styles, particularly in small colleges that prize dynamic, high-quality teaching, make it difficult for faculty to adopt someone else's instructional materials—courseware and otherwise. Many faculty feel that someone else's software would cover the wrong details of the subject matter or just wouldn't support their teaching approach. If it isn't modifiable, the teacher who would like to adopt the courseware can't adapt it to his or her course. Perhaps the program that a professor develops for personal use is not robust enough to be used by someone else who doesn't understand it intimately (Kemeny 1990).

General institutional barriers to the use of computers also affect a professor's ability to adopt instructional software. One problem is that computerization doesn't really reduce or eliminate other instructional costs, such as laboratory equipment or library books. If a professor is to adopt a piece of courseware, there must be some kind of delivery mechanism. The cost of equipping a student computer lab, along with the cost and availability of physical space for it, can pose serious problems for the institution. Yet most liberal arts colleges are not prepared to require, or even strongly recommend, that students buy their own personal computers. Without enough computers for student access, professors cannot realistically make computer use a required component of their classes. The courseware is relegated to a role on the sidelines of the class, a far cry from truly integrated instructional technology.

Finally, one barrier to educational computing is the faculty itself. Faculty members have generally not been as interested in developing or adopting academic software as computer staff may have hoped. In an informal phone survey, Bob Ehrlich (1990) found that for physics professors, a major obstacle to computer use was that it crowded out other essential topics. Another obstacle is the lack of time to restructure a course. All faculty have many competing demands on their time and energy. Computer projects are just not the sort of work most professors choose to do in their "spare" time. These are all legitimate concerns. Of course, there usually is a core of sophisticated faculty computer users at most liberal arts colleges. They work very hard to apply computers creatively in their teaching and research. Though notable exceptions exist, there will probably always be a relatively small number of faculty dedicated to educational computing, while most faculty choose to focus on other issues. This seems to be true even when a variety of enticements are available to promote faculty involvement.

Teaching and Computers

The mixed results we have experienced in the eighties do not portend the failure of instructional computing or courseware development. Nor do they imply that computing cannot have meaningful curricular impact at small colleges—that the skeptics were right all along. They *do* mean that we must begin to apply the lessons of the last decade. We need to develop new strategies for using computers in ways that explicitly support liberal arts education. These strategies must grow from our needs as educators.

Of course it is hard to figure out successful ways to use computers to enhance learning. We have a hard time even understanding the learning process, or defining good teaching. Even within small colleges there is a tremendous diversity of teaching methods and precious little agreement on how to improve education or what the curriculum should include. However, we can identify instructional approaches, as well as educational problems, that are common among small liberal arts colleges. With this as a basis, we can then think about how computers might be expected to support liberal education and identify those areas where it can't.

Most liberal arts colleges focus on providing a comprehensive, rigorous undergraduate curriculum. While some colleges have expanded to offer advanced degrees or courses in nontraditional areas, the emphasis still remains on well-rounded undergraduate education. Students are expected to take a broad variety of courses in the arts, humanities, sciences, and social sciences. One educational challenge is to help the student integrate knowledge gleaned from such a diverse array of subjects. Ideally, as students progress, they gradually focus on their chosen major and develop a depth of understanding in that field. The emphasis is on methods of inquiry—how to learn—rather than on simply teaching facts or skills. As a result, the distinctions between instruction and research are usually blurred. Conference style classes, frequent and high-quality professor/student interactions, independent student research, and the culminating senior project are all hallmarks of liberal teaching methods.

As teachers, professors play several basic roles. The first, and perhaps the most mundane, is the role of transmitting information. Professors possess knowledge of the subject matter which they try to pass on to their students. The professor is also a guide, who helps the student discover new ideas and learn to think independently. Finally, for many students a professor is a mentor, a source of inspiration and motivation who truly cares about students. This last function may be the most important role a professor can play for a student (Boyer 1987, 157). These elements certainly interact and support each other. A teacher who lacks basic knowledge of the subject usually can't excite the students and prompt them to explore the subject on their own. Similarly, if a teacher lacks the ability to motivate students, it is very difficult to pass on information. Exactly how these components interact to make for a good teaching/learning environment is a subject of endless debate. The element that is clearly common to all aspects of good teaching, however, is the teacher's dedication to students.

Liberal education faces many obstacles and problems in the nineties. Foremost in the minds of many are instructional challenges that professors face. Students often have difficulty integrating information from different classes and subjects. When students can't integrate knowledge from different disciplines, distribution requirements can actually serve to fragment their educational experience, rather than to promote broad, liberal learning. Students also have many problem areas that affect learning in all disciplines—critical thinking and the ability to formulate strong arguments, clear writing and communication, as well as quantitative thinking, the ability to understand and express ideas in nonverbal forms. In addition, as the incoming student body grows more diverse, institutions are seeing greater variation in students' preparedness for college. Many professors report a growing need for remedial instruction (Boyer 1987, ch. 5).

The most basic educational problems center around the curriculum itself. Liberal arts colleges are facing student demands for increased curricular diversity—demands that may become more salient at small colleges as they face enrollment shortfalls in the early nineties. A growing trend toward early specialization and vocationalism also threatens the college's ability to maintain a traditional, liberal curriculum. Sometimes the curriculum, along with other aspects of the college environment, does not promote active involvement on the part of students (NIE 1984). As a result, it does not seem able to address many of the instructional problems teachers face. Yet, at many colleges and universities the curriculum is in disarray and there is surprisingly little comprehensive curricular planning (AAC 1985). Small colleges, with relatively few classes and small faculties, have little room for curricular change. So, while higher education is facing many fundamental instructional challenges, some colleges do not have mechanisms for making unified curricular decisions on a college-wide basis.

Other challenges have to do with time, or rather the lack of it. Time management is an age-old problem for teachers, but, in many ways, the information explosion is making this problem worse. The vast quantity of available material makes it increasingly difficult for students to sort through and synthesize raw information into some usable form. Professors who have too much information to cover in a particular class are forced to become ever more specialized in their teaching. Faculty members also find it increasingly difficult to keep up with rapid change in their disciplines, which affects both their teaching and research. At small liberal arts colleges, which value both teaching and research, many faculty find it impossible to do both to their satisfaction.

Many of these issues are discussed quite thoroughly in *College: The Undergraduate Experience in America* (Boyer 1987). And while these problems are generally thought to plague only larger universities, small selective liberal arts colleges are clearly feeling their effects as well. If we are to use computers more effectively, we should explore ways in which they might address these fundamental educational issues. What can we expect computer technology to do for education in small colleges? What is the appropriate role for computing?

At the broadest institutional level, answers to these questions fall into a few basic, not necessarily exclusive, categories. Many educators reason that computers are information tools and as such have a natural place in higher education. Reed College adopted this philosophy in the early eighties and continues to cultivate the idea that computers play an important, though supporting, role in instruction. Curricular reform is not a primary goal. Instead, this approach emphasizes the role of computers as tools that enhance, rather than transform, instruction.

Another approach characterizes the computer as a vehicle for educational reform. Those who adopt this philosophy often compare the changes offered by instructional technology to those afforded by movable type. Computers allow such basic changes in the way information is manipulated and presented, that they can't help but cause, and require, changes in the way we think and learn. This philosophy focuses on using computer technology explicitly to solve curricular problems, and thereby improve education. The Association of American Colleges, for example, suggests that technological developments can "ease the burden" of creating a broader, more effective minimum curriculum (AAC 1985).

Another strategy emphasizes the importance of educating people about computers and technology in general. Many institutions feel obliged to provide an education that prepares young people for their future economic and civic responsibilities. Any such well-rounded general education should include the study of computers. Similar concerns, for instance, led the Sloan Foundation to develop its New Liberal Arts program in support of new courses enabling students to "obtain some greater feeling for those 'technical' fields which do so much today to determine their lives." (Morison 1984, 1). Teaching classes with and about computers has been a major component of the Sloan New Liberal Arts grants, which have been awarded to 36 colleges and 14 universities (Goldberg 1990, 1).

These broad themes help to define the institutional culture and attitude toward computing. All three of these strategies attempt to target instructional issues indirectly, by using computers to provide solutions to more general curricular or time management problems. But they do not help faculty address more specific instructional questions or guide them in implementing the technology successfully. Within the broader institutional culture, other factors influence the way in which computers are used. Departmental attitudes toward computers have a strong effect on how, or even whether, computers can find a way into the curriculum. In addition, faculty members must also consider what computers can and can't do for them in support of their own teaching. Educators need to find areas in which computers offer a clear advantage over traditional methods, support their personal styles, are consistent with the methods used in their disciplines, and are consistent with the institutional culture. That's a tall order. Rather than preaching the computer gospel, or pushing computing on uninterested faculty, computer support staff should help those who are interested find creative, realistic ways to use computers in pursuit of these goals.

What Can We Expect from Computers?

If used with creativity and forethought, computers have a lot to offer:

- Computers can provide a breadth of information that can exceed the scope of a single course or instructor.

- Computers can present information in ways that books cannot.

- With computers students may gain new and different perspectives on traditional subject matter.

- Computers make new methods of inquiry possible.

- Computers are useful for acquiring new information.

Unfortunately, computers also have limitations:

- Computers cannot replicate the complex personal interactions that students enjoy with their teachers.

- Computers are less accessible than books.

- Computers can erect barriers between students and learning experiences.

· Computers make it easy to oversimplify subtle
information.

Computers can't replace teachers. Let's hope the days are past when
teachers feel their very jobs are threatened by computerization.
While computer technology is well suited to support some aspects of
the teacher's role—transmitting information, exposing students to
new information or new ways of looking at information—they do so
in a much more limited way than a teacher can. Teachers interact
with their students and respond intuitively to subtle signals indicating
that the student is or is not grasping the subject matter. Though
computers can be quite interactive, they cannot achieve this level
of flexibility. Nor can computers provide the sort of personal
encouragement that is such an important element of the teacher's
role. As a result, computers should not be expected to improve
learning in the absence of considerable guidance—an investment in
time and energy—from the professor.

It also seems quite unlikely that computers can replace books.
Books have many physical advantages over computers. They are
easier to read for extended periods without eye strain, they are much
more portable, and despite considerable talk about courseware at
textbook prices, they are much cheaper to use. Faced with growing
concern about computer health risks, many people are looking for
ways to take a break from their computers for a while. Most people
still prefer reading from a printed page, particularly in certain cases,
such as browsing. In fact, few of our standard paper publication
formats lend themselves to electronic publication, with the exception
of reference materials, where the user wants to look up specific
information. The lack of electronic publication standards, as well as
channels for distribution, severely curtail the audience that can be
reached through electronic "books." When information is available
only on computer, it causes serious problems of equity in access to
information. Only those privileged enough to have a computer, and
the right model at that, can use the information.

Of course, many of the same limitations we now see with computers, once held true for printed materials. It does appear likely that
many of these pragmatic concerns will be solved in the future.
Visionary ideas like Alan Kay's Dynabook, an extremely powerful but

portable notebook-sized computer (Kay and Goldberg 1988) and Ted Nelson's *Xanadu* project, which is a standard electronic storage and retrieval system for all the world's texts, provide glimpses into a future in which computers really could replace books (Nelson 1987). In the meantime, we should not use computers simply to emulate the types of information and presentations that are possible in books, "doing nothing except making slight improvements to activities that have been conducted almost as well without computers in the past" (Nielsen 1990, 12).

Though there have been some isolated successes, in general computers cannot replace laboratory experimentation and many other forms of scientific exploration. The eighties saw the development of many laboratory simulation packages. Students can get something of the experience of performing chemical titrations, running rats through an operant reinforcement schedule, or using a microscope. This approach may save some of the expense and inconvenience of conducting student labs, especially for large numbers of students. However, when students work with simulated or videotaped experiments, rather than the real thing, they lose the experience of discovering anomalies, or handling subjects that don't behave the way they're supposed to. Students don't get a feel for what it is like to conduct their own experiments and solve the pragmatic problems that scientists face.

In a similar vein, while computers can help students do calculations that would otherwise be quite time consuming, they can actually conceal interesting irregularities and anomalies in the data. As Dan Styer (1990), a professor of physics at Oberlin College observes, if students blithely apply statistical applications (for example, Runge-Kutta or Monte Carlo), they can learn to solve problems in physics mindlessly, without developing insight into the underlying nature of the problems.

Computer technology can augment traditional instructional methods, support the teacher in various roles, and extend the professor's capabilities, without replacing them. Since computers are good at storing and presenting information, they can be used to provide a breadth of information that extends well beyond what any one professor could be expected to offer. This means that computers might be useful in helping students integrate information from a variety of subjects.

Computers can also augment readings by presenting information in ways that books cannot, thereby providing a new perspective on a topic. *Hypertext*, simply defined as "non-sequential writing" (Nelson 1987, *Dream Machines* 29), is one clear example of how computers can break away from the traditional book format. Books present information in a fixed, linear organization. Authors can escape such limitations to a certain extent, using footnotes and side bars, but the basic structure is inherently sequential. Hypertext programs, such as *HyperCard*™, *Guide*™ and Brown University's *Intermedia*, enable teachers to develop rich, interlinking webs of related, but nonlinear, information. Hypermedia, a more recent incarnation of the hypertext concept, lets the author add graphics, sound, and video to the mix. *Hypertext and Hypermedia* by Jakob Nielsen (1990) offers a good comprehensive discussion of hypertext and its many applications.

Hypertext and hypermedia also afford advantages over traditional computer assisted instruction. Unlike most CAI, in which the software controls the information, hypertext lets the student direct the flow of information. Ideally, with hypertext, neither the teacher nor the computer can create a barrier between the student and the subject matter. This approach makes it easier for the developer to avoid the unnecessary complications required to present prearranged sequences of material and to anticipate all possible responses. Software that puts the student in charge is more likely to excite and involve students.[1] Finally, since hypertext lends itself to creating linkages between diverse but related materials, it is well suited for the liberal arts environment. Hypertext can help students integrate information from various disciplines and promote interdisciplinary studies.

Computers can also foster, rather than obstruct, insight if they are used to simulate phenomena that otherwise could not be studied in class, or would be considered too advanced for undergraduates. Subjects that are well suited to this kind of simulation include, for example, archaeology, history, astronomy, and population biology, all because the subject matter cannot be reproduced in the classroom.

---

1. See Nelson 1987, *Dream Machines,* 129–136, for a complete discussion of hypertext versus CAI.

For example, Robert Kaplan in the Reed biology department uses both a statistical analysis package and population simulations to help students understand basic quantitative methods—statistical analysis and data graphs—as well as principles of population biology. In introductory biology classes students first conduct a small population study using data based on students in the class. They then use *StatView*™ on the Macintosh to run statistical analyses on their data. For ensuing lab assignments students work with programs that simulate population growth, demography, population genetics, and predator–prey interactions. In their final lab segment students perform statistical analyses on data generated by the simulation programs. Without computers this type of study would be impossible to perform given the time constraints of population growth and the length of the semester.

In some fields, computers are leading to the emergence of new methodologies, for both teaching and research. For example, in chemistry, molecular modeling of very large molecules was so cumbersome before the advent of computers, that it simply was not practical. According to Arthur Glasfeld in the Reed College chemistry department, it would take about six months to create a complex molecule with 6,000 atoms using a ball and stick model. The only other alternative for students was to try and visualize three-dimensional molecular structures from two-dimensional pictures. With a color graphics system and molecular modeling software, students can easily visualize the molecules discussed in class or problem sets. While computerized molecular modeling has not changed the basic theories of molecular structure and interaction, it has had a significant impact on research methods. In the past, such theories could only be explored on paper, making it impossible for researchers to test theories that involved more than the tiniest molecules. Now, analyses of quite complex molecules can be studied, even by undergraduates. For example, one thesis student at Reed is examining how positive and negative charges affect molecular binding in neurological dopamine systems. Using a molecular modeling system, she can visualize the location of charged ions and make predictions about how chemical reactions will propagate. Without today's computer tools, this type of study would be beyond the reach of most undergraduates.

In addition to manipulating and presenting information, computers are well suited to acquiring new information. Computers can make scholarly tools available to students that were previously only available to graduate students or professors. Rather than replacing laboratory work with simulations, computers can be used to make research-quality laboratory equipment more accessible for students (see Henderson 1989 for a good discussion of this idea). Music students work with computers interfaced to sophisticated synthesizers, compose their own scores, and hear then played in many different voices. Linguistics students conduct textual analysis of on-line documents. Students in physiological psychology can record and analyze neurological responses to visual or auditory stimuli. In all these examples, students get to work on research projects that would not have been possible without computers. When students can use computers to conduct their own research, they can become much more involved with the information and take a more active role in their education.

Any of the preceding approaches, if used in conjunction with traditional materials, can help students understand the multidimensional aspect of many intellectual problems. In turn, this can encourage students to become more actively engaged in the class and foster better student discussions. Of course, none of this will happen unless professors provide guidance to their students in how to effectively integrate the varied information offered by lectures, discussions, readings, and computers.

Examples of Instructional Research Labs

Despite many of the criticisms levied against traditional courseware, many liberal arts colleges, including Reed, have continued to investigate ways of using computers that address some of the problems that have been discussed. One approach to teaching with computers that has met with success is the use of combined teaching and research labs. The two examples that follow are meant to show how this model can work in two different disciplines—psychology and political science.

The Reed Psychology Core Lab is a computer-based laboratory for operant animal experimentation developed by professor Allen Neuringer and supported, in part, by a grant from the National

Science Foundation College Science Instrumentation Program. A versatile physical arrangement with laboratory cubicles around the edge and a lecture and conference section in the center supports multiple instructional uses—a variety of lab classes, conference-style discussion, seminars, and independent research. Students in introductory psychology classes learn operant conditioning on rats as part of their lab assignments. Upper-division classes that involve experimentation with either pigeons or rats use the same stations. During off hours, the lab is used by students working on thesis projects as well as professors conducting their own research. Because the Psychology Core Lab is a heavily used multifunction facility, it is an efficient use of the college's limited physical space.

The configuration of computerized lab stations is equally versatile. Each station consists of a Macintosh and an operant chamber, connected by interface hardware that can control the chamber and send data back to the Macintosh. The software consists of low-level communications routines, which most students never see. Experiment control programs, written in True Basic, are an easily modifiable top layer. Introductory psychology students don't do any programming. They work with preprogrammed experiment parameters and focus their attention on the experiment and its results. More advanced students who wish to develop their own experiments write their own programs—generally no longer than about 350 lines.

The Psychology Core Lab offers many benefits for psychology students, as well as the department. Students have a chance to work with sophisticated laboratory equipment early in their learning. "Psych Lab" is not just an exercise of working through canned laboratory assignments or predetermined simulations. The focus of laboratory work is on learning research methods and gaining familiarity with the subjects and equipment. Computers are enabling tools that make real research more accessible to students. This allows the development of techniques the student will be able to use in future independent research. Some of these skills involve specific technology and software and, some may argue, will be of limited value as the technology changes. On the other hand, the more general process of developing an experimental methodology to test a particular hypothesis, using the computer to control the experiment and collect data, will probably not change dramatically. The Psychology Core Lab also creates an environment that supports collaboration since students and faculty work closely together, often on different aspects of the same research.

Laboratory experimentation has always been a fundamental component of Reed's psychology curriculum. In addition, the psychology department has a long history of computer use and continues to be one of the most active departments in exploring new computer applications. With this background, computers are a natural fit for an existing curriculum. The faculty did not have to revamp their courses significantly in order to integrate computers. Thus, the primary advantages of computers in the Psychology Core Lab are that they make experimental research more accessible to students and permit a wider range of experimentation.

The Public Policy Workshop (PPW) is a computer facility created through a Sloan Foundation New Liberal Arts grant to Professor Stefan Kapsch of the political science department. The PPW was designed with three basic goals in mind:

1. To create a relaxed, attractive atmosphere in which students who are uncomfortable with computers— recalcitrant computer users—can become more comfortable with the technology and develop computer skills

2. To help students interested in public policy issues develop expertise with more quantitative, rather than solely verbal, forms of analysis

3. To support student and faculty collaboration on public policy research

The facility itself is a small classroom with ten Macintosh stations. The instructor's station is connected to a large screen monitor. A table is available for small conferences or for laying out printouts and other paperwork. A lounge area provides a comfortable setting for reading journals and other materials. There has been relatively little emphasis on developing custom courseware for the PPW. Students and faculty primarily use standard, off-the-shelf software—word processors, spreadsheets, statistical packages.

While computers were able to slide into existing psychology courses, a new public policy curriculum had to be developed in order to exploit what computers had to offer. Students in the public policy analysis class, which was created through the Sloan grant, worked in teams to do public policy research for groups outside the college. In 1990 some students worked in conjunction with Planned Parenthood to conduct a public opinion poll on reproductive rights. Another group worked under a local grant to evaluate a residential drug treatment program. Students studying introductory political science learn to use a program for calculating cross-tabulations. The pedagogical principle is that it is desirable for students to learn some basic data analysis techniques while working with relatively simple statistics, rather than jumping straight into complicated statistics such as multiple regression.

Like the Psychology Core Lab, the PPW is a combined teaching and research facility. However, at Reed there is not as strong a tradition of empirical research in political science as there is in psychology. With the exception of sociology, the social sciences take an analytic, rather than an empirical, approach. As a result, students who gravitate toward the social sciences are often more oriented toward verbal, instead of quantitative methods. While they are adept at understanding and picking apart prose arguments, they do not have the same facility with quantitative arguments—and while the PPW was designed to address these problems, success comes more slowly, dampened by the very problems it seeks to change.

Advantages and Disadvantages of Instructional Labs

There are many advantages to the use of combined teaching and research labs. At Reed it is natural to use computers in support of student research. This approach is consistent with the college's educational mission, which emphasizes the development of independent thinking and scholarly skills. It is also consistent with Reed's philosophy that computers are empowering tools that enhance scholarly activity. Education takes on the aspect of an apprenticeship, in which students learn by working with their teachers. In addition, departmental computer facilities create a forum in which students in that department, or in related areas, can work and socialize together.

This approach helps exploit the dynamic interaction between teaching and research, by merging many aspects of the two activities. As Cornell University has discovered after many years of developing academic software, "Incorporating original software into the curriculum is much more likely [to succeed] if it has origins in the research interests of the developer" (Galloway 1989, 230).

Combined instructional/research facilities are not without their drawbacks, however. In many ways, they are subject to the same problems that can plague any instructional computing effort. For example, the mechanics of using computers can dominate class time and divert attention from the real subject at hand. Department facilities often put a heavy burden on the professor and department since the academic computer center may have difficulty supporting the specialized computer applications required by different departments.

Even though professors can make extensive use of off-the-shelf software, it may still be necessary to have software development expertise on campus to provide specialized programs. These software development efforts are not typically focused on courseware in the traditional sense. At Reed we have found that our student programmers spend more time developing research tools that students and faculty can use to design their own experiments. Fortunately, it seems to be easier to develop software for research tools, than it is to develop courseware to be used in a classroom.

Finally, the extensive use of computers in laboratory classes and student research, raises some access issues. While computers can make laboratory tools more accessible, they can also discourage or intimidate students who are not comfortable with computer technology. If computer-based tools are the only way to conduct a certain project or course assignment, then students who find it difficult to work with computers will be disenfranchised. Perhaps the day will come when none of our students have these problems, but it is not here yet.

Computing Strategies for the 1990s

Like courseware, the combined teaching/research lab model is not a panacea. The successful examples mentioned in the previous section illustrate how computers can be implemented in a way that is consistent with the institution's philosophy and can support a professor's style and instructional goals. The type of application that works well, and is a natural fit at one institution, however, may be quite different from the approach used at another. In many cases creative, useful applications will extend well beyond the traditional concept of courseware.

Computers and networks can be used to improve traditional instructional methods by providing access to a wealth of information. For example, educational software can use information resources from all parts of a campus or from other institutions to provide a depth and diversity of information that is not possible in just one stand-alone computer. *Executive information systems*, for example, provide easy-to-use tools for accessing and analyzing large, complex data sets. The desktop computer, whether a microcomputer or a more advanced workstation, acts as the window into a variety of information sources located on other remote systems. The larger computers working behind the scenes, as well as the data network that transmits the information, must be fast enough to give the user the sense that all the information is right there on the desktop.

The idea of executive information systems has gained popularity lately in the corporate world, as well as in university administrative computing centers. The *Mandarin Project* at Cornell University and the *University Workstation* at the University of Texas at Austin are two examples of network-based information systems designed explicitly for university administrators. Executive information systems are attractive for corporate or administrative executives who presumably have neither the time nor the patience to sift through an endless maze of data, but who need direct access to pertinent information nonetheless. This description also fits most students and faculty in the liberal arts and there is no reason why the concept of executive information systems can't be applied to academic as well as administrative problem solving. Anthropology, history, linguistics, political science, and sociology are all disciplines that make use of large, diverse information sets and could use the executive information approach to their advantage.

To give a concrete example: A monumental event in Irish history is the 1846 Great Potato Famine which, through excessive mortality and massive emigration, reduced the population by more than 40 percent in less than ten years. Numerous factors contributed to the calamitous nature of the famine—rapid population growth, widespread and extreme poverty, poor agricultural practices, a large number of inadequate subsistence farms, and overdependence on the potato for humans as well as animals. Against this backdrop, successive years of potato blight had a disastrous result. Of course, controversy continues over the exact social and economic causes of the famine, as well as the extent to which it could have been predicted.

Historians use many different types of information to study the causes and results of the famine, such as records of marriages, births and infant mortality, employment and wage information, census records, descriptive examples from poorhouse records and traveler's diaries, records of agricultural practices and crop yields, and ships' logs. To understand fully the great famine, much of these data must be examined for changes over time, as well as regional differences. Some of these variables have complicated interactive effects. This varied assortment of data has been collected and compiled by researchers, but it is rarely available in a form accessible to students. A useful instructional program would incorporate access to relevant databases, whether local or remote, preprocess the raw data so they can be reduced and then presented in a meaningful way. For example, students might want to look at a graph of population growth over time, the interaction between population growth and the availability of food, or maps showing crop losses and emigration by county. Like any good networked database system, the program should also have easy querying tools so students can retrieve, sort, and analyze both textual and numerical data.

The Irish famine is but one example of a complex data environment that could promote an exciting new type of learning for undergraduates if it were made accessible through advanced technology. This type of network-based courseware is appealing in the liberal arts because it helps students to integrate diverse types of information. Network access is designed into the courseware structure, so networked resources are more than just an afterthought. Availability of sophisticated querying tools lets students control the flow of information, so they can quickly zero in on items that are of greatest interest to them.

However, there are hurdles that must be jumped before this type of project can be successfully implemented. Many small colleges do not have campus-wide networks, and of those that do, many do not have access to datasets available through national networks like the Internet. Numerous standardization and legal issues make it hard to get and use interesting data, even if a network is in place. And finally, the scale of such a project is beyond the reach of faculty at small colleges.

Collaborative courseware projects provide a way for faculties at small colleges to get involved in large-scale, content-rich development efforts, like the Irish famine example that was proposed. By joining forces with colleagues at larger universities, faculty from liberal arts colleges can partake of some of the resources that universities can more readily attract. Such collaboration also provides a mechanism for faculty to influence courseware design and development in order better to address the instructional needs of liberal arts institutions.

The Perseus project,[2] for example, is a hypermedia project that focuses on classical Greece. The package consists of a large CD-ROM–based HyperCard stack[3] linked to a set of video disk images. For example, students use a mouse to click on a map of Greece to zoom in on cities and archaeological sites. From the diagram of the site or artifact, the student can click on various views, which are displayed on the video disk monitor. The stack also includes a catalog entry and list of references for each monument. The goal of the Perseus project is to help students experience classical monuments in a way that may not be possible even by visiting the site, since many artifacts have been removed or dispersed in pieces. "We want the student, guided by the professor, to learn methodology by tackling significant examples of the kinds of problems that scholars grapple with daily" (Harward 1988, 18).

---

2. The Perseus project is based at Harvard University, where Gregory Crane is the director and Elli Mylonas is the managing editor.

3. HyperCard is a development tool based on the metaphor of a stack of file cards, with each card containing related but nonsequential information. The developer can easily create a collection of cards with text and graphics, as well as menus, windows, and buttons that link the card to other relevant cards or to resources like CD-ROMs and video disks. In HyperCard lingo, a *stack* is the file created in the development process.

As Perseus has evolved and expanded, it has come to include several liberal arts colleges, largely because key individuals moved to these schools and continued their collaboration on the project. Kenneth Morrell got involved in Perseus while a graduate student at Harvard University. He is now in the classics department at St. Olaf College and continues to work on the Perseus executive committee. Other Perseus contributors from the liberal arts include Tom Martin at Pomona College and Neil Smith at Bowdoin College.

The Perseus history highlights one way that small colleges can become more involved in educational computing projects—by attracting and keeping new faculty members who are actively engaged in using computers. Many new faculty just out of graduate school who have been involved in using computers in their research are likely to continue using them for teaching. Recent graduates also bring fresh perspectives on interesting computer applications and can help colleagues develop more innovative uses of computers. Caveats are in order however, since most liberal arts colleges do not explicitly reward courseware development efforts by their faculty. It is extremely unfair to encourage new faculty to invest in such development efforts if the institution does not consider this work when it comes time for a tenure decision.

Another example of collaboration is the Consortium for Upper-level Physics Software (CUPS), headed by Robert Ehrlich at George Mason University (Ehrlich 1990). In contrast to the Perseus project, where several scholars contribute to one huge database, faculty involved in the CUPS project are working to create a suite of programs. CUPS consists of 27 faculty developers working in teams of three to create computer programs for nine standard upper-division physics courses. Four of the 27 participants are from small liberal arts colleges. The primary goal of CUPS is to develop simulations that can be used for class demonstrations and by students outside of class. It is also important that the simulations work with existing courses without displacing other critical materials or reforming the curriculum. A National Science Foundation grant to CUPS will be used to pay programmers and cover administrative costs for the consortium. It is expected that each contributor has institutional support for his or her portion of the project in the form of a student programmer and a computer. This investment is significantly less than would be required if the faculty member were undertaking such an extensive development independently, and as such, is manageable by most small liberal arts colleges.

Though large scale collaborative projects like Perseus and CUPS are attractive, they are certainly not the only approach that can find success in the liberal arts. In many cases it simply is not necessary to make such a massive effort. There are numerous ways in which much smaller, and more realistic, courseware projects can support liberal arts instruction.

Much has been made of the increased communication offered by electronic mail and other network services. Networks have been particularly useful in making it easier for faculty to collaborate on research projects. However, electronic communication can also be used for more explicitly pedagogical purposes. In 1989, Reed political science professor Darius Rejali began directly incorporating communication via electronic mail into his classes. In two upper-division political science classes, students who did not participate in class discussion on any given day were required to participate in e-mail discussions on that particular topic within 24 hours after the conference. Students who had talked in class were encouraged to participate as well. The primary motivation for creating the e-mail forum was the tendency for a small vocal minority to dominate conference discussions, often to the point of frustrating other less vocal students. E-mail was "expected to play to their strengths if [the students] were better writers than speakers" (Rejali 1990).

As predicted, e-mail provided a lively forum, promoting active out-of-class discussions. Students became more familiar with each other. Also as expected, e-mail made it easier for students to react emotionally—"flaming" in reaction to heated arguments. Some other positive, and unexpected, results were increased feedback to the professor on his teaching, increased student creativity both in and out of class, an explosion of student participation, and the creation of a better mechanism for communicating with students on more mundane administrative topics.

Electronic mail can also be used to facilitate communication among students on writing assignments. At Skidmore College, Michael Marx of the English department found that students in the writing seminar were inhibited about criticizing each other's writing. To circumvent this problem, students were required to use BITNET electronic mail to exchange papers and critiques with students in a similar class at Babson College. Students who used BITNET tended to take more time with their critiques and explain their comments more carefully, because they couldn't fall back on face-to-face discussions to explain their comments (Marx 1990, 13). The e-mail approach also served to promote a novel means of interaction among students at different colleges.

Two other specialized programs that can be used to promote student communication are the *Electronic Dialectical Notebook* (EDN) and *Conversations*, both developed at Lewis and Clark College. EDN was developed by Dan Revel and Susan Kirschner to replace the traditional practice of exchanging notebooks and critiquing each other's essays in the freshman Basic Inquiry class. Using EDN, the teacher writes scripts to compose exercises which are then distributed to the microcomputers in the classroom. The student's computer shows the instructions for the current exercise and windows for reading and writing. For example, the instructions might tell the students to read a poem in the reading window, write a short essay, and then exchange essays with their partners. After sending critiques to each other, the students can turn in their work electronically and also save copies for themselves.

Conversations, also developed by Revel, is a much less structured approach to student communications. This program uses an AppleShare file server as the basis for a semipublic space in which students in Basic inquiry, or upper-level literature courses, can carry on class discussions. Kirschner, who teaches English at Lewis and Clark and directs the Basic Inquiry core program, will sometimes initiate discussions, but in other cases will propose that students originate the conversation and suggest topics on which they might focus. Participation is required and counts for roughly one-third of their grade, along with class discussion and papers. One advantage of using Conversations is that students who might be wary about voicing opinions that are not "politically correct" or popular, find it easier to diverge from the majority view. And, when students use both

EDN and Conversations, Kirschner finds that they develop a more sophisticated understanding of how to adjust their writing voice for their audience, becoming more formal for public conversations or more personal and focused for peer critiques.

In these electronic mail examples, faculty members take the relatively simple approach of incorporating existing communications tools into their courses. Though it does require time and energy, the investment is significantly less than would be required to develop a new piece of courseware. Programs such as EDN and Conversations take much more time to develop than the e-mail applications described earlier, since they involve custom software development and require in-house programming expertise. The advantage of these programs, though, is that they meet a specific need and allow more sophisticated types of student communication. In all these classes electronic communication works because it is integrated in a way designed to solve specific instructional problems, not just tacked on as an adjunct to class assignments. In addition, because electronic communication requires a certain critical mass—it is harder to use e-mail when only some of the people you want to talk to also use it—these professors increased their likelihood of success by requiring all students to use it.

Another example of small ways computers can be used to make a big difference, is the *pamphlet* approach, described by Eric Lane of the University of Tennessee at Chattanooga. Lane won a 1987 EDUCOM/NCRIPTAL award for his physics program, *Standing Waves*, which he developed to help students understand dynamic physics better by means of animated examples of basic wave concepts. Lane views *Standing Waves* and his other animations, "as little pamphlets that illustrate a particular idea or concept" (1989, 58). And while his animations can be used quite flexibly for classroom and laboratory demonstrations or for out-of-class assignments, each program is quite focused on the particular topic, and does not try to do too much. As Lane points out, "I want to use the microcomputer in the way that the student responds to it best and not try to make it be all things to all students. This means using it as a complement or supplement to class lecture, laboratory and individual study, not as a replacement" (p. 57).

Faculty who want to use computers in their classes can also use templates from readily available commercial software. Considering the difficulty of developing software, it is surprising that more faculty have not made better use of such programs in their classes. According to Gordon Galloway, then at Cornell University, "Using standard commercial packages to create curricular applications often produces good results with minimal problems" (1989, 230). For example, science texts in the Dynamic Models series edited by David Barkley, make extensive use of the electronic spreadsheet, "a powerful, ubiquitous, nonprocedural programming language that permits rapid and intuitive construction of sophisticated simulations" (Atkinson et al. 1990, viii). Each workbook, currently available for biochemistry, chemistry and physics, opens with an introduction to spreadsheets. Subsequent chapters cover the subject at an introductory level and incorporate spreadsheets into all the examples and problems. Students can use any standard spreadsheet in conjunction with the book, and templates are available from the publisher in both DOS and Macintosh formats.

Roberta Bigelow, in the physics department at Willamette University, uses *Dynamic Models in Physics* in her upper-division mechanics course. In the past students have done their own programming to perform Runge-Kutta calculations and graph the results. Homework assignments demand that students learn to interpret these graphs, which they often find very difficult. Using the spreadsheet templates, Bigelow found that more students understood the concepts of Runge-Kutta. In addition, students that may have avoided the class because they didn't like programming, did like the spreadsheet approach.

Design Issues

The difficulty with courseware development, particularly when it involves large-scale, content-rich programs, is that a vast amount of material must be organized in a way that is simple to use. One example of a superbly designed program is the NOVA *Animal Pathfinders* interactive video, developed with HyperCard. The stack presents a wealth of information, including an animal database, student activities, and tools the teacher can use to construct custom lessons. Video is fully intermingled into all aspects of the stack. The user interface design is elegant and straightforward. Of course, the development team at WGBH in Boston, where the software was created, was supported by a slew of talented designers and a professional video production staff.

There are other examples that courseware developers can learn from, not all of which are computer programs. For example, in *The visual display of quantitative information*, Edward Tufte (1983) describes how charts and graphs can maximize the information presented and yet retain a clear, simple design. Data graphics are similar to software interface designs in that both endeavor to present as much information as possible in a way that is intuitive and economical. Many of the principles of graphical elegance that Tufte develops can be readily applied to the user interface design of content-rich educational software. For instance, in addition to merely showing the data, graphical designs should (among other things):

- Induce the viewer to think about the substance rather than about methodology, graphic design, the technology of graphics production or something else

- Encourage the eye to compare different pieces of data

- Reveal the data at several levels of detail, from a broad overview to the fine structure (p. 14)

These ideals are achieved through designs that maximize the amount of ink (pixels in our case) dedicated to the information being conveyed and reduce, as much as possible, the space given to decoration or incidental imagery. Above all, the graphical display must reveal, rather than interfere with the communication of information.

> The best designs . . . are *intriguing and curiosity provoking,* drawing the viewer into the wonder of the data, sometimes by narrative power, sometimes by immense detail, and sometimes by elegant presentation of simple but interesting data (p. 121).

Unfortunately, graphical interference is a particular problem in software design. While a graphical interface is a true advance over older text-based systems, the interface can easily get cluttered up with extraneous, uninformative debris. It is easy for courseware developers to go overboard with a graphical interface, often mistaking abundant decoration for good design. All too often the user's attention is drawn to the bells and whistles of the program, rather than to the content. When software does not have a strong underlying design plan, users find themselves awash in a sea of icons and menus, and much of the development effort invested in the graphical interface is wasted.

Fortunately, there is no particular mystery to good graphical design, and informative books like *The visual display of quantitative information* provide reasonable design guidelines for faculty who want to develop clean, well-planned courseware, but who do not have access to professional interface designers.[4]

Where Will Students Use These Computers?

As computers become increasingly integrated into the liberal arts curriculum, the question arises as to where students will use these computers. Throughout the eighties most small colleges and universities created laboratories where students could use computers, usually for free, and primarily for word processing. Will the student lab continue to be the best way to provide access to computers? Probably not. It is unrealistic for faculty to require extensive computer use outside the class when there is a limited number of computer systems available in just a few locations. As a result the professor can't truly integrate technology into the curriculum. Some professors try to get around this problem by creating lab sessions for traditionally non-lab classes. The faculty can reserve a computerized lab or classroom for their courses and thereby ensure that students get the access and assistance they need. The burden is then on the institution to provide enough computers in the laboratory/classroom environment. Both physical space and up-to-date computer equipment are at a premium on small college campuses. Scheduling and management problems also make it difficult for the institution to

---

4. Other useful books that provide guidelines for graphical user interfaces include
   Apple human interface guidelines: The Apple desktop interface, and *HyperCard
   stack design guidelines.* Though these books deal primarily with Apple
   Macintosh design principles, they do provide many useful design guidelines that
   can be readily applied to software developed on other platforms.

operate many computerized labs, whether they are for general student access or restricted to departmental use.

The increasing variety of computer applications in the liberal arts curriculum will also make the centralized lab increasingly untenable. Multimedia applications, with sound and video, can't peacefully coexist in the traditional word-processing lab, where students are trying to compose and revise their papers. As students use computers for research and information acquisition, it will become increasingly impractical for students to go to a special, isolated computer room to use this important resource.

The rapid decrease in the cost of a personal computer, coupled with an increase in its curricular uses, has resulted in a dramatic rise in the number of students at liberal arts colleges who own their own computers. Among some colleges similar to those represented in this volume, private ownership of microcomputers in 1991 was reported to be as high as 70 percent. Though the average percentage of private ownership was 34.5 percent, this is still considerably larger than the 8.6 percent average of only four years earlier (1986–87).

The impact of increased student ownership of personal computers is that more computing now takes place in dormitory rooms or in off-campus dwellings than ever before. Adding fuel to this trend is the fact that many liberal arts colleges are extending their campus-wide networks to include dormitories, thereby providing students with access to laser-printing facilities, college-owned software, electronic mail systems, library resources, inter-campus data communication, and other services, all from the convenience of their own rooms.[5]

---

5. Among the CLAC schools, networking to individual dormitory rooms rose from less than 5 percent to more than 15 percent between 1987 and 1991. Although this is a significant increase, the majority of liberal arts colleges are able to cover the cost of network connections to individual dormitory rooms only when the dormitories are due for general refurbishing, including the installation of telephone service and/or new power wiring.

Conclusion

Should an institution invest in a software development effort? Should it develop academic software? It depends. Most institutions that have fostered academic software development have first created an environment that is supportive of computing in general. Those institutions, whether large universities or small colleges, have made an effort to provide computers for all faculty and students to use and have invested in an infrastructure to support those users in their everyday work. Computers are welcomed as useful tools, not treated with hostility or viewed as a luxury. In this fertile environment, students and faculty will use computers in increasingly sophisticated ways and ideas for interesting instructional applications will flourish.

For the institution, it is most fruitful to cultivate development projects in curricular areas where they arise naturally, rather than to promote computerization by those who are less inspired. As many educators have pointed out, "It is very difficult for schools to stimulate the creation of instructional materials from the top down" (Jones and Smith 1989, 32). This approach has several implications. First, an institution that is interested in promoting instructional computing should be prepared to respond to and support interesting possibilities when they arise. The promising projects may not be the most grandiose and they may not involve any actual software development. Successful projects can make creative use of off-the-shelf hardware and software. Support can be in the form of equipment and software for the faculty member, released time, funds for a student programmer or technical writer, or facilities where students can use the software. Support that will make the project proceed more smoothly may be much more important than financial incentives alone.

Second, the academic disciplines that are receptive to instructional computing will vary from school to school. At Reed, as at many liberal arts colleges, student research is an essential component of the educational process. It makes sense that computers were first used in research labs and then found their way into the classroom. Other colleges may focus on different instructional goals and subject matter. This is one reason why it is difficult for colleges to learn from the experiences of peer schools—each school has a different educational culture.

Third, if computer staff take an essentially responsive posture there is a risk that individuals who are the most demanding, or departments that most typically make use of computers, will attract most of the resources. Faculty who need more encouragement and prompting may not get the support they need and interesting development opportunities can be lost. So, in spite of all that has just been said, there is a need for computer staff who can help faculty, especially those who might not be the most obvious candidates, cultivate an interest in educational computing. It probably won't work just to give them a computer and wait for results. Faculty in this position will need a lot more prompting with interesting ideas, technical assistance, and general moral support.

Faculty should think long and hard before starting an instructional computer project. Development projects have a way of growing huge and out of control—*Godzilla vs. the Unsuspecting Professor*. Large computer projects that seek to incorporate a wide range of material are appealing for the liberal arts because they support instructional goals and make it possible to integrate a variety of related, but often diverse sources of information. Unfortunately such large-scale projects are usually too unwieldy for a professor in a small college, unless it is possible to collaborate with others in the development effort. Despite the appeal of such comprehensive efforts, faculty should look for less ambitious and more realistic ways that computers can be used to support liberal education. Start with a small project and see how it works. Consider where students will use the materials that are developed. If they are going to use them outside of class and without supervision, they will have to be relatively "bullet-proof." You may have to coordinate with your computer support staff to ensure that students are getting the help they need. Above all, make sure that the development is based on clearly articulated instructional needs, rather than the lure of the technology itself, and that it truly supports your teaching style.

The lessons learned from the failures of CAI and other courseware efforts of the past three decades have been painful ones. If we have acquired any insight at all, it is that there is no revolution in educational computing that is waiting for us just around the corner. But we have also learned that educational computing is not simply a fad of the late twentieth century. It is a feature of the liberal arts college landscape, much like the library or the laboratory, which is destined to grow, evolve, and play a continuing role in the undergraduate learning experience.

References

Apple Computer, Inc. 1987. *Apple human interface guidelines: The Apple desktop interface.* Reading, Mass.: Addison-Wesley.

Apple Computer, Inc. 1989. *HyperCard stack design guidelines.* Reading, Mass.: Addison-Wesley.

Association of American Colleges (AAC). 1985. *Integrity in the college curriculum: A report to the academic community.* Washington D.C.

Atkinson, Daniel, Douglas C. Brower, Ronald W. McClard, and David S. Barkley, ed. 1990. *Dynamic models in chemistry.* Marina del Rey, Calif.: N. Simonson & Company.

Boyer, Ernest L. 1987. *College: The undergraduate experience in America.* New York: Harper & Row.

Cavalier, Robert. 1990. *Developer tools: Promise, reality and hope.* Pittsburgh: Center for Design of Educational Computing at Carnegie Mellon (distributor). Videotape.

Ehrlich, Robert. 1990. A project to develop computer software and supplementary texts for nine upper-level physics courses. In *Computing in advanced undergraduate physics,* ed. David M. Cook, 204–208. Appleton, Wis.: Lawrence University.

Galloway, Gordon L. 1989. Cornell University: An institutional perspective on using information technologies to add value to teaching and learning. In *Computing across the curriculum: Academic perspectives,* ed. William H. Graves, 213–233. Reading, Mass.: Addison-Wesley.

Glick, Milton D. 1990. Integrating computers into higher education. *EDUCOM Review* 25: 35–38.

Goldberg, Samuel, ed. 1990. *The new liberal arts program: A 1990 report.* New York: Alfred P. Sloan Foundation.

Graves, William H. ed. 1989. *Computing across the curriculum: Academic perspectives.* Reading, Mass.: Addison-Wesley.

Harward, V. Judson. 1988. From museum to monitor: The visual
explorations of the ancient world. *Academic Computing* 2: 16–19,
69–71.

Henderson, Robert W. 1989. Microcomputer-based instructional
computing in psychology: Where, what, when, why, and who? In
Computing across the curriculum: Academic perspectives, ed.
William H. Graves, 15–25. Reading, Mass.: Addison-Wesley.

Jones, Loretta L., and Stanley G. Smith. 1989. Case study: Exploring
Chemistry. In *Computing across the curriculum: Academic perspectives*, ed. William H. Graves, 27–33. Reading, Mass.: Addison-Wesley.

Kay, Alan, and Adele Goldberg. 1988. The Dynabook—Past, present
and future. In *A history of personal workstations*, ed. Adele Goldberg,
249–263. New York: ACM Press.

Kemeny, John G. 1990. Computers in education: Progress at a
snail's pace. *EDUCOM Review* 25: 44–47.

Lane, Eric T. 1989. Developing *Standing Waves*. In *Computing
across the curriculum: Academic perspectives*, ed. William H.
Graves, 51–66. Reading, Mass.: Addison-Wesley.

Marcus, Marvin, Stanley Nicholson, and Llad Philips. 1990. A
college-wide model for developing computer-integrated instruction.
Paper presented at Annual Apple University Consortium Conference,
Santa Cruz, California.

Marx, Michael S. 1990. In *Computers and learning: A combination
that is paying off for higher education*. Milford, Conn.: IBM.

Meiss, Richard A. 1989. Development of teaching software: Some
hindsights. In *Computing across the curriculum: Academic perspectives*, ed. William H. Graves, 43–49. Reading, Mass.: Addison-Wesley.

Morison, Elting E. 1984. The Sloan new liberal arts. In *Technology
and science: Important distinctions for liberal arts colleges*, ed.
John N. Burnett, 1–5. Davidson, N.C.: Davidson College.

National Center for Research to Improve Postsecondary Teaching and
Learning (NCRIPTAL). 1990. *Catalog of winners from the 1987–90
EDUCOM/NCRIPTAL higher education software awards*. Ann Arbor.

National Institute of Education (NIE). 1984. *Involvement in learning: Realizing the potential of American higher education.* Washington D.C.: Department of Education.

Nelson, Theodor H. 1987. *Computer lib / Dream machines.* Redmond, Wash.: Microsoft Press.

Nielsen, Jakob. 1990. *Hypertext and hypermedia.* San Diego: Academic Press.

Potter, Frank, Charles W. Peck, and David S. Barkley, ed. 1989. *Dynamic Models in Physics.* Marina del Rey, Calif.: N. Simonson and Company.

Rejali, Darius. 1990. QuickMail in the classroom: Adventures in electronic communication. *At Reed* 1:16–22.

Styer, Daniel F. 1990. Using computers to build insight. In *Computing in advanced undergraduate physics,* ed. David M. Cook, 201–203. Appleton, Wis.: Lawrence University.

Tufte, Edward R. 1983. *The visual display of quantitative information.* Cheshire, Conn.: Graphics Press.

The Library Intersection: Roles and Models for Information Services

Gai Carpenter
Hampshire College
and
Ann Carey Edmonds
Mount Holyoke College

Gai Carpenter is director of the Harold F. Johnson Library Center at Hampshire College in Amherst, Massachusetts. Since 1981 she has also served as project manager for the Five Colleges Library Automation Project. In 1990, she assumed responsibility for all campus computing services at Hampshire and is engaged in the integration of academic, administrative, and networking services for the campus.

A graduate of Mount Holyoke College, she did graduate work in political science at Duke University and received her M.L.S. from Indiana University. She has worked at Hampshire since the college opened in the fall of 1970. She has served as a member and chair of the board of NELINET, the New England library network, and as a member of the OCLC Users Council.

Ann C. Edmonds has been college librarian at Mount Holyoke since 1964. She is responsible for the administration of the library, including archives and audio-visual services. As a member of the Librarians' Council of Five Colleges, Inc., she participated in the development and implementation of LS2000, the automated system linking the libraries of the five institutions: Amherst, Hampshire, Mount Holyoke, Smith, and the University of Massachusetts.

She holds a B.A. in history from Barnard College, an M.S. in library science from the School of Library Service, Columbia University, and an M.A. in geography from Johns Hopkins University. She has been active in library affairs, serving as president of the Association of College and Research Libraries in 1970–71, and Chair of the Board of NELINET, Inc. (New England Library Information Network) from 1982–1984. She has also served on evaluating committees of the Middle States Association of Colleges and Secondary Schools and the New England Association of Schools and Colleges.

> Many other work settings need and use information to achieve their purposes, whether it be the making of motorcars or the making of money. Only the academic institution has information, the creation of information, the assessment of information, the transfer of information as its total raison d'être.
>
> Bernard Naylor (1988)

The awareness of technology on the campuses of undergraduate liberal arts colleges has taken a quantum leap in a relatively short number of years. From isolated beginnings in separate departments the spread of automation has coalesced into interrelationships that impinge much more immediately and visibly on the total academic, as well as the administrative, college community.

In such a period of rapid growth, confusion and conflict concerning the definition of roles and responsibilities are inevitable. This is true for two organizations on the campus that see their primary responsibility as providing services to support the scholarly endeavors of faculty and students. These are the traditional library and the emerging academic computing center.

That such tension—either real or imagined—does exist, is seen in the flurry of articles that have appeared over the past five years in library literature, taking issue with what the computing community has stigmatized as the "two cultures," to the detriment of the librarians. While the shrillness of the librarians' cry has abated, there is still an uneasiness about our relationship, and apprehension about how each of us is viewed by our constituencies and by our administrations.

We would like to bury the hatchet dividing the two cultures and propose another culture, one that binds the library and the academic computing center in a common mission of service to the information seeker, the scholar/researcher, and the student. These information seekers are both demanding and independent; they do not particularly care who furnishes them with information, provided they get what they want.

For the hatchet to remain interred, we need to understand one another better. When C. P. Snow presented his classic lecture "The Two Cultures" in 1959, he viewed an unbridgeable chasm between the scientific and humanistic cultures. Several years later, when he wrote a commentary on his earlier perceptions (Snow 1965), he emphasized that the real message of his work was the importance of putting the powers of technology to work to meet primal human needs.

Snow's discussion is relevant to our present debate; we have moved, in western society, from the decades of the industrial revolution to those of the scientific revolution. Now we are in the midst of the information revolution, which, like the previous two, has the potential to empower or to disenfranchise, to create a world of haves and have-nots or to bring people together in the sharing and use of information on an unprecedented level.

We believe that there is much in the experience of librarians that can inform and strengthen the work of computer specialists, just as there is much in computing that can expedite and enhance the work of libraries. We are not yet ready to abandon spirited and constructive debate about the structures that can best support information services, the differences between information *access* and information *use,* the moral and intellectual dilemmas of providing raw information, and the human and humane requirements of information service. These issues are replacing the territorial ones in the library dialogue, signaling an acceptance of computer technology and its potentials. And these are the issues that all information-service professionals, whatever their current labels, must consider carefully if we are not to create an information-rich and knowledge-poor society.

In this chapter, we examine the intellectual and automated library systems that are models for information management systems, based on our experience in the Five Colleges library system. In addition, we explore the issues we all face as a result of rapid changes in media, technology, and the ongoing convergence of campus information services.

Where Have We Been?

It cannot be too strongly emphasized that the introduction of automated systems in libraries is an overlay onto their existing operations and is but one aspect of the many responsibilities that devolve upon libraries: developing collections, organizing them, preserving them, making them available, interpreting them. Whether in the form of clay tablets, papyrus scrolls, manuscripts, the codex, microfiche, videotapes, or electronic databases—the format does not matter—it is the content of the package that concerns the librarian. Over the centuries many devices have been developed to accomplish this mission, computerization being but the most recent.

Writing in the 1940s, Jesse Shera, a library historian, clearly articulated the mission of libraries. "Knowing books and men— knowledge of the materials and their sources, and empathy with the patron and his needs—these are the twin pillars upon which library service rests" (1976). Generations of librarians have collected materials to form libraries in order to satisfy users' needs. They have developed systems of cataloguing and classification that reflect the contents of these collections. For more than a hundred years, the library's card catalogue has been one of the major arcana of the academic community, and its creation, maintenance, and interpretation were the mysteries of librarianship and scholarship.

The wealth of information sources now available to scholars is a recent development. The individual scholar may develop a personal database application with any of several sophisticated software packages, but is the design of that application wholly personal? Or are there standards and rules that should be applied at all levels of information organization if it is to be truly useful? Here we believe the experience of libraries in automating databases is particularly instructive.

The logical underpinnings of library automation lie in the development of the Machine Readable Cataloguing (MARC) standard which was developed in the late 1960s. Designed as a communications format for the exchange of bibliographic data, MARC embodied a flexibility that was unusual at the time. Any record could have a variable number of fields, and any field, or sub-field, could be of variable length. This standard was, moreover, linked to another—the Anglo-American Cataloguing Rules—which defined for libraries the forms of entry used for data to describe a book, journal, film, recording, musical score, or any other medium.

The adoption of the second edition of the Anglo-American Cataloguing Rules (AACRII) meant wholesale change in the choices of entry (Samuel Clemens became Mark Twain, for example). In addition, the Library of Congress was constantly updating and changing terms, from the names of geographical entities to the terminology of subject headings. It was clear that no one could keep up with the pace of revision in a card catalogue, and that only an automated system that allowed across-the-board change would give us any currency.

The MARC format codes such details as the distinction between personal, corporate, and conference authors, or the music publisher's number, or the provenance of rare books. Each of these is regarded as important both in the physical description of a work and in the provision of scholarly access to the work. These standards have flowered in the creation of the national databases of the Library of Congress, the Online Computer Library Center (OCLC), and the Research Libraries Information Network (RLIN). Starting in the early 1970s, OCLC provided Ohio libraries, and eventually libraries worldwide, on-line interactive access to a database that now numbers over 22,000,000 bibliographic records.

Libraries are traditionally labor intensive and in the early years of on-line systems like OCLC there was little in automation that could change that characteristic. The initial service of this major database was the production of catalogue cards, which reduced the work of ordering preprinted cards from the Library of Congress or typing them in-house, but which relieved none of the work of filing in card catalogs. Initially the on-line database was perceived as a fancier method of card production. Cataloguing standards were subject to individual interpretation, and the database could be augmented by any participant in the on-line system. As a result, the growing OCLC database was only as perfect as most human endeavor.

The Five College System

Five Colleges, Inc., is a consortium of Amherst, Hampshire, Mount Holyoke, and Smith colleges and the University of Massachusetts at Amherst. When we began our adventure in library automation, we already had a history of library cooperation which stretched back to the founding, in 1951, of the Hampshire Inter-Library Center (HILC), and which included cooperative collection development, extensive interlibrary lending, and direct student and faculty access to the libraries of all the consortium members. The University had developed automated systems for acquisitions, a serials union list, and circulation. Each library had been using OCLC for its cataloguing for several years and our recommendation in 1977 to the presidents of the five colleges that we explore automation had been warmly endorsed.

Each of the librarians had different motives for embarking on the venture and did so with enthusiasm ranging from tepid to passionate. We did achieve early agreement on some guiding principles; we would share a union catalogue, and the system CPU would be located at the University. We were looking for the then-elusive integrated system that would support both an on-line catalogue and all the other functions that depend on the bibliographic database: circulation, serials control, acquisitions, interlibrary loans, management information, and so forth.

We are still seeking that grail in all its perfection, but we have developed a far more mature and worldly appreciation of the possible. Our cooperative experience has some special characteristics, distinct from those of colleges that have automated individually, but we believe that there is a commonality of experience.

We have learned a great deal since the late 1970s when, in our quest for a multifunctional system, we began to look at the automated systems that were then available commercially. A few institutions had embarked on in-house development of systems, and some of these have survived and become commercial successes as other colleges and universities have adopted them. Most of the choices were among commercial systems that seemed to cover a broad spectrum of flexibility. Some turn-key offerings were of the Procrustean variety—the library could adapt to the software, or perhaps pay the vendor to do significant modifications, but the system was not designed with inherent flexibility. Later systems showed more tolerance for variety, and allowed the end-user to define and modify functions without programmer intervention.

Most systems were aimed at the management of circulation activity, and few were capable of supporting the full MARC format with all its complexities. Circulation was viewed as an inventory control problem, in which some identification of the book and the borrower was needed. Mechanisms for linking the two, unlinking them, and enforcing penalties if the unlinking didn't happen soon enough were the essence of control. Some vendors used tapes of a library's bibliographic records, stripping them of most data to load a database for circulation. Some said they could support the MARC format, but close scrutiny revealed that they could not handle diacritics, or that the detailed character of the MARC record's coding would be compressed into fewer, less well-defined groups of fields.

Most automation vendors developed an early relationship with one or more libraries in a particular market segment, thereby defining the subsequent perception of that vendor's place in the library automation marketplace. That market is small and demanding. One major vendor has reorganized twice in Chapter 11 bankruptcy proceedings, yet still commands a significant market share. Some vendors have entered and then withdrawn from the library market after deciding it was not a commercially attractive venture. Many companies have failed and, as is generally true in the software industry, the flexibility of any vendor to modify its products varies inversely with the size of the installed user base. Most librarians would, however, agree with the observation that automated systems are converging, and that the functionality demanded by librarians is resulting in systems that are both increasingly similar and increasingly adaptable to localized or special needs.

The lead time from conceptualization to installation of a working system has contributed to one of the headaches of automation: by the time any system has developed reasonably mature functionality, its hardware and operating system platforms may be obsolete. Some systems have been designed on hardware platforms that are part of a turn-key package, manufactured by the vendor who wrote both the operating system and the applications software. Others are hybrids, and few are at the cutting edge of computer technology. Each new system can leapfrog past its older competitors. The newest systems, written in C and based on the UNIX operating system, are capable of supporting current data communications protocols and have the greatest capacity for modification and portability.

The next generation of systems will be built upon operating systems, object-oriented programming languages, and communications standards that are still evolving in the computing community. Yet it is likely that they will copy much of their functionality from the systems that have separately evolved in parallel with the evolution of computing technologies.[1]

Transforming Libraries: How Do We Change?

If the development of administrative computing services was commonly characterized by centralization, control, and standards, and if the microcomputer revolution has meant decentralization, flexibility, and individualism, the automation of libraries has meant wholesale organizational and intellectual upheaval. Even where there have not been visible signs of organizational turmoil, there have been fundamental changes in the ways work is performed, and often unresolved tensions in the changing dynamics of the library workplace. The creation of on-line public access catalogues has turned the comfortable world of Jesse Shera upside down, and many librarians have been left in an intellectual *terra incognita*.

The MARC record is capable of being manipulated in many and wonderful ways. In a database like that of the Five College system, there are 36 named and structured indices in addition to a keyword index which accesses terms in virtually any field of a bibliographic

---

1. We sometimes find ourselves the objects of condescending—at best indulgent—scrutiny by campus computing and networking experts, for having acquired a system that isn't based in UNIX. In fact, such systems were unavailable when we were shopping for library automation, and those now running in such environments still offer few improvements in their management of the complexities of library applications software.

record. Most systems have developed reasonably cordial user interfaces—in many cases the library's on-line catalogue is far easier for the novice to approach than an MS-DOS environment, or even the iconography of the Macintosh. There are instructions, helps, labels, and, if all else fails, the librarian to assist in the search. But the seductive simplicity of the on-line catalogue can be its greatest weakness; it is hard to persuade users of an on-line catalogue that they should consult a card catalogue when some of the holdings of the library are not yet machine readable. It is harder still to explain that there are alternative ways of searching that, because of the way the database and indices are structured, may yield additional "hits." But it is perhaps most difficult to teach the academically unsophisticated user of any catalogue or database that not all of its contents are of equal value.

Some years ago, studies were undertaken to evaluate user success in finding materials in the library through the card catalogue that tested the concepts of *collection failure* and *catalogue failure*. Collection failure occurs when a library simply does not own the work the researcher is seeking. Catalogue failure occurs when the subject access, or other aspects of the precis which is the card (or on-line) catalogue entry, contains insufficient information for the catalogue user to locate relevant information. Catalogue failure is an inadvertent product of the librarian's work. Despite the librarian's understanding of the intellectual content of the work being catalogued, it is possible to provide only a finite number of access points for any work. For many years it was the practice of the Library of Congress to assign only broad and general headings to the books it catalogued, and when libraries did their own cataloguing, they mimicked that practice.

In the on-line environment, a key-word search that accesses the title and subtitle of a book, or its contents notes, might overcome the deficiency of subject entry alone, but only if the title, subtitle, or note contains the key word. The process of converting records to machine-readable form has been a copyist's task. Except where obvious changes were required, the records have been copied from the national database and edited to match the card catalogue. Although cataloguing practice now favors fuller elaboration of access points, there has been neither time nor money to enrich the earlier records.

What Price Automation?

Libraries have stood at the periphery of campus debates about the centralization or distribution of computing services, and aloof from the turf wars of administrative and academic camps. But while the computing environments for faculty, students, and staff have evolved from those for the curious few who crunched numbers on massive mainframes to utilitarian word processing for everyone, the libraries of most liberal arts colleges have developed independent, sophisticated, and often-misunderstood systems of their own, the place of which in the broader campus environment has not always been thoroughly coordinated with the activities of other computing interests.

In the decade of the 1990s, the central concern of libraries in many liberal arts colleges is no longer automation. The preservation of the crumbling codex—the often transitory printed word—and the still escalating costs of print media, particularly scholarly journals, are far more compelling concerns. Although some college libraries are now in the process of automating for the first time, others are looking toward the next generation of systems. The seemingly insurmountable problems of the early years of library automation have been overcome, and the issues now are of refinements and movement to new standards.

If we accept that automation should function not to replicate complex manual systems at high speed but rather to initiate a fundamental re-examination of both process and content, we come to one of the thorniest problems in libraries. For all that librarians were recently praised in a *New York Times* article (Lewis 1990) for their advocacy of standards and cooperative development, there is in the very nature of standards a common trait of resistance to change. Magnified by our multi-institutional environment, there have been problems in the adoption of our automated system. We may reflect on institutional culture, individual rigidity, technophobia, and demonstrable necessity as factors affecting the adaptability of libraries and their staffs. There is no simple answer, but each plays a role in the adoption of the system, in the development of new policies and procedures, in the relinquishing of individual autonomy, and in the presentation of the system to its end users, the students, and the faculty.

The library is the object of a kind of love-hate relationship with its institution; lauded as the heart of the campus, it is also seen by the administration as a bottomless fiscal pit. The explosion of publishing and spiraling costs have left even the finest liberal arts colleges struggling to meet the needs of their faculty. Automation doesn't help. David B. Truman, the wise and pragmatic president of Mount Holyoke College in the 1970s, characterized library automation as a baby gorilla, a rapacious eater whose growth could not be controlled.

In the 1970s, when library automation was innovative and on the agenda of foundations and government agencies, generous grant monies were available. (The Five Colleges were the fortunate recipients of one such award.) But novelty is no longer a factor and institutional resources must now provide both ongoing costs and support for the next-generation system. It is possible to save money by automating, but none of us would pledge to reduce costs; new tasks arise, and new opportunities for mediating the research process. The fiscal fallacies of library automation are many; it is never a one-time cost. At the initiation of an automation project, costs can be expected to increase sharply for several years.

There are at least five significant cost centers that must be supported. First, the system itself, its hardware, software, data communications, installation, insurance, and housing, represents a major capital outlay, even if it can be phased in over several steps of system acceptance. Second, the database requires at least the loading of new records in machine-readable form which may have been produced on OCLC; more often, there will be an additional cost of retrospective conversion for older materials, and there may be the cost of having the database "massaged" to update headings and to correct errors. Third, there is the process by which individual physical items are linked to their bibliographic records; again there are several options for bar coding, but all are labor intensive at some point in the process and may require additional staff. Fourth, there is the ongoing cost of system support and maintenance, both for the hardware and software; software support follows the usual pattern of general updates in functionality and bug-fixes.

Finally, there are the human costs of training and staffing the system. While computing centers generally have been able to add new staff during the past decade, libraries have often been forced to assign the support of new systems to existing staff. Every library staff member must not only learn the specific subset of functions that constitute that job, but must also become aware of the relationships among functions that are no longer so discrete as they were in a manual and compartmentalized system. At some level, everyone becomes a systems person, translating old routines into the new structure, modifying procedures to take advantage of the system's capabilities, or chafing at the system's inability to present some data in the form in which they were maintained in the old system. In each library, there are some individuals who adapt more easily than others, and some who quickly get "inside" the system and understand it at an intuitive level.

Libraries' organizational structures reflect a division of labor, loosely characterized as *public* and *technical* services, yet it is on the technical side that decisions are made that most fundamentally affect the library's users—what subject headings are assigned, how a book is classified, whether a cross-reference is needed in the catalogue— decisions which the public side must then interpret. Library staffing tends to be hierarchical in nature, and computer literacy has not long been part of the equipment of the profession. As we automate, those in power may not necessarily be those in the know.

Once a system is fully installed and functional it is indeed possible that some libraries may be able to reduce costs, primarily in staffing. In a system like ours, where the database is shared, some of the tasks of maintaining the database are no longer performed in each institution, and many routines are completely eliminated. But the changes that will allow such reductions come only if the system's users fully utilize it; in an almost unconscious way, some staff tend to build elaborate new routines around the system, and to check on its performance. If a library chooses the goal of cost/staff reduction, it is likely that only thorough top-down redefinition of work flows will produce the desired results. It is not clear that we know yet how to let good ideas percolate up in the organization without the individual staff members perceiving that such ideas may threaten their own job security.

In the community of student and faculty computer users, there is an excitement, curiosity, and generosity in exploring new software, devising new applications, and sharing information in largely egalitarian ways. To the extent that libraries' structures inhibit that kind of interaction and flow of information, they risk underutilizing automated systems and staff talents, or creating tensions and conflicts that exacerbate the stress of change. For many staff, it is difficult to accept that the acquired system falls short of the utopian vision developed in a request for proposals. At the RFP stage, everyone is encouraged to develop desiderata, and each becomes particularly enamored of some set of functions that would satisfy a long-felt need. As the process engages staff in the idea and process of automation, it creates a revolution of rising expectations. Some staff, of a hacking mentality, enjoy the thrill of making the system do what they want, while others cannot. Some cannot because the system does not perform the function they'd like, others because they cannot redefine the problem in ways appropriate to a computer solution.

Intellectual Challenges: What Do We Know?

For decades, librarians have helped students and faculty to learn to do research, whether using a card catalogue, locating material, or guiding scholars to other pertinent collections. New technologies have modified this role and expanded librarians' responsibilities as teachers. Technology has routinely extended the library's reach well beyond the local environment, even in a cooperating cluster like the Five Colleges.

In recent years, librarians have increasingly used terms like *mediator* to describe their relationship to student and faculty users of the library. That interaction has developed more intensively in the use of on-line database services, where either the complexity of the data file, or the costs associated with its use, or both, have encouraged librarians to try to conduct searches as efficiently and effectively as possible. Even though Dialog and other services can be accessed on individual accounts, the tendency is to process requests through the library. The development of CD-ROM databases extends those database searching activities radically, by placing the database in the hands of the end user. Medline or Biological Abstracts is a far richer database than the library catalogue; they contain an abstract of the work, and they deal with publications at the level of individual articles. Sources like the Science Citation Index even link articles by cited works. The local on-line catalogue is a slender reed by comparison, yet it represents in the Five College environment close to three million titles—surely the bulk of the information that the undergraduate student is likely to require in many disciplines.

For all the emphasis we now place on machine-readable data, the codex will persist. It is unlikely that the means of converting print to machine-readable form will become so automated or so inexpensive that the most obscure texts will ever be converted. And, as Neff suggests, while the database may be most desirable for reference and browsing, the book or other forms of hard copy will likely continue to be the preferred form for study in most disciplines (1985).

Some authors suggest that the new role of the library or information center is in the reorganization and repackaging of materials in a variety of media. This vision is partly due to the temptation of technology and the excitement of hypertext, but it is also an interesting contrast to the traditions of scholarship in which the production of knowledge has been the work of the scholar. This scholarship has used and gathered information in many forms, and reorganized and repackaged it. For a number of years, libraries have been engaged in the collection and organization of many media, and the provision of hardware to support different types of software. The traditional tools of the library have already been used to colocate media—in the catalogue, if not physically—and the entries in the on-line catalogue have now expanded to include even audio-visual hardware.

We question Neff when he says "The computer . . . has a distinct role to play in the library because the computer offers to both library user and librarian a new function that is wanted: the capability of customizing information retrieval to satisfy a library user's particular need. [Computers] can be programmed to rearrange and edit text, . . . they can compare two or more information items, and they can synthesize information from many sources. Thus the computer can make information dynamic, whereas the library can only make it available" (1987).

We must continue to distinguish the apparatus of scholarship from that of information retrieval. It is the user's definition of need that does the customizing, just as it did when print indices were used, but library staff do indeed interpret and translate requests into the languages of the research tools, thereby making information dynamic, rather than simply available, as Neff asserts.

The repackaging that we believe appropriate is that of the multimedia virtual library, in which text, data, sound, and image can all be selectively transmitted to the end user. The issues of intellectual property rights and copyright, however, are substantial. The revisions to the copyright laws have really not begun to encompass the potential effects of full text-retrieval systems, and the laws regarding software are, like those that have limited photocopying for classroom use and interlibrary loan, largely unenforceable. It may be argued that monitoring the use of on-line information systems will actually be easier than the self-regulation demanded in the use of printed information, and that the author at least will be more justly compensated for the use of his or her work. The nature and extent of the publisher's surcharge for access will reflect the increasing treatment of information as a commodity that does not depreciate with use. Pricing structures for CD-ROM databases make them less attractive than their paper counterparts in purely financial terms. The outright purchase of paper has been replaced by the opportunity to lease a CD-ROM file, and to continue to pay prices equal to or greater than the annual cost of a paper subscription.

Where Are We Going?

As computing networks have grown, the ideas of the *scholar's workstation* and the *virtual library* command our attention. Limited resources alone will demand more dependence on the conceptual scholarly library, rather than a particular physical entity, and networks already significantly enable use of that virtual collection. If a faculty member can search the abstracting and indexing services for scholarly journals from office or home, or use the Internet to scan the holdings of other libraries, the legwork of research can be drastically reduced.

International lending agreements allow us to borrow the book, or copy the article, or access the data file for that researcher, and to minimize the time spent in information gathering.

We find ourselves exploring the concept of a virtual library, and articulating its technical mechanisms with little understanding of the intellectual ones. A virtual library, by definition, is the product of purposive searching in a somewhat structured universe of information; it is not often described as resulting from a series of random events. *Serendipity* and *accident* are not words that often appear in the discussion of information networks and information services, yet they play an important role in intellectual growth and the seemingly spontaneous generation of new ideas. Neff concurs when he asserts, "Browsing in the electronic research library of the future should be developed to permit both physical and logical serendipity to occur" (1987). Moholt agrees, saying, "The matter of freedom of choice is very important: it allows for serendipity, happy accidents, chance associations, and similar creative glitches. . . . If my wanderings through the literature are too tightly channeled and controlled, I may well find the process highly unrewarding and spend my time calculating ways to circumvent it" (1985).

In the current literature we find a preoccupation with mechanisms, and less focus on content and structure. Models are discussed that ignore the wide gap between existing data and those data that would be available only with massive conversions of text. The two cultures of the humanist and the scientist conflict; access to older materials will be of far greater concern to the humanist than the scientist, and computer-assisted browsing of manuscripts, archives, and rare books is unlikely to prove an economically feasible offering of the virtual library. In a recent article, one librarian echoes our concerns, "Establishing access to the world of information . . . has . . . been necessary and wonderful, but as long as we take that accomplishment as the model for the understanding of the real processes of communication and conceptualization, we limit ourselves to static, external relationships with those processes" (Swan, 1990).

And what about the undergraduate? The local on-line catalogue alone can provide an overwhelming array of choices. The first-year student who wants to do a paper on Virginia Woolf can be intimidated by the sheer volume of material, and perhaps frightened by the notion that all of it should somehow be mastered before writing a term paper. Here, the role of the librarian as mediator may be apparent, but it is still not clear. How do we, and how do the faculty, teach students to distinguish the wheat from the chaff? Is it the librarian's responsibility, or is it the function of the liberal arts college to imbue its students with discernment by some magical osmotic process?

Perhaps we should simply purge the chaff from our libraries, and modify our standards for judging libraries (as indeed some of the regional accreditation standards have done) from quantitative to qualitative. We would judge ourselves, and be judged, not by the size of our buildings, or even our budgets, but by the ease with which our students and faculty can locate and retrieve the general information and specific texts they require. We would emphasize the interpretation of information and instruction in its retrieval and use in addition to acquisition and preservation of "information containers."

Studies of library use consistently show that older materials are less used than newer ones, and while there are variations among disciplines there is evidence that in the undergraduate liberal arts college the patterns are the same as those in larger, research university collections. Our database totals over three million titles; can our librarians help a student to select the five or ten volumes on a particular subject that will focus precisely on the term paper topic? More information is not, we conclude, necessarily better information, and while the virtual library is a realizable dream for the trained scholar, it may be a frightening overload for the undergraduate.

We have spoken of the next generation of library systems that we can imagine but cannot yet see in the marketplace. The conceptual system would include not only the on-line catalogue—which for the foreseeable future will continue to suffer the limitations we have already discussed—but also the local availability of on-line databases, whether in networked CD-ROMs or locally mounted data files and search engines. Moholt describes "a personal model" of an "Information Support Center" (1985). It is unfortunate that that vision must be bounded by what we know is currently feasible. Some institutions have formal plans, some are simply stumbling toward implementation of what she describes, but she describes nothing that is not already possible. As we observed earlier, the start-up for systems that support libraries has generally been lengthy; we need to be sure that the conceptualization of new systems does not preclude the later incorporation of technologies and services that are now only laboratory experiments.

Admittedly, the patterns of access and utilization of information that Moholt describes are not yet widespread, and the varied protocols of software and telecommunications today would require the researcher to have considerable wizardry to access, browse, extract, massage, integrate, and disseminate information. The user interface for such systems will be a continuing problem; each system has its own controlled thesaurus and its own search protocols, and despite experiments in creating a transparent user interface, there is no standard yet available. Text retrieval will be on the desiderata list, but the utility of a retrieval linkage will depend largely on the availability of central sources for document requests, or the development of uniform protocols for such requests.

Who Will Lead Us?

Discussing the convergent services of libraries and computing centers, Naylor asserts that "the new service group will be remarkably important to the institution" and estimates that "it will perhaps spend over ten percent of the total budget" (1988). In the current economy, when most liberal arts colleges and many universities are facing increasing budgetary restraints, it will be imperative that all the campus information providers act in concert to maximize the cost effectiveness of systems and services.

We believe that there are areas of computing in which the faculty and staff who have become the computing experts are reinventing solutions that are part of the librarian's repertoire; to the extent that the solutions evolve from a series of trials and errors, they are costly. We do not believe that computing professionals have "stronger magic" than librarians, but that there are new areas of technical expertise that can contribute to the broad mission we have always pursued— that of providing free and unrestricted access to information. In the context of these organizations, Naylor observes, "It is interesting to note that it is librarians who seem most often to be asked to take the lead in heading any new combined service; the factor which is most often identified is the librarian's longstanding commitment to a service role, by contrast with the computing specialist who is preoccupied with the technology itself" (1988).

Librarians have been particularly preoccupied with the user interface and with ideas of user friendliness. In each new generation of students, we have more sophisticated computer users who may need less of this generic system cordiality than we have thought. At the same time, the kinds of database applications we are describing do involve manipulations of multiple systems and demand selectivity in choosing among the arrays of citations that may be retrieved. We must recognize that among our faculty there is a wide spectrum of sophistication both in the use of existing systems and in the understanding of potentials. While some faculty are demanding services that we must stretch to provide, others are still becoming acquainted with word processing and approaching on-line library catalogues with trepidation. They, no less than our students—and sometimes more—need our help in understanding and utilizing the new media formats and technologies.

We see recurrent references to the need for programmer support for faculty. The computing revolution has caught a generation of scholars in mid-career; indeed both the computer specialists and librarians now working with automation have often acquired their skills as a kind of retooling from their previous areas of expertise and concentration. One of the effects of this revolution on scholarship, however, is to create an underclass of accomplished scholars whose training did not include a now-critical set of tools. The scholar's use of computing has parallels in traditional scholarship, and models for support already exist. We characterize computing support for faculty as having several levels of sophistication.

Academic computing support parallels library experience and established patterns in faculty research. Data gathering and data entry are the equivalent of basic bibliographic research and gathering of documents from a traditional print library, a task assigned to the undergraduate student assistant. The design of appropriate applications for commercial software may require the expertise of a graduate assistant; the equivalent of culling the raw data and references for the truly relevant material. Where a research design requires new manipulations of data, the programmer becomes the laboratory assistant; the chemist has been able to call upon a glass blower to construct a laboratory apparatus, now he or she may call upon a programmer to design a model for the laboratory process.

The issue here is not whether faculty need support from computing staff, but at what level. We are witnessing retraining on a grand scale, but it is a temporary phenomenon. We already see students entering college who are far more computer literate than many faculty, staff, and administrators. As they emerge into their professional lives, knowledge of the computer will be taken for granted as competence in foreign languages, statistics, or experimental design is already taken for granted by many academics. To pose the issue in a completely different way, how would we respond if the faculty, administration, and staff of an institution all needed to learn Chinese to perform their work? How would we structure the training and continuing education? How would we allocate resources, manage the program, recruit the teachers, and determine priorities? If we regard computer literacy in this context, we may see the same pattern we describe elsewhere in our discussion of the costs of library automation: high start-up costs followed by a level-funding phase, followed by some potential for savings based on the intelligent utilization and management of the new resources.

The more we discuss the next-generation system, the more our description sounds like that of the network managers or computing services staff, who talk about the need to provide users with access to a range of systems and services. If we are clear about the role of automation in libraries, we are less sure of the role of librarians in automation. Librarians have embraced new technologies, but unlike the academic computing or networking staffs, they have not started from a *tabula rasa*. As we mentioned earlier, automation is an overlay to the traditional tasks of the library, which involve the management of the physical objects that constitute the collection. As the collection has changed from one of books and journals to one that includes audio and video recordings, films, and even the microform manifestations of print, we have developed larger collections of hardware, and have confronted the issue of standardization in media formats.

The newest of the Five Colleges, Hampshire, was founded in the late 1960s as an experimental institution. Part of the Hampshire experiment was to create a non-traditional library, which from its inception included non-print resources and media production facilities. The campus was designed with a coaxial cable network connecting both its academic and residential buildings, and it was expected that the college's students would eventually be able to sit in their dormitory rooms and access the library from computer terminals. The concept was daring, yet it was the idea of the scholarly workstation and virtual library on a less global scale. Technology has now made the concept attainable, but it has lost much of its charm. We are not social psychologists, but we do understand the importance of community among scholars. For the faculty, the "informal college" of colleagues, with whom one formerly interacted at meetings and through correspondence, has been drawn closer together by electronic mail. For the student, the community is that of one's cohort, and the library as physical space provides opportunities for interaction and support in the processes of learning.

The individual librarians of the Five Colleges have formal and informal relationships to other computing activities on campus. There is among the institutions a range from one at which the librarian is currently responsible for all computing on the campus, to those where the librarians are members of campus computing advisory and planning committees, to those where the librarians are informed through administrative channels of the activities of computing personnel, but who have no role in planning or policy making.

Computing has become a major competitor for institutional resources and has become politically powerful with the administration at many liberal arts colleges. In many cases it is the new fiscal bottomless pit, and it may be capitalizing on some of the same factors that have kept money flowing into libraries. Administrators accept that computing and a "computing presence" are important to attract students and support faculty, just as they have accepted the need to maintain a strong library. Most administrators, however, neither understand the technical details nor want to do so. They trust the emerging computer experts. Administrators and faculty believe that they understand libraries, because they have used them throughout their academic careers; computing still has the cachet of the new and unknown. We believe that administrative insight, collegiality, and individual assertiveness will place the librarians in their appropriate roles in the development of campus computing services.

Many of the articles by librarians do not distinguish accurately between academic and administrative computing services. Several authors make broad generalizations about computing services, which are directly contradicted by others. Each has evidently extrapolated from individual experience of structures and personalities and assumes that those organizational and personal behaviors are normative. There is agreement that administrative computing should be viewed as dealing with internal information, while both library and academic computing deal with a mix of locally held and external information and are more apparently convergent in their operations.

We know of no examples of librarians having been instrumental in the design of administrative computing systems, yet they are trained and experienced in the range of issues that such automation must address. We managed very large databases and developed standards for their organization, and we developed records-management programs, long before we had computers as tools. In decentralized or partially decentralized computing environments, where the controls of centralized management may begin to erode, we again have experience in file design and data management that are of universal applicability. In the corporate world, the librarian has become the information manager or specialist. The renaming affects compensation more than content.

A key issue, at the heart of the two-cultures dilemma, is the administrative structure and organization of the emerging information-services system in academic institutions. In purely economic terms, one may question how many distinct administrative units are needed to develop and maintain the combination of services that are now divided into libraries and computing services. In some institutions, the units of computing are even more delicately nuanced, with separate entities for networking, user services, microcomputer systems, and so forth. How much overhead can the contemporary liberal arts college afford in this range of activities, and what divisions of labor and spheres of influence are most compatible with the coherent provision of instruction and support for students, faculty, and staff?

Another manifestation of the dilemma is apparent in the language used to describe computing: Is it "systems" or "services," or just computing? In libraries, we speak of systems both in automated and manual operations; in each case, they are sets of routines that manage objects and their movement into and out of the physical system of the library. Services, on the other hand, are wholly user centered. Does the choice of nomenclature in computing reflect an underlying set of assumptions about priorities?

Finally, we must return to the role of the academic administration in determining the shape and direction of the new information services. To the extent that both computing and libraries are regarded as necessary and expensive but not understood, administrators may be persuaded not by any overarching model for the emerging service but by the claims and counterclaims of individuals with personal stakes in the outcomes. Despite the experiences of several universities that have administratively merged libraries and computing, there is still no clear direction for colleges. Continuing education and dialogue between librarians and computer specialists, monitored and encouraged by the administration, may help us both to greater appreciation of the assets we bring to the shared endeavor. We must also be willing to take administrative risks, to test organizational models, and to report dispassionately on the strengths and weaknesses we discover in those alternatives.

References

Bechtel, Joan. 1988. Libraries and computing centers working together: A success story. *Libraries & Computing Centers; Issues of Mutual Concern,* no. 7, March 1988 insert to *Journal of Academic Librarianship* 14.

Cargill, Jennifer. 1987. Cooperative cohabitation: Libraries and computer learning centers. *Library Software Review* 6:344–348.

Cimbala, Diane J. 1987. The scholarly information center: An organizational model. *College and Research Libraries* 48:393–397.

Dougherty, Richard M. 1987. Libraries and computing centers: A blueprint for collaboration. *College and Research Libraries* 48: 289–296.

Lewis, Peter H. 1990. Executive computer. *New York Times,* May 13, sec. 3, p. 8, col.1.

McDonald, David R. 1988. The ingredients of a good relationship: the library's point of view. *Libraries & Computing* Centers; *Issues of Mutual Concern,* no. 6, insert to *Journal of Academic Librarianship* 13.

Miller, Ellen G. 1985. Managing automation for results: The role of the campus computing center. *College and Research Libraries News* 46:160–165.

Moholt, Patricia. 1985. On converging paths: The computing center and the library. *Journal of Academic Librarianship* 11:284–288.

Moholt, Patricia. 1987. On converging paths: The computing center and the library. *Libraries & Computing Centers; Issues of Mutual Concern,* no. 1, insert to the *Journal of Academic Librarianship* 1:32a–32b.

Moholt, Patricia. 1989. What happened to the merger debate? *Libraries & Computing Centers; Issues of Mutual Concern,* no. 13, insert to the *Journal of Academic Librarianship* 15. [An editor's note in this issue announced the publication of the insert was being suspended.]

Naylor, Bernard. 1988. The convergence of the library and the computing service: The central issues. *British Journal of Academic Librarianship* 3:172–186.

Neff, Raymond K. 1985. Merging libraries and computer centers: Manifest destiny or manifestly deranged? An academic services perspective. *EDUCOM Bulletin* 20:8–12.

Neff, Raymond K. 1987. Computing in the university—The implications of new technologies. *Perspectives in Computing* 7: 14–22.

Plane, Robert A. 1982. Merging a library and a computing center. *Perspectives in Computing* 2:14–21.

Shera, Jesse. 1976. *Introduction to library science.* Boulder: Libraries Unlimited.

Snow, C.P. 1965. *The two cultures and a second look: An expanded version of the two cultures and the scientific revolution,* Cambridge: Cambridge University Press.

Swan, John C. 1990. Rehumanizing information: An alternative future. *Library Journal* 115:178–182.

Woodsworth, Anne. 1988. Computing centers and libraries as cohorts: Exploring mutual strengths. *Journal of Library Administration* 9:21–34.

Index